Afterlives of war

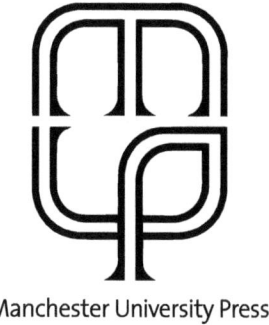
Manchester University Press

Cultural History of Modern War
Series editors

Ana Carden-Coyne, Peter Gatrell, Max Jones, Penny Summerfield and
Bertrand Taithe

Already published

Carol Acton and Jane Potter   *Working in a world of hurt: Trauma and resilience in the narratives of medical personnel in warzones*

Michael Brown, Anna Maria Barry and Joanne Begiato (eds)   *Martial masculinities: Experiencing and imagining the military in the long nineteenth century*

Quintin Colville and James Davey (eds)   *A new naval history*

James E. Connolly   *The experience of occupation in the Nord, 1914–18: Living with the enemy in First World War France*

Lindsey Dodd   *French children under the Allied bombs, 1940–45: An oral history*

Peter Gatrell and Liubov Zhvanko (eds)   *Europe on the move: Refugees in the era of the Great War*

Julie Gottlieb, Daniel Hucker, and Richard Toye (eds)   *The Munich Crisis, politics and the people: International, transnational and comparative perspectives*

Jessica Hammett   *Creating the people's war: Civil defence communities in Second World War Britain*

Grace Huxford   *The Korean War in Britain: Citizenship, selfhood and forgetting*

Linda Maynard   *Brothers in the Great War: Siblings, masculinity and emotions*

Duy Lap Nguyen   *The unimagined community: Imperialism and culture in South Vietnam*

Lucy Noakes   *Dying for the nation: Death, grief and bereavement in Second World War Britain*

Juliette Pattinson, Arthur McIvor and Linsey Robb   *Men in reserve: British civilian masculinities in the Second World War*

Beatriz Pichel   *Picturing the Western Front: Photography, practices and experiences in First World War France*

Spyros Tsoutsoumpis   *A history of the Greek resistance in the Second World War: The people's armies*

Centre for the
Cultural History
of War

https://www.alc.manchester.ac.uk/history/research/centres/cultural-history-of-war//

Afterlives of war
A descendants' history

Michael Roper

MANCHESTER UNIVERSITY PRESS

Copyright © Michael Roper 2023

The right of Michael Roper to be identified as the author of this work has been asserted by them in accordance with the Copyright, Designs and Patents Act 1988.

An electronic version of this book is also available under a Creative Commons (CC-BY-NC-ND) licence, thanks to the support of Knowledge Unlatched, which permits non-commercial use, distribution and reproduction provided the author and Manchester University Press are fully cited and no modifications or adaptations are made. Details of the licence can be viewed at https://creativecommons.org/licenses/by-nc-nd/4.0/

Published by Manchester University Press
Oxford Road, Manchester M13 9PL

www.manchesteruniversitypress.co.uk

British Library Cataloguing-in-Publication Data
A catalogue record for this book is available from the British Library

ISBN 978 1 5261 5403 3 hardback

First published 2023

The publisher has no responsibility for the persistence or accuracy of URLs for any external or third-party internet websites referred to in this book, and does not guarantee that any content on such websites is, or will remain, accurate or appropriate.

Typeset
by Deanta Global Publishing Services, Chennai, India

In memory of my father Stan Roper, 1926–2016, and my mother Ailsa Roper (née Sefton), 1928–2021

Contents

List of figures	*Page* ix
Preface and acknowledgements	xii
Introduction	1

Part I: Researcher

1 The evidence of afterlives	29
2 Family transmission	61

Part II: Observer

3 National narratives in the Centenary	89
4 *Meeting in No Man's Land*: motives for remembrance among British and German descendants – Michael Roper and Rachel Duffett	109

Part III: Historian

5 Fathers and the habits of home	139
6 Playing at war and being at war	173
7 Daughters, care and citizenship	197

Part IV: Descendant

8 Father and son on Bob's war	221
9 Dysentery and the Anzac legend	234

10 Legacies of dysentery   260
11 Stomaching peace   282

Epilogue   297
Appendix I: Afterlives *interview profiles*   309
Appendix II: Meeting in No Man's Land *interview schedule*   319
Select bibliography   321
Index   339

List of figures

All rights reserved and permission to use the figures must be obtained from the copyright holder.

0.1	Camilla Jarvis and her family's war heritage. Courtesy of Camilla Jarvis.	Page 3
0.2	Granddad and his lemon tree, Surrey Hills, Melbourne, circa 1964. Author's own.	9
0.3	Hanne's cigar box with her grandfather's honour medal. Courtesy of Hanne Kircher.	10
0.4	Winifred Spray's photograph of her father John Hickson who died in 1916. Courtesy of Marian Parry-Jones and Peter Blakebrough.	12
1.1	British Guardsman on home leave. www.pinterest.co.uk/pin/416512665539382288/. Accessed 8 September 2022.	38
1.2	'Goodbye Daddy! God Bless!', Bamforth & Co. postcard. Courtesy of the Army Children Archive.	39
1.3	Harriet Pollock and her daughters. Author's own.	44
2.1	Mary Burdett's father George, a Royal Army Service Corps motor engineer, on a Clyno motorcycle. Courtesy of Mary Burdett.	67
2.2	Marie-Anne Careless wears the ring that her father smuggled out of Frontstalag 220. Courtesy of Marie-Anne Careless.	79
4.1	Hilary and Dieter meet in no man's land. Courtesy of Age Exchange and Dieter Filsinger.	111
4.2	Jürgen had recently found this photograph of his grandfather in 1892. Courtesy of Age Exchange and Jürgen Müller-Hohagen.	114

4.3	Postcard of Delia's grandfather in 1933 dressed as a centurion. Courtesy of Age Exchange.	130
4.4	'Three cheers for the fennel flower!' Postcard sent home by Christel's grandfather. Courtesy of Age Exchange and Christel Berger.	131
5.1	Savile Lumley recruitment poster, 'Daddy, what did you do in the Great War?' (London: Johnson, Riddle and Co. Ltd., 1915). Imperial War Museum Art (hereafter IWM), PST 0311.	140
5.2	Richard Reiss, *The Home I Want*, 1918. Courtesy of the Mary Evans Picture Library.	147
5.3	Francis Long playing with his children at the beach. Courtesy of Margaret Seabrook.	158
5.4	Margaret Seabrook and her brother playing in the garden. Courtesy of Margaret Seabrook.	159
5.5	Page from Margaret Seabrook's photo album, 'Happy Daddy!!' Courtesy of Margaret Seabrook.	160
7.1	A girl leading a blind Australian soldier from St Dunstan's Hostel. Model by Clare Sheridan, 1918. IWM Museum Exhibits Collection, Q 66143.	198
7.2	Louis Raemaker's sketch of a blind soldier and his guide. Courtesy of Blind Veterans UK.	199
7.3.	St Dunstan's postcard 'Blinded for You', 1916. Courtesy of Blind Veterans UK.	200
7.4	'You've Not Said How I've Growed, Daddy!', Thomas Henry, circa 1916. Courtesy of the Mary Evans Picture Library.	204
8.1	Granddad with the Roper grandchildren at Surrey Hills, circa 1964. Author's own.	224
8.2	Reconstituted family in the backyard at Montmorency, circa 1977. Author's own.	225
8.3	Granddad on horseback in the Anzac march, circa 1977. Author's own.	226
8.4	Robert Henry Roper studio portrait held by the Roper and Toohey families. Author's own.	230
9.1	David Barker, 'APRICOT AGAIN!' Courtesy of Bridgeman Images.	240

9.2 Otho Hewett, 'Each One Doing His Bit'. Courtesy of C. E. W. Bean (ed.), *The Anzac Book. Written and Illustrated in Gallipoli by the Men of Anzac* (London: Cassell & Co, 1916). 245

9.3 C. E. W. Bean, 'Turkish Divisional Orders'. Courtesy of C. E. W. Bean (ed.), *The Anzac Book. Written and Illustrated in Gallipoli by the Men of Anzac* (London: Cassell & Co, 1916). 251

Preface and acknowledgements

The First World War was a global cataclysm and, like all traumatic events, its effects were long-lasting. The impact was not restricted to the generation that took part but was felt by their children and their children's children too. The traces left by the war could take many forms, in objects such as letters, trench art and foreign exotica stored in family lofts and garages, posted on digital genealogy platforms or put up for sale on eBay. But the conflict also left more intimate and inchoate traces – stories and silences, behaviour and emotions – that were transmitted through the generations. *Afterlives* explores the legacies of the First World War in families in Australia, Britain and Germany. It is about the shadow that the First World War cast over the descendants, how it shaped their identities and how they draw on its history to make sense of their ancestors and themselves.

The book combines military and genealogical records, interviews, personal memory and 'co-research' with descendants carried out over a decade. It is at once historical and personal, a reflection on the past and the present. The research was conceived in 2011 as an oral history of British descendants. At the same time, my father and I were researching my grandfather Robert Henry Roper's war service in Gallipoli and the Middle East and the legacies of his war in our family. The 2014–18 Centenary commemorations in Australia, the UK and Germany gave new prominence to descendants. I watched these developments as an observer as much as a historian, taken aback by the surge of public interest in the First World War, much of which – in Australia and the UK – was state-sponsored. What had started off as an academic study and a family project, I now realised, was part of a cultural phenomenon, and the Centenary also became part of the story. I debated the structure of the book over many months with friends, colleagues, readers of the manuscript and my editor, and eventually decided on a form that reflects the roles I adopted after 2011. I was at various points a researcher interested in the memories of those who came after and an observer during four years of remembrance. But I was also a historian of descendants, and I was myself a descendant. *Afterlives* reveals the legacies of the First World War through methodological meditations on what it means to come after, commemoration-watching, social history and memoir.

It has been a privilege to hear, record and bring to a new audience the testimonies of the ninety descendants who feature in *Afterlives*. I would also like to thank the friends, children, grandchildren and carers who acted as gatekeepers for the interviewees. The initial call for participants in 2011 was made possible by Fran Adams, who was then publicity officer at the University of Essex and got it circulated in local newspapers across the UK. Rachel Duffett has worked on the project throughout, providing suggestions about research, reading drafts, planning and hosting events at the First World War Engagement centre at the University of Essex between 2014 and 2018 and producing her own insightful articles on children's culture and legacies of the First World War. Chapter 4, '*Meeting in No Man's Land*' was co-written with Rachel. I admire her energy, creativity and ability to organise, and I am lucky to have had the opportunity to work with her. Elijah Bell marshalled into files the chaos of emails, letters and phone calls that arrived after the 2011 call for participants. James Wallis did a fantastic job researching the family backgrounds of the interviewees. Marion Haberhaugh transcribed the interviews, and Bethany Morgan undertook the herculean task of coding them all in Nvivo, suggesting, too, useful avenues to pursue. Many thanks to them all.

I met David Savill, Creative Director of Age Exchange, in early 2015 at a film screening of their London project *Children of the Great War*. His enthusiasm and ability to make things happen are extraordinary. Through David, it became possible to extend the project into a study of descendants making history. We invited Age Exchange to a collection day at the University of Essex in the summer of 2015 and in early 2016 we joined their project *Meeting in No Man's Land*, which brought together German and British descendants in Bavaria in April 2016. I would like to thank David's co-organisers, among them Debbie Clark, Suzanne Lockett, Jürgen Müller-Hohagen, Hanne Kircher, Elfriede Pauli, Hedvig Petzet, Simon Purins, Ivan Riches, Melanie Sommer, Karin Wimmer-Billeter and Margarita Wolf. I am grateful to the participants in the Essex collection day and *Meeting in No Man's Land* for allowing Rachel Duffett and me to observe, interview and use their interviews in our research. Sarah Lloyd led the Hertfordshire Everyday Lives in the War First World War Engagement Centre from 2014 to 2018 and provided fantastic support for the Essex branch of our centre. Barbara Peirson, who was Director of the Lakeside Theatre, set in train a verbatim testimony production based on my interviews. *Voices of the Great War* was written by Annecy Lax, directed by Robert Price and performed by final-year drama students at Essex in June 2016.

The initial interviews were funded by a British Academy Small Grant in 2013, and the collaboration with Age Exchange during 2015–16 was made possible through Arts and Humanities Research Council (AHRC) and Heritage Lottery funding. I would like to thank the Leverhulme Trust for the award of a Research Fellowship in 2017–18 (RF-2016-284), which allowed me the freedom to reimagine the project. All three grant proposals were improved immeasurably by Gary Williams at the Research and Enterprise office at Essex. A Fellowship at Newcastle University in NSW during 2017 permitted time for research and I would like to thank Philip Dwyer for facilitating this. I also gained much from discussions with graduate students over the past decade who were also working on war, biography and generation, among them Allan Hildon, Catherine Hickman, Christos Peristianis, Alice Sage and Terry Smyth.

I am grateful to Robert Baker, the Information and Archives officer at Blind Veterans UK, the archivist Gary Haines at the V&A Museum of Childhood, Jane Brown at the Institute of Tropical Medicine, David Flegg at the State Library of Victoria and staff at the Imperial War Museum for help in locating archival materials. I had fascinating discussions on the gut and war with the gastroenterologist Martin Veysey, Dr Richard McClelland and Janet McCalman who is leading the 'From Diggers to Veterans' project at Melbourne, whose expertise was much appreciated. Bruce Scates, Rebecca Wheatley and Laura James helped me gain access to my grandfather's pension files in 2016 and were warm hosts and sources of helpful advice during my

Centenary visits to Melbourne. The Channel Island historians Gilly Carr and Louise Willmot provided clarification of events on the island during the Second World War. Bruce Scates and Raelene Frances organised the tour of Gallipoli in 2015 which brought together First World War historians from around the globe, and I would like to thank them for their hospitality. Janet Butler discovered a copy of my grandfather's memoir in the Liddle Collection in Leeds and kindly got in touch to let me know. I have benefited greatly from discussions with Jill Barnard, Johnny Bell, John Murphy, Kate Murphy and Alistair Thomson, colleagues on the Australian Research Council History of Australian Fatherhood project who read and commented on drafts. I would like to thank Penny Summerfield for providing access to her interview transcripts. Many thanks also to my stepmother Robyn Roper for contributing her knowledge of the Roper family history, and for access to my father's papers.

Draft chapters (in some cases, multiple drafts of the entire manuscript) were read by Shaul Bar-Haim, Graham Dawson, Rachel Duffett, Richard Hall, Sean Nixon, Paul Thompson, John Tosh, James Wallis and Bart Ziino. Their comments and conversations helped to develop and deepen my thinking, and I am fortunate to count many of them as friends as well as colleagues. I gained much from conversations with David Bell, Marion De Landmeter, Peter Doyle, Matt Ffytche, Karl Figlio and Ross Wilson. Tracey Loughran and I co-organised *The Historian's 'I'* conference at Essex in 2019 with help from the AHRC and I would like to thank Tracey and the participants for their reflections on subjectivity in historical work. Coffee with Jonathan Lichtenstein – who at that time was writing his descendant memoir *The Berlin Shadow* – was always a pleasure. Anne McElroy, Alice Roper and Thomas Roper lived with the book for more than a decade. Their scepticism about my ability to finish it became a family joke, but in truth, it could not have been completed without them, not least because of their insightful comments on drafts in recent months.

Lastly, I would like to thank Cath Roper and Lyndal Roper, whose own experience of the First World War's legacies in our family and thoughts about subjectivity, mental health, family transmission and social history inform the entire study. Since our parents' deaths, we have had to find new ways to communicate with each other across barriers of time difference, geography and a global pandemic. *Afterlives* is the result of one such communication and I look forward to others.

Permissions

An earlier version of Chapter 4 was published as M. Roper and R. Duffett, 'Family Legacies in the Centenary: Motives for First World War Commemoration among British and German Descendants', *History and Memory*, 30: 1 (Spring/Summer 2018), 76–115. An earlier version of Chapter 7 was published in the Proceedings of the British Academy, 'Little Ruby's Hand: Young Women and the Emotional Experience of Caregiving in Britain after the First World War', in L. Noakes, C. Langhamer and C. Siebrecht (eds), *Total War: An Emotional History* (Oxford: Oxford University Press, 2020), 59–77.

Introduction

The last German veteran of the First World War, Erich Kästner, died in 2008, the last Australian veteran, John Campbell Ross, in June 2009 and the last British veteran, Harry Patch, a month later. All that remains of the contemporary witnesses are the ghosts that endure in grainy snatches of black and white film, audio recordings and the ephemera held by families and archives. Today, children and grandchildren are the final remaining links to the living memory of the conflict.

I began conducting oral history interviews with British descendants in 2011, the very moment when the contemporary witnesses died out. The war had sometimes affected their children and grandchildren profoundly, but they did not necessarily consider that they had a legacy of their own. As she described her mother cleaning and bandaging the hole in her father's face – a wound caused by infected shrapnel that eventually killed him – Marion Armstrong suddenly paused and exclaimed: 'It's my mother's life that's interesting!' She went on to tell me that she had trouble getting to sleep as a small child because her father 'was on morphia, and he was moaning in the next bedroom – as I say, a little cottage'. Her infant insomnia felt as nothing compared to her parents' distress.

When the reminiscence arts organisation Age Exchange organised a collection day for First World War descendants at the University of Essex in July 2015, Camilla Jarvis arrived with a suitcase full of objects which she laid out on two tables. Her grandfather Philip, a pilot in the Royal Flying Corps (RFC), had died in a mid-air crash in 1919, and his daughter Léonie was born a month later. On one table was the memorial book put together by her great-grandmother, with photographs of her grandfather playing in a sailor suit, his school reports and photographs of him as a dashing young recruit dressed in the uniforms of the Army Services Corps and RFC. Camilla had a lock of Philip's hair that may have been taken from the corpse: his hair was the 'very same colour' as her own, Camilla observed. On the second table was the baby book kept by Philip's widow Eileen, documenting Léonie's life 'from the day of her birth to the day of her marriage'. Day one recorded a child 'perfect in limbs and health' who in the hours after her birth 'began to resemble her father'. The book recorded Léonie's christening, first Christmas, nicknames, toys and poems, sketches and hand-tinted photographs. Camilla was wearing the sapphire engagement ring that Philip gave her grandmother, and at home she had the dressing table set that had been his engagement gift. All these items had been passed to her by her mother, a private treasure trove that documented the life of the First World War serviceman, kept by three generations of women.

Scars and missing limbs were a common sight for children growing up in the 1920s and 30s, but as Camilla's suitcase of objects shows, the war past was also present in collections of letters and postcards and photographs, souvenirs and medals. Its legacies could sometimes be benign or even positive. Rosemary Gitsham's father had served in Gallipoli and the Somme and had a hole in his elbow that was 'large enough to put an egg in' but he showed no other signs of trauma.[1] Love of travel and technology were the main legacies of his war. There were framed photographs of the Egyptian desert and pyramids on the walls at home, and in the loft were old maps, flight logbooks and drawings of aeroplane engines. Inspired by his war service as a mechanic, he joined the RAF in the mid-1920s and was 'mad about flying'. Rosemary inherited his passion: she had spent her entire career working for an aviation firm and had flown, she told me proudly, 'in everything except a helicopter, and a microlight!'

The subjects of this book are the generations in Britain, Germany and Australia born after the First World War who lived in its shadow.[2] Growing up with a war in the family, some of them went on to become history-makers, researching their ancestors' war pasts, signing up for heritage events and interviews and seeking out the connections between their family's story and the public history of the conflict. In Britain, their pasts and their stories had largely escaped historical attention prior to the Centenary, even though in 2013 almost half

Introduction

Figure 0.1 Camilla Jarvis and her family's war heritage.
Courtesy of Camilla Jarvis. All rights reserved.

the population claimed to know a relative or community member who had been involved in the war in a combatant or auxiliary role.[3] Professional historians typically treated the war in the family in a last chapter or epilogue – as my own book *The Secret Battle* did – or merged it into a grand narrative of aftermath which assumed rather than investigated the personal impact on successors. 'After' was sometimes delimited as 1919, before most of the descendants still alive in 2013 were born.[4] As the Centenary dawned and professional historians reflected on popular beliefs about the First World War in Britain, some took aim at amateur family historians for uncritically repeating the 'pity of war' narratives of senseless slaughter on the Western Front that they learned from the war poets and *Blackadder Goes Forth*. British history of the First World War, remarked David Reynolds in 2013, had become 'stuck in the mud and stalled on the Somme', and descendants, it seemed, were partly to blame.[5]

Afterlives brings the histories of descendants like Marion, Camilla and Rosemary to the fore. It documents the varieties of war heritage in their homes as children, reconstructs their relationships with the 'contemporary witnesses' and ruminates on how the war past in the family shaped them.[6] It reveals their efforts to piece together the war histories of parents and grandparents, and how they interact with different national traditions of remembrance. Finally, it seeks to understand the personal motivations that draw descendants into research on the First World War, how they 'use' history and what history means to them as a social and emotional pursuit.

Most descendants grow up with a 'lived history' of the war in the family before they possess a 'learned history'.[7] When I began interviewing British descendants, I was initially taken aback by how little they knew about what their mothers and fathers did during the war. Some turned to fiction to fill in the gaps. Rosemary Game's father was a tunneller who died of war-related rheumatism in his forties, she told me in 2013. Yet it was only after reading Sebastian Faulks's *Birdsong* in the 1990s that she began to appreciate what he must have gone through. As a Mass Observation directive in 2014 showed, other descendants had also formed their impressions of the First World War by reading *Birdsong*.[8] Shuttling between the war and the efforts of a granddaughter in 1978 to reconstruct the life of the grandfather she never knew, *Birdsong* spoke to their own experience of coming after.

At the same time, perhaps because some descendants grow up with an afterlife in the family that does not fit the popular imagination of the First World War, they develop a critical understanding of received narratives. June Teape, my first interviewee, had donated a substantial archive of her father Walter Hempshall's artefacts to the Imperial War Museum. There are photos of Walter in the familiar ruined landscapes of France and Belgium, but there are also images of him standing outside a hospital tent in Kenya with a pet monkey, pictures of Kikuyu and Masai warriors and of Walter posing with East African soldiers. Speaking to me in 2011, June thought historians should talk more about the global dimensions of the First World War. Brian Keys brought another theatre of the conflict into view in 2015. His paternal grandfather had served in Murmansk in 1918 supporting the White Russian Forces in their campaign against the Bolsheviks. Illness and disease were the main killers. Brian marvelled at his grandfather's stoicism, poorly fed, snow blowing into their huts, the chilblains on his feet a permanent legacy of the campaign. Brian was irritated that the Western Front dominated public discussion of the First World War and that the Russian campaign, 'another Churchill embarrassment', was largely forgotten.

The history-making of descendants like Brian and June goes back a long way and in Britain they have played a central role in the history and popular memory of the First World War. Ted Hughes's poetry evoked his father's war in Gallipoli and France and the Calder Valley communities of his childhood which mourned their losses, and his commentaries on Wilfred Owen during the 1960s helped bring the war poets to prominence.[9] In his popular 1960s BBC radio programme *The Long Long Trail*, presenter Charles Chilton mixed facts about the war with songs and excerpts from interviews with veterans. It was Chilton's format and ironic tone that Joan Littlewood subsequently adopted in her production of *Oh, What a Lovely War!* Chilton's stance on the war was informed by a personal history: born in 1917, his father was killed in the conflict and his mother died when he was five from an abortion that went wrong.[10] *The Long Long Trail* was inspired by the discovery of his father's name on a memorial at Arras dedicated to his memory.

In recent times it is the third generation that has kept the First World War within the mainstream of national culture. Pat Barker's 1990s *Regeneration* trilogy, with its themes of masculinity, homosexuality and trauma, was at one level a commentary on the contemporary age, the historical setting serving as a 'backdoor onto the present'.[11] Yet it was the product of an earlier time, too. As Barker told *The Guardian* in 2012:

> My grandfather had a horrific wound in his left side. I used to see it every Friday night when he got stripped off for a wash at the kitchen sink before setting off for his weekly night out at the British Legion. It was a bayonet wound, but he never talked about the war. So there was a wound, and there was silence. But that kind of silence becomes compelling. It's a space which invites imaginative exploration.[12]

Barker describes a motivation common among descendants, who are drawn to imagine – perhaps through literature, perhaps through history – the backstory of the marks of violence. The sense of recognition felt by readers like me was not just because the *Regeneration* trilogy resonated with the psychological sensibilities and victim culture of the *fin de siècle*, but because it spoke to personal histories of war and their aftermaths.[13]

Two of the cinematic 'blockbusters' of the First World War Centenary were produced by grandsons. In Peter Jackson's interview about *They Shall Never Grow Old* – a masterpiece of haunting which transforms black-and-white footage of the Western Front into full colour and gives voice to its silent soldiers – he explained that 'it's a war I grew up with in my household'. Jackson's grandfather died in 1940 from multiple wounds and Jackson never knew him: a family loss had brought the First World War into his home, while *They Shall Never Grow Old* employed lip readers, oral testimony, colouring techniques and 3D to bring the soldier on the Western Front back to life. Growing up, his grandfather's compulsion to wash his hands made Sam Mendes curious about his war. After five decades of silence and then in his seventies, his grandfather began to talk about the mud on the Western Front and how they could not keep themselves clean. Mendes's film *1917* stitches together the episodic horrors of trench warfare into 'one long shot', as if the family war stories, in the way Mendes experienced them growing up, were a singular cataclysm.[14]

Descendants were thus prominent among the filmmakers, broadcasters, theatre directors, novelists and poets who put the First World War on the cultural map in mid-twentieth-century Britain and Australia. They were, and are, people who grew up with the memory of war and, as adults, sought to render it in poetry, novels, radio and theatre.[15] Through research and imagination, they could reconstruct scenes their fathers and mothers, grandmothers and grandfathers had witnessed.

Many of the historians who became First World War specialists in the twentieth century also had a family link to the conflict. Martin Middlebrook, whose 1971 book *The First Day of the Somme* described the 'blackest day in the history of the British army',[16] was profoundly affected by his mother's stories of a sister trapped in Belgium, a brother hit in the stomach and killed at Ypres in October 1915 and another who died from chronic bronchitis after being gassed and made a prisoner of war.[17] Denis Winter's unsparing account of trench warfare *Death's Men* draws on the testimony of his uncle Joe and father Harry.[18] Patsy Adam-Smith was among the first wave of historians in Australia to interview veterans, and the introduction of her 1978 bestseller *The Anzacs* is a poignant statement of what it means to come after: 'You were too close, nearness blinded, deafened, stupefied you with its immensity', she comments, a feeling which in later life prompted a wish 'to answer my own perplexities' and gather the testimonies of other First World War returned soldiers.[19] A family history of war can encourage the historical turn and be a source of creative insight. The second edition of Alastair Thomson's *Anzac Memories*, published nineteen years after the first in 1994, includes an essay about his grandfather Hector who suffered from bouts of mental illness after the war. Joan Beaumont, a staunch critic of the commemorative excess surrounding the Anzac legend and the role of descendants in perpetuating it, nonetheless begins her *The Broken Years* with an arresting description of how the war affected her uncle; in effect, intimating the power of an intergenerational transmission about whose effects on historical understanding she is at the same time sceptical.[20]

During the past half century, the cultural circuits in Britain and Australia that link families and the public memory of the First World War have grown and become increasingly sophisticated. Descendants can now subscribe to powerful online research tools like Ancestry.com, peruse digitised official records, and access resources from institutions like the Australian War Memorial and the Imperial War Museum. Yet, as I have come to understand since starting the book, the national absorption in First World War history in Britain and Australia and the active involvement of descendants in contributing to it cannot simply be explained as a generational transfer in which the descendants get their ancestors' war story on the record as the contemporary witnesses pass away. The efforts of descendants are underwritten by the state and a media that thrives on hidden histories of war. When in 2011 I put out an appeal in local newspapers across Britain asking people born in the 1920s and 30s to get in touch, I was deluged by letters, emails and phone messages. The respondents were not just animated by the sense that their family story might otherwise be lost, but by the belief that it deserved to be heard and would reach a sympathetic public.

The Anglo-Australian historical culture is strikingly different from Germany's, as I discovered in 2016 when Rachel Duffett and I took part in the Age Exchange project *Meeting in No Man's Land*, which brought together British and German descendants to share family heritage and stories of the conflict. Prior to the planning meeting in January, Creative Director David Savill asked us to bring along an object that represented the war in our family. I brought a photograph of my grandfather underneath the lemon tree in the backyard of his suburban Melbourne home and a cassette of the interview I had done with him in 1980, both artefacts already in the public domain and part of my family heritage.

But among the German organisers, the ephemera of the First World War, if it existed, was not claimed as family heritage, and had not been shared publicly. Hanne Kirschner, one of the organisers from Munich, brought along a cigar box which she and her cousin had retrieved from the outbuilding of the family joinery works just days previously. The box contained the Honour Medal that belonged to her grandfather, issued in 1934 as part of Hitler's effort to rehabilitate the veteran, and decreed by the National Socialists to be the only legitimate award of military service. Her grandfather had been a soldier in Hitler's Sturmabteilung ('Storm Detachment'), and Hanne was 'ashamed' of him. The medal had lain in the cigar box since his death in 1951, an object that – like her grandfather's part in the Nazi regime – was in the family but not spoken about. The British descendant Camilla Jarvis, by contrast, had paid for her grandfather Philip's Military Cross to be mounted in a special silver frame and kept it on display at home.

Meeting in No Man's Land exposed the differences between Anglo-Australian and German consciousness of the First World War among descendants. In Germany, during the Centenary it was the Second World War that dominated public discussion about the family legacies of war, as children and grandchildren continued to confront family ties to the Nazi regime and a past they wanted to bury. The sense of responsibility made it difficult to disclose the suffering that families had gone through, for as the debates in the early 2000s about the firebombing of German cities show, those who sought to acknowledge the domestic casualties also seemed to want to downplay German guilt.[21] The mournful tones of descendants in Britain and Australia assume a war of victims, while German descendants often deal with shame and complicity as they explore the impact of war on the family.

Figure 0.2 Granddad and his lemon tree, Surrey Hills, Melbourne, circa 1964. Author's own. All rights reserved.

What kind of history of the First World War can be written through the lives and historical activities of descendants? This study engages with three overlapping fields: social history, memory studies and studies of inter-generational transmission. In the tradition of history from below, *Afterlives* seeks to reconstruct the lived experience of home and family among those who were born after the First World War but had a war history in the family. Its themes – the environments of home, children's play, the cultures of interwar boyhood and girlhood, motherhood and fatherhood, love and loss, discipline and care and the impact of war – have been well developed within the social history of interwar Britain.[22] Oral history has been at the forefront of much of this work. As Tamara Hareven pointed out in 1978, momentous events like war or economic collapse create a cast of mind, conditioning the ways in which people react to later events in life, so that, for example, the children of the Great Depression continued to scrimp and save even in the post-Second World War age of prosperity.[23] And as Paul Thompson and Raphael Samuel insisted in a pioneering volume in 1992, the errors and distortions

Figure 0.3 Hanne's cigar box with her grandfather's honour medal. Courtesy of Hanne Kircher. All rights reserved.

in our accounts of the past can shed light on both history and the psyche. Hopes and desires infuse experience and the ways in which we attribute significance to historical events. Family stories, their shapes and mistakes, are interesting precisely because of the emotional investments they reveal, which transmit from ancestors to become the 'myths we live by' in each new generation.[24]

But we do not remember in a vacuum. Cultural milieux shape family stories about the First World War. The 'public memory' approach within oral history – widely adopted in studies of war in Australia and Britain – works with the concept of a cultural circuit in which individuals compose personal testimony through the public narratives which are available to them. The historian is primarily interested in the cultural context of the memories people compose, rather than the past of which they speak.[25] In an interview, a narrator will draw on the available heritage of war stories to compose an account that fits the norm and makes sense to themselves, the listener, and a future imagined audience. The participants in this study framed their accounts through tropes such as the pity of war, the soldier as the archetypal victim, trauma discourse and emotional codes that had shifted from stoicism to confession during their lives. As Lynn Abrams puts it, the public memory approach emphasises 'outside influences – including the filtering process over the intervening years between the experience and the interview, whereby layers of discourse shape the ways we recall and retell experience'.[26]

However, this conception of oral history does not so readily account for emotional experiences in childhood, a temper that could erupt from nowhere, a father caught in a moment of melancholy or a weeping mother and grandmother. The emotions attached to these memories were sometimes felt to have little connection to public remembrance and would only later be placed in a cultural and historical context. Winifred Spray, whose father died in the war, refused to go to school on Armistice Days after one of her teachers told the class to be quiet, and 'would they think of me'. As a child, Winifred had her own memento, a studio portrait of her father in uniform: 'perhaps it happens to photographs when they're big – his eyes followed me around, and I often ... and I often used to go and look at this photograph. But my mother never talked about him at all.' That photo sat beside us on the mantle during the interview, a talisman of the father she never knew.

Theories of transmission can shed light on silence and forgetting, and emotions from the past that stay with the witness and travel down the generations. Whereas the popular memory approach is concerned with the media, state and public institutions as conveyors of *post hoc* memory, these approaches ask how the emotional residues of experience are carried through life and time. They offer a rich account of subjectivity and of how we experience emotions in relation to others, especially as children. As the German historian Mary Fulbrook explains, transmission studies focus on formative events and the role of descendants in 'carrying the traces and impact of earlier events forwards, with implications for subsequent actions and attitudes, as well as transmission to those born later'.[27]

Family transmission has been particularly important in studies of the victims and perpetrators of the Holocaust. In Germany, the approach developed from the late 1960s as part of a generational movement, as young people in West Germany – influenced by international youth and anti-war movements, and the ongoing discovery of evidence about the extent of Nazi crimes and the participation of ordinary German people in the regime – began to confront their parents. Oral historians and sociologists developed a rigorous form of life-story interviewing that could expose the silence in families, revealing, often in the face of considerable resistance, the

Figure 0.4 Winifred Spray's photograph of her father John Hickson who died in 1916. Courtesy of Marian Parry-Jones and Peter Blakebrough. All rights reserved.

interviewee's part in the Nazi past, and how they had been drawn into participation.[28] Convinced that the involvement of the parental generation in evil had to be confronted, the personal effects on the second generation – facing a burden of guilt denied by their forebears – drove the analysis. As Gabriele Rosenthal, one of the proponents of the method, explained: 'As a sociologist and non-Jewish German woman, I am concerned with the question of how the past influences our present time. This question has been socially imposed on my generation, born in Germany after 1945, because of the Nazi past.'[29] The method has almost juridical rigour. A single question is asked in the first interview and then, having analysed the transcript, a second interview targets silences, gaps and vague responses, aiming to expose the involvement of the narrator in events now considered shameful.[30] Rather than pity or admiration at the toughness of a survivor, this approach confronts the historian with people they cannot sympathise with, and poses questions about the limits of empathetic understanding.[31]

The drive to expose hidden relationships with the Nazi period also impels the third and fourth German generations. As the psychoanalyst and philosopher Roger Frie explains in *Not in My Family*, 'Because my parents were children during the war and my grandparents were participants in the war, I am defined by my past and what it means to be third generation.'[32] Harald Welzer and his colleagues have shown how the history of the Nazi period that young people are taught at school and university is often at odds with the war stories told by their grandparents and great-grandparents. The 'learned history' reveals widespread support for the Nazis among German families but the 'lived history' is often about victims, resulting in the development of a double consciousness. Intimate family relationships often lead descendants to want to exculpate their grandparents from evil. Through small acts of omission and forgetting, they turn away the finger of blame, constructing a family narrative of resistance to evil and 'cumulative heroization'.[33] Transmission involves complicity between generations, as family loyalties motivate the descendants to protect their loved ones from moral judgement even when evidence to the contrary stares them in the face. The impetus behind this interview method is quite specific – to expose the guilt that descendants refuse to hear – but has broader implications, showing the subtle but profound influence of the war past on family relationships and how that past may shape the subjectivities of descendants. These transmission studies reverse the popular memory approach: here the cultural circuit, the 'learned history' of Nazi Germany, has only a superficial impact and is incapable of shaking myths constructed within the family.

As in the German literature, transmission is a central theme in studies of the impact of the Holocaust on Jewish families.[34] Here the second generation has acquired an identity and field of study of its own.[35] Descendants describe being aware of their parents' suffering from a very young age, before they possessed historical understanding. Transmission to the second generation typically occurs through silence: the primary experience is the unarticulated pain of survivor mothers and fathers, which inspires the child's search for understanding. Only at *that* point do cultural forms become part of the picture, as the children turn to photographs, film and fictional accounts of the Holocaust to fill in the gaps in their imagination. The descendants of Holocaust survivors typically engage with the cultural circuit as they try to make sense of emotional experiences in childhood that had no narrative.

In contrast to the public memory approach, transmission studies tend to assume that the narrator is never fully in command of the telling. Implicitly or explicitly, they adopt a notion of the unconscious, assuming that the knowledge of war is not only communicated through talk but through the body and emotional enactments, and that even silence transmits something. Freud's method sought to discover the causes of his patients' neuroses in unresolved early experiences. He believed that their early experiences were not readily available to him through memory, glimpsed at best in clues whose significance was connoted by their very remoteness from the animating impulse, usually a distressing or unpleasant event, or one that had overwhelmed the young child.[36] Memory was always a construction and not a reliable record of the event, time and place: a patient's recollection might post-date the affective experience that animates it, or be a response to an earlier point in time than the apparent content of the memory suggests. Nonetheless, vestiges of the past were always in the present for Freud: our behaviour and states of mind reflect the ongoing impact of early conflicts, imperfectly expressed in memory.

Marion Armstrong told me that when she woke up the morning after her brother Eric died during the Second World War, and 'every morning for ages after, my cheeks were stiff with salt. I couldn't ... I must have cried all the time I was asleep, because I worshipped him – he was my father. I hadn't had a father for a long time, and he took the ... and he was a lovely lad.' She had been encouraged to be a brave girl after her father died on her ninth birthday, 'Yes, my ninth birthday, because I couldn't have a party', and when Eric died a decade later, the tears came as she slept. As Marion talked about her father's death and the loss of Eric, I felt myself become tearful. The emotion of losses that had occurred more than seventy years ago was transmitted to me, her interviewer.

There is nothing mystical about reactions like these, and yet historians are sometimes shy to acknowledge that their explanations draw on notions of unconscious motivation. When Harald Welzer discovered that the family narratives of grandchildren distanced their ancestors from the evils of National Socialism, he implicitly worked with the Freudian concept of a reaction-formation, where an emotion (in this case, guilt) is denied through repeated insistence on its opposite: my grandfather was not a Nazi. Omissions, misremembering and fabrication reveal a past that exerts its influence behind the teller's back.

Afterlives draws on elements of the three approaches outlined here, while recognising that they are epistemologically diverse and often in tension with each other. It is in part a social history that reconstructs aspects of childhood in the 1920s and 30s to place the war within the physical space and family relationships of home. It explores domestic routines and the ways in which the First World War past entered children's play. Working with the concept of popular memory, it explores the received beliefs that shape descendants' contemporary perceptions of the First World War in Britain, Australia and Germany. At the same time, it draws on transmission theories to explore the emotional afterlife of the First World War within families, and the emotional investments that descendants make as they come forward to be interviewed or put their family ephemera on display.

The war's legacies in my own family shaped my path to becoming an historian of descendants and the historical cultures they create. My paternal grandfather was the subject of my first ever oral history interview, undertaken in 1980 as part of an Australian social history course. The topic of the interview was the Great Depression of the 1930s, but as Granddad fumed at the behaviour of the bosses and politicians who had cut the wages of the workers, he returned to the war:

> But there were some fellows that, well I don't know, I thought of them anyway, and they thought the same as me, we were mates [*sound of cutlery being put away in kitchen*], and we just got the wrong end of the stick. And we learned to, you know, we learned to hate. For instance, we wouldn't go near … our Regiment's get-together every year, our reunion, because of what we thought of them.[37]

Hoping to discover more about the war that taught Granddad to hate, I did a second interview with him a month or so before his death in September 1980. Until then, my knowledge of the war consisted of fragments of memory, a twisted little finger and a patch of translucent skin at the edge of Granddad's singlet. Historically speaking, I was ignorant. As a contribution to scholarly understanding, my interview was a disaster: I assumed the Dardanelles was in France because the name *sounded* French, and that the Second Battle of Gaza was in Gallipoli since, from Granddad's recollections, it was a bloodbath. Listening to the tragic stories of men like Simpson and his donkey which were broadcast through the school tannoy every year around Anzac Day, it seemed obvious that a rout such as Granddad remembered at Second Gaza could only have taken place at Gallipoli. There was tension between us as Granddad, trying to present an account that would pass muster among historians, sought to tell his war experience in chronological order, while I pressed him to tell his tales of freak deaths. Horrible history though my interview made, it helped me to understand the figure from my childhood who cared deeply for us and had a sense of fun – hosing us down in the heat of summer and allowing us to cuddle up in bed with him and Granny in the winter – but who was prone to unpredictable rages and whose flashbulb memories became lodged in my mind.

I was around seven or eight when he began to relate his stories of horror and part of my reason for interviewing him in 1980 was to get them on record:

> some fellow ... he was up on the parados, and these doctors must have been talking, see this chap turned around, and the next thing is, he fell into the doctor's arms. And the doctor turned him over, to push him off, I suppose, and the fellow had a beautiful smile on his face, and the bullet went straight through the jugular vein. And there he was dying, with a beautiful smile on his face.

'Those are things', he went on to say, 'you know, that you'd think were impossible. The impossible happens.'[38]

At the age of fifteen, in one of my first attempts to write poetry, I tried to capture the contradictory legacies of Granddad's war – hatred of man's inhumanity to man, hatred of the bosses and nostalgia for the comradeship of the rank-and-file.[39] Granddad was then in his mid-seventies and would spend his time in the sleep-out of their suburban Melbourne home writing about the war. He produced at least three memoirs in elegant cursive hand although his fingers were stiffening with age, as he explained to the British First World War historian Eric Liddle.[40] My grandmother would talk about the local boys who never came home, the grief of their families, and the returned soldiers in the outlying suburb of Frankston where they lived in the 1920s who lost their homes in the Great Depression. She could still reel off their names fifty years later. When I read Paul Fussell's *The Great War and Modern Memory* in 1980 it was a revelation: here was a text that made *emotional* sense, in which I recognised my grandfather's bitterness and sharpened antennae for hypocrisy, and how irony helped manage the memory of shocking events.[41] Spending time with my grandparents, I became immersed in their war.[42]

Looking back on the interviews forty years later has made me think about my practice as a social historian and interviewer. The hold of the Anzac legend over me as a young man may help explain why it was Granddad's war, not Granny's, that took my attention, despite her interjections, which I experienced at the time as annoying. I wonder now about the premium I put on empathy and moving stories, and why it was the piteous aftermath of Granddad's experience at Lone Pine – the weeping nineteen-year-old left on his own all night in a sap, defended by the dead bodies that he piled together into a barricade – that I wanted on the record. Granddad had told us that when they rushed a trench of Turkish soldiers 'there was a lot of blood kicking around'.[43] Why were my sister Cath and I so attentive to his pain, yet never thought to ask who he attacked and how, and what it felt like to kill? The downplaying of violence is not just a personal blind-spot, but a characteristic of British and white ex-colonial Allied perceptions, professional and public.[44] Granddad's memoirs say nothing about why he joined up. If ever he felt the stirrings of patriotism, that sentiment was replaced by hatred towards British officers. We never thought to ask if he had visited prostitutes or joined the drunken gangs that sacked the brothels in Cairo.[45] Yet in 1978 he had written to an ex-comrade in the Camel Corps that half the men in no. 2 Company went AWL (absent without leave) when they were stationed in Abbassia in 1917, and 'we did tarry a little longer than necessary in one den of iniquity'.[46] He never mentioned the fifteen thousand Indian troops on Gallipoli, or the French forces whose numbers were equivalent to the Anzacs. In Britain, Australia and Germany, perpetrators and victims remain split along boundaries determined by the outcomes of the First and Second World Wars, contributing to a lop-sided vision in which the 'bad characters' and sanctioned military violence of the BEF or Anzacs are forgotten, and the 'good German' dismissed as a myth.

The research for *Afterlives* took place between the deaths of contemporary witnesses early in the new century and the end of the Centenary commemorations in 2018. It entailed a combination of oral history, consultancy, 'co-research', commemoration-watching, public lectures, memoir and family history. Although it draws on observations of the German descendants in *Meeting in No Man's Land*, it is in essence a two-nation study. I began by interviewing British descendants born between 1920 and the mid-1930s, based at the time of interview in the south-west, East Anglia, the north-east and the Home Counties. I did clusters of interviews among residents who had grown up in Middlesbrough, Norwich and Bristol. These cities were bombed in the Second World War and this experience pervaded their memories of growing up and the war before their time. I interviewed 35 descendants, and in the summer of 2016, had the extraordinary experience of seeing their interviews dramatised in the verbatim testimony production *Voices of the Great War* at the University of Essex Lakeside Theatre.[47]

The Conservative government's plans for the Centenary included provision for community First World War projects, and from 2014 the First World War historian Rachel Duffett and I became involved in a range of Heritage Lottery Fund heritage projects through our membership of the HLF/AHRC Everyday Lives in War Engagement Centre run by Sarah Lloyd at the University of Hertfordshire. In June 2015 we teamed up with Age Exchange to host a collection day at the University of Essex where the stories and First World War heritage of Camilla Jarvis, Brian Key and twelve other descendants were recorded and digitised.[48] In April 2016 we joined Age Exchange again as they brought together twenty-three British and German descendants in Bavaria for four days of interviews and sharing of family war heritage. *Meeting in No Man's Land* generated a digital archive of filmed interviews and domestic ephemera which formed the basis of an Age Exchange film that premiered at the British Film Institute in the summer of 2016 and has since been shown in venues across the UK and Germany.[49]

During the Centenary I was also travelling backwards and forwards from the UK to visit my family and colleagues in Australia. My father was then in his mid-eighties and keen to look again at the impact of the First World War on his father. In September 2015 and again in February 2016, I interviewed Dad about his early life and memories of his mother and father. Until Dad's death in June 2016, I would receive regular emails with copies of service histories, battalion diaries and carefully edited transcript copies of Granddad's memoirs. Part IV of the book gives an account of our history-making and where it led.

Afterlives is as much a participant history as a commentary on descendant culture from the outside. I eventually decided to frame the book around the four principal roles I have assumed since 2011. Part I, 'Researcher', is about approaches and methods. Here I discuss the challenge of interviewing informants who are not eyewitnesses to the events at stake and how theories of transmission illuminate 'second hand' testimonies like theirs. Part II, 'Observer', reflects on the activities of British, German and Australian descendants during the Centenary. It begins with an account of the national frames of war memory in each country, and then discusses the motivations for remembrance among the British and German descendants brought together by the reminiscence arts organisation Age Exchange in 2016 to share their family stories.

Part III, 'Historian', traces the family legacies of the First World War among the so-called 'second generation' in Britain who were born in the 1920s and 30s and came to adulthood in the Second World War. Part IV, 'Descendant', tells the story of afterlives from the inside out. It describes the journey of researching Robert Henry Roper's war during the Centenary and meditates on how our relationships with family members now and in the past work their way into the family histories we produce. Opening with the dysentery epidemic that led to the Allied retreat from Gallipoli in December 1915, it ends with an investigation of its legacies in the Roper family. It brings 'family history' home.

Afterlives is a composite portrait of the generations born into families with a First World War history and a descendant's meditations on the private and public memorials they create. It reveals how, although the war was often little more than a ghostly presence in their early lives, descendants can, and have, enriched the historical consciousness of the First World War. At points its interpretations are tentative but drawing as it must on the speculations of those who are no longer in touch with the contemporary witness, perhaps this is a necessary condition of a descendant history.

Notes

1 Letter from Rosemary Gitsham to author, 4 August 2014.
2 Generation in this study is defined principally in familial terms, i.e., as steps in the line of descent from the 'war generation' to their children (second generation), grandchildren (third generation) and so on.
3 British Council, *Remember the World as Well as the War: Why the Global Reach and Enduring Legacy of the First World War Still Matter Today*, 2014, www.britishcouncil.org/sites/default/files/remember-the-world-report-v4.pdf, 7. Accessed 1 November 2021. A YouGov poll carried out in 2012–13 found that 47 per cent of respondents claimed to have a relative in the First World War. British Future, *Do Mention the War: Will 1914 Matter in 2014?* (London: British Future, August 2013), 18.
4 J. Nicholson, *The Great Silence 1918–1920: Living in the Shadow of the Great War* (London: John Murray, 2009); T. Tate and K. Kennedy, *The Silent Morning: Culture and Memory after the Armistice* (Manchester: Manchester University Press, 2013).
5 D. Reynolds, *The Long Shadow: The Great War and the Twentieth Century* (London: Simon & Schuster, 2013), xviii, 387. Also G. Sheffield, 'The Centenary of the First World War: An Unpopular View', *The Historian* (Summer 2014), 22–6. On the limitations of family history see H. McCartney, 'The First World War Soldier and His Contemporary Image in Britain', *International Affairs*, 90: 2 (2014), 304–7. Martin Francis struck a different note in 2014, asking historians to consider the 'millions of Britons' who 'believed that the Great War had violently shattered their lives to an extent that might be irreparable'. M. Francis, 'Attending to Ghosts: Some Reflections on the Disavowals of British Great War Historiography', *Twentieth Century British History*, 25: 3 (2014), 355–6.

6 On the role of families in transmission, see J. Winter, 'Forms of Kinship and Remembrance in the Aftermath of the Great War', in J. Winter and E. Sivan (eds), *War and Remembrance in the Twentieth Century* (Cambridge: Cambridge University Press, 1999), 40–61; J. Winter, 'Sites of Memory and the Shadow of War', in A. Erll and A. Nünning (eds), *Cultural Memory Studies: An International and Interdisciplinary Handbook* (New York: de Gruyter, 2008), 61–77.

7 On lived and learned histories, see B. Tint, 'History, Memory and Intractable Conflict', *Conflict Resolution Quarterly*, 27: 3 (Spring 2010), 240; H. Welzer, 'Collateral Damage of History Education: National Socialism and the Holocaust in German Family Memory', *Social Research*, 75: 1 (Spring 2008), 287–314.

8 Mass Observation 2014 Directive. Part 1. The First World War, www .massobs.org.uk/images/Directives/Autumn_2014.pdf. Accessed 1 November 2021.

9 Hughes, wrote the literary critic Dennis Walder, was a 'war poet at one remove, writing out of the impact of memory – the individual memory of his father, and the collective memory of English culture'. H. Melody, 'Ted Hughes and War', www.bl.uk/20th-century-literature/articles/ted -hughes-and-war. Accessed 1 November 2021. J. Winter, *War Beyond Words: Languages of Remembrance from the Great War to the Present* (Cambridge: Cambridge University Press, 2017), 193–6.

10 V. Dowd, 'The Birth of *Oh! What a Lovely War'*, *BBC News Magazine* (12 November 2011), www.bbc.co.uk/news/magazine-15691707. Accessed 1 November 2021; D. R. Allen, 'Charles Chilton Obituary', *The Guardian* (14 January 2014).

11 K. Westman, 'Generation Not Regeneration', in S. Monteith, M. Jolly, N. Yousaf and R. Paul (eds), *Critical Perspectives on Pat Barker* (Columbia: University of South Carolina Press, 2005), 163.

12 P. Barker, '*Regeneration* by Pat Barker', *The Guardian* (31 August 2012); R. Nixon, 'Interview with Pat Barker Conducted by Rob Nixon', *Contemporary Literature*, 45: 1 (Spring 2004), 6.

13 In his introduction to the interview with Barker, Nixon describes his great-grandfather's grief after he lost his son in the First World War, and his father's silence about his experience in North Africa in the Second World War: 'Imaginatively and emotionally, the book and its author spoke my language.' Nixon, 'Interview with Pat Barker', 4.

14 Catherine Shoard, '"The Stupidest Thing Humanity Ever Did to Itself": Sam Mendes and Colin Firth on 1917', *The Guardian* (3 January 2020).

15 Dan Todman observes that the second generation came to adulthood in a society characterised by views about the war that ranged from pacifism to continued belief in sacrifice. Having experienced a second

global conflict as young adults, they were led 'back to the First World War as they reached middle age' during the 1960s and 70s. D. Todman, *The Great War: Myth and Memory* (London: Hambledon and London, 2005), 225.

16 M. Connelly, 'An Interview with Martin Middlebrook: Reflections on Fifty Years of Researching and Writing on The First World War', Gateways Event, University of Kent, 15 October 2015; Todman, *Great War*, 201–3.

17 M. Middlebrook, 'The Writing of the First Day on the Somme', December 2004, https://web.archive.org/web/20060215034015/http:/ /www.fylde.demon.co.uk/middlebrook2.htm. Accessed 1 November 2021.

18 D. Winter, *Death's Men: Soldiers of the Great War* (London: Penguin, 1978), 131.

19 P. Adam-Smith, *The Anzacs* (Melbourne: Penguin, 1991), 6.

20 J. Beaumont, *Broken Nation: Australians in the Great War* (Sydney: Allen and Unwin, 2014), 1–5.

21 R. G. Moeller, 'On the History of Man-Made Destruction: Loss, Death, Memory, and Germany in the Bombing War', *History Workshop Journal*, 61: 1 (Spring 2006), 103–34. In Roger Frie's view, Jorge Friedrich, the author of *Der Brand*, implicitly equates aerial bombing with the horrors of the Holocaust through terms such as 'annihilated', 'crematoria' and 'extermination'. R. Frie, *Not in My Family: German Memory and Responsibility after the Holocaust* (Oxford: Oxford University Press), 101–2.

22 On young women: Sally Alexander, 'Becoming a Woman in the 1920s and 1930s', in S. Alexander, *Becoming a Woman and Other Essays in Nineteenth and Twentieth Century Feminist History* (London: Virago, 1994); C. Langhamer, *Women's Leisure in England, 1920–1960* (Manchester: Manchester University Press, 2000); K. Milcoy, *When the Girls Come Out to Play* (London: Bloomsbury Academic, 2017); S. Todd, 'Young Women, Work and Leisure in Interwar England', *The Historical Journal*, 48: 3 (2005). On young men: M. Tebbutt, *Being Boys: Youth, Leisure and Identity in the Inter-War Years* (Manchester: Manchester University Press, 2012). On parenthood: L. King, *Family Men: Fatherhood and Masculinity in Britain, 1914–1960* (Oxford: Oxford University Press, 2015); T. Fisher, 'Fatherhood and the British Fathercraft Movement 1919–39', *Gender & History*, 17: 2 (2005), 441–62; L. Abrams, '"There Was Nobody Like My Daddy": Fathers, the Family and the Marginalisation of Men in Modern Scotland', *Scottish Historical Review*, 78: 206 (October 1999), 219–42; E. Roberts, *A Woman's Place: An Oral History of Working Class Women 1890–1940*

(Oxford: Wiley-Blackwell, 1995); E. Roberts, *Women and Families: An Oral History 1940–1970* (Oxford: Wiley-Blackwell, 1995).
23 T. Hareven, 'Cycles, Courses and Cohorts: Reflections on Theoretical and Methodological Approaches to the Historical Study of Family Development', *Journal of Social History*, 12: 1 (Autumn 1978), 97–109.
24 R. Samuel and P. Thompson, 'Introduction', in R. Samuel and P. Thompson (eds), *The Myths We Live By* (London: Routledge, 1992), 5; D. Bertaux and P. Thompson (eds), *Between Generations: Family Models, Myths and Memories* (Oxford: Oxford University Press, 2005); S. Pooley and K. Qureshi (eds), *Parenthood Between Generations: Transforming Reproductive Cultures* (New York: Berghahn Books, 2016).
25 A. Thomson, *Anzac Memories: Living with the Legend* (Melbourne: Monash University Press, 2013). See also G. Dawson, *Soldier Heroes: British Adventure, Empire and the Imagining of Masculinities* (London: Routledge, 1994); P. Summerfield, *Reconstructing Women's Wartime Lives: Discourse and Subjectivity in Oral Histories of the Second World War* (Manchester: Manchester University Press, 1998); R. Wilson, 'Still Fighting in the Trenches: "War Discourse" and the Memory of the First World War in Britain', *Memory Studies*, 8: 4 (2015), 454–69; R. Wilson, *Cultural Heritage of the Great War in Britain* (Aldershot: Ashgate, 2013).
26 L. Abrams, *Oral History Theory* (London: Routledge, 2010), 55; P. Summerfield, *Histories of the Self: Personal Narratives and Historical Practice* (London: Routledge, 2018), 106–34.
27 M. Fulbrook, *Dissonant Lives: Generations and Violence through the German Dictatorships* (Oxford: Oxford University Press, 2011), 16.
28 G. Rosenthal, 'German War Memories: Narrability and the Biographical and Social Functions of Remembering', *Oral History*, 19: 2 (Autumn, 1991), 34–41; R. Sieder, 'A Hitler Youth from a Respectable Family', in Bertaux and Thompson (eds), *Between Generations*, 99–121.
29 G. Rosenthal, 'Veiling and Denying the Past: The Dialogue in Families of Holocaust Survivors and Families of Nazi Perpetrators', *History of the Family*, 7 (2002), 225–38.
30 G. Rosenthal, 'Reconstruction of Life Stories: Principles of Selection in Generating Stories for Narrative Biographical Interviews', *The Narrative Study of Lives*, 1: 1 (1993), 59–91.
31 These problems are discussed by Thomas Kohut in his study of members of the Weimar youth generation who joined Nazi youth groups in the 1930s, became committed Nazis during the Third Reich and were members of the Free German Circle after the Second World War. 'As I complete this book', he writes bluntly, 'I have become aware that I do not particularly like the interviewees.' At the same time, he seeks to

'reduce the intellectual and emotional distance separating us from them, in part by thinking our way inside their unique historical circumstances, in part by recognizing that they were as we are and that we have within us the capacity to be as they were'. T. Kohut, *A German Generation: An Experiential History of the Twentieth Century* (New Haven: Yale University Press, 2012), 16–17.
32 Frie, *Not in My Family*, 9.
33 Welzer, 'Collateral Damage', 289.
34 There have been collaborative programmes between descendants. Dan Bar-On's first book was based on interviews with the children of Nazi war criminals; his second major study, *Fear and Hope*, focused on three generations of Holocaust families, and in tandem with this research he promoted meetings between descendants on each side. D. Bar-On, *Fear and Hope: Three Generations of the Holocaust* (Cambridge, MA: Harvard University Press, 1995). Bar-On worked with Rosenthal on her study *The Holocaust in Three Generations: Families of Victims and Perpetrators of the Nazi Regime* (London: Bloomsbury, 1998).
35 For examples see E. Hoffman, *After Such Knowledge: A Mediation on the Aftermath of the Holocaust* (London: Vintage, 2005); M. Hirsch, *The Generation of Postmemory: Writing and Visual Culture after the Holocaust* (New York: Columbia University Press, 2012); A. Stein, *Reluctant Witnesses: Survivors, Their Children and the Rise of Holocaust Consciousness* (Oxford: Oxford University Press, 2014) and Jonathan Lichtenstein's memoir of his Kindertransport father, *The Berlin Shadow* (London: Scribner, 2020).
36 S. Freud, 'Screen Memories', *The Standard Edition of the Complete Psychological Works of Sigmund Freud*, Vol III (London: Vintage, 2001), 322.
37 R. H. Roper interview, 'Great Depression', 1980.
38 R. H. Roper interview, 'First World War', 1980.
39 My grandfather has a very powerful car
He wears a toad of toad hall cap
When he is driving it
His voice is powerful
When I was a boy his voice was frightening
It made others feel secure
He curses the capitalists
And he curses the communists
He thinks wars are terrible
But enjoys talking about the war he was in
He likes to feel that people need him
I love him

40 Letter from R. H. Roper to Eric Liddle, 30 January 1979.
41 P. Fussell, *The Great War and Modern Memory* (Oxford: Oxford University Press, 1975).
42 M. Roper, 'The Bush, the Suburbs and the Long Great War: A Family Memoir', *History Workshop Journal*, 86 (Autumn 2018), 90–113.
43 R. H. Roper interview, 'First World War'.
44 Among soldiers charged with killing, comments Joanna Bourke, 'contradictory emotions existed side by side, but historians have tended to examine only one half, assuming that the pleasure was "sick" or "abnormal" while the trauma was "normal"'. J. Bourke, *An Intimate History of Killing: Face-To-Face Killing in Twentieth-Century Warfare* (London: Granta Publications, 1999), 373.
45 P. Stanley, *Bad Characters: Sex, Crime, Mutiny, Murder and the Australian Imperial Force* (Sydney: Pier 9, 2010), 28–37.
46 Letter from R. H. Roper to Rory, 1 September 1978.
47 Lakeside Theatre, *Voices of the Great War*, 24–25 June 2016: https://lakesidetheatre.org.uk/events/voices-of-the-great-war/. Accessed 1 November 2021.
48 Age Exchange, 'Children of the Great War with the University of Essex and the First World War Centre at University of Hertfordshire', www.age-exchange.org.uk/what-we-do/arts-projects/project-gallery/children-of-the-great-war-with-the-university-of-essex-and-the-first-world-war-centre-at-university-of-hertfordshire/; https://everydaylivesinwar.herts.ac.uk/2015/06/children-of-the-great-war-memorial-collection-day/. Accessed 1 November 2021.
49 Age Exchange, *Meeting in No Man's Land*, www.age-exchange.org.uk/what-we-do/arts-projects/current-projects/meeting-in-no-mans-land/. Accessed 1 November 2021.

Part I

Researcher

1

The evidence of afterlives

One of my first interviews for this project was with Kathleen Skin, aged ninety-two and living in assisted housing in Cambridgeshire. My experience of that interview in September 2011 continues to challenge my thinking about oral history and memory. Kathleen was a lively narrator, with an eye for detail. Her father, she explained, had been blinded in one eye and lost most of the muscle in his leg when he was hit by shrapnel during the First World War, for which he received a 100 per cent pension.

Kathleen remembered a Christmas during the 1930s when her father was in hospital recovering from an attack of malaria:

> KS: And anyway, came Christmas, and we'd gone to bed, and there was a knock at the door – but, of course, we didn't know, I was sound asleep, I think – and at the door stood a chauffeur, and he had a sack, and he had boxes, and there was also a valet, all dressed up in uniform, you know, from the household … it was the Brown Owl's family, and she must have said to the others, you know, 'We've got this family here, and we've got to do something.' So they did. And we all got a present at Christmas, and we … had a roast dinner … everything that we wanted for Christmas was there. And coal! And … [*laughs*] … oh yeah, what my mother … affected her more than anything, was not that these things came from this wealthy family, was that the chauffeur came back, and he pressed sixpence in her hand, and he was hard up, and he'd got children … and I think that upset her more than anything. Anyway, I can see it all! [*sounds tearful*] Anyway, Dad came home on Christmas Day … all wrapped up in a blanket, and so we had a good Christmas. [*starts to cry*] I don't know how they managed … so we went up, and we went down. [*stops crying*] Now, I want

you to see this, because every now and again, my father kept having a letter saying, 'Come and be examined', because they tried to take away his pension, because they found out that he could dig the garden and grow vegetables ...
MR: I'll read this out then, shall I?
KS: That was when he was at Wickford, you see, that one.
MR: '24th February, 1923. The Ministry of Pensions. Dear Sir, Arrangements have been made for you to attend Special Surgical Hospital, Shepherd's Bush ...'

I want to make three observations about Kathleen's interview, both in relation to the women and men who grew up in the 1920s and 30s after the war's end and about the practice of oral history. Firstly, there is tension between the vivid scene she depicts and its status as testimony. At the time I pictured Kathleen as an eyewitness, and it was only on reading the transcript of the interview some months later that I realised she had said she was asleep. Kathleen's mother must have told her this story, and yet as Kathleen becomes upset, it is as if the experience is her own: breaking into tears, she says, 'I can see it all'. The affective intensity of her mother's reaction pulls the daughter and the historian onto the scene.

This moment in Kathleen's interview captures the situation of the so-called 'second generation' in Britain, who were not present during the events that shaped their parents' lives, yet whose own lives were shaped by those events, and who have often had occasion to imagine themselves on the scene. It is an example of what Maurice Halbwachs called a 'gripping abbreviation', which condenses the experience of coming after into a single image.[1] Marianne Hirsch, in her study of the children of Holocaust survivors, calls the imaginative reconstructions of the second generation 'postmemories'.[2]

Because Kathleen's story encapsulates the experience of living with the consequences of a war before her time, I have often used it in presentations and papers. In so doing, however, I have cherry-picked from her interview, which became more improbable as it proceeded. Like the central character in Woody Allen's 1983 film *Zelig*, she was on the scene of many key events in the mid-century. In the late 1930s, she told me, she went on a trip to Germany and stayed with the family of her father's friend. She had seen Hitler, Himmler and Goebbels at rallies and had been on a twenty-mile Nazi Youth march, suffering terrible blisters, but 'I never gave in'.

She practised parachute jumping with the Luftwaffe cadets and had seen children with tags being evacuated. She took photographs of international shipping in the Kiel Canal before being hurried across the border to Holland, sending her pictures to British intelligence officials on her return. During the war she was a Land Girl, a nurse and an armourer, putting guns in aircraft. She had done an operation for Special Operations Executive (SOE), rowing a boat to Guernsey under cover of the night to rescue a Polish prisoner of war who was an expert in radar.

Kathleen brought out a coin with filed edges, which she claimed SOE gave its agents as a form of identification in case they were captured, and instructed me 'don't tell anybody about my gold coin!' She had ended the war as a 'Bletchley girl', the most revered of all servicewomen. After the war she lived in Malaya, where her fiancé collapsed during their engagement party at the Dog pub, eventually dying from cancer after a hospital bedside wedding. The cause of his cancer was radiation fallout from the British nuclear tests in Australia. Kathleen also got cancer due to the fallout from the Hiroshima and Nagasaki nuclear bombs and had to have a hysterectomy. Her accounts became more macabre as the interview continued and she ended by telling me that her mother had helped the coroner cut open her six-month-old baby on the kitchen table after it died from mumps.

It is difficult to establish the points of departure from actuality in Kathleen's account. The letter was evidence of her father's disability, and other sources corroborate much of what she described, like the Strength Through Joy rallies, or the club in Kuala Lumpur colloquially known as the Spotted Dog. Campaigners in Britain and Australia have shown that there were elevated cancer rates among British servicemen and local indigenous communities exposed to nuclear tests in Australia in the 1950s. I have been unable to locate records of Kathleen's Second World War service and historians of intelligence and the Channel Islands tell me that there is no record of SOE operations involving the rescue of prisoners by boat.[3] It seems unlikely that Kathleen appeared in as many roles and theatres of the Second World War as she claimed.

In our interview, Kathleen created a seamless web from remembered experience, the emotions animated by remembering, shared cultural references (Christmas saved by the kindness of strangers) and her present concerns (to convey the injustices perpetrated by the Ministry of Pensions). Movements like these often occur in oral history and were apparent in other interviews too, a function perhaps of reconstructing memories of childhood among people in late life whose unconscious controls may be lifted, as well as the displaced relation that descendants have to the First World War, a past before their own. When interpreting such interviews, oral historians tend to go in one of two methodological directions.[4] Some will seek to ascertain and defend the value of their sources against assumptions about the retrospective standpoint of oral testimony. Kate Fisher and Simon Szreter in their study of sex and marriage between the wars argue that hindsight can actually be an advantage, the relatively permissive standards of today enabling their elderly interviewees to reflect on their sexual behaviour in a more open way than would have been possible when they were young.[5] Archaeologists have used oral history to investigate the uses of household goods in the first half of the nineteenth century, retrieving complete examples of crockery and pottery from shards, and bringing together groups of older people who recognise the objects from their grandparents' homes, and who relate memories of how they were used and where they were placed in the home.[6]

Oral history projects like these rely on triangulation to help assess accuracy and account for the effects of memory as they retrieve an aspect of the past which may otherwise be inaccessible to historians. Such a stance need not stem from naïve empiricism: discussing the methodological issues involved in interviewing child survivors of the Holocaust, Rebecca Clifford shows how their memories, fractured though they may be, nevertheless reveal the life-long implications of broken parent–child relationships in a way that the archival records of aid agencies cannot. Without oral history, Clifford concludes, a history of family reunification after the Holocaust from the child's perspective would scarcely be possible.[7] Contemporaneous sources do not tell us 'what happened afterwards. They do not tell us how these reunions were subjectively experienced, nor what long-term implications the process had.'[8]

On the other side, historians of memory tend to be as concerned with the way the interviewee remembers, and the cultural scripts and emotions that condition their recall, as with the experiences and events to which they testify. Alistair Thomson's *Anzac Memories* is a notable example of this approach: he found that when Australian veterans of the First World War remembered the conflict in the early 1980s, they did so through the Anzac legend of laconic, brave and egalitarian masculinity.[9] They responded unwittingly to the pressure to conform to public narratives and re-told their war through the frames of mid-twentieth-century Australian nationalism.[10] In Mark Roseman's study of the Holocaust survivor Marianne Ellenbogen, he draws on a rich variety of sources – interviews, official documents, diaries, memoirs and mementoes – to identify the inaccuracies in her testimony, and to document how her memory of the war changed over time. Marianne's errors and fabrications, he argues, do not undermine the value of the testimony but on the contrary, provide important clues about the emotional burdens that survivors carried. To an oral historian like this, 'misremembering' or 're-remembering' has value as the divergencies between event and memory signal where emotional legacies of loss and hope, psychic defences and unfulfilled wishes break in.[11]

An interview is always more than a chronicle from which facts can be plucked, as Elizabeth Tonkin once put it, 'like currants from a cake'.[12] But as Roseman shows, it also tells us about more than the here and now of remembering. When people reminisce, they bring an aspect of the personal past into relation with the present. The experience involves more than memory; it brings 'a sense of the past in the present', as Kurt Danzinger puts it.[13] Sometimes that sense can be so compelling that the interviewer feels plunged into the scene too, and the perception of time is telescoped, as I experienced during Kathleen's story about Christmas.

Some of Kathleen's account of her early life is supported by external documentation and has value for First World War historians. For example, it shows the consequences for families of the Ministry of Pensions policy of subtracting the cost of hospitalisation from a man's war pension. But Kathleen's more improbable recollections can also be understood as evidence of the war's impact, revealing the subjectivity of a generation that was surrounded from birth by the war-bereaved and damaged veterans, but who had no social identity as victims themselves. Their *mothers*, they would tell me, were the ones who suffered, had to be resourceful and had to swallow their pride. 'We were lucky', Kathleen said, 'we had a good mother who managed to make food out of practically nothing.' And later, 'Oh, my mother had a hell of a time. And she was a very strong woman, a very good woman. Marvellous, she was.' Far-fetched though it seems, Kathleen's story about the post-mortem reveals her wish to convey how tough her mother was, and how capably she held the family together in the face of her father's incapacity. Like other daughters in this study, in late life Kathleen still felt her mother's predicament in the 1920s and 30s: it was remembering her *mother's* distress that led Kathleen to break into tears. In the Second World War, however, Kathleen had become a hero and a victim in her own right. Her account might be thought of as a form of what Alessandro Portelli calls a 'uchronic dream', an imaginative compensation for a childhood hidden in the aftermath of the First World War, which put her at the centre of events in the mid-century and gave her a history of her own.[14]

The narrative in oral history is always produced within a context and it is always more than talk. The communication in a psychoanalytic session, says the psychoanalyst Betty Joseph, needs to be understood within the 'total situation' of the encounter, and something similar can be said of oral history.[15] It is an event, the context of which includes the communication beforehand, the initial meeting between the two parties, the surroundings in which the interview is held and what happens during and after the recording. Two people – often unknown to each other beforehand – form a relationship, the evidence of which consists of looks, gestures and silence as well as talk. Much that takes place around the visible and audible cues is opaque. This includes the emotions felt by the interviewee as they remember, and those felt by the historian as they conjure in their minds the scenes described by the interviewee. One cannot separate the 'knowledge' of the past that is obtained in such an interview from the feelings and imagined pasts which transpire in the encounter. Ruminating on the possibilities of clinical techniques in qualitative social research, Duncan Cartwright describes how a cough, repeated word or digression may point to unconscious meanings. He calls this phenomenon 'noise', a metaphor that re-centres the auditory but points to the significance of the total context.[16]

There are good reasons why oral historians sometimes hesitate to explore this broader context and prefer to distil their evidence in words. We might accept that emotions animate many of the stories that people tell us in an interview, and notice moments when psychological defences break in on each side, but we do not possess the training to fathom their meanings. Even judged by the standards of the most intensive life-story interview and the least intensive therapy, moreover, the encounters in oral history are relatively fleeting. We simply do not know our informants that well.

At the same time, however, precisely because our concern is a past in mind that is composed of a mixture of reconstruction and fantasy, it is helpful to consider how the emotional state of the interviewee might bear on the narrative they construct and how the interviewer feels as they ask questions, observe and listen.[17] Each party draws on imagination to fill in gaps in experience, memory and knowledge, and to manage the affect that is connected to events in the past and aroused by remembering. When the transcriber of Kathleen Skin's interview inserts '[*starts to cry*]', this denotes an emotional register picked up from listening. It is not a transcription of speech, and for every mood the transcriber picks up, many others flit between the interviewer and the interviewee and are not recorded. Sometimes the past appears as an enactment, such as when Kathleen hands me the letter from the Ministry of Pensions, and I offer to read it out. Conventionally in oral history, the audio recording is thought of as the raw data which is then converted into a transcript, the written document being easier to retrieve and analyse, and fitting the historian's preferred forms of communication, the essay and book. The evidence changes form twice as the encounter becomes sound and then text.[18] By that stage, the interview seems more akin to a story than a meeting between two people.

The discussion in this chapter draws on my experience of oral history since the early 1980s but is particularly concerned with the thirty-five interviews I conducted with British descendants between 2011 and 2014. I kept a journal in which I noted the location and surroundings of the interview, my impressions of the interviewee, and what happened during the sessions. The interviews were recorded and transcribed in full and were coded using Nvivo, but in developing my interpretations I often found it helpful to return to the recordings – or listen to them while reading and marking up the transcript – rather than rely in the first instance on the transcripts or thematic categories.[19] Audio, remarks the radio documentary maker Siobhán McHugh, is a powerful source of affect. It stirs up emotions and thoughts in the listener, who makes associations with the situation of the speaker based on their personal experience, knowledge and imagination.[20] Digital recording makes it comparatively easy to locate particular moments in the interview, and in listening again, I found I was able to reanimate a sense of the encounter in the round. Reconstructing scenes from the interviews, my direct memory was part of the evidence and helped form my interpretations.

In what follows, I view the encounters in oral history alongside the ideas of the psychoanalyst and paediatrician Donald Winnicott. My aim is not to advocate the use of clinical techniques in oral history interviews, but to shed light on what oral history itself entails as an encounter, particularly when it concerns the inter-generational impact of war.[21] Winnicott's thinking here provides a vantage point from which to think about the relationships in the past that people recall and those that occur within the interview, as each is apprehended through the senses and imagination of the teller and the listener.[22] The next section considers the interview as a form of 'intermediate space' between past and present, the external and the internal worlds. The final section describes four ways in which, in my interviews with descendants, I sought to maintain a sense of the whole experience, the emotional communication and the acts of imagination that go on within it.

Oral history as an 'intermediate space'

The 'transitional object' is probably Winnicott's most influential idea and belongs in his terms to an area of intermediate experience. The blanket or teddy chosen by the infant exists in the world but at the same symbolises the mother and is a creative source of what Winnicott called 'illusion'.[23] Winnicott believed that through play the infant developed a capacity to live in the world, and in his Paddington clinic he watched children move back and forth between the mother and the objects of their play, thus establishing a creative space between the 'me' and the 'not me'. Through such activities, Winnicott believed, the 'pure subjectivity' of the newborn infant was accompanied by an increasing capacity for objectivity.[24] The struggle to relate inner and outer reality goes on throughout life and illusions retain a positive value in managing the strain between them.[25] Unlike Freud, for whom growth depended on the recognition of the reality principle, Winnicott had a more positive view of illusions.[26] Although he did not theorise the relation between them, Winnicott believed that there was a 'direct continuity' from play to cultural experience and the creativity of the adult. Innovations in science, art or literature or belief in religion were 'little madnesses' that allowed the adult to foster illusions like those of the child at play.[27]

What then if we consider the oral history interview as a form of play? In playing, says Winnicott, the child displays 'the ideas that occupy his life', and something analogous happens in an interview through the oral historian's encouragement to talk about the past.[28] Creativity in the space of the interview entails work with what Winnicott calls 'inherited tradition' or 'the cultural store': stories, myths and images of the wider culture that are transmitted from the past and to which the individual brings their own experience, inner world and preoccupations.[29] Let me give an example. Winifred Spray's father was killed in 1917 when she was two and a half. When I asked her in 2011 if she had any memories of him, she responded:

> Well, I'm not sure, but I remember my mother going to ... we lived at Old Basford ... the top of a hill, and I remember walking down this hill, the grassy banks on each side of it, and we'd gone to meet a soldier. I don't ... I don't ... I think it could have been my father, it could have been my mother's brother, because he came home on leave about that time, but I think it was my father. And my mother let go of my hand – I'd be two and a half – to let me run to meet him. And he picked me up, and put me on his shoulder. And that's the only memory I have. And it might not even have been my father, it might have been my mother's brother, but I think it was my father. But ... there's no means of knowing.

As Winifred described this scene and each time I re-hear or re-read it, images of family separations and reunions in wartime come to mind from photographs, films, interviews, books and histories.[30] Occasionally I trawl through online images – the contemporary historian's 'cultural store' of first call – hoping to identify Winifred's memory of being hoisted into the arms of a home-bound soldier. Winifred composes her account in the intermediate space between

Figure 1.1 British Guardsman on home leave.

personal experience and tropes of the veteran's return, and her story hovers between fantasy and historically minded assessments. At one moment she claims the serviceman she remembers was her father, but at another, acknowledges that this may not be the case. She has an explanation of the identity of the man she remembers if it wasn't her father (interestingly, she doesn't call him her uncle), but takes pleasure in the thought that it was really him. At times Winifred is drawn towards an understanding that there may be elements of fantasy in her memory; at others, she fosters the illusion that her father was not always lost to her.

Winifred related this memory in the first couple of minutes of our interview and went on to recount other childhood dreams and apparitions of her father. Our interview gave Winifred an opportunity to rejuvenate these illusions. Her mother did not tell Winifred that her father was dead until she was six or seven, and here she talks about her hope that he would return:

The evidence of afterlives 39

Figure 1.2 'Goodbye Daddy! God Bless!', Bamforth & Co. postcard. Courtesy of the Army Children Archive. All rights reserved.

I prayed so hard, I thought, 'This is going to happen.' And I remember the … [*laughs*] somebody knocking at the door, when my grandmother was there, and I thought, 'This is him!' And it was somebody came and said … 'I've brought you some rhubarb! [*laughs*] I met your mother, and I said, "I've got some spare rhubarb!"' I always remember this wretched rhubarb! And I thought it was my father [*laughs*] having lost his memory, and suddenly remembered where he was. And when I was little, there used to be a lot of horses go by the … our front garden … well, our road, which fronts onto a road which went near to one of the … well, two hospitals, where there were a lot of wounded Tommies, and soldiers recuperating, and I used to go to the gate and search all these men's faces, thinking, 'Perhaps one of them's my father, and he's forgotten where he is, who he is.' Of course, it wasn't.

This kind of remembering draws on the post-war trope of the soldier who has lost his memory. When in 1922 the Ministry of Pensions in France published a photograph of the amnesiac soldier Anthelme Mangin in national newspapers, dozens of families from among the 250,000 missing French servicemen came forward to claim the man as their own.[31] Children orphaned by the war held on to the hope that perhaps their fathers were not dead after all.[32] Winifred draws on the shared post-war imaginary of the amnesiac soldier to express the deep personal wish that her vanished father would return.

Her memory of childhood was structured around the moments of his possible reappearance:

> I was once very feverish, with probably just a sore throat and cold, sitting on my mother's knee, on that rocking chair, and … the back door opened, and there's a door into this kitchen/living room, and this soldier walked in, and I was sure it was my father. Whether it was … I don't really believe in ghosts, but … I remember saying to my mother … 'That's my daddy coming in', and she just … she said I was delirious. Well, probably I was. And I still see it … in his Army uniform.

Winnicott believed that hallucinations fall outside the definition of play because the person hallucinating has lost a sense of the external reality.[33] When Winifred says 'I still see it', she is not hallucinating, but conveying a memory of her hallucinations, and is thus in the transitional space. Preparing for our interview the day before, she had written notes about her memories and apparitions (she handed them to me at the end of the interview) and had dreamed about her father that night. Her interview was, in essence, a history of her dreaming, a transitional object in reverse which created an illusion of reality around the father she never knew.

Winifred's interview illustrates the complex shifts that take place in oral history between imagination and experiences of the world. The genre might be considered a transitional space in two senses. Firstly, it shifts between orientations in time, crossing between past, present and an imagined future. Adam Phillips remarks that the analyst must ask, 'what am I being used to do?', and that is a question the historian should also ask. Both the interviewer and interviewee imagine a future audience as they work in the present on the past, and each uses the other to help them reach that audience.[34] As I shall describe below, in the *Afterlives* project it has been important to understand where the interviewee wants to go via the oral historian.

Secondly, oral history interviews straddle the internal and external worlds. They belong in Winnicott's terms to 'an intermediate area of *experiencing* to which inner reality and external life both contribute'.[35] The interviewee moves between the inner and outer worlds: at one moment Winifred Spray is immersed in her memories, and at another, she reflects on their status as dreams or hallucinations. In 'Uchronic Dreams', Alessandro Portelli notes that fantasy may be more prominent in interviews with elderly people as the conscious controls on memory diminish and the narrator is less able or concerned to locate their account in relation to actuality.[36] Substitution and fabulation may also be common among descendants, for whom an 'inherited culture' of war and its aftermath takes the place of experience. When the narrator did not witness the events of whose consequences they speak, 'composure' leans hard on established cultural forms and learned histories.[37]

Oral history leads in two directions: it supposes that the interviewee will try to describe their experience as accurately as they can – this, after all, is the presumed value of the 'eyewitness' – but at the same time recognises that nobody tells it as it was. I opened the *Afterlives* interviews by asking about the dates, places of birth and occupations of family members. I asked people to describe the houses in which they had lived as children, their relationships with siblings and parents, and their memories of growing up. I sought clarification when the account seemed unclear or was at odds with my assumptions, and sometimes pressed people for more exact descriptions, bringing them into touch with historical themes. Being interviewed by a historian, the interviewee may make a conscious effort to align their accounts with known historical events and conventional understandings. Kathleen Skin's memory was jogged by the coming visit of the historian, and she found herself remembering a time when she personally witnessed a 'historic' occasion:

> I suddenly thought of something last night, and I wrote it down, about watching the '101' disappear into the distance in 1929. I was lying on the grass, looking up at the sky, and I saw this silver ball going along. I called my father, and he was milking the goat, so he had a look, and he said, 'Oh, it's an airship!' And it was the last voyage of the '101' and it crashed in France. And that was the last airship they used. So that's historic, but it was also during the War … I mean after the War, in the thirties … no, '29 it was, I think it crashed. You can look it up.

Talking to the historian, an interviewee may feel anxious that their recollections do not fit in with accepted versions of the past and might be proved wrong: Kathleen prevaricates about the date of the '101' crash (October 1930) and eventually passes to me the responsibility for accuracy. Our presence can invite what Winnicott called a 'compliant' attitude, a pressure to construct a self that is congruent with prevailing historical accounts and satisfies the imagined requirements of the historian.[38] Some of my interviewees, for example, having volunteered for an interview about family legacies of the war, were embarrassed when I asked about their parents' war service as they had few details. Some had contacted me in the hope that I would help them find out more. They knew the war not as participants or historians, but as children growing up afterwards.

At other points in an interview, our attitude and questions may work in the direction of fantasy. As Portelli puts it, 'We want our narrators to tell us not only what they remember seeing but also how they perceived events, how they felt and dreamed about them, what meanings they take away, how they see their place in history.'[39] An approach like this entails the interviewer helping to create a space in which the interviewee can enter what Winnicott calls a 'non-purposive state … a ticking over of the unintegrated personality', in which the illusions attached to the past are brought to mind.[40]

The oral historian's research questions and epistemological assumptions will tend to take them in one direction or another. Our informants, however, reminisce in a transitional space between experiences in the world and fantasy, and their accounts do not belong wholly in either. Winnicott believed that the analyst should not ask the child 'Did you conceive of this or was it presented to you from without?' Oral historians often ask themselves whether a testimony is accurate or 'true' to the historical record, but when gauging matters of fact, they might also ask how history writes itself on the psyche and how people draw on memory, culture and emotions to work on past experience. As the historian of women in the Soviet Army, Svetlana Alexievich, comments, 'Remembering is not a passionate or dispassionate retelling of a reality that is no more, but a new birth of the past, when time goes into reverse. Above all it is creativity. As they narrate, people create.'[41]

The oral historian participates in this productive space, drawing on the store of cultural and historical knowledge to compose his or her own illusions about the past of the interviewee. This is part of the appeal of oral history, which is often pursued with enthusiasm and a sense of mission that goes beyond the strictly professional. Part of the allure is the promise to transport us to a different time and place and be in the skin of another. Vivid pictures of the interviewees' pasts often come to my mind during an interview: when Kathleen sees her mother accept sixpence from the hard-up valet, or Winifred has a vision of her father at the kitchen door, so do I. Listening again to an interview or reading a transcript, we consolidate these images and construct further scenes in our heads.[42] No matter how vivid our imaginings, however, we know that they are not replicas of past times and places. More than once I have been pulled out of a reverie about the interviewee's childhood to see the elderly person in front of me struggle to get up from their chair and disentangle themselves from the lapel mic. Visions of the past fill the imaginations of both the interviewee and the historian, composed from experience and the 'cultural pool' of images and narratives about the past.[43]

The *Afterlives* interviews have made me think about how the oral historian's situation of coming after might relate to the children's sense of coming after, as both parties work with phenomena that are before their time yet are sometimes experienced as if they were in the present. It is not just our interviewees who construct illusions about the past, the historian does too: we seek to reanimate the past and make it intelligible to the present while knowing all the time that history is only in our heads. Below I will describe four ways in which I have sought to capture a sense of the total situation of the oral history interview as it weaves between past experience and imaginative reconstruction.

Places and things

My interviews took place in the homes of the interviewees, where they were sometimes only just managing to live independently. Even now, a century after the war, its effects could sometimes be seen in the location of the house. Winifred Spray was living just outside Oxford where she had brought up her three children. Her mother, she said, gesturing towards the bottom of the garden, had lived just over there. The local council allocated her a house on the estate that backed onto Winifred's house, and there was a connecting gate between the two properties. The arrangement reflected the sense of obligation and responsibility that she – and the local council – had felt towards the elderly war widow living on her own.

Harriet Pollock's two daughters sat with me throughout her interview, two generations of war-bereaved daughters. Both Harriet's father and her husband had died from war-related health conditions. She had lived close to her mother in Middlesbrough, as had her daughters. Harriet had a bed in each of their houses and would go from one to the other. The north-east is characterised by strong matriarchal relationships, as Elizabeth Roberts showed, but in Harriet's case the absence of husbands and fathers had also brought mothers and daughters close.[44] Housing histories, then, could reveal the effects of the war across generations and the century.

Figure 1.3 Harriet Pollock and her daughters. Author's own. All rights reserved.

The war heritage in homes was also revealing. A pair of shell cases were on display in the front room of Marie-Anne Careless's house on the Welsh border. They had been engraved by an English soldier billeted at her grandparents' farm in Hazebrouck in northern France and depicted her mother and her mother's cousin, both of whom were engaged to British soldiers. The cousin's fiancé was later killed, but she never married and continued to wear the engagement ring. In the early 1920s, Marie-Anne's parents settled in Bertincourt, the scene of the 1918 Spring Offensive, where her father worked as head gardener in the local war cemetery.

During the Second World War, Marie-Anne's father was imprisoned outside Paris, and she and her mother moved into a tiny flat in Paris. The family returned to Bertincourt at the end of the war to find that most of their furniture and household possessions had been taken. The shell cases had survived, however, and were now on display in the front window of Marie-Anne's house on the Welsh border, where she lived with her British husband. Highly polished, they were symbols of the relationships between British soldiers and French families that had defined her family's history through the twentieth century and two world wars.[45] Yet despite their importance, Marie-Anne did not romanticise them. I emailed her later to ask whether the soldier who had crafted the shell cases had been the fiancé of Marie-Anne's aunt or mother. She replied that although this might make for a nice story, she did not know who the artist was. Sometimes it is the interviewee rather than the interviewer who moors the account in actuality.

I changed my approach to the interviews as I began to realise the significance of mementoes of the war and childhood, asking people in advance if they had any objects they wished to show me, and looking over them in the second half of the interview. I kept the recorder on, but there are only snatches of narrative in the transcript – it is a record of what was said in passing as we pored over photographs, trench art, medals, mementoes, official documents and letters. I became interested in the histories of these objects after the war: when did the descendant acquire them, and when had they been brought down from the loft and passed to grandchildren for school projects on the war? Were they usually on display, or had they been retrieved from a suitcase or cardboard box in anticipation of my arrival?[46]

Difficulties in understanding

Misunderstandings, resistance to questions, the forgetting or mishearing of what the interviewee has said and problems with the recording equipment can be instructive, although, as Valerie Yow notes, they tend to produce an immediate impulse to forget them.[47] The difficulties experienced by an interviewee can communicate themselves in such a way that they trouble the interviewer's competence. Early in the project, I interviewed an eighty-seven-year-old man who I shall call Mr Grey, who had served in the Navy in the Second World War. This was my second interview that day and I arrived slightly late, feeling tired. I struggled to keep the interview on track during the first hour and a half, as Grey talked at length and in a rather detached way about the village where he had grown up. We broke for afternoon tea, and Grey then began a detailed account of joining the Navy in the Second World War. I had a sense of the interview circling around and found it difficult to follow his train of thought. 'Where is he going with the interview?' I wondered. He described being aboard a Merchant Navy boat bound for the French coast where they had been sent to inspect landing facilities and realising that they had approached the wrong beach. He began to weep, but I could not fathom why, as there was, he said, 'nothing' on this beach. They checked their bearings, and eventually landed on Omaha beach. It was not the empty beach that Grey was upset about, but the corpses stacked up on the sand at Omaha beach from the landing the previous day. Breaking into tears again, he explained that at that moment, he saw how life could be taken away 'just like that', and he clicked his fingers. He had not told anyone about it for forty years – not even his uncle, who had worked with battle-stressed soldiers – until he travelled to the battlefields with his wife in the mid-1980s.

My interview with Mr Grey shows how the emotions attached to past experiences can be re-animated in an interview, and that the interviewer's reactions can repeat aspects of the problems the interviewee experiences.[48] On getting home, I realised to my dismay and intense embarrassment that I had failed to turn the recorder back on after tea. Discomfited by Mr Grey's difficulties in getting to the point – and sensing, perhaps, that his story might be about to lead somewhere difficult – I had enacted his feeling, not just that he might not be able to explain what happened to him, or that people did not want to hear his story, but that his story was unbearable and *unlistenable* to. Neither of us, at that moment, was able to sustain the interview as a transitional space.

Traumatic experiences can place exceptional emotional demands on the interviewer and are particularly likely to lead to mistakes, mishearings and suppression, in the process, exposing aspects of the emotional communication between interviewer and interviewee that are normally hidden.[49] Even a trifling misunderstanding, however, can tell us something about the subjectivity of the child growing up in the war's aftermath. Ray Burgin grew up in the remote village of Thurgoland in South Yorkshire where his father, blinded in 1917, ran a poultry farm. As he described his childhood, Ray often switched between the first and third person, and I sometimes found it difficult to follow who he was talking about:

> *RB:* He was … found his way around the farm all right. And I remember when I went to school, in the local school, he would walk along the lane, sort of meet me coming home, sort of as it was getting dark in the winter time. I don't think I was, you know, too pleased about doing that, but it was only a sort of straight lane …
> *MR:* You mean you weren't pleased about him doing that?
> *RB:* Yes. I wasn't pleased about me being, you know, out there alone!
> *MR:* Okay.
> *RB:* It was dark…. So he did that. But … if he walked anywhere else, it was always with my mother, basically. When he got … moved down to the South Coast, they walked quite a lot.
> *MR:* And how would he walk … would he be holding … she would hold his arm?
> *RB:* Yes, you would hold his arm. If you come to a step, you warn him. But otherwise, he just walked along.

Burgin switches perspective here, beginning with an account of his father's capabilities, then recalling a memory of himself walking down the 'straight lane' at dusk. The blind veteran who could 'walk alone' was considered the epitome of the war hero, and perhaps this is in the back of Burgin's mind, but what emerges is his childhood fear of being alone in the dark, a fear which his blind father had perhaps tried to assuage by meeting him.[50] There was no electricity at the farm in Thurgoland, only paraffin lights and then Calor gas lighting, so the winter evenings at home were also spent in the gloom. My confusion listening to Burgin, I realised, was a pointer to the double subjectivity he had experienced as a child, anxious about the unsighted world that his father inhabited, but encouraged from an early age to assist him ('You just hold his arm'). Burgin had gone on to become an electrical engineer and designer of fluorescent lights, an interesting choice for a man whose memories of childhood were marked by darkness.

Moments in which the interviewee resists a question or comment can reveal the differences between the emotional codes of the mid-twentieth century and those of today. Jefferey Flower told me that during the first bombing raid on Bristol in November 1940, he watched his father, who did not usually drink, finish off half a bottle of whisky: 'it must be terrible, I mean, the bombs were dropping around like nobody's business, and we were just there in the house … we didn't have no shelters at that time, no arrangements made'. Earlier in the interview, Jefferey had told me that his father was 'the only survivor' in his section after a shell burst over their trench on Christmas Day 1915. Thinking of that, I commented that the bombing raid 'must have been quite [...] disturbing to him'. Jefferey assented at first but on second thought he was not comfortable with my interpretation: 'Yeah, I think so. He didn't show it. You know, he wasn't saying, "Oh dear!" or anything like that. I mean when war was declared, he said, "Here we go again!"' Jefferey went on to describe one of the last raids of the blitz when an incendiary bomb landed on the roof of their house and his father fell through the rafters in the loft trying to retrieve it: 'But, I mean, to approach a flaring incendiary bomb, you know, that showed he had experience! [*laughs*]'

Casting my mind back to his story about the whisky, I was more explicit: 'this is someone who's had some bad things happen to him before, and it's coming back again?' 'No. No', he said, 'I think I was just telling tales! [*laughs*]'. It is not clear to me what Jefferey meant by this, whether he felt bad about mentioning his dead father's anxieties behind his back, or whether he was suggesting in a teasing way that I should not take his story seriously as he had made it up. Either way, the comment reveals Jefferey's resistance to my speculation that the bombing had brought back memories of the First World War. He responded with a counter-narrative that positioned his father within the norms of what Jessica Hammett calls the 'useful masculinity' of the civil defence worker and veteran, whose familiarity with combat was a source of sound judgement and calmness under fire.[51] As Jefferey explained, 'he'd had war experience, he'd had bomb experience, grenade throwing and all the rest of it … He wasn't scared of picking up a flaming bomb … he was more scared of his house burning down than possibly getting hurt.'

This exchange reveals a generational tension between the understandings of war and masculinity that Jefferey inhabited as a young boy in the war and those of the historian of war today. Jefferey recognises that my questions position his father as a victim, and he responds by trying to convince me otherwise. Fleeting thought it is, the push and pull between interviewer and interviewee reveals emotional worlds in tension, one associated with the two wars, which values endurance, the other with the psychological culture of confession and victimhood in the early twenty-first century. Clients in psychoanalysis, remarks Winnicott, have contrary impulses: they willingly subject themselves to its pressure to uncover their deepest thoughts and feelings, but also want to remain hidden. Jefferey Flower's reaction is an instance of the desire to avoid his memories being fixed by the interviewer's interpretations.[52]

Voices

In 'The Listening Guide', Carol Gilligan, Renee Spencer, Katherine Weinberg and Tatiana Bertsch establish a methodology for discerning the 'invisible inner world' of an interviewee through attention to voice. Voice, they argue, provides the 'footprint of the psyche, bearing the marks of the body, that person's history, of culture in the form of language, and the myriad ways in which human society and history shape the voice'.[53] Their approach involves listening for repeated metaphors and images that indicate the plot of the story, constructing 'I' poems based on key words repeated by the interviewee and detecting the 'contrapuntal' voices, often in tension, that may be detected in the course of the interview.

In this study, focused as it was on vertical relationships, I found that attention to voice provided a sensitive register of feelings about parents and how the interviewees had internalised parental authority and norms. Describing the excitement of the Blitz as a twelve-year-old child, John Frost paused, then said he had done 'two really bad things'. He had taken home an unexploded incendiary bomb that fell in the woods in Kingsdown, Kent, where he had been evacuated with his cousin, but panicked when he woke up the next morning: 'I thought, "Dad'll kill me if he sees this" ... [*laughs*], so I put it in my coat, and as I was walking to the bus stop, I threw it over somebody's garden, front garden.' Here the internal voice of conscience and authority, Freud's super-ego, takes the persona of John's father.

John went on to remark in a serious tone that 'I mean, the house is still there', as if he still half-feared that it might have been blown up. Traces of the panic he felt then surface in the interview. When I tried to put to Frost that he must have been thinking to himself, 'Did it go off? Did someone get hurt?', he replied quickly, 'No, it didn't', as if his mind was still fixed on the potential disaster.

The voice of Winifred Spray's mother can be detected as she describes what it was like for mother and daughter to live off the widow's pension. As a child, Winfred had sometimes felt ashamed of her mother. Winifred was given 'the best of everything ... the very best quality of everything, lovely toys and ... the practical things, I didn't suffer at all. But my mother used to look a bit shabby, I used to think.' On one occasion Winifred's school friends passed by when Winifred was having coffee in Nottingham with her aunt, 'who was always well-dressed'. The girls assumed the woman was Winifred's mother: 'I just let it pass. And forever after that, I was so afraid of them seeing me with my mother, looking so ... not exactly shabby, but ... she bought good clothes which had to jolly well last, and ... it's a dreadful thing to deny your own mother, isn't it?'

There are three voices in play at this point in Winifred's account: those of her mother, herself as a child and the elderly woman who now feels ashamed of the 'dreadful thing' she did. Her mother's voice is apparent when Winifred corrects her initial description of her mother's clothes as 'shabby' and endorses the value of economy ('clothes which had to jolly well last'). That phrase, we might conjecture, is one which the young Winifred had heard her mother say, and as she utters it, the memory of her mother presents itself with such force that she immediately breaks out in self-reproof. She follows up the story with redoubled assertions of her mother's goodness, which seem designed to countermand the shame she had felt as a child. She 'was a wonderful mother really', who 'would sacrifice her own pleasures for me, and ... as I say, never married again, never ... would never have married again, I don't think'. Her mother's single-minded devotion to Winifred, however, had clearly also been a cause of some difficulty for Winifred. When I asked her later in the interview if she would have liked her mother to remarry, she said yes, and described her regret that her mother had rebuffed a suitor from next door, a man who was also widowed and had a daughter. Alongside the voice of the ninety-four-year-old, asserting what a good mother she had had, it was possible to hear the voice of a child who at times had felt ashamed of and responsible for her mother.

Repetition of words or phrases can also point to emotional states in the past that were unresolved or difficult to express. Reading through the transcript of Marion Armstrong's interview I realised she had used the phrase 'not deprived' four times:

> She was very very good. I was lucky. I don't have visions of a ... a deprived childhood. We had no money, but we had everything that mattered. She was very loving, very kind, very capable, and I had good grandparents.
>
> And I actually had a holiday every year ... I've had holidays at York a lot, Skipton a lot – that's where her sisters were – as I say, don't imagine it was a deprived childhood, it wasn't.
>
> She was thrilled with the ... winter coat he got [a gift to her brother for grammar school] ... it was very good quality – and this was all paid for by the British Legion, because my dad had been an Army man, you see. But as I say, don't think of it as a deprived childhood, it wasn't. We had everything that matters.
>
> It wasn't a deprived childhood at all. He met us from school every day. He had a sweet in his pocket for me, 'Don't tell your mum, because she says I'll spoil your dinner!'

Marion here measures her experience by the standards of a working-class northern childhood: she had a loving mother and father, annual holidays, good clothes and treats. There seems to be a voice telling her that she should feel grateful, and in each of these moments in the interview, her gratitude felt genuine. Yet there was a history of bereavement in the family which leads me to consider Marion's statements as more than a testimony of a happy childhood: by her late teens Marion had lost both her father and brother, but the family was stoic throughout.[54] The repeated negative '*not* deprived' in Marion's interview could be a kind of reaction formation, which in the very act of asserting what she had, expresses what she lost. Statements like these reveal the emotional situation of the sons and daughters of war disabled, growing up in a society which did not recognise them as 'secondary' victims.

Many such voices can be detected in an interview, and as 'The Listening Guide' suggests, in identifying them, we learn much about the subjectivity of the interviewee. The voices I heard during my interviews, however, while they represent aspects of the selfhood of the person being interviewed, were often evocations of actual people, mothers and fathers in particular. Animated by the invitation to remember, the interviewees gave renditions of characters and relationships from childhood. Winifred's remark about clothes lasting, for example, felt almost like ventriloquism. At the same time, voices form only part of the communication with an interviewer, who on occasion may be being invited to hear and experience something different from what the words on their own assert.[55]

Motivations

Voices, then, need to be heard within the overall situation of the interview and that includes the interviewee's reasons for putting themselves forward as a participant. It is commonly assumed in psychoanalysis that the analysand has an unconscious project into which they will try to draw the analyst. As Betty Joseph remarks, 'Much of our understanding of the transference comes through our understanding of how our patients act on us to feel things for many varied reasons; how they try to draw us into their defensive systems.'[56] Oral historians think at length about what they want to achieve in their interviews, and what kinds of approach and questions will best facilitate their aims, but in a parallel vein to the clinician, we might also ask about the motives of the interviewee and the kinds of projects which they seek to enlist us in, conscious and unconscious.

This is a question I needed to think about from the start of the project, when over one hundred people got in touch in response to an appeal for descendants published in local newspapers across the UK. I was astonished – and overwhelmed – by the response, and spent the next few weeks ploughing through emails and letters and answering phone calls and phone messages. People sent me written recollections of their childhoods and their parents' lives, photographs and military records.

In addition to the reasons people got in touch, I have tried to think about how they wished to make use of the interview. When Kathleen Skin passed the letter from the Ministry of Pensions to me, for example, I was unsure what to do. She had only just recovered her composure and having been passed the letter, I felt a pressure to do something with it. What was going on here? I was, I think, responding to Kathleen's wish that the Ministry of Pensions be called to account for submitting an unwell man to constant reviews. As the interview is an aural record, and the letter, being a written text, offers no proof, I offer to read it aloud. In so doing, I commit her testimony to the record.

Winnicott writes that creativity occurs when the individual contributes to the store of common culture, and when they 'have somewhere to put' what they find. The oral historian might be thought of as an agent in this process, offering the prospect of a home for memories composed from experience and the 'cultural pool' of publicly circulating heritage of the past.[57] The second generation understands that their experience of having lived amidst the aftermath of the First World War will soon be lost, and that historians will then possess the monopoly on historical understanding. As their historian, I ask myself: how do they wish to make use of me in navigating between the evanescent past of 'communicative' family memory and the enduring forms of 'cultural' memory of the First World War?[58] What do they want to get on the record before they pass?

I have tried to describe here what I learned during my interviews with the sons and daughters of those who witnessed the First World War firsthand. I did not set out to adopt an experiential method. In the early interviews, I did not think to ask people to show me their material heritage of war, and my journal notes were as much an aide-memoir of their stories as my experience of the interviews. I did not envisage listening to the recordings to renew my memory of the encounters but found this valuable because it picked up clues about context – tones of voice and shifts in emotional states, the 'extraneous' noise of people getting up and down, the presence of others in the house, the voices from the past that echoed in interviews. I was certainly aware of misunderstandings and my lapses of professional competence, and it took some deliberation before it was possible to glean their significance as evidence of the situation of the second generation, mediating between the war's eyewitnesses and the historian.

An approach like this is not without its problems. Reflecting on the methods of documentation used by psychoanalysts, Donald Spence describes the degradation of meaning that occurs in the transition from the clinical encounter to the written case study, likening the former to a rain forest and the latter to a mud field.[59] The analyst's 'on-site observations' are subjective and impermanent: the resulting case studies are often written up long after the event and are based on a diminished memory of the sessions. Notes and even recordings are poor substitutes, amenable to 'retrospective falsification' and the forgetting of embarrassing moments or gut reactions that do not fit conventional understandings. The result, says Spence, is a tendency to confirm existing theoretical preconceptions: 'Only by looking in great detail at the actual session can we displace our comfortable assumptions about how psychoanalysis is practised and find out what actually happens and how a given session was understood by both parties', he concludes.[60]

An experiential method in oral history faces some of the same issues. It too is subject to the historian's reconstruction of the event, and a flattening out of the encounter. Referentiality to the interviewer's personal experience may make it difficult for another person to assess the interview.[61] The relative brevity of the encounter may limit the oral historian's capacity to test their interpretations through experience, and to establish what motivates the interviewee to create the illusions they do.

The attempt to account for the context as comprehensively as we can, however, is a counterweight to the tendency in oral history, and in qualitative research more generally, to treat the enduring artefacts – the audio recording and the transcript – as self-contained entities. A study of voice that does not find a place for the person who speaks, or a narrative methodology that disembodies the narrator, is impoverished. Studies in which the researcher delegates the interviewing or relies on previous interviews (the so-called 'secondary use' increasingly promoted by funding councils) must do without direct personal experience of the interview, and this tends to increase the reliance on text. Attention to the interview relationship provides more than supporting evidence 'off the record' but is crucial to understanding how aspects of the past of the interviewee appear in the present.[62] Pausing over mistakes and technical glitches, listening again and using the transcript to re-imagine the encounter help to mitigate the 'smoothing tendency' that occurs as the relationship becomes a record and, ultimately, part of a work of history. As Portelli remarks, the value of oral history lies in the evidence it gives of the 'creative imagination' of the interviewee.[63] That evidence, however, is not wholly contained within the stories the narrator tells, but inheres in everything that happens in the interview, a creative relation in which the 'oral' is just part.

Notes

1 Quoted A. Erll, 'Locating Family in Cultural Memory Studies', *Journal of Comparative Family Studies*, 42: 3 (2011), 307.
2 The historian of women in the Soviet Army, Svetlana Alexievich, was born in 1948 and grew up in a rural Russian village. She describes the sensibility of the second generation growing up after the Second World War: 'We didn't know a world without war; the world of war was the only one familiar to us, and the people of war were the only people we knew.' S. Alexievich, *The Unwomanly Face of War* (London: Penguin, 2017), xii.
3 Many thanks to Louise Willmot and Gilly Carr for their responses.
4 On the status of oral testimony as evidence see P. Thompson with J. Bornat, *The Voice of the Past*, 4th edn (Oxford: Oxford University Press, 2017), 188–238; P. Summerfield, *Histories of the Self: Personal Narratives and Historical Practice* (Abingdon: Routledge, 2019), esp. 101–15; and Lynn Abrams on the evolution of oral history from the 'recovery mode' of the 1970s and 80s to a contemporary concern with subjectivity and the cultural environments of memory. *Oral History Theory* (Abingdon: Routledge, 2010), 5–9.

5 S. Szreter and K. Fisher, *Sex Before the Sexual Revolution: Intimate Life in England 1918–1963* (Cambridge: Cambridge University Press, 2010).
6 J. Webster, L. Tolson and R. Carlton, 'The Artifact as Interviewer: Experimenting with Oral History at the Ovenstone Miners' Cottages Site, Northumberland', *Historical Archaeology*, 48: 1 (2014), 11–29.
7 R. Clifford, 'Families after the Holocaust: Between the Archives and Oral History', *Oral History*, 46: 1 (Spring 2018), 42–3.
8 Clifford, 'Families after the Holocaust', 45.
9 A. Thomson, *Anzac Memories: Living with the Legend*, 2nd edn (Melbourne: Monash University Press, 2013).
10 Alesandro Portelli makes this point in his classic essay 'The Death of Luigi Trastulli: Memory and the Event'. The significance of oral history, he concludes, often lies 'not in its adherence to fact, but rather in its departure from it'. A. Portelli, *The Death of Luigi Trastulli and Other Stories: Form and Meaning in Oral History* (New York: State University of New York Press, 1991), 51.
11 M. Roseman, 'Surviving Memory: Truth and Inaccuracy in Holocaust Testimony', in R. Perks and A. Thomson (eds), *The Oral History Reader*, 3rd edn (Abingdon: Routledge, 2016), 320–34. See also M. Roper, 'Re-Remembering the Soldier Hero: The Psychic and Social Construction of Memory in Personal Narratives of the Great War', *History Workshop Journal*, 50: 1 (Autumn 2000), 181–204.
12 E. Tonkin, *Narrating Our Pasts: The Social Construction of Oral History* (Cambridge: Cambridge University Press, 1992), 6.
13 Quoted in P. Hamilton, 'Oral History and the Senses', in Perks and Thomson, *Oral History Reader*, 107. For a nuanced defence of the 'authenticity of experience' in the wake of the memory turn in oral history, see T. Kohut, *A German Generation: An Experiential History of the Twentieth Century* (New Haven: Yale University Press, 2012), esp. 237–42.
14 A. Portelli, 'Uchronic Dreams: Working-Class Memory and Possible Worlds', in P. Thompson and R. Samuel (eds), *The Myths We Live By* (London: Routledge, 1990), 145.
15 B. Joseph, 'Transference: The Total Situation', *International Journal of Psychoanalysis*, 66: 4 (1985), 447–54.
16 D. Cartwright, 'The Psychoanalytic Research Interview: Preliminary Suggestions', *Journal of the American Psychoanalytical Association*, 52: 1 (Winter 2004), 228.
17 For an example see Richard Hall, 'Emotional Histories: Materiality, Temporality and Subjectivities in Oral History Interviews with Fathers and Sons', *Oral History*, 47: 1 (Spring 2019), 61–71.

18 Much of what is conveyed in oral history, Timothy Ashplant remarks, is lost in transcription. 'Fantasy, Narrative, Event: Psychoanalysis and History', *History Workshop Journal*, 23: 1 (1987), 170.
19 Wendy Holloway and Tony Jefferson comment on the problems with qualitative software packages which house data 'outside the mind' rather than encouraging the capacity to hold in mind a sense of the whole interview. W. Holloway and T. Jefferson, *Doing Qualitative Research Differently: Free Association, Narrative and the Interview Method* (London: Sage, 2000), 69.
20 S. McHugh, 'The Affective Power of Sound: Oral History on Radio', *Oral History Review*, 39: 2 (Summer/Fall 2012), 194.
21 On the similarities and differences between the aims and practices of oral history and psychotherapy, see K. Figlio, 'Oral History and the Unconscious', *History Workshop Journal*, 26: 1 (1988), 120–32; M. Roper, 'Analysing the Analysed: Transference and Counter-Transference in the Oral History Encounter', *Oral History*, 31: 2 (Autumn, 2003), 20–32; V. Yow, 'What Can Oral Historians Learn from Psychotherapists?', *Oral History*, 46: 1 (Spring 2018), 33–42. On the application of psychoanalytic methods in social research, see K. Stamenova and R. D. Hinshelwood, *Methods of Research into the Unconscious* (Abingdon: Routledge, 2018); Holloway and Jefferson, *Doing Qualitative Research Differently*; Cartwright, 'The Psychoanalytic Research Interview'.
22 For essays that consider social research as form of intermediate space, see A. Kuhn (ed.), *Little Madnesses: Winnicott, Transitional Phenomena & Cultural Experience* (London: Bloomsbury Publishing, 2013).
23 D. W. Winnicott, *Playing and Reality* (London: Penguin, 1988), 16.
24 A. Phillips, *Winnicott* (London: Penguin, 2007), 114.
25 Phillips, *Winnicott*, 122.
26 M. Jacobs, *D. W. Winnicott* (London: Sage, 2008), 52.
27 Winnicott, *Playing and Reality*, 118.
28 Winnicott, *Playing and Reality*, 50.
29 Winnicott, *Playing and Reality*, 116–17.
30 See Melvin Bragg's semi-autobiographical novel *The Soldier's Return* (London: Hodder and Stoughton, 1999), and A. Allport, *Demobbed: Coming Home after the Second World War* (New Haven: Yale University Press, 2009), esp. 51–80.
31 J. Y. Le Naour, *The Living Unknown Soldier: A Story of Grief and the Great War* (New York: Metropolitan Books, 2004), 2.
32 R. Van Emden, *The Quick and the Dead: Fallen Soldiers and Their Families in the Great War* (Bloomsbury: London, 2011), 8.
33 Winnicott, *Playing and Reality*, 6.
34 Phillips, *Winnicott*, 118; Figlio, 'Oral History and the Unconscious', 120.

35 Quoted in Phillips, *Winnicott*, 119.
36 Portelli, 'Uchronic Dreams', 144–5.
37 On composure see G. Dawson, *Soldier Heroes: British Adventure, Empire and the Imagining of Masculinities* (London: Routledge, 1994), 22–6; Thomson, *Anzac Memories*, 10–15; P. Summerfield, 'Culture and Composure: Creating Narratives of the Gendered Self in Oral History Interviews', *Cultural and Social History*, 1: 1 (2004), 65–93.
38 Winnicott, *Playing and Reality*, 76. Yow observes how the wish to be eloquent and to impress the interviewer may lead the interviewee to embellish. 'What Can Oral Historians Learn from Psychotherapists?', 35.
39 Quoted in Yow, 'What Can Oral Historians Learn from Psychotherapists?', 36.
40 Winnicott, *Playing and Reality*, 60, 64.
41 Alexievich, *Unwomanly Face of War*, xv.
42 Yow describes the 'deep impression' that an interview can make on the interviewer: 'the words so deep they last a lifetime'. 'What Can Oral Historians Learn from Psychotherapists?', 39–40. For me the impression is visual as much as aural. I hold vivid memories of people and places long after the interview and continue to imagine the events and people from the past that the interviewee describes.
43 Winnicott, *Playing and Reality*, 117.
44 It was not only daughters who took on responsibilities like these as the war generation aged. After his wife died, David Smith's father came to live with David and his family. The grandchildren learned to clear their toys away and keep doors closed so Granddad would not trip over. Interview with David Smith, 10 January 2013.
45 Nicholas Saunders describes the therapeutic value obtained by descendants in polishing the war ephemera of their ancestors. 'Bodies of Metal, Shells of Memory: "Trench Art" and the Great War Re-Cycled', *Journal of Material Culture*, 5: 1 (2000), 59.
46 See Michèle Barrett and Peter Stallybrass on the domestic history of a First World War family archive: 'Printing, Writing and a Family Archive: Recording the First World War', *History Workshop Journal*, 75: 1 (2013), 1–32.
47 Valerie Yow, '"Do I Like Them Too Much?": Effects of the Oral History Interview on the Interviewer and Vice-Versa', *Oral History Review*, 24: 1 (Summer 1997), 67.
48 Eelco Runia describes how the problems being investigated by the researcher may repeat themselves in the analysis. E. Runia, '"Forget about It": "Parallel Processing" in the Srebrenica Report', *History and Theory*, 43: 3 (October 2004), 295–320; McHugh, 'Affective Power of Sound', 194.

49 Dominick LaCapra comments of historians interviewing Holocaust survivors that: 'His or her manifest implication in an affectively charged relationship to the survivor or witness and the special, stressful demands this relationship places upon inquiry may have more general implications for historical research, especially with respect to highly sensitive, emotionally laden, and evaluatively significant issues.' 'Holocaust Testimonies: Attending to the Victim's Voice', in D. LaCapra, *Writing History, Writing Trauma* (Baltimore: Johns Hopkins Press, 2001), 87.
50 J. Anderson, *War, Disability and Rehabilitation in Britain: 'Soul of a Nation'* (Manchester: Manchester University Press, 2011), 52.
51 J. Hammett, '"It's in the Blood, Isn't It?" The Contested Status of First World War Veterans in Second World War Civil Defence', *Cultural and Social History*, 14: 3 (2017), 358.
52 Phillips, *Winnicott*, 148. On the interviewee's resistance to the historian's interpretations, see K. Borland, '"That's Not What I Said": Interpretive Conflict in Oral Narrative Research', in S. Gluck and D. Patai (eds), *Women's Words: The Feminist Practice of Oral History* (New York: Routledge, 1992), 63–76.
53 C. Gilligan, R. Spencer, M. K. Weinberg and T. Bertsch, 'On the Listening Guide: A Voice-Centred Relational Method', in P. M. Camic, J. E. Rhodes and L. Yardley (eds), *Qualitative Research in Psychology: Expanding Perspectives in Methodology and Design* (Washington, DC: American Psychological Association, 2003), 157.
54 See Introduction.
55 Cartwright describes the gaps between what the interviewee says and how the interviewer feels about the communication. 'Psychoanalytic Research Interview', 227.
56 Joseph, 'Transference: The Total Situation', 447.
57 Winnicott, *Playing and Reality*, 117.
58 On the distinction between communicative and cultural memory, see J. Assmann, 'Communicative and Cultural Memory', in A. Erll and A. Nünning (eds), *Cultural Memory Studies: An International and Interdisciplinary Handbook* (New York: de Gruyter, 2008), 109–19.
59 'It is probably the lack of context', Spence remarks, which accounts for 'why recorded segments of sessions often seem dull, pointless and boring to a degree that we rarely experience in an actual session'. D. Spence, 'Rain Forest or Mud Field?', *International Journal of Psychoanalysis*, 79 (1998), 643.
60 Spence, 'Rain Forest or Mud Field?', 644–5. Ironically, perhaps, Spence recommends the methods of history from below to clinicians since those who practise it 'can almost always count on being surprised by the actual fabric of specific happenings' (645).

61 Gabriele Rosenthal suggests, however, that the formulation of interpretations in groups can help counteract this. G. Rosenthal, 'Biographical Research', in C. Seale, G. Gobo, J. F. Gubrium and D. Silverman (eds), *Qualitative Research Practice* (London: Sage, 2004), 55.
62 A. Sheftel and S. Zembrzycki (eds), *Oral History Off the Record: Toward an Ethnography of Practice* (London: Palgrave, 2013).
63 Portelli, 'Uchronic Dreams', 145.

2

Family transmission

When a descendant shares their personal archive with an oral historian or brings it along to a heritage event, they respond to the historical culture around them. But it is not just their own: they also respond to a history within the family, memories of ancestors and the feelings associated with them and the backstory of how they came to hold the family heritage. This chapter investigates the role of families in preserving the First World War past and the forms that family transmission may take, from objects to emotional enactments.

Families are characterised by deep relationships across and within generations: our family histories help make us who we are.[1] The family therapist John Byng-Hall describes how a 'family script' may be repeated across generations. Scripts are patterns of interaction distinctive to each family which children learn as they watch family dramas from the wings of everyday life. 'The past is made present', he remarks, 'by bringing scripts for family life from the family of origin.'[2] Such scripts are not sealed off from history. The impact of war, economic disasters or other 'external' events may be carried through the habitual behaviour of the parent even when the event is not spoken about, and the effects on the descendants may be just as profound as the effects on the parent. Around half the British recruits in the First World War were volunteers, but every descendant is in a sense a conscript. For them, the war's legacies were present from birth and were sometimes felt to have determined life chances. Brian Mullarkey wanted to make clear the financial impact of his father Albert's breakdown due to the war. He began our interview by comparing himself and his cousins whose father was a decorated veteran. They had gone to private schools and had careers in the law and military, but because there was no breadwinner in Brian's family, he was not able to stay on at school, and eventually joined the fire service. Jean Brown had her first long-term relationship when she was in her seventies after the death of her blind father, for whom she had been the primary carer.

Sometimes the legacies of the war were so taken for granted that they were scarcely perceived as such. Mary Burdett's father used to allocate chores to each of his children, and his standards were exacting: 'I mean, we always all had jobs in the house – various things we were expected to do … if we did a job, he would expect it to be well done … he had a great eye for detail, and he expected, you know, not to be messed up.' Behaviour like this was evidence of the mark left by military training, but in the children's eyes, it was just how their fathers were.

At the same time, for some descendants, the war could serve as an explanation for family troubles whose origins were perhaps ultimately undeterminable. The claim of legacy allowed them to locate the cause of family troubles in an external event. Brian Mullarkey believed that his father's breakdown, which he dated to 1923, was due to 'what was then known as "shell-shock"'. The family's financial struggles resulted from the fact that 'Shell shock was not recognised as a medical condition and he was refused an Army pension.'[3] According to the Norwich Union, who paid his pension, Albert had retired in 1930, and the company newsletter on his death in 1956 described him as having a 'kindly if rather eccentric disposition'.[4] Albert may well have been suffering from war trauma – delayed onset is now recognised as a feature of PTSD – but in locating his decline from the early 1920s, Brian brought the war and his father's breakdown closer together in time, and framed his treatment by the Ministry of Pensions within a political narrative of post-war betrayal of the war generation.

The naming of a legacy was as much a *social* as a medical process, a question of what families believed and the family scripts through which children understood their fathers' conditions. Mental illnesses were perhaps particularly liable to be explained as war wounds. A condition caused while a father was serving his country might make it feel less shameful. Families reckoned with ideas of causality in different ways, some belatedly discovering the war in behaviour they had taken for granted, others understanding early on that the war was responsible for the man their father was.

Age and life stage also motivate the decision to present the family history as a war story, and there were stark reminders of the second generation's mortality during my research. We took a break in one interview so that a carer could administer oxygen to my interviewee. Brenda Aubrey and her husband had planned to do their interview together, but he died in the period between our initial contact and the interview. David Smith, who appeared to me to be a remarkably fit and lively eighty-four-year-old, died three days after our interview.

Their age makes these descendants particularly aware of being the last generation to grow up in the war's shadow and that this might be their last chance to get information on the record. Responding to my newspaper appeal, George Elders enclosed in his letter the notification of death form that had been sent to his wife's parents in Whitby after George Dixon died in 1916. Worn through and torn along the folds, the form had been opened countless times, but George's wife had passed away, and neither she nor he had surviving relatives. Unwell and dependent on carers, George felt that the artefact would find an appropriate home with a First World War historian.

Jan and Almeida Assmann have coined the terms 'communicative memory' and 'cultural memory' to describe the different accounts of the past that circulate within families and public institutions. Communicative memory is transmitted by word of mouth in everyday interactions and plays a crucial role in the 'affective ties that bind together families, groups and generations'.[5] Cultural memory is produced by memory professionals such as historians and museum curators and inheres in formal and enduring artefacts and public institutions – the book, the TV or radio broadcast, the exhibition and the archive. The two forms of memory have different timeframes. Communicative memory is evanescent, lasting for three or at most four generations or around 80 years, while cultural memory may endure over centuries. Descendants stand at the junction of these two types of memory. When the link between the personal memories of family members and official commemorations weakens, Jay Winter observes, a 'powerful prop' of remembrance is lost.[6] Historians are not the only ones to see this: the second generation knows that time is short and is compelled by the moment of generational passing – providing that the wider culture is receptive – to transmit their 'lived history' to a wider audience. Linde, who had volunteered for *Meeting in No Man's Land*, remarked on how pleased her father would be that 'he can once more have a voice through me'.

For the Assmanns, communicative and cultural memory are temporally discrete. Drawing on the historian of oral tradition, Jan Vansina, they describe a 'floating gap' that shifts with each generation.[7] Yet what strikes me from my interviews and the Centenary commemorations are the close inter-relations between these forms of memory. When I asked Marion Armstrong why she had volunteered to be interviewed, it became clear that she wanted the Ministry of Pensions put in the dock. Her mother had lost the right to the war pension after her husband died because the couple had married after he incurred his disability:

> *MA:* I just thought it might do some good, because I feel very bitter that my mother didn't get a pension, and I thought if somebody ... that that actually did happen, somebody might do something about it. I don't know whether they do that now or not, but that was the law then.
> *MR:* It was the fact that she had married ...?
> *MA:* Yes, she married after he was wounded. If she'd have married him before, she'd have had the full pension all the time we were little. And I thought it might do some good that way, that was all ... because it isn't fair.

Marion wanted people today to understand the injustice and hurt caused to her family because the Ministry of Pensions would not pay benefits to the family if a veteran had married after incurring his disability.[8] For her interview to 'do some good', it had to find its way into a permanent record. Marion was using me, her historian, to negotiate the 'floating gap' between family memory and history. Bart Ziino concludes from his study of the war memoirs published by Australian descendants that they were acting in a spirited 'defiance of ossification of memory', and the same could be said of the participants in this study.[9]

Descendants will often seek out cultural producers who might help them transmit the family story to a wider public. The work of the reminiscence organisation Age Exchange over the past three decades, for example, has revolved around oral testimony which is then worked into cultural memory as theatre productions, films and educational aids.[10] The historical pursuits of descendants are more than life rafts onto which they cling before the tide of cultural memory eventually washes over them. A century on, well beyond the supposed span of communicative memory and precisely because their numbers are thinning, descendants are key agents in transmitting the cultural memory of the First World War. The following sections investigate the social, generational, psychological and material mechanisms that animate this transmission.

Silence and sentience

The British descendants who answered my newspaper appeal in 2011 have witnessed profound shifts across the twentieth century in the norms that govern privacy and the sharing of intimate confidences. They put themselves forward at a moment when the disclosure of family secrets and traumas was not only encouraged, but had social cachet, a movement in which oral history itself was deeply immured as a technology of modern confession.[11] Yet 'silence' was often the first word to come to mind when I asked what they remembered hearing about the First World War as children. Looking back, they were puzzled by the lack of talk. Clive Jones remembered the veterans in the village near Ludlow where he grew up: 'They rarely discussed it, particularly the men ... and there were people who had been wounded, they'd been frostbitten, they were ... they were still suffering, and ... they never ... they never discussed what happened to them.' Bill Swann, whose father was a double amputee, grew up amidst the disabled soldiers in the Oswald Stoll Mansions. Marked though they were by the war, Bill reflected,

> none of these men ever talked about the detail of it at all. And the more I think about it – you started me thinking back, you know – and I think it's odd, they never did talk about it. And it's the same with the kids at school, all their fathers must have been in the War, but nobody ever talked about it! Huh!

Bill expresses a paradoxical feeling that was shared by many interviewees: they got in touch with me because the project seemed to speak to their experience, but once in the interview, felt they had little to say. Elizabeth Game's father was 'like a lot of veterans, he never spoke of his ... experiences in the First World War, and from what I read, very few of them ever did, and he was one of them. The only thing he talked about was something ... you know, if anything funny happened.' He had a heart condition due to rheumatic fever in the war, and although as a girl Elizabeth was very aware of his father's health problems, the war itself was an absent presence: 'You grow up with a scene, don't you. You grow up with the knowledge that this ... your grandfather did this, and your father did that ... and Uncle Jack was killed in the War. You know, we didn't know him, as children.' Allan Pentney was eighteen when learned how his father lost his leg; it was his cousin who told him.

Silence was not necessarily a response to distress, however. A relatively benign war might also be absent from family memory. Mary Burdett's father, who set up a successful machine tool company in Peterborough after the war, owed his career in part to what he learned as a motor engineer in the RASC during the war. Even in a family where there was no trace of horror and, in some respects, the war's legacies were positive, it was, in Mary's words, 'conspicuous by its absence'.

Memories of the war were more accessible in some families than others. David Smith's father didn't volunteer anything but would respond if David and his brother asked direct questions. Jeffery Flower's father 'wasn't mum', but he rarely spoke about the war either. Some gave seemingly *verbatim* renditions of stories their fathers had told. Repetition might help the veteran dispel the memory of horror, but could trouble his children. Joyce Fey's father was in the Machine Gun Corps, and twice in our interview, she repeated his story about men who sank into the mud carrying their tripods and were unable to get up again. Margaret Reardon remembered how her father 'used to sit, sit me on the lap' in his armchair of an evening, and tell her about the men who slipped off the duckboards shouting, '"help me. Help me comrade!", but the others behind couldn't stop, because if they stopped, they would all fall ... the pressure on people coming behind them would have pushed them in, so they went ... and people were dying in the mud.' Margaret thought that her father's war stories were his way of 'getting it out of him'.

Figure 2.1 Mary Burdett's father George, a Royal Army Service Corps motor engineer, on a Clyno motorcycle. Courtesy of Mary Burdett. All rights reserved.

Fragments of the war past such as these could be difficult for a child to make sense of. Brian Mullarkey recited the words spoken by his unkempt father as he wandered up and down the house: '"Chocolade, chocolade, demi franc, demi franc", and he thought that was funny.' His father was not capable of giving Brian a coherent account of his war, but Brian had watched him shake at the sound of thunder, and hover with his hands poised over the front door knob, too afraid to open it.

It was not only the fact that their parents said little that the descendants found puzzling, but that they had not asked questions. Lacking a context as children, they searched for clues later. Hedley Green gave his father a copy of *In Flanders Fields*, Leon Wolff's graphic account of the mismanaged and bloody campaign at Passchendaele in 1917: 'he just gave it back to me and said, "That's right, boy" – his only comment. I know he'd got shrapnel still stuck in his arms … and I know he did say that it was a bit hairy driving ammunition wagons at night, with no lights, because of the shell holes at the Front, and that was all he ever said.'

Feelings of unsettlement like this tell us about the emotional cultures of the present as well as those of the past. Silence and oblique mentions led some interviewees to conclude that their fathers were traumatised. Although too young to witness the transformation themselves, they were convinced that war had changed their fathers' personalities. June Marriage thought her father's experiences had 'quietened him'. Bill Swann believed that his father and the other disabled men in Oswald Mansions didn't talk about the war because it was 'way too horrible', and he appreciated the 'deliberate effort' it must have taken *not* to talk. When I asked Pat Stamp how her mother and father reacted to the outbreak of the Second World War, she replied: 'memories must have come flooding back, one way and another. But no, they never discussed anything like that with us. Nothing.' The contrast in emotional cultures between then and now seemed to demand an explanation, which some descendants found through a trauma frame of repression and repetition.

The survivors believed that the best way to deal with distress was to try and forget. Dennis Johnson quoted his father's advice:

> He always said to me, I'm always struck by his theory and I teach my children and the grandchildren, he always said to me, 'Think of this word ...' Them days they call ... they never call you by your first name, Dennis, it's always 'son'. 'Now, listen to me, son. I'll tell you something.' He said, 'Always be positive in your life, right?' He said, 'Think positive. Act positive. And be positive in your life, and you'll never go wrong.' He said, 'Just think of the word "tab" – T A B – think, act, and be positive in your life, and you'll never go wrong.' And I stuck by it, and, touch wood ... [*laughs*] ... I've never gone wrong!

During his life, William Johnson had many reasons not to feel positive. His first wife died in childbirth in 1916 when he was in Britain recovering from a shrapnel wound in the buttocks and back.[12] Facing the prospect of returning to France, he decided to place baby Edna and his sons William and Raymond in a National Children's Home and Orphanage. After the war, he returned to Stockton to live with his sisters, effectively a single man until he remarried a year and a half later, when Raymond and William moved in with him. Baby Edna stayed in the home in Cheshire, her existence kept secret from his new family. Raymond died in 1929 aged nineteen, and

Sydney, a son from his second marriage – Dennis's brother – was killed at Dunkirk in 1940.[13] William Johnson had suffered multiple losses but tried to follow the principle of staying positive and looking to the future. Dennis approved of his father's attitude, but it left a mixed legacy. He was shocked to learn in 1984 that he had a half-sister, and spent a lot of time trying to 'visualise what went through' his father's mind after the death of his first wife, and why after remarrying, he had not told Dennis that he had a sister: he 'didn't wanna, like, look back on that life, because he'd got another one now, you know'.

People like Dennis grew up in a different emotional climate from that of today, and the tensions between emotional expectations then and now surface when they remember their parents.[14] Dennis explained his father's behaviour as a traumatic reaction to the loss of his wife and the disintegration of his family. His father's secretiveness troubled him, but at the same time he admired his efforts to live according to the creed of 'T-A-B'. Dora Kneebone was also ambivalent about the changes in emotional expectations. On one occasion she had come across her father in the backroom 'in the chair, and just sitting like this [*puts her head in her hands*]'. She wondered if he had argued with her mother, or whether

> he had just thought about somebody, or something to do with the First World War deaths. I asked our vicar about this a few weeks ago, and told him just the same as I've told you, I said, 'Now, should I have gone to him to comfort him?' I said, 'I didn't.' You know, again, it wasn't my business.

Looking back from a time when the mental impact of combat is much discussed, Dora wondered if she should have come to her father's aid, but then reminds herself of the family scripts of her childhood, repeating a phrase she may even have been told by her mother or father: 'it wasn't my business'. Dora did not approve of public displays of emotion. She had recently watched the award ceremony for the Victoria Cross winner Josh Leakey and was 'furious' to see the Head of the General Army Sir Nick Carter embrace him after presenting the medal. 'This General should not have comforted him like that', she told me, before going on to admit that the world had changed, and her attitudes were 'Victorian'.

Bill Swann had a similarly split perception of why the war generation had been silent, and what he felt about the attitude of serving soldiers today. Among his parents' generation, the traumas of the war were simply too great to take in, and the only way to live with the past was to forget. Amnesia was a kind of social defence: 'It was never talked about. I get the feeling, somehow, that it was a sort of general feeling that you had to forget the War. It was certainly ... or perhaps it was too horrible to even talk about – because it was a horrible war, wasn't it!' Yet Bill did not have much sympathy for returned soldiers from Afghanistan and Iraq who claimed to suffer from PTSD, and he wasn't convinced that a talking cure would help them: 'I'm afraid that I think the old ways were best – put up a stiff upper lip sort of thing, because all this talk about counselling and that, I think it just makes people weak. I think so, anyway.' As they sought to understand their parents' silence, the second generation drew on PTSD diagnostic terms like exposure to overwhelming shock, delayed onset and disturbed memory. Yet they shared their parents' belief in 'moving on'. The more expressive emotional culture of the late twentieth and early twenty-first centuries makes them uneasy, and unlike the children of Holocaust survivors or the 1968 generation in Germany, they are not convinced of the psychological and social benefits of challenging silence.[15]

Silence about emotions and silence about the war seem more striking to the descendants in an age where trauma stories saturate the media and the shell-shocked soldier's hysterical enactments symbolise the horrors of mass warfare.[16] Raised in a culture that believed distress should be kept private and silence was a virtue, they are now living in an age of confession. British children of the war generation face two ways. They perceive their parents' silences through a trauma lens but approve of their stoicism. They recognise family silence as a legacy of the conflict, but this makes it hard to know what to say.

Gender

Social norms about silence and confession shaped the accounts of descendants, but they were also shaped by expectations about where in the family the war story was to be found. These expectations, I soon discovered, were not just held by the interviewees, but by me too. Initially, *Afterlives* was conceived as a 'soldier-centred' history. The first sentence of the information sheet given out to participants in 2011 described the project as a study of 'the impact of the First World War on the children of soldiers'. Realising the problem with this formulation after the first tranche of interviews, I modified the sheet to read 'the impact of the First World War on children born after the war's end', hoping in this way to broaden the study to include mothers, the war on the home front, non-combatants, pacifists and conscientious objectors. My own bias in the selection of historical significance was revealed.

Yet the project's focus on fathers was not just an artefact of the way I had positioned the research, as I soon discovered that many of my interviewees also assumed that the war's effects travelled down the paternal line. It was their fathers' war that they had researched, and it was the gaps in their military service that sometimes embarrassed them. Their mothers, however, had lived through the war too. They also did war service, experienced raids, had loved ones who served and were bereaved. The asymmetry in the visibility of mothers' and fathers' wars can partly be explained in terms of the gender scripts with which this generation had grown up (a transmission to which I was clearly not immune!). In her analysis of Mass Observation diarists writing on the eve of the Centenary, Lucy Noakes observes that female descendants often act as the repositories and carriers of memory of the conflict. The suffering of the soldier/veteran tends to come before that of others, a historical outlook that reflects conventional expectations about women and emotional labour.[17] Like the Mass Observation diarists, the interviewees in this study had grown up watching veterans assemble each year on Armistice Day and their 'soldier-centred' perspective was reinforced through novels, films and TV programmes about the mud and blood of the Western Front. They were preoccupied with their father's war and its aftermath, even when their mothers had also been in uniform.

Some described their mothers' war experience in a manner that made it seem incidental. Pat Stamp thought her mother might have worked during the war 'in a factory of some description or the other', possibly munitions, but knew more about her mother's career as a shop-girl in Selfridges before the war. The evidence of her father's war, however, was seared into her memory, as he 'had holes in his legs … sort of like that – in both legs he had holes' big enough to put a finger in.

When I asked Dora Kneebone what her mother did in the war, she replied: 'Oh, just this hand sewing work, in London.' Dora talked mainly about her father, who had a wound on his leg that Dora's mother told her she must never look at. Yet during the interview, it was revealed that the war had profoundly affected her mother too. There was a floral memorial at the entrance to the family home in Wembley called 'Harry's window' which her 'soft-hearted' mother maintained in memory of a soldier who was in the same Company as her brother and may have been her sweetheart. Her mother had had a traumatic experience of her own during the war. Trying to escape from a zeppelin raid on London, she tripped down some stairs and broke her collarbone. She accepted a cigarette to calm her nerves and this 'started off her liking for cigarettes', a habit that helped calm her down when she was nervy but ended in her death from lung cancer in 1964. Sometimes the war pasts of their mothers emerged bit by bit as backstories which were not felt to be formally part of the war's history.

The war was more prominent in memory when mothers had done work that challenged gender norms and had stories of adventure and sexual independence to tell. George Elders's mother worked at the munitions factory in Gretna, and he proudly (and correctly) stated that ten thousand women had worked there at its peak. She found the work of filling shells boring but enjoyed the excitement of being away from home. As a child, he used to look through his mother's autograph book with its plaid cover and rhyme at the end, 'By hook or by crook, I'll be last in the book.' Risqué pictures hinted at the exciting life his mother had led, one showing a woman's hair grip with the caption: '"This was found in a soldier's bed, does it belong to you?" [*laughs*].'

Hedley Green's account of the war focused as much on his mother as his father. She had joined up out of a sense of adventure and ran an officer's mess in France with her friend Amy: 'her friend was the cook, and she was the waitress, and did the table laying and all the rest of it. And apparently she was quite speedy. She could manage six soups of plates – six plates of soup – on her arm!' Meeting up with an acquaintance of his mother during the Second World War, he learned more about her exploits. On one occasion she put on the full Highland uniform and went to check out a local brothel. Hedley painted a picture of a feisty woman with an active romantic life before her marriage to his father. She had become engaged to an officer from a wealthy local family who later broke off the relationship and in revenge, she took a hammer to the engagement ring. Returning to Sudbury, she arranged three dates one Saturday night in the town centre. She would occasionally tease his father by reminding him that, as a Sergeant in the war, she outranked him. His mother, said Hedley proudly, 'didn't take prisoners gladly'.

The children were fascinated by the gender reversals that a mother's war work could entail. Perley's mother was in the Land Army, and her father was in the Royal Scots Regiment. As in Hedley's family, there were family jokes about 'my dad wearing a skirt, and my mum wearing riding breeches!' Mary Kerslake conveyed a similarly strident impression of her mother, Ivy Dean, who joined the Queen Mary Army Auxiliary Corps as a VAD in 1917.[18] She had needed great strength to lift the 'dead weight' of wounded men up and down the stairs to the operating rooms, Mary explained. On one occasion Ivy had tried to steal some fresh strawberries by wriggling through the broken pane in the hospital pantry door, but she got stuck and had to be pulled out by the Sister. These were feminine equivalents of an old soldier's tales and, like them, resonated with historical narratives of the conflict. Yet in contrast to Arthur Marwick's 1965 study *The Deluge*, which portrayed the war as a time of personal liberation for women, Ivy Dean's war story was ultimately one of a disappointed return to domesticity. She had wanted to train as a nurse after the war but her father refused to pay for it and instead Ivy took over the care of her baby sister and another sister's child: 'She was terribly upset', said Mary, 'because she desperately did want to be a nurse, and [was] told it was her duty to stay at home'. Mary had kept Ivy's training certificates: the war history transmitted from mother to daughter was one of both pride and frustrated ambition.

Even in families where the mother's war was part of family lore, however, there could be a tension between personal experience and expectations about what counted as a war legacy. I was initially surprised when, having related long and funny descriptions of his adventurous mother, Hedley commented that 'as far as I'm aware, the War had had no effect' on her. He was comparing his mother with his father and two uncles, all of whom had died in their early seventies. Hedley put their deaths down to psychological stress, as 'I mean, they never spoke about it, any of them.' The war stories in his family went down the maternal line, but the negative impact was felt through the men, a legacy of horror, the repressed memories of which had shortened their lives.

It was not just the soldier-centred frames of popular memory that led interviewees to focus on the father's war; it was also the fact their earliest knowledge of the conflict often came from seeing misshapen or missing limbs or the erratic behaviour of ex-servicemen. June Teape remembered a 'big and handsome man' who used to ride a bike around the village, 'goodness knows how he managed to make a living, but ... it was the fact that he was on the bike, and the bike was shaking and everything ... You were always terribly aware of the sadness of this business from the First World War.' Born in 1915, Winifred Spray lived near two hospitals and used to watch 'wounded Tommies and soldiers recuperating' pass by her front gate. Their most intimate glimpses of war damage were the bullet and shrapnel wounds on their own fathers' bodies. George Elders moved from the awestruck child to the remembering adult in a single sentence: 'I say you could put your knuckles in – in this hole in the back – so how it missed his spine I don't know.' Bees were attracted by the smell of his father's amputated arm, John Mingay told me, and would swarm around it while he was at work on their smallholding. Seeing disabled veterans from Iran and Afghanistan on TV, Swann was taken back to his childhood:

> *BS:* I know when I used to see them, I didn't like the look of them! [*laughs*] They looked horrible!
> *MR:* No. Can you describe what they were like?
> *BS:* Well, you know, there was just the stump, with a sort of loose end. You know, you've seen pictures of them coming back from Afghanistan ... well, you know, it puts me off when I see that – the young blokes now doing the same. And that's how it is, you know, two short stumps ... that was all it was. Yeah. Yeah.

Words like 'just' and 'all it was' convey the foreshortening of time as Swann experiences again the unnerving sensation of severed limbs. Marks like these made a deep impression on children before they possessed the mental capacity to explain what they were seeing, and contributed to the 'soldier-centred' perspective. Yet in terms of gender, the legacy of wounds could be double-edged. The more damaged the father, the more central the war became to the family story, yet the more central the mother was likely to be in keeping the family going. The soldier-centred approach not only placed children on the margins but obscured the figure upon whom the life of the ill veteran would often most depend: the wife and mother. In a restoration of the gender order, the disabled soldier's place in the memory of the war was maintained through his identification as a victim supported by the invisible labours of women.

Trauma

> The second generation after every calamity is the hinge generation, in which the meanings of awful events can remain arrested and fixed at the point of trauma; or in which they can be transformed into new sets of relations with the world.
>
> *Eva Hoffman*[19]

The concept of transmission is perhaps most familiar within the literature on trauma, which as Hoffman describes here, is concerned with what happens to a trauma after the event, and how its afterlife is experienced and shaped by future generations. Developed initially within psychoanalysis and in clinical work with the children of Holocaust survivors, the reach of transmission theories has expanded well beyond psychoanalysis and psychotherapy over the past two decades to embrace cultural studies, sociology and oral history.[20] Transmission theories show how the emotions associated with a trauma can travel. Eva Hoffman recalls the fragmentary phrases of her survivor parents that 'lodged themselves in my mind like shards'.[21] Transmission might show itself in the clinical setting when the patient presents an aspect of their parent's history in response to an analyst's interpretation, as if their own behaviour can only be explained through the past before their time.[22] Trauma theory assumes that memory is not only transmitted through intentional activity but may be most powerful when it is not conscious.[23] Haydée Faimberg describes a 'telescoping of generations', a sense of foreshortened time among descendants caught in the grip of their parents' past.[24] Marion Armstrong reprised her mother's history as she tried to explain why she found it difficult to cry.[25] Relatives and neighbours respected her mother because of the brave way she coped with her husband's death in the early 1930s. When her son Eric died a decade later, she 'just cried for two days. She just was ... she was working – because she was a worker – at home. I mean, she was cooking and doing everything, she didn't give into it, but she was just crying as she walked around.' It was important to Marion that I should know that her mother had kept going and her tears lasted just those two days. Even in private she was working on her emotions, keeping busy, controlling her grief and sustaining an attitude of restraint.[26]

Successor generations carry the impact of traumas before their time through day-to-day interactions with the survivors. Transmission may occur through what the psychoanalyst Ilany Kogan calls 'primitive identification', when the children internalise the damaged parent's self-images and feel responsible for their suffering.[27] Dora Kneebone's daily ritual of taking off her father's shoes when he came home from work shows the sensitivity she developed towards his pain, which reversed the usual relations of care between the generations.[28]

A trauma may also cross generations through the damaged aspects of the self that the parent projects into the child. In a psychic process that Kogan calls 'deposited representation', the members of the second generation become repositories for the unbearable feelings of the survivors.[29] My father Stan and uncle Lin admired their father's toughness. Bob was one of twelve children born in a poor rural town in north-eastern Victoria, who had made his own way as an itinerant labourer from the age of twelve and was a Gallipoli hero. But why did Lin's dreaminess as a child, and dislike of shaving as a teenager, drive my grandfather to violent rage? Seen from a transmission perspective, it is possible that Lin showed a vulnerability that Bob despised in himself. Formidably stoic, the only pain he ever complained of was indigestion.

Faced with silence and the effects of unconscious transmission, the second generation can either 'buy into' their parents' defences or oppose them.[30] Rejection is likely when the legacy is one of guilt or shame. Yet, as studies of the 1968 generation in Germany show, neither acceptance nor rejection frees the successor generations from being haunted by their elders' experiences. As Chapter 4 explains, the German participants in *Meeting in No Man's Land* who were born during or after the Second World War were preoccupied with their relationships with their fathers, and traced tensions that went right back to the First World War. Whether hostile or sympathetic, transmission of this kind engages fantasy and imagination, and generates 'cultural memory' as the second and third generations investigate the traumatic scene. Drawings, literature and photographs capture what the children have long imagined.

History can perform a similar function, as it provides frames of meaning and generalised descriptions that allow descendants to come closer to the precipitating events in their parents' and grandparents' lives and locate them as part of a group which faced common circumstances. The second generation's trajectory of understanding, observes Hoffman, works the opposite way around from the adult world's response to events. While the adult 'asks first "what happened?", and from there follows its uncertain and sometimes resistant route towards the inward meaning of the facts, those born after calamity sense its most inward meanings first and have to work their way outwards towards the facts and the worldly shape of events'.[31] When Hedley Green gave his father *In Flanders Fields*, he was looking for confirmation of the hazy reality he had sensed as a child.

Psychological defences like denial, repression and sublimation are commonly observed in clinical work with the children of survivors, but the habits and scripts which each family adopts to manage a trauma are unique. Each family has its own patterns of conscious and unconscious exchange between generations. Transmission is thus a vertical and inter-generational process, but it can also bring horizontal and intra-generational relationships into play. As second-generation Holocaust survivors transform a 'lived history' of war into a 'learned history', undertake therapy and theorise transmission, they develop a generational identity and establish transmission as a collective phenomenon. Their iterations of family history strengthen what Hirsch calls the 'affiliative' ties among the second and third generations.[32] The historian who enquires into the war's impact on descendants may also become part of this transmission and experience something of the obligation that the second generation feels to repair the damage of a violent past.³³ Ghosts, Avery Gordon insists, are social figures, conveying memory traces that unsettle later generations, but whose investigation promises to lead 'to that dense site where memory and subjectivity make social life'.³⁴ Inviting the second and third generations to compare notes on the war in the family, the Age Exchange project *Meeting in No Man's Land* created 'affiliative ties' that have continued in emails and get-togethers since 2016. At the time of writing, the participants are planning to create a graphic novel from their stories. Exchanging family letters, war ephemera, official records and personal artworks from across the divide, they are constructing a shared historical and cultural landscape as descendants. The ghosts of the First World War dead, they discovered, were not just closeted in the home: despite the very different legacies of victory and defeat in Britain and Germany, haunting was also a shared generational experience, a part of how they all came to be and a history worth telling.

Heritage

Transmission can thus engage deep social and psychic processes as the second generation tries to navigate the legacies of a trauma. Yet the marks of war in homes afterwards could also be unremarkable, and go unremarked, like the trench art on windowsills and fireplaces that were part of the 'house-worlds' of children growing up in the 1920s and 30s.³⁵ Jefferey Flower described a doorstopper made from a shell case as 'part of the scenery' of his childhood. Sometimes the significance of the object only became apparent later. Alex Seabrook paused when I asked her if there were any First World War objects in her family, and she then recalled a doorstopper made from the driving cone of a shell that her ninety-four-year-old mother still uses today. The domestic utility of war heritage was sometimes more apparent to descendants than its historical importance.

Such ephemera could have many functions in family memory – a symbol of patriotism and service, of military identities, or of loss and dislocated lives. The ring fashioned from a French coin with the Union Jack etched into its face condensed the effects of two world wars on Marie-Anne Careless and her family.

Her parents had met when her father was fighting in France during the First World War and they settled in Bertincourt in the early 1920s where her father was a gardener for the Imperial War Graves Commission. During the Second World War, he was imprisoned at Frontstalag 220 in St Denis after trying to escape to Britain with his family. The ring, with the Union Jack on its face, had been smuggled out of Frontstalag 220, a present for Marie-Anne from a father she could barely remember and a gesture of defiance towards his captors. Marie-Anne recalled how it 'was made for me, especially. Made for me specially.' She seemed to speak simultaneously as a child and adult when she remembered the beauty of the ring and the

Figure 2.2 Marie-Anne Careless wears the ring that her father smuggled out of Frontstalag 220. Courtesy of Marie-Anne Careless. All rights reserved.

risks her father had taken in getting it to her: 'And it was colourful. That was really … if he'd been caught with that, he would have been in trouble! [*laughs*].'[36]

Marie-Anne's story shows how objects can act as focal points for 'communicative memory' within families, particularly when they have been displaced. As the Centenary reveals, however, the artefacts of war can also act as a material junction or bridge between familial remembrance and cultural memory. Material heritage bobs about in the 'floating gap' between the remembering descendant and the present, and the direction of drift, from the loft, shed or garage to the museum curator, archivist or digital imager, tells us about the changing social role and self-identities of descendants.[37] Earlier in life, the second generation had taken the ephemera of the war for granted. Flower remembered seeing his father's officer training manual as a child, but 'never read it through'. As a young woman, Dora Kneebone found the letters her uncle had written to her mother 'very boring' and passed them on to her aunt, who threw them away. War heritage might be pressed into everyday service. Winifred Spray would take her father's cane with her while out walking the dog until she lost it in the local woods. He had been killed in 1916 and the cane was among the handful of personal effects returned after his death. Postcards of French cities and towns, Egypt and the pyramids encouraged an interest in faraway places but the children did not necessarily think of them as valued legacies of war.

Curiosity among the third and fourth generations had sometimes sparked the second generation's interest in long-held objects. The First World War medals awarded to Marie-Anne Careless's father, for example, had been affixed to a cardboard sheet by her granddaughter for a school presentation. Mary Kerslake kept her father's war diaries safe and had 'known they've always been there', but when her son found them and said, 'this is interesting', and took them away to transcribe, she herself took more interest and read them through. From the diaries, she and her son reconstructed her father's war movements. Stimulated by TV programmes like *Antiques Roadshow*, *Who Do You Think You Are?* and the intensification of commemoration as the last survivors passed and the Centenary approached, objects which had lain undisturbed for decades in suitcases and attics could appear on walls, shelves and sideboards. Burgin had recently found a letter written by an officer at the hospital in Boulogne to his father's brother, which informed him of the seriousness of his father's wounds. It had always been among his father's personal effects but 'I couldn't remember we had it'. He 'only really came across it' when his granddaughter asked him for help with a project on the First World War. Aware of their roles as gatekeepers, the second generation sometimes worried about the decisions they made. Brenda Aubrey had given her brother permission to gift their father's bayonet to a neighbour as a thank-you for helping to look after his dying wife, but part of her regretted it: 'I couldn't say it in front of her, I'm not that type, you know! And I said, "Yeah, that's all right." But I was quite upset really.'

The journeys of domestic war ephemera over time and space can reveal the ways in which, in Nick Saunders's words, 'emotion, memory and imagination' of the First World War coalesce among successor generations.[38] That journey is not just about the eventual eclipse of living memory by physical remains as the territory of the family historian is ceded to the archaeologist. A focus on descendants suggests that the process is more attenuated than this. Objects maintain a direct link to the war past in the absence of the participants.. They hark from the time and are part of it, and in handling them, descendants touch the things their loved ones touched. Objects also connect those with a living link to those without: as these descendants introduce their war ephemera to their grandchildren and great-grandchildren, or bring it to museums, exhibitions and commemorative events, they deepen historical knowledge and, inspired by the increasing transmissibility and social currency of First World War heritage, create new communities of exchange.[39] The domestic ephemera of war helps to sustain the affective intensity and longevity of communicative memory. It re-animates personal attachments that have passed into memory and projects the family story into the historical consciousness of future generations.

Transmission has many facets. The impact of war on successor generations is perhaps most telling where a trauma is not verbalised, registers unconsciously and is transmitted in enactments. Yet among British descendants born between the wars, silence was not necessarily the result of an unspoken trauma. Many of them approved of silence as a coping mechanism. Their ambivalence about the value of confession was at one level a repetition of the parental script – it is best to forget – while at the same time, silence compelled them to understand the war that shaped their parents. Not all transmission affects later generations in such profound ways. It can also be a matter of routine as fathers adapted their military training to the home and parenting. It can be a question of who keeps what artefacts and why, where they are kept, how they figure in the home and who passed what on to whom and why. Transmission models from psychology and psychoanalysis privilege the internal dynamics of family transmission, but it is a profoundly historical process: notions about where the family legacies of war lie, who the key historical actors and victims are and who provides the support reveal social expectations about gender, ageing and responsibilities between generations. Family transmission is simultaneously a social, generational, material and psychic process, and rather than being eclipsed by history as living memory passes, is inseparable from it.

Notes

1 A. Erll, 'Locating Family in Cultural Memory Studies', *Journal of Comparative Family Studies*, 42: 3 (2011), 306.
2 J. Byng-Hall, 'Family Scripts: A Concept Which Can Bridge Child Psychotherapy and Family Therapy Thinking', 3, https://icpla.edu/wp-content/uploads/2015/04/Byng-Hall-J.-Family-Scripts.pdf. Accessed 1 November 2021; J. Byng-Hall, *Rewriting Family Scripts: Improvisation and Systems Change* (New York: Guilford Press, 1995), esp. chs 2 and 3.
3 Brian Mullarkey, letter to author, 11 September 2011.
4 *Norwich Union Magazine* (September 1956), 3.
5 J. Assmann, 'Communicative and Cultural Memory', in A. Erll and A. Nünning (eds), *Cultural Memory Studies: An International and Interdisciplinary Handbook* (New York: de Gruyter, 2008), 111.
6 J. Winter, 'Sites of Memory and the Shadow of War', in Erll and Nünning (eds), *Cultural Memory Studies*, 72.
7 Assmann, 'Communicative and Cultural Memory', 112.
8 By contrast, the Australian repatriation authorities continued to pay pensions when a marriage was contracted after discharge. C. Lloyd and J. Rees, *The Last Shilling: A History of Repatriation in Australia*

(Melbourne: Melbourne University Press, 1994), chapter 11 'Out of the Limelight', 85.
9   B. Ziino, 'Introduction: Remembering the First World War Today', in B. Ziino (ed.), *Remembering the First World War* (Abingdon: Routledge, 2015), 6, 8.
10 R. Duffett and M. Roper, 'Making Histories: The Meeting of German and British Descendants of First World War Veterans in "No Man's Land", Bavaria, 2016', *The Public Historian*, 40: 1 (February 2018), 13–33.
11 D. Cohen, *Family Secrets: The Things We Tried to Hide* (London: Penguin, 2013), esp. epilogue 'Genealogy and Confessional Culture', 241–53; A. Freund, '"Confessing Animals": Toward a Longue Durée History of the Oral History Interview', *Oral History Review*, 41: 1 (Winter/Spring 2014), 1–26.
12 William John Johnson RASC pension card, Yorkshire Region, 16 November 1920.
13 Death Index, Gertrude Johnson, 'Deaths registered in January, February and March 1916', 110; Marriage Index, William John Johnson and Mary Frater, 'Marriages registered in January, February and March 1920', 290; H. Sugden, *Children on Wheels: Adventures with the Children of the NCHO on Tour, 1920* (London: Epworth Press, 1928), 50–4; Sidney Johnson Commonwealth War Graves Commission records, Dunkirk Town Cemetery, 14.
14 For an account of the emotional codes surrounding grief in interwar Britain, see L. Noakes, *Dying for the Nation: Death, Grief and Bereavement in Second World War Britain* (Manchester: Manchester University Press, 2020), 45–72.
15 On post-war generations in Germany, see M. Roseman, *Generations in Conflict: Youth Revolt and Generation Formation in Germany 1770–1968* (Cambridge: Cambridge University Press, 1995); M. Fulbrook, *Dissonant Lives: Generations and Violence through the German Dictatorships* (Oxford: Oxford University Press, 2011).
16 N. Haslam and M. McGrath, 'The Creeping Concept of Trauma', *Social Research: An International Quarterly*, 87: 3 (Fall 2020), 509–31.
17 L. Noakes, '"My Husband Is Interested in War Generally": Gender, Family History and the Emotional Legacies of Total War', *Women's History Review*, 27: 4 (2018), 610–26.
18 Ivy Deane, Service Medal Award Roll, Queen Mary's Army Auxiliary Corps Service Records, 14 April 1920; Ivy Tunnah, 'Growing Ivy' ms, 4 October 1991, 4–6.
19 E. Hoffman, *After Such Knowledge: A Mediation on the Aftermath of the Holocaust* (London: Vintage, 2005), 103.

20 For cultural studies, see M. Hirsch, *The Generation of Postmemory: Writing and Visual Culture after the Holocaust* (New York: Columbia University Press, 2012); sociology, A. Stein, *Reluctant Witnesses: Survivors, Their Children and the Rise of Holocaust Consciousness* (Oxford: Oxford University Press, 2014); social history, R. Clifford, *Survivors: Children's Lives after the Holocaust* (New Haven: Yale University Press, 2020).
21 Hoffman, *After Such Knowledge*, 11.
22 H. Faimberg, *The Telescoping of Generations: Listening to the Narcissistic Links between Generations* (London: Routledge, 2005), 50; W. Bohleber, 'Transgenerational Trauma, Identification and Historical Consciousness', in J. Straub and J. Rüsen (eds), *Dark Traces of the Past: Psychoanalysis and Historical Thinking* (New York: Berghahn, 2011), 72–3; V. Volkan, 'The Intertwining of the Internal and External Wars', in M. G. Fromm (ed.), *Lost in Transmission: Studies of Trauma Across Generations* (London: Karnac, 2012), 90.
23 D. Bar-On, *Fear and Hope: Three Generations of the Holocaust* (Cambridge, MA: Harvard University Press, 1995); I. Kogan, 'The Second Generation in the Shadow of Terror', in Fromm (ed.), *Lost in Transmission*, 5–21.
24 Faimberg, *Telescoping of Generations*, 11.
25 See Introduction.
26 As Lucy Noakes observes, the interwar emotional economy 'validated restraint, and increasingly saw expressions of sadness, anxiety and fear, as problematic, unsuitable behaviour'. Noakes, *Dying for the Nation*, 67.
27 Kogan, 'Second Generation', 5–8. See also Hoffman on the 'obligation of compassion, of extra altruism' felt by many children of Holocaust survivors, *After Such Knowledge*, 98.
28 See Bohleber, 'Transgenerational Trauma', 70, on generational reversal; A. Hass, *In the Shadow of the Holocaust: The Second Generation* (Ithaca: Cornell University Press, 1990), 33.
29 Kogan, 'Second Generation', 7.
30 S. Frosh, *Hauntings: Psychoanalysis and Ghostly Transmissions* (Basingstoke: Palgrave Macmillan, 2013), 47–8.
31 Hoffman, *After Such Knowledge*, 16.
32 M. Hirsch, 'The Generation of Postmemory', *Poetics Today* 29: 1 (2008), 114; Frosh, *Hauntings*, 10–11; A. Bloch, 'How Memory Survives: Descendants of Auschwitz Survivors and the Progenic Tattoo', *Thesis Eleven* (September 2021), 1–11. On the importance of the second generation as a social movement see Stein, *Reluctant Witnesses*, 16.
33 J. Winter, 'Thinking about Silence', in E. Ben-Ze'ev, R. Ginio and J. Winter (eds), *Shadows of War: A Social History of Silence in the Twentieth Century* (Cambridge: Cambridge University Press), 29.

34 A. Gordon, *Ghostly Matters: Haunting and the Sociological Imagination* (Minneapolis: University of Minnesota, 2008), 8. See also Frosh, *Hauntings*, 38–66.
35 N. Saunders, 'Material Culture and Conflict: The Great War 1914–2003', in N. Saunders (ed.), *Matters of Conflict: Material Culture, Memory and the First World War* (London: Routledge, 2004), 5; N. Saunders, 'Bodies of Metal, Shells of Memory: "Trench Art" and the Great War Re-Cycled', *Journal of Material Culture*, 5: 1 (2000), 59.
36 When Marie-Anne's father died, they found a further sign of his resistance among his personal effects: 'like a lapel badge, and you looked on the back of it, I don't know what was on the front, but on the back it was an oath that they had … as an Englishman, he would never trade with a German again'.
37 A. M. Foster, '"We Decided the Museum Would Be the Best Place for Them": Veterans, Families and Mementos of the First World War', *History & Memory*, 31: 1 (Spring/Summer 2019), 87–117; M. Barratt and P. Stallybrass, 'Printing, Writing and a Family Archive: Recording the First World War', *History Workshop Journal*, 75 (Spring 2013), 1–32; On the 'cycles of significance' of family objects, see L. Gloyn, V. Crewe, L. King and A. Woodham, 'The Ties That Bind: Materiality, Identity and the Life Course in the "Things" Families Keep', *Journal of Family History*, 43: 2 (2018), 163–4.
38 Saunders, 'Material Culture', 15.
39 On the role of objects in sustaining inter-generational relationships see A. Woodham, L. King, L. Gloyn, V. Crewe and F. Blair, 'We Are What We Keep: The "Family Archive", Identity and Public/Private Heritage', *Heritage and Society*, 10: 3 (2017), 203–20.

Part II

Observer

3

National narratives in the Centenary

This chapter considers the national histories that have shaped descendants' perceptions of the First World War in Germany, Australia and Britain. Growing up in the 1920s and 30s, the second generation often experienced the war's aftermath in person, but their conscious understanding of the conflict was gleaned from family stories and what they learned at school, in the media and on remembrance days. There was a lived history in the home, but because this was a war before their time, they relied on external narratives to explain it.

Public memory of the First World War has evolved in different ways in these three countries, shaped by the aftermaths of defeat and victory, the political extremism of the mid-century, the Second World War and its legacies, the Cold War and the military conflicts in Iraq and Afghanistan. When Erich Kästner died in 2008 there was no public marking of the moment in Germany or in Austria where he was born. Kästner was believed to be the last surviving veteran, but there was no confirmation as Germany did not keep official track of its veterans.[1] 'That is the way history has developed', his son Peter explained to reporters from the Associated Press, 'In Germany, in this respect, these things are kept quiet; they're not a big deal.'[2] When in the same year, the bodies of twenty-one German soldiers from the First World War were found in an underground shelter in Alsace, there was little response from the German press and public. The headline in *Der Spiegel* read: 'WWI Grave Find Tells Story Germans Want to Forget'.[3]

Germany does not have a national day of remembrance like Britain's Armistice Day or Australia's Anzac Day. A day of mourning or *Volkstrauertag* was proposed in 1919 but never became official.

Memorials to the more than two million First World War dead were erected across Germany in the immediate aftermath of the conflict, but no national memorial was constructed. In Nazi Germany, the emphasis shifted from mourning to celebrating the front-line soldier and a national holiday was declared, as Martin Bayer puts it, 'to establish the Frontkämpfer ... as a unifying myth of heroism and sacrifice'.[4] Defeat, and the central place that the Frontkämpfer subsequently took in Hitler's vision of the German nation, contributed to the forgetting of the First World War after 1945.

This ambivalence about the First World War was reflected in the official approach to the Centenary in Germany, where it was decided not to hold a centrally organised event in 2014. David Cameron's ambitious plans for the Centenary in austerity Britain worried the German government, which feared that the commemorations might stir up anti-German sentiments, and an ambassador was dispatched to Britain to urge its government to agree on a pan-European narrative emphasising the human costs of the conflict. The exchange revealed how sensitivities surrounding the Second World War continued to frame reactions to the First World War in Germany. It also revealed the German government's anxieties about the revival of extremist tendencies in Europe, tendencies which ultimately, despite Cameron's leadership of the Remain campaign, contributed to Britain's decision in 2016 to leave the European Union. Playing up the importance of service and sacrifice for one's country alongside the remembrance of loss, Cameron's vision of the commemorations sought to promote national unity at a time of social division and did not exclude anti-European sentiments.[5]

Despite reluctance by the federal government in Germany, there were signs of renewed interest in the First World War as the Centenary approached, the impetus coming from non-state and voluntary agencies. Some predicted that the war, in Arndt Weinrich's phrase, was 'about to assert itself, to emerge from the shadows cast by the Holocaust and the Second World War'.[6] The ninetieth anniversary in 2004 coincided with the publication by Gerhard Hirschfeld, Gerd Krumeich and Irina Renz of a thousand-page *Encyclopaedia of the First World War*, aimed at a general audience and presenting a pan-European and transnational perspective on the conflict.[7] The public reaction to the Centenary surprised some commentators, overshadowing the seventy-fifth anniversary of the outbreak of the Second World War.⁸ A survey in 2014 found that 69 per cent of respondents expressed interest in the First World War. Sales of books about the First World War were outselling those about the Second, while new documentary films brought the war 'back to life and into German living rooms'.⁹ Regional and local museum exhibitions during 2014, such as Berlin's *War of the Empires*, drew large numbers.¹⁰ The flurry of public interest was encouraged by Christopher Clark's book *The Sleepwalkers*, which sold over 350,000 copies in Germany and at last count was in its twentieth German edition.¹¹ The media debates about the book illustrate the different tendencies that animated the re-emergence of the First World War, some seeking to locate it within a longer history of conflict in the twentieth century that includes the rise of Nazi Germany and the Holocaust – a so-called 'Second 30 Years War' – others drawing attention to Clark's emphasis on the pan-European roots of the conflict to counter accusations of German aggression and exceptionalism.¹² As Annika Mombauer comments, the controversy over *Sleepwalkers* was in some ways a re-run of the debates in Germany during the 1960s, when Franz Fischer challenged the orthodoxy that the causes of the First World War were to be found in a failure of the European alliance and insisted instead that Germany bore the main responsibility. In the Centenary re-run, however, those who pursued war guilt were now branded the 'old fashioned traditionalists'.¹³

We witnessed the enthusiasm for learning more about the First World War when we arrived in Rosenheim in the spring of 2016 for *Meeting in No Man's Land*. Two of the German participants had recently read *Sleepwalkers*, and many were curious to learn more about the 'British obsession' with remembrance. They had retrieved family heritage of the war from attics and outbuildings, and some had recently visited local archives and came armed with fresh discoveries about their fathers and grandfathers. The historical importance of Theodora's family story about her grandfather, who survived a massacre of twenty-one Catholic Journeymen by the *Freikorps* in Berlin on 6 May 1919, had become clearer to her as the centenary of their deaths approached and plans for a memorial were announced.¹⁴ This was 'the first catastrophe' that her grandfather would face after returning from the war; others would follow. For Theodora and for the Catholic descendants of the murdered journeymen, the lesson a century later was one of 'reconciliation' and political and religious tolerance.

Our meeting was clearly tapping into a collective moment, but many of the German descendants felt ambivalent about the war histories in their families. For some, it was better not to ask questions. The only evidence of his grandfather's war that Wolfgang possessed was a dozen postcards, a French bayonet and a letter opener. The bayonet had lain in his grandmother's attic until she died and was then passed to his father. It was Wolfgang's 'favourite' piece of First World War ephemera and he had mounted it on the wall in his home. When I asked Wolfgang what he appreciated about the bayonet, he answered simply 'I just like it'. It was just a domestic ornament, and its history did not concern him: 'I don't know how my grandfather got this bayonet', Wolfgang explained. The back story – a trophy taken from a French *poilus* that his grandfather had captured or killed perhaps? – was lost.

For many of the German participants, family memory continued to be dominated by the Second World War. Theodora conveyed the way in which it had eclipsed the First World War in her family. She had recently learned that the Dachau concentration camp had been a munitions plant in the First World War, and that her own grandmother had worked there. Growing up in Dachau in the 1950s and attending the 'death march' commemorations each year, her memory was fixed on the significance of the site in Germany's history of genocide. The family connection to Dachau had come full circle, as her son had recently moved to the area. In contrast to Britain, the First World War could not furnish a model of citizenship for the German participants and their emotional connections to First World War ancestors were hedged about with guilt.[15]

The funding devoted to Centenary commemorations indicates the place that the First World War holds in the national culture of the three countries. While Germany was estimated to be spending in the region of 3.5 million euros, David Cameron put aside 50 million pounds, and the Australian government is reported to have made over 562 million dollars available, potentially outstripping the combined expenditure of all other countries and spawning what has been described as a 'memory orgy'.[16] The inclusion of two ex-prime ministers in the National Commission set up in Australia in 2011 to plan Australia's commemorations shows the reverence with which the First World War is treated.[17] It was not always thus. Numbers attending the Anzac Day parades fell in the late 1970s and early 1980s when I was in my teens, and the news headlines on Anzac Day in those decades were dominated by the scuffles between veterans and feminists protesting against rape in war.[18] Since then the event has grown exponentially. Its popularity has increased with the passing of the survivors, the city-centre marches on 25 April accompanied by dawn services at the local war memorials of virtually every town and city in Australia.

The First World War is commemorated in Australia as a moment of national becoming, the Act of Federation which created a Commonwealth from the six self-governing territories having taken place just fourteen years earlier in 1901. The Gallipoli campaign announced the nation's arrival on the international stage; the phrase 'baptism of fire' was one we often heard as children. The comparatively high casualty rate, the significance of the Gallipoli campaign as a foundation myth (albeit built on a retreat), the prosperity of its citizens and its remoteness from the principal theatres of war in Europe and the Middle East have helped make Australia a world leader in battlefield tourism.[19] Gallipoli is its most hallowed ground. Fourteen people were present at the official dawn ceremony in 1957, but 42,273 applied to attend the commemoration at Anzac Cove in April 2015.[20] When I visited the peninsula a month later as part of a delegation of historians from Britain, Australia and Turkey, the roads around Çanakkale were still busy with busloads of Australian and New Zealand tourists. But though this tourism has become international, its reference points remain national. Busloads of Turkish tourists were visiting the peninsula at the time, some of whom had been given free trips to the site by President Erdogan during his campaign for re-election, as the AKP sought to re-position the narrative of the Çanakkale campaign as a Muslim nationalist struggle.[21] Turkish and Antipodean crowds stood side by side at Chunuk Bair, the Turks looking at a statue of Ataturk, the gaze of the Antipodeans fixed on the memorial to the New Zealand soldiers who fought at the site on 8 August 1915. This was state-centred mass tourism in parallel, with no personal contact between the two groups although some undoubtedly shared a history as descendants.

Australian citizens have turned battlefield pilgrimage into an art in the thirty-five years since I emigrated to Britain, as I discovered when visiting the cemetery at Lone Pine where my grandfather fought. Our group gathered into a circle shortly before we were due to depart, and I was invited to swig from a flask and say a few words in Bob's honour. I felt flustered and had no idea how to respond. Standing among colleagues who were critical of Anzac's nationalistic overtones, on the soil where Granddad witnessed the full force of what he called 'man's inhumanity to man', I nevertheless felt no desire to acknowledge publicly what he had gone through.

Later that year I visited the Canberra War Memorial with my father, and after a day in the archives we were invited to attend a Last Post ceremony in the courtyard. At first, I thought we must have stumbled on a significant anniversary, but it turned out that the Memorial had started conducting daily remembrance services in April 2013. We listened as a member of Australia's armed services told the story of a soldier whose name is listed on its Roll of Honour, his history carefully researched by Memorial staff who respond to written requests from members of the public. The Memorial assumes that those who submit requests will be descendants, as the form asks for information about nicknames and 'Family Anecdotes'.[22] My father and I stood awkwardly as we listened to a moving tribute that was officiated by serving members of the Australian Defence Forces and supported by the Returned Soldiers' League – an organisation once shunned by my grandfather and reviled and ridiculed by the Left when I was a youth. The militarisation of history and commemoration in Australia was revealed, as a family's story of loss was coaxed into a national narrative by historians and army officials.[23]

The First World War is seen by Australians as an event in family history as much as the history of the nation. When the ex-Premier of Victoria, Ted Baillieu, was made chair of the committee to organise the state's commemoration in 2013, he declared that families must be at the centre, because people needed to make personal connections to the conflict: 'You have to have descendants identified in order to make a commemoration because if there is not a connection you have only got an exhibition, and we've had exhibitions galore.'[24] Baillieu had gone on his own pilgrimage in 2008, phoning his mother on her deathbed from Vlamertinge cemetery in Belgium to describe the place where her father lay.[25] 'The symmetry of it was spooky', he told *The Age*: 'My mother had a stroke and would die as a consequence of that stroke and I was sitting beside my grandfather's grave at that moment, but I was able to speak to her from that place.' Australia's plans for the commemoration of the Gallipoli landing in 2015 reflected the importance attached to descendants. When a ballot was held for the 10,500 places at the dawn service, first in the 'cascading hierarchy of memory credentials' were the ten surviving widows of veterans, and four hundred school-children, representing the generational span from the veteran to future generations. Next in line were 'direct descendants', with sons and daughters privileged over later generations, followed by veterans and, finally, members of the general public.[26]

Descendants were also at the centre of the 2009 campaign to disinter the remains of 250 soldiers placed by the Germans in six mass graves after the Anzac's first engagement on the Western Front at Fromelles in July 1916. More than three thousand people put their names down on the Relatives Database and over one thousand came forward for DNA tests, believing that they might be related to the missing soldiers. The bodies of 203 Australians were identified, the announcement of their names in 2010 and the reburial service at a new Commonwealth War Graves cemetery at Pheasant Wood – the first to be constructed for over half a century – finally bringing 'closure for the families of the men', according to the Australian War Memorial.[27] Families attended the services and were invited to add a personalised inscription to the headstones. Pheasant Wood cemetery, the Musée de la Bataille de Fromelles and the Australian Memorial Park form part of the 'Australian Remembrance Trail', funded by the Australian Government to the tune of $10 million.[28]

The visibility of descendants through the Centenary met with a mixed reaction among Australian historians, who noted the parochial and sentimental tone of much public commemoration.[29] The grafting of nationalism onto pity and mourning concerned some: sharpened by the 'trauma age', sympathy with the horrors suffered by Anzacs at Gallipoli and on the Western Front often co-exists with the desire to honour the nation through the sacrifices of its forefathers. In the public imagination, remark Carolyn Holbrook and Bart Ziino, the Anzac is simultaneously 'on the couch' and 'waving the national flag'.[30] The historian movement Honest History, meanwhile, whose aim is to 'challenge the misuse of history to serve political or other agenda', added a 'Centenary Watch' to its website which aimed to expose the excesses of remembrance and provide an outlet for critical interpretations.[31]

War is a family story for many Australians and forms a powerful source of emotional connection to ancestors and the nation. Australia's vibrant culture of genealogy consists in large part of people who are researching a First or Second World War ancestor.[32] Descendants have spawned a boom in volumes of First World War letters and memoirs, from fewer than a hundred publications in the 1980s to 215 in the decade after 2000, many of them privately funded.[33] The Australian government actively supports their historical work through the National Archives, which have digitised the service and repatriation records of all serving First World War personnel. Despite cuts elsewhere in archival services in recent years, this 'gift to the nation' enables family historians to undertake the kind of research on the military service and post-war health of their ancestors that descendants from other nations can only envy.[34]

Although underwritten by the state, however, descendants in Australia do not just prop up a militarised image of Australian society. As Holbrook and Ziino conclude, their research is motivated by life stage and loss, the wish for connection with loved ones and the search for one's own identity. Descendants' memoirs can convey a critical relationship with the public memory of Anzac and enlarge historical understanding through personal knowledge of the war's impact.[35]

Britain sits between Germany and Australia in terms of the First World War's significance in the public consciousness and the prominence of descendants in commemoration. Its frames of remembrance remained relatively stable in the fifty years between the publication of Alan Clark's withering attack on the competence of military leadership, *The Donkeys*, and the eve of the Centenary. The 'Lions led by Donkeys' theme was carried through theatre productions like *Oh, What a Lovely War!* and the twenty-six-episode BBC television series *The Great War*, screened in 1964 to commemorate the fiftieth anniversary. The shift from top-down military history to the social history of the trench soldier went hand in hand with a critical vision of the war as a senseless slaughter. Reflecting this, in the second half of the twentieth century the Battle of the Somme and its sixty thousand British casualties on 1 July 1916 – the most lethal day in the history of the British army – eclipsed Ypres as the principal site of

British First World War remembrance.[36] This statistic – taken from Fussell's *Great War and Modern Memory* – was one of the few facts about the war that I was able to recount to my grandfather in 1980 and has been recounted to me numerous times since by descendants.

In the run-up to 2014, the perceived hegemony of the 'pity of war' narrative was the subject of animated debate in Britain. The First World War, declared David Reynolds in 2013, was 'a saga of personal tragedies, illuminated by poetry not history, a subject for remembrance rather than understanding', the British public immune to historical scholarship that showed the range of theatres of war and diversity of soldiers drawn into the conflict from across the Empire.[37] The pity of war perspective occluded other histories: the contribution of African and Indian soldiers to the war effort, women's participation on the home and war fronts, the histories of non-combatants and conscientious objectors, popular patriotism and the reasons why British people were motivated to join the war effort. Descendants were thought to have helped entrench a narrow memory of the war, lacking the confidence, expertise and critical facility to look beyond the war poets they learned at school.[38]

In the speech announcing his plans for the Centenary, David Cameron sought to inflect the pity of war perspective with a patriotic note. He spoke of loss and mourning but emphasised the sacrifices made by the British people, and expressed his hopes for a commemoration that, like the 2012 Diamond Jubilee celebrations, 'captures our national spirit in every corner of the country, something that says something about who we are as a people'.[39] The organisers not only wished to promote civic participation, but to emphasise the value of military service at a time when the British public was regularly witnessing the aftermath of conflicts in Iraq and Afghanistan.[40] They wished to reach young people in particular. As Catriona Pennell shows, the 6,500 pupils whose visits to the Western Front battlefield were sponsored through the scheme underwent an intensive education in military citizenship, accompanied by a team of senior Army officers who organised war games and displays of military hardware, and stood with the children throughout the commemoration ceremonies.[41] It was in response to plans like these, and the potentially celebratory tone of the plans for the Centenary, that counter-movements like the No Glory campaign were formed in 2014 by literary and media figures, while the historian and Labour MP Tristram Hunt argued that the Centenary should help create a more global view of the conflict, revealing the 'multiple histories' of combatants throughout the Empire.[42]

Descendants were not at the top of Cameron's remembrance list in 2012 but seemed to become more prominent during 2014–18. Many had long-standing interests in First World War history, represented through organisations like the Western Front Association, founded in 1980. Their stories featured in newspapers and TV productions as the Centenary approached, giving intimate glimpses into the long-term effects of the conflict that promised to engage readers and viewers with no personal connection to it.[43] The money awarded by the Heritage Lottery Fund (hereafter HLF) through the First World War Then and Now stream went to around two thousand community projects which ranged from research on the names of local war memorials to projects about the home front and the impact of the war on local communities, conscientious objectors and 'hidden' wars, including non-European combatants.[44] The most common were military-based, covering themes like war memorials, military life and conflict, military anniversaries and theatres of war, but applicants seemed to become more interested in legacies and inter-generational themes as the Centenary progressed.[45] Descendants were prominent among the five million visitors to the highly successful *Blood-Swept Lands and Seas of Red* exhibition at the Tower of London in 2014 and were keen to relate their family histories of the conflict.[46] Unlike the Last Post ceremony at Australia's War Memorial, the services each evening at the Tower commemorated, not an individual, but 180 troops from across the Commonwealth, whose names were nominated by members of the public. Perhaps because of Britain's role in the Empire, the emphasis was broader and more collective, a commemoration that British descendants could attach meaning to, but which was not only for them.

Descendants had a more central part in the *Shrouds of the Somme* installation by Rob Heard, which commemorated the Commonwealth soldiers with no known grave and toured Exeter, Bristol and Salisbury in 2016 and Belfast and Thiepval in 2017–18. The project culminated in an exhibition at Queen Elizabeth Olympic Park in Stratford in 2018 where seventy-two thousand miniature shrouds, each striking a different pose, were laid out on the grass. *Shrouds* was unique among the large-scale art projects in the UK because it relied primarily on private funding. Heard began sewing the shrouds after a serious car accident, transfixed by the numbers of casualties and a belief that 'each man needs his one last moment in time'.[47] He was affected by the response to his exhibitions. A visitor to the 2016 installation in Exeter told Heard that his uncle's body was never recovered and that the shrouds were 'the first time his Uncle had lain on British soil for one hundred years'.[48] The merchandise from the 2018 exhibition suggests the premium placed on a family connection: 'certified' shrouds for £65 included the name and regiment of an individual serviceman, while unidentified shrouds were priced at £30.[49] Like the Tomb of the Unknown Soldier, *Shrouds* symbolically brings the dead back 'home' to British soil, but instead of standing for *any* soldier, the eight-five thousand visitors could imagine each shrouded figure as an individual and were able to leave a personal tribute.[50]

New digital technologies helped descendants to undertake research on their ancestors, share it and contribute to the historical record. The Europeana project *1914–1918*, set up in 2013 to record family heritage of the First World War, achieved its success through the willingness of descendants to connect and contribute to the historical record.[51] The Imperial War Museum's digital platform *Lives of the First World War* appealed to a similar constituency, inviting individuals to upload private collections of photographs and records which were curated by a team of twenty-five volunteers. A total of 7,686,232 life stories had been gathered by the time the appeal closed in March 2019.[52] Platforms like these created new and lasting public memorials, helping, as Helen McCartney observes, to 'keep remembrance in the present' through instantaneous public access to the heritage of private households.[53]

By 2015, the British commemorations of significant battles were looking more like those in Australia, an instance perhaps of Colonial influence in reverse. Entrants in the public ballot to take part in the official commemoration ceremony at Passchendaele in 2017 were invited to fill out a form 'Sharing Your Personal Connection', the assumption being that these were the people most likely to want to join. Their stories provided moving material for the BBC's official coverage and other press reports. The attending dignitaries, celebrities and royalty, reported *The Guardian,* were 'in the presence of the sons and daughters, nieces and nephews of the hundreds of thousands of allied soldiers who died in the blood and mud of the Ypres salient'.[54] Speaking at Tyne Cot, Prime Minister Theresa May declared that 'It is an honour to be joined today by so many descendants of those men'.[55] At the Battle of Amiens commemoration a year later the spotlight was on descendants again. Planning the event, the Department of Culture, Media and Sport put out an appeal for 'descendant stories', urging relatives with a 'personal connection' to get in touch. A number of participants had their ancestors' medals pinned to their chests, a tangible marker, the invitee and historian James Wallis notes, of the personal significance of the event for them.[56] A similar emphasis was evident in the service at Westminster on Armistice Day 2018. Her grandfather was 'accompanying me in spirit', wrote one attendee in the Western Front Association *Bulletin*, while another explained that she had taken some mementoes of her family to the service to help 'keep in perspective the reasons for my attendance'.[57] The official thankyou letter to attendees singled out those with an ancestral link: 'In particular, it has been a privilege to help descendants to remember their ancestors'.[58]

In Australia and increasingly in Britain during the Centenary, remembrance found its most poignant expression through descendants. Their moving stories revealed the war's hidden impact on families, but tended to traverse the well-trodden paths of Gallipoli and the Western Front, and fold the global conflict back into national history. While descendants in Australia are vaunted even when the family war story is one of tragedy, and in Britain they rub shoulders with the elite, German descendants are wary of staking claims around a common inheritance from the First World War past.

These differences became apparent in *Meeting in No Man's Land* when members from each country were placed in pairs to interview each other. The German participants presented their research on First World War ancestors as an individual quest. Nobody in the family knew anything about her grandfather's war, Theodora explained. She had to collect the information herself and eventually, she said proudly, 'I assembled a picture of him.' The Germans were curious to know why the British were so fond of commemoration and battlefield tours. Why, Franziska asked Diana with amazement, did the British award so many medals, and did *all* soldiers receive them? Talking to Diana made her feel that 'we are just not open enough, or messed up in some way. We can't talk freely about these things.' The British descendants had no compunction about putting their medals on show, but the history of medal-giving under Hitler made the Germans wary: Hanne, having produced her grandfather's 1934 Honour Cross in the planning meeting, did not bring it to her paired interview.[59] Their country's history of extremism was always close to the surface. Christel became embarrassed as she read out the inscription on her grandfather's prayerbook: '"The German soldier is a hero in God's eyes". It is very difficult to read it.'

In Germany, the research of descendants fills a gap into which the state is unwilling to venture. Their research brings home the ambiguous legacies of being a descendant, as many among the second generation were socialised within the Third Reich, and the third generation grew up amidst the generational revolt against the denial of what had happened in the Second World War.[60] Australian and British descendants feel no such qualms about introducing their family histories into local and national arenas, and their links to the contemporary witnesses provide the affective pull in the Centenary commemorations.

The claim to be a descendant carries unquestioned authority and authenticity in Britain and Australia. Yet such claims are always selective, and often a matter of politics. Communities of German descent long pre-dated the First World War in Australia, but after the outbreak of the war, seven thousand people of German descent – naturalised Australian citizens among them – were detained in internment camps and deported to Germany at the end of the war. Their plight is a 'sobering counter-projection to the story of the heroic Anzacs', remark Nardine Helmi and Gérard Fischer.[61] Some of Australia's Asian population today will have ancestors who fought with the Imperial forces in the First World War yet are descendants without an identity, as their histories do not form part of the white settler story of nation founding. Although there have been attempts to extend the Anzac commemorations to Indigenous Australians, minority ethnics, women and gay and lesbian service personnel, none carries the mantle of the white digger.

In Britain, despite the efforts of the HLF and First World War Engagement Centres to increase the diversity of commemoration, only 8 per cent of participants identified as Black or minority ethnic compared with 13 per cent in the UK as a whole.[62] The Imperial War Graves Commission's decisions not to erect individual headstones for many of the non-white colonial forces soldiers who had died in the war were exposed at the end of the Centenary in a high-profile campaign that highlighted the racial hierarchies implemented by the commission's founders.[63] Only white soldiers, it appeared, had been deemed worthy of equal treatment. Artistic commemorations like *Shrouds* or Jeremy Deller's *We're Here Because We're Here* conveyed the jolt of a national trauma to a contemporary age but represented a largely white heritage despite the involvement of non-white actors, while the channelling of project funding to local community groups sometimes added to the challenge of broadening the narrative in the transfer of remembrance to new generations.[64]

Descendants in all three countries were vocal actors throughout the Centenary. Standing in for the victims and survivors, they personalised the history of the conflict and created an emotional community of remembrance that bridged the First World War generation to contemporaries who have no living link to the conflict. Digital reproduction technologies and social networks unavailable to their ancestors enhanced their affective reach. Yet the children and grandchildren in Germany, Britain and Australia, while they share an identity as descendants, stand in a different relation to the dominant national narratives of war in the twentieth century. While families in Australia and Britain take pride of place in national remembrance and commemorations, as the next chapter shows, Germany's history of extremism dominates the family story, and the recovery of its First World War past takes place predominantly in private, local and regional spaces.

Notes

1 D. Crossland, 'Last German World War I Veteran Believed to Have Died', *Spiegel International*, 22 January 2008, www.spiegel.de/international/germany/aged-107-last-german-world-war-i-veteran-believed-to-have-died-a-530319.html. Accessed 4 November 2021.

2 D. Rising, 'Erich Kaestner; May Have Been Germany's Last WWI Veteran', *Boston Globe*, 27 January 2008, http://archive.boston.com/bostonglobe/obituaries/articles/2008/01/27/erich_kaestner_may_have_been_germanys_last_wwi_veteran/. Accessed 4 November 2021.
3 D. Crossland, 'WWI Grave Find Tells Story Germans Want to Forget', *Spiegel International*, 27 October 2011, www.spiegel.de/international/europe/pocket-books-and-prayer-beads-wwi-grave-find-tells-story-germans-want-to-forget-a-794103.html. Accessed 4 November 2021.
4 M. Bayer, 'Remembrance Revisited? The First World War Centenary in Germany', *Cultural Trends*, 27: 2 (2018), 136–7.
5 In retrospect, however, surveys show a remarkable degree of national solidarity about the commemorations even at the height of national tensions over Brexit in 2018, reflecting a feeling that the Centenary should 'not be used as a political football'. L. Buckerfield and S. Ballinger, *The People's Centenary: Tracking Public Attitudes to the First World War Centenary 2013–2018* (London: British Future, 2019), 4, 8; E. Hanna, L. M. Hughes, L. Noakes, C. Pennell and J. Wallis, *Reflections on the Centenary of the First World War: Learning and Legacies for the Future* (June 2021) 22, https://reflections1418.exeter.ac.uk/wp-content/uploads/2021/10/Reflections-on-the-Centenary-of-the-First-World-War-Learning-and-Legacies-for-the-Future.pdf. Accessed 25 January 2023.
6 A. Weinrich, 'Un Siècle – Deux Trajectoires. Les Mémoires Françaises et Allemandes de la Première Guerre Mondiale, 1918–2014', *La Grande Guerre. Politsche, Kulturegeschichte der Vork reigszeit*, https://grande-guerre.hypotheses.org/2009#identifier_13_2009. Accessed 4 November 2021; J. Winter, 'Commemorating Catastrophe', *War and Society*, 36: 4 (2017), 242.
7 G. Hirschfeld, G. Krumeich and I. Renz (eds), *Encyclopaedia of The First World War* (Paderborn: Ferdinand Schoningh Verlag, 2003). 'The war is back in German history', wrote Tillmann Bedikowski in his review of the book. www.deutschlandfunk.de/gerhard-hirschfeld-gerd-krumeich-irina-renz-hrsg.730.de.html?dram:article_id=102196. Accessed 4 November 2021.
8 Weinrich, 'Un Siècle – Deux Trajectoires'.
9 A. Mombauer, 'The German Centenary of the First World War', *War and Society*, 36: 4 (2017), 285.
10 Exhibitions include Berlin's *War of the Empires – World War I 1914–1918*, at the Deutsches Historisches Museum, and the programme of exhibitions *1914. At the Heart of Europe. The Rhineland and the First World War*. For other examples, see Weinrich, 'Un Siècle – Deux Trajectoires'.
11 Mombauer, 'German Centenary', 280; Bayer, 'Remembrance Revisited', 136.

12 A. Wirsching, 'Christopher Clark's Sleepwalkers and the Germans: A Misunderstanding?', http://insidestory.org.au/christopher-clarks-sleepwalkers-and-the-germans-a-misunderstanding. Accessed 5 November 2021; Mombauer, 'German Centenary', 280; M. Bayer, 'Commemoration in Germany: Rediscovering History', *Australian Journal of Political Science*, 50: 3 (2015), 553.
13 Mombauer, 'German Centenary', 281.
14 A plaque commemorating the deaths of the journeymen was unveiled on Munich's Karolinenplatz in 2019, https://vor-ort.kolping.de/kolpingsfamilie-muenchen-zentral/gedenkveranstaltung-gesellenmord/. Accessed 20 September 2021.
15 On the rationalisation by descendants of the involvement and complicity of ancestors, see H. Welzer, 'Collateral Damage of History Education: National Socialism and the Holocaust in German Family Memory', *Social Research*, 75: 1 (Spring 2008), 287–314.
16 Mombauer, 'German Centenary', 279; J. Beaumont, 'Commemoration in Australia: A Memory Orgy?', *Australian Journal of Political Science*, 50: 3 (2015), 541; *Honest History* editorial, 'Kaching! Australia's Anzac Centenary Spend Hits $A562 Million', *Honest History*, 11 January 2016, http://honesthistory.net.au/wp/kaching-australias-anzac-centenary-spend-hits-a562-million/. Accessed 5 November 2021; R. Fathi, 'Is Australia Spending Too Much on the Anzac Centenary?', *Honest History*, 14 April 2016, http://honesthistory.net.au/wp/is-australia-spending-too-much-on-the-anzac-centenary-a-comparison-with-france/. Accessed 5 November 2021.
17 Beaumont, 'Commemoration in Australia', 537.
18 On the transformation of Anzac Day, see C. Twomey, 'Trauma and the Reinvigoration of Anzac', *History Australia*, 10: 3 (2013), 85–108; C. Holbrook, *Anzac: The Unauthorised Biography* (Sydney: New South Books, 2014); C. Holbrook, 'How Anzac Day Came to Occupy a Place in Australians' Hearts', *The Conversation*, 24 April 2017, https://theconversation.com/how-anzac-day-came-to-occupy-a-sacred-place-in-australians-hearts-76323. Accessed 5 November 2021.
19 On casualty rates, see J. Murphy, *A Decent Provision Australian Welfare Policy, 1870 to 1949* (London: Routledge, 2016), 109. B. Scates, *Return to Gallipoli: Walking the Battlefields of the Great War* (Cambridge: Cambridge University Press, 2006). For a critical commentary on the rise of battlefield tourism in Australia, see M. McKenna and S. Ward, '"It Was Really Moving, Mate": The Gallipoli Pilgrimage and Sentimental Nationalism in Australia', *Australian Historical Studies*, 38: 129 (2007), 141–51. The debates between Scates and McKenna and Ward are summarised in C. Holbrook and K. Reeves, 'Making

Sense of the Great War Centenary', in C. Holbrook and K. Reeves (eds), *The Great War: Aftermath and Commemoration* (Sydney: University of New South Wales Press), 6–9.
20 V. Kant, 'Remembering Gallipoli in Contemporary Turkey', in B. Ziino (ed.), *Remembering the First World War* (Abingdon: Routledge, 2015), 153; Beaumont, 'Commemoration in Australia', 538.
21 Kant, 'Remembering Gallipoli', 156–7; P. Daley, 'Turkish Islamist Push May Be to Blame for Removal of Atatürk Inscription at Anzac Cove', *The Guardian*, 16 June 2017.
22 Australian War Memorial, 'Request for a Last Post Ceremony', www.awm.gov.au/form/request-for-a-last post-ceremony. Accessed 8 July 2019.
23 M. Lake and H. Reynolds, with M. McKenna and J. Damousi, *What's Wrong with Anzac? The Militarization of Australian History* (Sydney: New South Books, 2010), iii.
24 *The Age*, 12 December 2013, www.theage.com.au/national/victoria/connecting-with-our-heroes-20131212-2z9xq.html. Accessed 8 July 2019. See also C. Holbrook and B. Ziino, 'Family History and the Great War in Australia', in Ziino (ed.), *Remembering the First World War*, 51–2.
25 M. Baker, 'Connecting with Our Heroes: Ted Baillieu Wants as Many People as Possible to Connect with Their Family's Involvement in the Great War', *The Age*, 12 December 2013.
26 Beaumont, 'Commemoration in Australia', 538–9.
27 Australian Army, 'The Fromelles Project', www.army.gov.au/our-work/unrecovered-war-casualties/fromelles/the-fromelles-project. Accessed 8 July 2019; A. Pegram, 'Fromelles: Identifying the Fallen', Australian War Memorial, 19 March 2010, www.awm.gov.au/blog/fromelles-identifying-the-fallen. Accessed 8 July 2019.
28 Australian Government Department of Veteran Affairs, 'Australians on the Western Front: Visiting Fromelles', https://anzacportal.dva.gov.au/history/conflicts/australians-western-front/australian-remembrance-trail/vc-cornerfromelles/visiting. Accessed 8 July 2019; Trip Advisor, 'Musée de la Bataille de Fromelles', www.tripadvisor.co.uk/Attraction_Review-g2359641-d2331324-Reviews-Musee_de_la_Bataille_de_Fromelles-Fromelles_Nord_Hauts_de_France.html. Accessed 8 July 2019.
29 J. Damousi, 'Why Do We Get So Emotional About Anzac?', in Lake et al., *What's Wrong with Anzac?*, 94–109.
30 Holbrook and Ziino, 'Family History', 41; Twomey, 'Trauma and the Reinvigoration of Anzac'.
31 'About Centenary Watch', *Honest History*, http://honesthistory.net.au/wp/category/centenary-watch/. Accessed 5 November 2021.

32 Holbrook and Ziino, 'Family History', 39.
33 Holbrook, *Anzac*, 145.
34 In mid-2021 the Australian government was forced to do a U-turn after a successful campaign by historians to reverse funding cuts to the National Archives that would have resulted in the destruction of audio and film collections. At the same time, funding for the War Memorial was being increased. www.abc.net.au/radionational/programs/breakfast/historians-issue-desperate-plea-for-national-archives-funding/13383658. Accessed 20 September 2021.
35 Holbrook and Ziino, 'Family History', 52–3.
36 H. McCartney, 'The First World War Soldier and His Contemporary Image in Britain', *International Affairs*, 90: 2 (2014), 291.
37 D. Reynolds, *The Long Shadow: The Great War and the Twentieth Century* (Simon & Schuster, 2013), 387.
38 McCartney, 'First World War Soldier', 305–7; C. Pennell, 'Taught to Remember? British Youth and First World War Centenary Battlefield Tours', *Cultural Trends*, 27: 2 (2018), 91. Professional historians, James Wallis observed presciently in 2014, would have to reach an accommodation with family historians given that this was 'inevitably be one of the ways through which members of the public can attain a degree of personal relevance to the events of 1914–18'. 'Great-Grandfather, What Did *You Do* in the Great War?', in Ziino (ed.), *Remembering the First World War*, 24.
39 *The Guardian*, 11 October 2012.
40 K. Jeffery, 'Commemoration in the United Kingdom: A Multitude of Memories', *Australian Journal of Political Science*, 50: 3 (2015), 562–7.
41 Pennell, 'Taught to Remember?', 83–98; M. Harrison (ed.), *The Centenary of the First World War: How the Nation Remembered* (London: DCMS Centenary Publications, 2019), 9.
42 Quoted in Jeffery, 'Commemoration in the United Kingdom', 564.
43 For a selection, see T. Helm, 'WW1 Memories: My Grandfather's Story', *Observer*, 3 November 2013; S. Norton-Taylor, 'Ghosts of Soldiers: Memories of My Grandfather's First World War Service', *Observer*, 3 August 2014; L. Moody, 'Lewis Moody: Why I Retraced My Great-Grandfather's WWI Journey', *Telegraph*, 11 November 2014.
44 L. Noakes, 'Centenary (United Kingdom)', in U. Daniel, P. Gatrell, O. Janz, H. Jones, J. Keene, A. Kramer and B. Nasson (eds), *1914–18 Online*: *International Encyclopaedia of the First World War* (Berlin: Free University, 2019). https://encyclopedia.1914–1918-online.net/article/centenary_united_kingdom?version=1.0. Accessed 5 November 2021; Harrison (ed.), *Centenary*, 19.

45 S. Lloyd, J. Moore, A. Maunder and R. Smith, 'HLF First World War Projects Focus Group Analysis Notes', 15 March 2018. Thanks to Rachel Duffett for research on the HLF project themes.
46 J. Kidd and J. Sayner, 'Unthinking Remembrance? Blood Swept Lands and Seas of Red and the Significance of Centenaries', *Cultural Trends*, 27: 2 (2018), 74–5.
47 'Shrouds of the Somme – Interview with Artist Rob Heard', www.youtube.com/watch?v=uMcUUfVZG58. Accessed 5 November 2021.
48 'The Story of the Shrouds', www.shroudsofthesomme.com/our-story/. Accessed 5 November 2021.
49 www.shroudsofthesomme.com/product/shrouded-figure-framed/. Accessed 5 November 2021.
50 H. McCartney, 'Commemorating the Centenary of the Battle of the Somme in Britain', *War & Society*, 36: 4 (2014), 297. Thanks to James Wallis for additional information.
51 Europeana Collections 1914–18, www.europeana.eu/en/collections/topic/83-1914-1918. Accessed 5 November 2021.
52 Imperial War Museum Lives of the First World War, https://livesofthefirstworldwar.org/. Accessed 5 November 2021; Harrison (ed.), *Centenary*, 238.
53 McCartney, 'Commemorating the Centenary', 298.
54 D. Boffey, 'Passchendaele, 100 Years On: A Final Great Act of Remembrance', *The Guardian*, 29 July 2017.
55 'The National Commemoration of the Centenary of Passchendaele – The Third Battle of Ypres', The Commonwealth War Graves Commission's Tyne Cot Cemetery, 31 July 2017, https://assets.publishing.service.gov.uk/government/uploads/system/uploads/attachment_data/file/633773/Final_Tyne_Cot_Commemorative_Programme_English.pdf. Accessed 5 November 2021.
56 Email correspondence with James Wallis, 22 February 2019.
57 *Western Front Association Bulletin*, 112 (December 2018), 7.
58 Email from caroline.rowley@culture.gov.uk to National Armistice Service 2018 Mailbox, 9 January 2019 (forwarded courtesy of James Wallis).
59 See Introduction.
60 On German generations, see M. Roseman, *Generations in Conflict: Youth Revolt and Generation Formation in Germany 1770–1968* (Cambridge: Cambridge University Press, 1995); T. Kohut, *A German Generation: An Experiential History of the Twentieth Century* (New Haven: Yale University Press, 2012); M. Fulbrook, *Dissonant Lives: Generations and Violence through the German Dictatorships* (Oxford: Oxford University Press, 2011).

61 N. Helmi and G. Fischer, *The Enemy at Home: German Internees in WWI Australia* (Sydney: New South Books, 2011), 41.
62 Hanna et al., *Reflections on the Centenary*, 24.
63 M. Barrett, 'Sent Missing in Africa: Briefing Paper for *The Unremembered*', www.michelebarrett.com/wp-content/uploads/2019/11/Sent-Missing-in-Africa.pdf. Accessed 21 September 2021. For studies of Indian troops, see G. M. Jack, *The Indian Army on the Western Front: Indian Expeditionary Force to France and Belgium in the First World War* (Cambridge: Cambridge University Press, 2014); S. Das, *Empire and First World War Culture: Writings, Images, and Songs* (Cambridge: Cambridge University Press, 2018).
64 On the enduring appeal of the British soldier on the Western Front in cultural memory of the First World War, see L. Noakes and J. Wallis, 'The People's Centenary? Public History, Remembering and Forgetting in Britain's First World War Centenary', *The Public Historian*, 44: 2 (2022), 56–81.

4

Meeting in No Man's Land: motives for remembrance among British and German descendants

Michael Roper and Rachel Duffett

In April 2016 the London reminiscence organisation Age Exchange brought together twenty-three German and British people with a First World War history in the family. Funded by the National Heritage Lottery, *Meeting in No Man's Land* took place over four days in Bavaria, and involved a mixture of filmed interviews, creative workshops and social events aimed at facilitating and sharing family legacies of the war. This chapter asks what compels British and German descendants to engage with the First World War pasts of their ancestors, and how their relationships to that past are shaped by family histories of war and the different commemorative practices and histories of violence in the two countries.

The meeting began in a large room at the Catholic welfare organisation Caritas in Rosenheim where some of the German organisers were based. Descendants from each country were put into pairs and invited to step into the centre of the room with an artefact that represented their family's connection to the war. People came forward with letters, postcards, trench art and photographs in their hands and related a memory of their ancestor which was translated *in situ*. Ally brought the diary of his great uncle, a talented illustrator. On Tuesday 2 August 1921, the young veteran had written, 'I know the TB has gotten to my stomach – it will soon carry me home – the doctors are helpless.' The last entry was written by his family: 'passed away 4.20am, Wed 24/8/21'. Dieter brought his father's patriotic books on the First World War. The books had been part of his 'house-world' of war since childhood, but now became a medium for sharing memories and making history.[1] If on the one hand, the meeting sought to elicit 'lived' rather than 'learned' histories of war, on the other, the prospect of taking part in the event encouraged many participants to undertake their own research and connect their family's story to regional and national histories of the conflict.

Acting as 'resident historians', Age Exchange's *Meeting* allowed Rachel Duffett and me to investigate how descendants had 'internalised their lived or learned history' of the conflict and how their outlooks were shaped by personal relationships with the survivors.[2] We wanted to know why they had agreed to take part in an event where they introduced their family's war past to an audience that included ex-adversaries, and what their hopes for the meeting were. We asked each participant to reflect on these questions during their interview.[3] Our roles oscillated between participant, observer, interviewer, lecturer, blog writer and researcher. We took part in the planning meetings in Rosenheim in January 2016, conducted some of the interviews with the German participants (assisted by translators), and watched the Age Exchange team conduct the remaining individual interviews. We watched the descendants interview each other. We joined the creative workshops and social events and then undertook an analysis of the records produced by the event, including over fifty-two hours of filmed, translated and subtitled interviews, and seven hundred digitised artefacts. Concurrent with our research, Age Exchange began work on the documentary film *Meeting in No Man's Land*, which was produced in the summer of 2016 and shown in the two countries in the autumn of 2016.[4]

The participants

The descendants who took part in *Meeting in No Man's Land* were a mixture of second, third and fourth generations. Six were born between 1918 and the Second World War and were children of survivors. Sixteen were grandchildren (eight German and eight British) born in the 1940s and 50s, and one was a great-granddaughter. Most were or had been employed in professional occupations, many of them in public sector jobs like teaching and social work. The British volunteers were recruited by Age Exchange and some were seasoned 'memory workers', having joined Age Exchange previously on projects including the theatre production *Children of the Great War* which was shown in London in 2014.[5] German

Meeting in No Man's Land 111

Figure 4.1 Hilary and Dieter meet in no man's land.
Courtesy of Age Exchange and Dieter Filsinger. All rights reserved.

participants came to the project from Caritas in Rosenheim and from Münchner Bildungswerk, a centre in Munich which develops learning programmes, training and workshops for citizens.

The group's members were conscious of being among a shrinking population which has direct memories of the survivors, and whose first knowledge of the war was acquired from them.[6] Ally recalled asking his grandfather 'stupid questions about guns' as a child. As a boy, Chris had frequent conversations about the war with his grandfather and father. It could be the subject of humour: on one occasion when a neighbour lit an incinerator and smoke began to billow into the back garden, Chris's grandfather strode up and down the boundary fence shouting 'gas attack, gas attack!' at the top of his voice. The stories of the British descendants were comparatively settled and well-rehearsed, and they engaged with the canons of British First World War memory: Martin brought a letter written to his great-grandparents by the memoirist Vera Brittain after their son's death and Peter had found a mention of his grandfather in Edmund Blunden's memoir *Undertones*. Delia recalled how deeply affected she was by seeing Joan Littlewood's production of *Oh, What a Lovely War!* and watching 'every episode' of the 1964 BBC series *The Great War*. Many had visited the sites where their forebears fought and died.

The accounts of the German descendants were less securely anchored in public or family narratives. The history of the First

World War had been 'shoved aside' at school, remarked Christel, and there was silence in the family as well. As Hanne observed, 'No one talked about the war, and him [her grandfather] being in the war.' She only found out that her grandfather was a First World War veteran when a cousin mentioned it. Watching the German descendants, we had a sense of First World War history in the making. Hanne had recently gone to her local war memorial to look at the names on it. Theodora had visited the war archives in Munich and was excited to find her grandfather's war records, which she proudly displayed during her interview. The thrill of discovery was inspired among some of the Rosenheim participants by the serialisation on local radio of a 1914 diary written by the mother of one of the group's members. Summarising the mood among German descendants during the First World War Centenary, Hanne remarked that 'finally it is being talked about'.

Yet it was not an easy history to broach. While it was clear from the individual interviews with German descendants that the National Socialist period was often a point of tension between the generations, they barely mentioned it in their paired interviews with British descendants. Perhaps this part of the family story felt too awkward to share: when Hanne learned that her father had been a member of the SS, she told her interviewer, she felt 'ashamed'. They did not expect pity. Linde mentioned that her father had been a prisoner of war and had returned home poor in health and underweight. Her only comment was that 'he suffered indeed, still many years, because of that'. Researching a father or grandfather's service in the First World War could help explain the family's relationship to National Socialism and extremism. Some of the Munich participants had been recruited after taking part in a seminar series at the Münchner Bildungswerk on the inter-generational impact of the Nazi past called *The Long Shadows of War*. The organiser of the series, Jürgen Müller-Hohagen, was a psychologist living in Dachau, whose academic and clinical work was closely connected to his experience of living nearby the camp and growing up with the personal guilt of being born to a family of 'Nazi bystanders'. Jürgen believed that the impact of extreme violence and guilt had been transmitted down the generations to descendants of the Nazi past, 'negated by the perpetrators themselves, but transported to the offspring via poisoned relationships'.

By comparison, the British participants felt little moral ambiguity about their forebears. According to the national script of 'lions led by donkeys', the Tommy had been plunged into senseless slaughter and was to be admired for his decency and stoicism. Insofar as the British were responsible for the cataclysm, as the 'war poets' had shown, blame lay up the chain of command among the old incompetents.[7] Even the descendants of men who had rushed to sign up did not question their ancestor's agency in the violence. Up to a point, the victim trope was universal. Descendants from each side talked about the miseries of the trenches, and in their paired interviews, Peter and Martin tried to forestall possible awkwardness among their German partners by pointing out that the British soldier had more in common with his German comrades than with his officers. National narratives of war and commemoration tended to strengthen the respect of British descendants towards their First World War forebears, while the German descendants' investigations into the conflict were troubled by questions about what their fathers or grandfathers did afterwards.

If on the one hand the meeting invited participants to consider their ancestor's war within the national frames of war memory, on the other, it encouraged them to commit personal memories to the historical record. Some simply wanted to communicate the fact that, although they were born afterwards, the war nonetheless had, in Ally's words, 'a huge effect on me personally'. He reckoned that no less than twelve members of his family had fought in the conflict. Knowing that the interviews were being filmed and the goal of the project was a documentary, some had stories to tell about the hidden effects of war. Their accounts challenged the established narratives and chronologies of 1914–18. Hilary talked about her grandmother, who was barely old enough to remember the war, but whose life changed dramatically afterwards when her father died from his injuries, leaving a pregnant wife who went blind with shock and was forced to place Hilary's grandmother and her sister in a workhouse. Theodora described her grandfather's plight in 1919 after returning from the war to Munich, recovering from wounds, both parents deceased in the past year, his job under threat and his friends killed in an attack by Freikorps soldiers. Hilary and Theodora had little to say about the war itself; they wanted to talk about events it set in train and spoke as direct witnesses.

Figure 4.2 Jürgen had recently found this photograph of his grandfather in 1892. In the interview, he notes his military bearing: 'upright, controlled'. Courtesy of Age Exchange and Jürgen Müller-Hohagen. All rights reserved.

The participants thus shared a perception of standing between an impermanent 'communicative memory' of war based on their relationships with the eyewitnesses and a 'cultural memory' that would endure in archives, museums and history books. The 'affective ties that bind together families, groups, and generations', Jan Assmann notes, are the stuff of communicative memory, and introducing a family member to the group – describing their appearance and temperament, quirks and interests – created a powerful emotional atmosphere.[8] The participants' relationships with the person whose war history they came to relate had not always been easy. Hanne claimed to have 'no feelings' towards her grandfather, and

Diana described her 'grampie' as moody and easily roused to anger. The participants did not work with history in the same ways or use it for the same ends. Each had their own reasons for joining the project and connected their family's past to the history of the First World War through different memory practices.

At the same time, irrespective of national background or the kinds of relationships that participants had with members of the war generation, there were common motivations for taking part in the project. Some of the reasons people gave for joining were prosaic – giving in to the urgings of the organisers, the prospect of a free trip to Germany or reviving Anglophone connections. Linde, who did her interview in perfect English, revealed that she had gone on a school exchange to London in 1951 organised by her father, who wanted young people to forget their enmity.

The participants drew on generic conventions as they narrated the First World War history in their families, but their stories were often deeply moving. Reflecting on the purpose of the meeting and assessing it as an emotional experience and a commemoration in the making, the following discussion identifies four types of motivation among descendants. Each is associated with different emotions, some that the organisers sought to elicit, others that transpired as the participants got to know and interview each other. The section 'Bearing memory and making history' explores the situation of the children and grandchildren as 'hinge generations'. It is concerned with loss and the wish to preserve memory and rekindle emotional ties with an ancestor through history. 'Lessons from history' describes how descendants highlight the destructive consequences of the First World War in the service of seeking peace or redressing damage from the past and is concerned with the social functions of anger. 'Breaking silence' examines the participants' attempts to confront difficult war pasts and the distorting effects of silence in their families. 'Restoring humanity' is about the counter-narratives of brutalisation, the wish among descendants to show that *their* father or grandfather had lived a blameless and fulfilling life. It is concerned with pride and shame, and the resistance to historical narratives that seem to impugn a loved one.

These motives do not exhaust the range of possible impulses for commemoration, and do not necessarily constitute 'ideal types' of commemorators; indeed, most descendants exhibited more than one motivation during the meeting. The typologies show the variety and vitality of the emotional ties that developed during the four days of our meeting, ties that may well be present in other communities formed around the memory and commemoration of war. In the spirit of the meeting, which sought to bring together participants from opposing sides, the typologies identify common impulses for commemoration, while the differences between the inter-generational legacies of war in Germany and Britain are discussed within each theme.

Bearing memory and making history

As the participants showed their ephemera, fished out official records and recounted stories about their ancestors, the responsibility they felt as bearers of the family history became apparent. At some point, they had become the ones to take on the mantle of family historians, to hold the artefacts and records and to do research.[9] Theodora was the only 'really interested' member of her family and her mother had told her she was 'mad' for wanting to unearth her father's war history. It sometimes bothered Ally that nobody else in the family had taken an interest in his grandfather's war and relied on Ally to share what he knew.

The reasons for undertaking history could go right back to early childhood: a relationship with a parent that had ended prematurely, or grandparents who provided a haven from troubles elsewhere in the family.[10] Ruth's father had died from TB when she was four and her last memory of him was as a frail man dressed in hospital pyjamas. After her mother died, Ruth's sister discovered a hundred letters written by her father to her mother, which showed him to be cheerful, funny and a wonderful writer. The letters revealed a side of him that she had never known. Similarly, reading her grandfather's war letters helped Rosemary to see her grandfather in a new light. He had died when she was twelve and she recalled his Victorian views about women. The letters he wrote to her grandmother, however, showed that he was someone who liked women.

Among the third generation of British descendants, growing up in the 1960s and 70s, the First World War had sometimes become central to relationships as they became aware of the history of the

First World War and recognised the significance of grandparents who were eyewitnesses. Ally described him and his grandfather as 'companions'. As a teenager Ally would accompany his grandfather Walter to the local Toc H bookstore in Wales and listen as veterans reminisced about the war.[11] As Walter grew older and his circle diminished, Ally made a point of visiting him each week. He wanted to hear his war stories, but the visits were also a way of helping to counter Walter's isolation. Ally was one of the creators of the website Europeana, which invites people across Europe to submit images of First World War heritage and tell the stories associated with them.[12] Coaxing his grandfather's war history as a boy, Ally had gone on to create an international enterprise based on digital preservation of the communicative memory of war. There was a link between Ally's role today and the way in which his grandfather and great-uncles recorded their war: the three brothers had gone to war with Kodak Brownie cameras, and Ally now was capturing in digital form the many hundreds of Kodak photos taken by soldiers like them.

The responsibility for bearing history frequently centred on objects. When he was in his twenties, Martin's grandmother told him that she wanted him to have her scrapbooks and crucifix after she died. She had been a VAD in a hospital in Buxton, and Martin's story focused on the puzzle of how the crucifix came into her possession. Leafing through her scrapbooks, he reconstructed an incipient romance between his grandmother and a sergeant who she was caring for. He had taken the crucifix from a ruined house in France, a miracle survivor like the statue of the Virgin on the church tower in Albert. In Martin's interview, he thinks about what the crucifix might have meant to the family on whose bedroom wall it had hung, to the soldier who took it and to his grandmother. Possession of the crucifix set in train a host of questions about lives lived in cataclysm and the importance of care, faith and romantic relationships. Martin had become a history teacher and attributed his career to having been given custody of his grandmother's war heritage.

As people who sought to care for that heritage, the thought that there might be nobody after them to hold it could be unsettling. Mariana was thinking of donating her father's war letters to the city of Vienna where he grew up as her brother did not want them, and Mariana's only son, who would have inherited them, had died young. His postcards and letters from the Dolomites were important to her as they brought back the memory of a 'very loving' father. He had separated from Mariana's mother when Mariana was a girl, and she regretted that she did not have the chance to live with him after the age of three.

Rainer's interest in the First World War was also motivated by war ephemera, in his case, a diary given to his mother in 1913 by her uncle Adolf. She had begun the diary in mid-1914, recording the assassination of Archduke Ferdinand and the hordes of newly mobilised soldiers in the local railway station in the small town of Bückeburg in Northern Germany. As he grew older Rainer became more interested in this 'inheritance', but it revealed a mother whose attitudes were hard to identify with. Rainer read out extracts in which the young girl described 'Fully equipped soldiers standing there, full of fighting spirit, strong and powerfully.' By contrast, his own early experience of war – the Second – was one of fright. As Rainer explained, 'my mother bore me into the war and I experienced war on-site from the age of one until seven'. Their smallholdings were bombed eleven times. Inspired by the wish to understand the strength of patriotism displayed by his mother in her diary, he had recently visited Bückeburg station, and had stood on the platform trying to imagine a time in which it 'was a great thing in the view of the society to go to war for the fatherland'. The diary intimated everything he loved about her – a passion for writing and painting, her lively interest in society and culture – and he could not understand how at the same time she could subscribe to such 'depressing' ideals. Her favourite uncle, who had given her the diary, died in the trenches just a year later, yet grief at his death did not shake the adolescent girl's support for war and the fatherland.

The diary presented Rainer with evidence of war enthusiasm that his generation, growing up after the Second World War, found 'incredible'. In a bid to better understand it, he had returned to the very spot where her patriotic fervour was stirred. Perhaps, however, these sentiments were not so unfamiliar to Rainer after all, for among his photos was one of himself dressed in the uniform of the Hitler Youth. When the interviewer pointed this out, Rainer replied that this was common among children of his generation. The First World War can stand as a surrogate for the Second: more distant temporally and emotionally, lying beyond the horizon of personal experience, its history can hold feelings and beliefs close to home.

All the participants in the meeting were engaged in preserving memory and making history. Loved ones seemed to come to life through the objects they brought with them. Martin became animated as he leafed through his grandmother's album looking for blank pages and damaged photos: in a fit of pique, she appeared to have ripped out images of the matron in charge. The damage to the album proved the intensity of her hatred. The transformation from private ephemera to historical artefact sometimes seemed to occur before our eyes. As she prepared for her interview, Christel transferred her grandfather's handmade postcards and decorations from an anonymous box into a wooden display case, wanting, she said, to 'present it more beautifully' and 'give it a place of honour'.[13]

The preservation of objects, the recording of family stories and the piecing together of war stories were key activities in the formation of the participants' identities as descendants. The meeting strengthened this identity, creating spaces and activities that brought descendants into relationships with one another. Yet while the event facilitated generational affinities and kindred memories, it also revealed the impact of different national histories and narratives of war, the British descendants protected by their national mythology from looking critically at the part their forefathers had played in violence, the German descendants immersed in reparative efforts to which the history of the First World War could contribute or from which it could provide a distraction.

Lessons from history

Some of the participants approached the meeting with didactic motives. They wanted to convey a message about the disastrous consequences of war and were using the event and their filmed interviews to reach a larger audience. For others, the moral impulse was more muted, a reflection that came towards the end of an interview that had focused on the personal cost of war to family members.

There could be a strong motivation to expose the hidden damage of the conflict among those who had seen firsthand the physical and mental impact of the war on a loved one. Being among a diminishing population with a living link to the war generation sharpened the sense of responsibility to take a stand. Hilary's reason for bringing her grandmother's story to the meeting, she explained, was because people needed to understand that lives had been 'turned upside down' by the conflict, and if she did not contribute her story, it would vanish from history. Ruth wanted to air the sense of injustice in her family about her father's death from TB when she was four years old. 'We think', she explained, that his death was due to the effects of gassing, but the Ministry of Pensions refused to acknowledge this and consequently her mother had to manage on a widow's pension which was less generous than the war pension. The family were short of money and although her sister passed the Eleven Plus, she was unable to go to grammar school. Echoing the interwar political narrative of betrayal of the war generation, British descendants expressed long-standing resentments about the failure of state provision.[14]

For some participants, the meeting was a vehicle through which to send a message to the future rather than a means of exposing past injustices. 'Never again' was their motivation. Les had three First World War veterans in his family, but personal reminiscence was less important to him than the urge to sway minds. He had been a Greenpeace activist and described himself as a 'combative pacifist'. Les recognised the contradiction in taking a bellicose stance in the cause of peace but attributed it to the fact that he came from a military family. Pacifist though he was, he was also a keen shot.

Les began his interview with an account of journeying from France to the Age Exchange interview in London, and of seeing the terrible conditions suffered by asylum seekers in the Sangat 'prison' on the northern coast. Four of Les's relatives had fought in the First World War, but he spoke mostly about his maternal grandfather who was wounded and gassed. Les relied largely on the information compiled by his uncle Doug, who had made a record of his grandfather's reminiscences of the Somme. Les had visited the spot where his grandfather fought and reconstructed the scene in his interview. After the order to attack, his grandfather was blown back into the trench, and after advancing, was forced to retreat. Les's account expressed the pathos typical of British narratives of the Somme as he imagined his grandfather 'paddling through blood and entrails and bits' of sixty thousand dead. Time and geography were condensed, his grandfather seeming to witness in one scene the aftermath of 141 days of fighting across fourteen miles of front. Les was aware that there was an element of mythology in his account but it served a purpose: his Somme, a sea of mud, blood and madness, explained why war must be stopped. Les wanted the meeting to act as a springboard for peace and his paired interview with Maria concluded with the pledge 'never again'.[15]

The anti-war message was more subdued among others but when asked during the interviews what had brought them to the meeting, many responded in terms of their hopes for peace. Britain's pending referendum on leaving the European Union was on everyone's mind, and Ruth seemed to speak for all when she proclaimed 'I'm a great European'. Theodora commented on the sorrow caused by the First World War, and her concern that the current generation has no connection to its upheavals. The lessons from that war 'need to be kept' as the world now faced another 'dangerous' moment of countries pursuing sectional interests and refusing dialogue. It troubled Wolfgang that conflicts were brewing up all over the world, but he believed that Germany 'had learned' from its violent past, and at the end of his interview he broke into English to proclaim, 'Peace in Europe and the World'.

Most participants declared their wish for peace, but among the Germans descendants, this stance bore a complex relation to the war past, particularly among those whose ancestors had been supporters of National Socialism. Angelika believed that, having seen the consequences of conformism, her generation (born in the 1950s) had a more questioning attitude towards authority than the generation who were young adults in the Second World War. The two 'catastrophes' of world war had led them to reject 'black and white' views. Christel, also born after the Second World War, believed that the political lesson was one of remaining sceptical. 'Don't simply believe', she counselled, but engage in debate and discussion: 'You can only appeal to all people to try and live peacefully.' Talking to British (and Australian) interviewers, and meeting the descendants of adversaries in two wars, the German participants probably felt a heightened need to show that the country had learned from its mistakes. But the structures of reconciliation were fragile, and some found it difficult to sustain them as memory opened the wounds of defeat.

Marga's account revolved around the death of her father when she was twelve. He had served in the First World War, and in the 1930s was a member of the SA and Stahlhelm. He volunteered in 1943 and served in Italy where he was taken prisoner, returning home in autumn 1945 underweight and 'completely depressed'. Marga described the patriotic atmosphere of her childhood, her father's slogans 'war guilt, lies', his boast that the King's Regiment in which he'd served was 'undefeated in the field' and his anger towards civilians for the 'stab in the back'.[16] Marga felt that her father had been 'enamoured' by the First World War, yet his death after the Second World War left a complicated legacy. The British Control Commission for Germany had taken away his electrical shop, believing that the ex-Nazi was 'not worthy' to run the business. Suffering poor health and worried about the loss of his business, in 1947 Marga's father attempted suicide, and he died in a psychiatric hospital two weeks later. Marga's account recapitulates a perception common among German people living in the West during the denazification period, who according to Svenja Goltermann claimed to feel 'completely at the mercy of the occupying forces'.[17] Marga believed that the effects of her father's death and the fears that surrounded the Allied Occupation had travelled down two generations: she suffers from anxiety, and so does her fifty-one-year-old daughter. Her anger about the way her father had been treated was clear. But faced with a British interviewer and audience, she also felt the need to distance herself from her father's patriotism.

In tracing the origins of the family tragedy back to the First World War, Marga may have hoped to defuse its emotional charge. Her anxiety, and that of her daughter, she now believed, 'has its cause in this primal catastrophe of the First World War'. Talking about the First World War, however, brought back the traumas of the Second. Marga did not return to the meeting after her interview. It had clearly aroused raw feelings and she did not find it easy to express them. There is a moral chasm between perpetrators and the suffering of their victims, and perhaps she did not wish to appear to be sympathetic towards her father given his Nazi past.[18]

Proclamations of peace exposed a variety of identifications with the First World War. For some, learning about the conflict was less important than its status as 'the war to end all wars', a cataclysm that must never be repeated. Others carried long-held grievances about the aftermaths of war that had been passed down across generations. Declarations of peace could also signify membership of a united Europe in the face of resurgent nationalist movements. Ruminating on war and peace, participants used the meeting to address multiple imagined audiences: people who might be lured into patriotism by official commemorations, people who remained sceptical that Germany had learned its lessons or those who refused to acknowledge the suffering that defeat and occupation in the Second World War caused to the German people.

Breaking silence

> And when I say: 'Show it! Show the wound that we have inflicted upon ourselves during the course of our development', it is because the only way to progress and become aware of it is to show it.[19]
> – *Joseph Beuys*

Regardless of national background, the remark we heard most often during the four days of the meeting was that parents and grandparents did not talk about the war. Shared histories of family silence drew the British and German participants together, and in reconstructing their ancestor's war past through archival records, photographs, mementoes and histories of the war, they broke that silence. Listening to others' stories, they came to view their experience as part of a national, cross-national and generational history. But the participants also came to the meeting with particular histories of silence, some felt to be relatively benign and others felt to have been harmful not just to them personally, but to generations in their family.

Physical legacies sometimes filled the silence.[20] Even Les, whose interview was least focused on the 'private' impact, entered a different register when he described seeing the scars on his grandfather's calf, buttock and shoulder as he emerged from the shower. Violent impacts on the body had created a deep impression on them as children. Diana's 'grampie' never spoke about the war, but there were scars on his scalp. The skin on Marga's father's neck was thin, a wound from which he had almost bled to death. Domestic ornaments also conveyed the non-verbal history of war. Delia brought along a Princess Mary Christmas gift box, one of over two and a half million given to those serving at home and abroad in 1914. She recalled running her fingers across the lid as a small child, fascinated by the feel of the princess's bust on its engraved lid, not knowing then the historical significance of the box. Sense impressions like these generated a demand for explanation. For some, the meeting functioned to create a narrative around the dumb heritage of the war they had known since a time when they themselves could barely talk.

Silence did not always have deeper connotations. Peter's grandfather and great-uncle were killed in the First World War, his grandfather dying in a failed attempt to avenge the death of his brother. His father did not talk about them, and Peter had learned of their deaths by chance while reading a book on the Tenth Essex Regiment that was on the bookshelves at home. Peter did not believe that his father's silence was a traumatic reaction; it just reflected the character of the man. For descendants like him, the lack of family discussion about the First World War was felt to be normal and did not demand a psychological explanation.

Others believed that family silence was a response to trauma. Volatile tempers or emotional detachment were put down to troubling memories that the survivors could not express and their families struggled to comprehend. Diana did not state directly that her 'grampie' had suffered a trauma, but her account drew on a trauma frame. On coming home from work he would head for his armchair and listen to music or the radio or read novels. The family had pieced together his military record in recent years and realised that he had gone through some of the bloodiest battles of the war: the Marne, First Ypres in late 1914 and Second Ypres in spring 1915. Knowing more about her grandfather's war, Diana now believed that his rigid routines and need for solitude had been a way of managing difficult memories. Diana was interviewed by her son David Savill, Age Exchange's Creative Director and the initiator of *Meeting in No Man's Land*, in a fascinating mix whereby the 'private' story of unspoken war legacies, passed from the veteran to his granddaughter, entered a public arena through the coaxing of the great-grandson. Their story sheds light on transmission across four generations, David's motivation for setting up the meeting being in part a response to the silence in his family.

For participants like Diana, the meeting was an invitation to place unspoken legacies within the family on the historical record, an impulse typical of successor generations. Among British descendants, pity was accentuated by the belated recognition that a silent father or grandfather was probably traumatised. For the German descendants, however, it was not possible to hold a sense of their ancestors simply as victims.

Unspoken guilt distorted relationships between generations. Jurgen and Theodore described a 'heaviness' in the family and Hanne recalled an underlying 'tense mood' throughout her childhood as her family 'covered' her father's participation in the SA during the Second World War and her grandfather's Nazi sympathies. The 'huge silence' in the family meant that 'nothing can grow out of it'. Forgetting had psychological consequences down the generations, Hanne believed, as 'we all carry the legacy whether we want it or not. If we let the war touch us or if we are looking at the terrible things or not, they are there.'[21]

Uncovering the histories of fathers and grandfathers in the First World War was significant for these participants as a way of breaking the cycle of family silence. Aware of the legacies of silence about the Second World War, they turned to the First World War to understand its origins. Hanne described a grandfather who 'had no emotion for the children. He had emotion for work, for helping others and for doing things properly.' Three generations of the family occupied the same house after the Second World War, and for a while she had shared a bed with her grandparents, recalling her fears lest she move about in her sleep and rouse her grandfather's anger. Her grandfather used to hit them with a stick if they misbehaved at mealtimes, and during the interview, she picked up a ruler and waved it around the table, just as he had done. She felt relieved after he died and enjoyed being able to snuggle up to her grandmother in bed. All she could remember about her grandfather was his strictness: 'I had no other feelings.'

To help prepare for the meeting, Hanne had gone to the archives in Ebersbach where her grandfather was born and lived before the war. 'It was very exciting', she explained, to learn that he had been a keen gymnast and had acquired his own fishing rights – this prompted a memory of him as an old man, filling the bath with fish. She learned that all four of his siblings had died in childhood, a pre-war 'tragedy' that she thought must have affected him deeply. She also knew now that he had seen 'horrible things' in the war.

From her reading of the archival sources and discovery of his war medals in an outbuilding, she had begun 'to get to know him' as a person. Participants like Hanne were not using history to *justify* the political views and conduct of grandfathers, as the myth of the 'stab in the back' would have it, or to recast them simply as victims. History for them is a handmaid of psychology, furnishing an external perspective on the complicity and silence of fathers and grandfathers. Hanne was an artist whose earlier work had addressed her father's Nazi past, and part of her contribution to the meeting was a workshop in which participants drew pictures of the war legacies in their families. At the end of her interview, Hanne recited the quotation from Beuys with which this section opens. In this way, she proclaimed her identities as a granddaughter saddled with silences from the two wars, an artist and a member of the Kriegskinder generation committed to breaking silence.

Breaking silence was felt to have personal as well as political value, and for the German descendants, it was not possible to seal family histories off from the national past. Where British participants might talk of fathers and grandfathers who were 'stern', the Germans described men who were 'authoritarian'. Part of the point of relating their story in the meeting was to expose the nexus between public and private histories of dogmatism.

Dieter's story illustrates this. His grandfather was commissioned in the war, but by 1917 he had become demoralised by having to send men into battle and see them return as casualties. He became a Democrat in Weimar Germany and remained an opponent of Hitler even through the early years of the Second World War when the invasion of France succeeded, and his veteran friends were applauding Hitler's ability to finish off the job. Dieter's father, however, opposed his own father's politics. He joined the Hitler Youth in the 1930s, and to Dieter's embarrassment and anger, even today he defends Hitler.

For Dieter, there was a cross-generational inheritance of overbearing authority. If his father 'commanded something', he explained, 'we had to follow this command absolutely'. His grandfather had opposed Hitler, but as Dieter discovered from his aunts, he was 'very aggressive and irascible' at home. Dieter believed that his father, in becoming a Hitler Youth and 'making Hitler his father', was rebelling against his own father, who, although he was a Democrat, behaved 'like a dictator' at home.[22]

Far from being buried in silence, in this family the First World War was the key event through which political and generational tensions were expressed. As a young man, Dieter had been urged by his father to read 'thick books' about the Treaty of Versailles age which made clear that Germany was wronged. Although he opposed his father's politics, at that age Dieter lacked the historical knowledge to argue with him. Later he read books that established Germany's responsibilities for the First World War. Here was a domestic First World War drama played out over three generations, presented to other descendants in the hope that resolution could be achieved by exposing the tensions between grandfather, father and son. Talking of authoritarianism, he said at one point that 'I can feel it in my family, I can feel it through my father'. His father, however, felt ambivalent about Dieter's attempts to banish the family taboo of looking at the past. Dieter's research had shown that his grandfather was barely an adult when he joined up. As a result, Dieter's father now realised that his own father had 'suffered, he was a victim', but was nevertheless still 'scared that too much is going to come to light'. Calls to end silence, as Jay Winter notes, may either result in a lifting of the interdiction or occasion its reiteration, and Dieter's father oscillated between these positions.[23]

Among the German descendants, Dieter was unusual in that the First World War, not the Second, was the conduit through which family conflicts were expressed. Even so, there were silences, as it was the *political* consequences that were discussed, rather than tyranny in the domestic sphere. Dieter believed that history could help gain a perspective on private legacies such as these. His had been a life in which 'everything separated into two worlds', and he had gone back to his grandfather's war in the hope of locating the roots of authoritarianism in the family. In sharing the traumas of his grandfather's war with his father during the meeting, he hoped that anger might 'find its end'.

Silence was a common theme in the descendants' accounts of family life, but its emotional import varied. Some British descendants saw it as typical of the war generations and did not believe it distorted family relationships. Others saw silence as a mark of trauma which they had not understood as children, but which, as they pieced together the war records of a father or grandfather, was now obvious. German descendants could not separate the family history from their country's role in the evils of the twentieth century. Historical research might help explain the origins of authoritarian tendencies in the family, but its legacies could not be wished away. Dieter felt that, in an effort to avoid behaving like his father and grandfather, he was sometimes too compliant with his work colleagues. Seek as he might to contextualise the struggles between fathers and sons in the history of the First World War, Dieter recognised that he had not escaped the authoritarian past.

Restoring humanity

The ability of an ancestor to sustain their humanity amidst the violence of war was emphasised by some participants, whose stories functioned as a counter-narrative to trauma.[24] As the British and German participants compared the letters and postcards of their ancestors in their paired interviews, they discovered that the preoccupations of the two sides were not so different. They missed their mothers' cooking and longed to be home and receive letters and parcels. There was animated agreement between Linde and Ruth as they compared photographs of their fathers in uniform, noticed how short they both were and agreed that they were just 'boys'. They identified with the soldier's innocence, caught up in a conflict that was not of his making.

Many participants admired the lives that their ancestors had made for themselves after the war. Delia's grandfather loved amateur theatre and cinema, and eventually became a cinema manager. The legacy that Delia took from her grandfather was not one of death and destruction – she had to discover for herself the horrors of trench warfare – but passion for life. Indeed, Delia's contribution to the meeting seemed at times to be an enactment of this legacy. She had taken part in the theatre production *Children of the Great War* and her energetic account of her grandfather's post-war career in the theatre and as a cinema manager had a theatrical twist.

Others emphasised the therapeutic effects of the leisure enjoyed by their fathers and grandfathers. The benefits could flow down the generations. Just like her 'grampie', Diana was an avid reader and had trained as a pianist, the first in her family to go to higher education. Recreations like hiking (or for the Bavarians, mountaineering), cycling, motoring, travel, languages, art, music, theatre and film and photography were often mentioned. After the war, Wolfgang's parents travelled around Europe in a mobile homemade by his father, who liked to paint the wilderness. Linde recalled how her emotionally rigid father softened with age and became a loving grandfather. When Linde was a girl, he would line up his pencils in neat rows and not let her touch them, but as an old man, he was happy for his grandchildren to use them however they wished.

For German descendants, it could feel particularly important to distinguish their grandparents from the stereotype of the brutalised front-line soldier. Christel emphasised her grandfather's compassion. He had served in Berezina in Russia and his postcards gave sympathetic portraits of the lives of the Russian peasants. The First World War had fostered his sympathies towards poor and blameless people caught up in conflict, an attitude which he showed again during the Second World War when he harboured Polish labourers to stop them from having to go to the Front. Her grandfather's postcards and decorations symbolised his attitude to war. Crafted by hand from the bark of silver birch, lichen, wheat stalks and flowers, they made 'something beautiful' out of destruction.[25]

Theodora (born 1954) admired her grandfather because he had taken a stand against extremism. During the Soviet Republic in Munich, the Communist-controlled baker's union tried to get him sacked because he belonged to the Christian Journeyman's union, and in 1937 the family lost their flat when the National Socialists were in power and he refused to join the German Labour Union. Theodora found many similarities between herself and her grandfather. She was also someone who did not go along automatically with her colleagues and would object if things weren't right. Given the kind of man he was, Theodora was sure that her grandfather had never been 'patriotic'; he would not have volunteered and would have been 'sad' to have to leave his parents. It was not clear from her interview, however, whether her father had taken the same defiant stance. He had also become a soldier at nineteen and the legacies of his war pervaded Theodora's childhood: 'I can't remember anything at all having been said about the First World War. That's also got to do with the fact that my father was in the Second World War and his story overlaid everything else. That's my feeling, that was the main topic in my family.' The Second World War may have

Figure 4.3 Postcard of Delia's grandfather in 1933 dressed as a centurion. Courtesy of Age Exchange. All rights reserved.

dominated her early life but was largely absent from Theodora's testimony at the meeting. Rather than dwell on the more tangled relationships of her parents to the Nazi past, she was inspired by her grandfather's resistance to extremism.

Others could not disentangle their ancestors from the 'difficult past' but wanted to convey that their father or grandfather was not simply an extremist.[26] Angelika started her interview by talking about her grandfather's love of travel, language and culture. Before the war, he had cycled through France, the Netherlands, the Balkans and Hungary. He fought against France in the war but was a Francophile. She described his curiosity about the world, the way he explained things to her as a small child and how calm and relaxed he was. But 'I have to add', she explained, 'that my grandparents were committed National Socialists'. Hitler had made people feel better, she said, and in joining the Party and enlisting as an

Figure 4.4 'Three cheers for the fennel flower!' Postcard sent home by Christel's grandfather. Courtesy of Age Exchange and Christel Berger. All rights reserved.

intelligence officer during the Second World War, her grandfather would have been motivated by the wish to come to the aid of his country. She was sure he had never done 'anything bad'; he was 'a good man'. Based on her childhood memory of a loving grandfather, Angelika presented herself as a kind of moral guarantor for her grandfather. Christel also drew on personal knowledge of her grandfather to draw conclusions about his part in history: being the peaceful person he was, he would not have volunteered in the First World War; 'the way I knew him', she said, he must have been a conscript. Among German descendants, faith in the moral integrity of the ancestor can work against the motivation to ask questions and find out more about their ancestors' war histories.[27]

Stories like these reveal elements of what Harald Welzer calls a 'heroising' tendency among German descendants, who focus on 'moral integrity' and acts of resistance, and thus 'manoeuvre' their ancestors away from the perpetrator group.[28] While at points the German descendants in our meeting strove to show that their fathers or grandfathers were not implicated in evil and were not responsible for Germany's extremism, at the same time they were not just seeking to escape guilt. Their motives for undertaking a family history of the First World War, and the uses to which they wished to put it, were ambiguous and conflicted. If on the one hand, a descendant might choose to memorialise the 'good' German, on the other, the meeting exposed their family story and could be personally confronting. Seeking figures who (whether in fact or in the narrator's imagination) resisted brutalisation and were not steeped in bitterness, they hoped that future generations would also value discussion and compromise and try in Theodora's words to 'understand the other side'.

Despite their different national backgrounds, the groups that Age Exchange brought together in the meeting were of a broadly similar political and social type. Middle-class, they were also pro-European. Their stories tended to converge on pity and loss. As descendants of those who had served their country on the home or war fronts, they were motivated by a common wish to connect their family's past to history, helped by the bureaucratic machinery of record-keeping that the First World War set in train. In filming the meeting and in creating a documentary, Age Exchange was helping to bridge the gap between descendants and history. The fact that participants were recalling early relationships with their own parents and grandparents stirred more intimate memories and identifications than those which a state-sponsored commemoration such as Armistice Day might produce. The meeting thus created an 'emotional community' of a singular kind.[29]

The four motivations for commemoration identified here suggest a more varied picture of the relationship between individuals, families, nation-states and the tropes of the First World War than historians have sometimes assumed. The British 'pity of war' narrative, for example, can be deployed in a strategic bid for peace through graphic iterations of the horrors of trench warfare. Or it can serve as the cultural backdrop of a personal tragedy, when for example an ancestor reads aloud a moving letter or diary from an ancestor who died. Pity may give rise to family stories that, despite the varieties of actual war service, assume the experience was universally traumatic, and marvel at what the survivors achieved afterwards.

Assisted by their national frames of remembrance and contemporary narratives of trauma that lock onto victimhood, the British descendants did not feel compelled to take stock of their ancestors' part in violence. By contrast, the impact of defeat and extremism was part of family history for all the German participants, and the meeting gave us insights into its intergenerational fallout. For some of them, as Mark Roseman notes, 'it was the perceived overlap between family and national experience that gave generational rebellion its symbolic and emotional force'.[30]

Amidst the pressures to end the silence about the Nazi past, the 'discovery' of the First World War among German descendants could serve a variety of ends, sometimes even within a single individual. Historical research could show how authoritarian fathers and grandfathers emerged from patriotic delusion and the disastrous aftermath of the First World War. At other times the First World War was perceived as a conflict in which moral valuations were less clear than in the Second World War, and *pace* Clark, Germany could be exculpated from sole responsibility. The British descendants felt no need to reflect on the bellicose sentiments of their ancestors – in their national mythology, patriotism was a subject for satire – but the German descendants were always conscious of the moral ambiguities surrounding the family history and, in the meeting, we observed them grapple with the legacies of evil, albeit retreating at times into historical bunkers.

The participants in our meeting were probably distinctive in their shared wish to reckon with the negative impact of military conflict across national boundaries and within families, however. We watched as, during the four days of the meeting, they united around the wish for peace. On the last day, we went on a walking tour of Munich past the police barricades where Pegida demonstrations and counter-demonstrations were held each Monday. A month later, the anti-immigration and anti-Islam AfD (Alternative for Germany) party would hold a meeting outside the Hofbräukeller tavern in Munich where, on 16 October 1919, Hitler made his first political speech.[31] Two months later, as Age Exchange worked on its documentary film of the meeting, Britain would vote to leave the European Union. The affective ties between the participants in our meeting were based on sharing and reconciling different pasts, but recent events in Europe suggest that the memory of the two World Wars can equally form the basis for groups drawn together through feelings of enmity.

Notes

1. N. Saunders, '"Bodies of Metal, Shells of Memory": Trench Art and the Great War Re-Cycled', *Journal of Material Culture*, 5: 1 (2000), 46, 59.
2. B. Tint, 'History, Memory and Intractable Conflict', *Conflict Resolution Quarterly*, 27: 3 (Spring 2010), 240.
3. The schedule was agreed between Essex and the Age Exchange team and is attached in Appendix 1.
4. The film can be viewed at www.youtube.com/watch?v=ZtOvjVihEfA. Accessed 30 August 2021. Age Exchange's approach to reminiscence work is further explored in R. Duffett and M. Roper, 'Making Histories: The Meeting of German and British Descendants of First World War Veterans in "No Man's Land", Bavaria, 2016', *The Public Historian*, 40: 1 (2018), 13–33.
5. Age Exchange, 'Children of the Great War', www.age-exchange.org.uk/cotgw/. Accessed 30 August 2021.
6. The family memory of war is a 'powerful prop' of remembrance, remarks Jay Winter, and without it, commemoration may become 'hollow'. J. Winter, 'Sites of Memory and the Shadow of War', in A. Erll and A. Nünning (eds), *Cultural Memory Studies: An International and Interdisciplinary Handbook* (New York: Walter de Gruyter, 2008), 72.
7. For accounts of this script, see R. Wilson, 'Still Fighting in the Trenches: "War Discourse" and the Memory of the First World War in Britain', *Memory Studies*, 8: 4 (2015), 454–69; R. Wilson, *Cultural Heritage of the Great War in Britain* (Aldershot: Ashgate, 2013).
8. J. Assmann, 'Communicative and Cultural Memory', in Errll and Nunning (eds), *Cultural Memory Studies*, 110–11. Family history is an 'emotional labour', and we struggle with emotions as we do it, notes the archivist and family historian Martin Bashforth. 'Absent Fathers, Present Histories', in P. Ashton and H. Keen (eds), *People and Their Pasts: Public History Today* (Basingstoke: Palgrave Macmillan, 2009), 206.
9. On the significance of family archives in identify formation, see L. Gloyn, V. Crewe, L. King and A. Woodham, 'The Ties That Bind: Materiality, Identity and the Life Course in the "Things" Families Keep', *Journal of Family History*, 43: 2 (2018), 157–76.
10. James Wallis notes that loss may be a powerful carrier of intergenerational bonds and First World War memory. 'Great Grand-Father, What Did You Do in the Great War? The Phenomenon of Conducting First World War Family History Research', in B. Ziino (ed.), *Remembering the First World War* (Abingdon: Routledge, 2015), 29.
11. Toc H was a Christian movement set up during the First World War and is an abbreviation of Talbot House, a rest and recreation centre

established by British chaplains in Poperinghe in 1915. Branches of Toc H were set up in the UK and Dominions after the war and included bookshops staffed by veteran volunteers.
12 Europeana's First World War collection is available at www.europeana.eu/en/collections/topic/83-1914-1918. Accessed 30 August 2021.
13 On the First World War objects preserved by family members and the creation of personal shrines, see M. Barrett and P. Stallybrass, 'Printing, Writing and a Family Archive: Recording the First World War', *History Workshop Journal*, 75: 1 (Spring 2013), 1–32. On the significance of objects in summoning back the dead, see Gloyn et al., 'Ties That Bind', 168–9.
14 J. Baxendale and C. Pawling, *Narrating the Thirties: A Decade in the Making, 1930 to the Present* (London: Macmillan, 1996).
15 Ross Wilson identifies the mobilisation of anti-war sentiment as one of the contemporary 'uses' of the First World War. Wilson, *Cultural Heritage*, 191.
16 Marga's account of her father accords with George Mosse's 'myth of the war experience'. According to Mosse, the myth constructs the war as a sacred event and highpoint of heroism and sacrifice, displacing the reality. G. Mosse, *Fallen Soldiers: Re-Shaping the Memory of the World Wars* (Oxford: Oxford University Press, 1990), 7.
17 S. Goltermann, 'On Silence, Madness, and Lassitude: Negotiating the Past in Post-War West Germany', in E. Ben-Ze'ev, R. Ginio and J. Winter (eds), *Shadows of War: A Social History of Silence in the Twentieth Century* (Cambridge: Cambridge University Press, 2010), 99.
18 'Former soldiers of the *Wehrmacht* did not cross over the boundary between perpetrators and victims', remarks Goltermann, and '[f]or this reason, their mental suffering never became part of the memory culture of the Second World War in Germany'. Goltermann, 'On Silence, Madness, and Lassitude', 111.
19 Quoted in A. Borer, 'A Lament for Joseph Beuys', in Borer (ed.), *The Essential Joseph Beuys* (London: Thames & Hudson, 1996), 25.
20 Wounds, writes Carol Kidron, facilitate 'somatic communication' between survivors and descendants. 'Breaching the Wall of Traumatic Silence: Holocaust Survivor and Descendant Person–Object Relations and the Material Transmission of the Genocidal Past', *Journal of Material Culture*, 17: 1 (2012), 11. See also C. Holbrook and B. Ziino, 'Family Memory and the Great War', in B. Ziino (ed.), *Remembering the First World War* (Abingdon: Routledge, 2015), 134.
21 Hanne's comments chime with Mark Roseman's observation that 'to grow up in post-war families was to grow up in stained silences'. M. Roseman, *Generations in Conflict: Youth Revolt and Generation*

Formation in Germany 1770–1968 (Cambridge: Cambridge University Press, 1995), 42.

22 Roseman suggests, in contrast to Dieter's family history, that the Nazi regime was able to mobilise youths 'without generational conflict'. Roseman, *Generations in Conflict*, 31.

23 J. Winter, 'Thinking about Silence', in Ben-Ze'ev, Ginio and Winter (eds), *Shadows of War*, 4.

24 See Kidron on life-worlds and death-worlds, 'Breaching the Wall', 4.

25 As war ephemera, Christel's postcards made of bark were strikingly different from the 'deep ambiguous' trench art constructed from shells and bullets. Saunders, 'Bodies of Metal', 55.

26 See also K. Wolnik, B. Busse, J. Tholen, C. Yndigegn, K. Levinsen, K. Saari and V. Puuronen, 'The Long Shadows of the Difficult Past? How Young People in Denmark, Finland and Germany Remember WWII', *Journal of Youth Studies*, 20: 2 (2017), 164.

27 Alexander Freund also notes how German descendants use their personal knowledge to distance ancestors from extremism. 'A Canadian Family Talks about Oma's Life in Nazi Germany: Three-Generational Interviews and Communicative Memory', *Oral History/Forum d'histoire orale*, 29 (2009), 14–15.

28 H. Welzer, 'Collateral Damage of History Education: National Socialism and the Holocaust in German Family Memory', *Social Research*, 75: 1 (Spring 2008), 310–13.

29 The phrase 'emotional community' is from Mabel Berezin, who notes the power of commemoration to engender and express emotional energies. 'Secure States: Towards a Sociology of Emotion', *Sociological Review*, 50: 2 (2002), 39.

30 Roseman, *Generations in Conflict*, 42.

31 J. Henley, 'Munich Police Brace for Rival Protests at Anti-Refugee Party's Meeting', *The Guardian*, 13 March 2016.

Part III

Historian

5

Fathers and the habits of home

In Savile Lumley's 1915 recruitment poster – among the most famous of all First World War propaganda images – a father sits in his armchair and looks towards the viewer with a discomfited expression. His son plays with toy soldiers in the foreground, and the attentive daughter on his knee asks what he did in the war. The poster pricks the conscience of British fathers-to-be who are yet to volunteer: what will your children think of you after the war if you cannot tell them how you served your country?

This forward projection of home life after the war is strikingly different from the retrospective accounts of children born in the 1920s and 30s, for whom the typical legacy of the war was not pride or even memories of horror, but silence. When he was ill in bed, Brian Mullarkey used to ask his father the very same question as the daughter in Lumley's poster: 'he used to come and sit by me, and ... the question was, you know, "What did you do in the War?", and he would never talk about it. Very rarely talked about it.' Brian's father had suffered a breakdown and rarely left the family home; his trembling hand would sometimes hover over the front doorknob for minutes at a time:

> In thunderstorms it was terrible, with the noise, he'd shake. He said nothing, but shook. And he wouldn't sit at the table with us, he sat in the kitchen on his own, and all the time in the house was spent virtually in the kitchen ... Who knows ... what was going on in his mind.

Brian's childhood was dominated by his father's mental illness, but he had no clue what had caused the 'smart and clean' clerk to become an unshaven figure with holes in his trousers that 'he wouldn't let Mother mend, he got a piece of string and tied round

Figure 5.1 Savile Lumley recruitment poster, 'Daddy, what did you do in the Great War?' IWM Art, PST 0311. All rights reserved.

it'. Two photographs mounted side-by-side in Brian's hallway wall contrasted the pre- and post-war father, one showing a dapper young man in a suit and tie, the other, a figure with half-closed eyes and a craggy white beard who Brian did not call 'father', but 'old Larkey'. As was the case for many children growing up in the 1920s and 30s, throughout Brian's childhood the war was a felt presence but not a remembered experience. It influenced family fortunes and could shape fatherhood itself, its legacies sometimes encouraging the 'involved father' imagined in Lumley's domestic scene, but constraining others to the point where the very title 'father' was revoked. The past war could be found in many places in the interwar home, on bodies, in states of mind and household routines, but talk was scarce.

The concept of inter-generational transmission can illuminate situations like these where the influence of the past was not only communicated in stories, but in actions, habits, material remains, forgetting or the refusal to remember. As Siân Pooley and Kaveri Qureshi observe, attitudes and ways of doing things are often passed unwittingly from generation to generation, formed as they are from everyday interactions and taken-for-granted assumptions. In addition to remembered experiences of childhood and parents' stories about their past, transmission can involve normative expectations about the right way to bring up a child or act as a citizen. It can entail moral precepts and judgements, sometimes religious, but often involving less coherent sets of attitudes towards the world.[1] Transmission can occur through habituation. It can involve objects, or it can be bodily, a matter of gesture, gait and posture.[2] It occurs through the roles children are drawn into. As a young girl, Margaret Reardon would plead with her father not to tell her upsetting stories, but as she grew older, she would say 'Tell me about the mud and the duck-boards', offering to be his listener and help get things off his chest, a role that reflects the gender expectations of young women between the wars.[3] Sometimes the impact of childhood experience communicated itself in the interview with a force that took me aback. I felt Brian Mullarkey's shame as he remembered how, when his friends asked who the dishevelled man was in the front window of his house, he told them it was his grandfather.

Silence itself could convey normative expectations between the generations, and it took effort to maintain. The children admired their fathers' ability to bear up. Pat Stamp's father had '[not] just a scar, it was, literally, a hole' in both legs due to shrapnel, and although he had difficulty walking he never used a stick: 'He was an amazing person really. I mean, you could tell by the way he walked along, and the look on his face, he did look as if he was in pain.' Yet 'he never complained, never heard him grumble at all. Never.' Fathers were respected for holding back memories and emotions. June Teape's father, Walter Hempshall, had been a stretcher bearer in the RAMC in East Africa and France. Although he almost never talked about the war, June believed that 'it coloured the whole of his existence afterwards. But he was a very private ... in many ways he was a very private person ... do you know what I mean?' His letters and postcards give few clues about what his war was like. He liked to photograph native Africans and game animals, and among the collection are photographs of four native Africans sentenced to hanging for the murder of an Englishman. Walter was fascinated by the ruins of French towns and sent his family dozens of postcards of bombed-out cathedrals and churches, most of which contain the phrase 'everything is as per usual'. The habit of keeping things private clearly went a long way back.[4]

June picked up signs despite this. As she explained, her father 'told me once something about when they were packing up at the end of the War, this chap who was in charge of their Unit was a doctor, and he said to them, he said, "Look at you", he said, "You go away without a scratch", he said, "and you're ruined for life."' Though voiced by a third party, the comment, June felt, had been Walter's way of intimating how he himself felt about the war. He had wanted to protect June from his memories: 'I think he was very aware of ... you know, he didn't want to pass on anything that was ... disturbing to me, when I was growing up. Do you know what I mean?' Raymond Burgin interpreted his father's silence in a similar way. A Sapper in the Royal Engineers, Walter Burgin had been shot in the head and blinded in 1917. Growing up with a disabled father, the war's legacies were very present to Ray, but Walter kept his memories to himself. He 'talked a little bit about trenches, but I don't remember a lot of detail. I don't think he belaboured the unpleasant side of it too much for a little youngster, you know.' Paternal silences like these were not simple instances of forgetting but resulted from what Luisa Passerini calls a 'self-decided attitude'.⁵ Silence was the sign of a caring father in the children's eyes. As Harriet Pollock commented, 'I don't think they liked us to worry.' The First World War serviceman, as Walter Benjamin observed, often 'returned from the battlefield grown silent – not richer, but poorer in communicable experience'.⁶ Silence, however, was not just a sign of the mental turmoil induced by the war, but could be proof of paternal love and care, a deliberate attempt to keep children 'sheltered', as Harriet Pollock put it.

The war may not have been much talked about, but it was in the background, and the remainder of this chapter investigates its everyday manifestations. It seeks to answer the question posed in Lumley's poster: how would the war figure in family life afterwards? The first section investigates the impact on housing, through fathers' capacity to earn and the networks through which housing was obtained. The second section investigates the influence of military service on domestic routines. The third section considers leisure, sometimes pursued by fathers as a means of forgetting, at other times initiated by wartime experiences. The final section is about violence, which, in contrast to the post-war trope of the brutalised veteran, was barely mentioned by the interviewees.

Kindness was the quality they remarked on most, but the 'good father' was an identity that had to be accomplished. The genealogy of this identity, moreover, was connected to the two wars, the hobbies and peaceable temperament of the suburban husband being aspects of national identity that were contrasted with Prussian militarism.⁷ The interviewees assessed their fathers against these interwar norms of domestic masculinity, but the 'good father' was also a counter-memory, which acknowledged the damage war had done, but sought to show that *their* father had not been brutalised. The war was thus an absent presence in the homes of children growing up in the 1920s and 30s. On the one hand, domesticity projected veterans into new identities as husbands and fathers and absorbed them in the lives of a 'hopeful generation' as yet untouched by war.⁸ On the other hand, the war appeared in the habits and routines that fathers drummed into their children, and in the insistence that their father was a 'good father'.

Housing and domestic space

Historians have taken different views on the significance of domesticity in the aftermath of the First World War. For Susan Kent, the interwar emphasis on women's domestic role constituted a backward step, the pre-First World War feminist critique of separate spheres, and calls for equality in work and politics, being followed in the 1920s and 30s by a reassertion of traditional ideals of femininity. Men returning from the war were 'in a violent frame of mind' and peace thereafter would depend on 'minimising the provocations of men to anger'.[9] For Alison Light, domesticity, rather than being a means of social appeasement of brutalised veterans, had a reparative role. The popularity of the whodunit, the crossword puzzle, board games and gardening in the 1920s and 30s, she observes, lay in their capacity to comfort citizens numbed by war. Suburban pastimes symbolised the emergence of a gentler conception of masculinity and the nation as the warrior became a husband and father: 'In the ubiquitous appeal of civilian virtues and pleasures, from the picture of "the little man", the suburban husband pottering in his herbaceous borders, to that of Britain itself as a sporting little country batting away against the Great Dictators, we can discover a considerable sea-change in ideas of national temperament.'[10] In her study of domestic interiors between the wars, Deborah Cohen describes how furnishings became simpler and more uniform, creating a 'peaceful, neutral background' in homes that were 'places of repose'. Rather than the simmering violence noted by Kent, or the playful distractions noted by Light, Cohen believes that mourning was the principal domestic legacy of the war: 'The home was to be, above all, quiet, reserved, and neutral.'[11]

Demographic trends indicate the popularity of domesticity between the wars. By the end of the 1930s marriage rates were higher than at any point in the previous century, with 41 per cent of the population between the ages of fifteen and thirty-nine being married (a 7 per cent increase on the rate in 1901).[12] The reduction in completed family size affected domestic relationships. The parents of my interviewees tended to come from families that were significantly larger than the families they themselves created, a characteristic which reflects the national picture: two-thirds of marriages in 1925 resulted in two children or less.[13] Smaller family size, shorter working hours and increased standards of living for many in the 1930s afforded new opportunities for home-based activities.

There were significant shifts in the roles played by veteran fathers within this domestic culture. These were noted by my interviewees, whose knowledge of their father's war may have been sketchy, but who had vivid memories of him at home. Laura King has described the growing involvement of fathers in guidance, moral training and play, a shift which would continue after the Second World War.[14] Yet the change may have had a 'pre-history' too, the First World War helping to bring the 'involved father' into being. Forgetting the war did not just entail reluctance to put memories into words, it could also occur through having children and being a father. Busying themselves with hobbies and 'masculine housework', guiding and disciplining children, men put the war behind them, while at the same time, it was through these very habits that children encountered the war past.

Many children in the 1920s and 30s were growing up in families formed by war. Marriages to disabled men involved support from the outset and were perceived as a form of womanly war service. Ray Burgin's father, who had lost his sight during the war, married a nurse from St Dunstan's Hostel after the Matron arranged what was literally a 'blind date'. David Smith's parents also met during his father's recovery. His mother had been a Red Cross nurse in Manchester and had nursed his father, who almost died after his leg was amputated above the knee. Smith thought this was 'quite romantic really'. Nursing may have offered a period of liberation from the strictures of the Edwardian family, but for Smith and Burgin's mothers, it had ended up in domesticity. This was not just the case for nurses; as Chapter 7 explains, in the aftermath of the war there was a broader social expectation that care would fall on women. Allan Pentney was sure that his mother would never have married his father had he been able-bodied. Coming from the same small village in Norfolk, however, she felt a sense of obligation: 'She took pity on him … And he needed help, and she gave him help. That was like it all her life. She looked after and helped him.' War was often entwined in parents' romances and marriage, establishing routines of care and sacrifice before children were born.

Bricks and mortar bore the signs of war. The importance of housing in compensating citizen soldiers for their war service, and easing their transition back into civilian life, was recognised during the war itself. As the President of the Local Government Board commented in 1919, 'To let them [our heroes] come home from horrible, waterlogged trenches to something little better than a pigsty here would, indeed, be criminal ... and a negation of all we have said during the war, that we can never repay these men for what they have done for us.'[15] The simultaneous vision of a national population fit for military service and home as a place of repose is portrayed in the cover image of the town planner and MP Richard Reiss's 1918 booklet *The Home I Want*.[16] At the bottom is a row of grim back-to-back tenements; at the top, the home of the future, a cottage surrounded by trees and green space, with its own garden.

The success of Lloyd George's 'Homes for Heroes' scheme is disputed, and the assessments of historians reflect the polarised legacies of reconstruction. Local authorities constructed almost 1.1 million of the four million new homes between the wars, and between 1931 and 1939, four-fifths of existing slum dwellers were rehoused.[17] At the same time, the ambitions of the 1919 Addison Act were curtailed by economic downturns and cutbacks in the 1920s, and despite progress under the Wheatley Act in the 1930s, still around a third of the working class were living in slum housing in 1939.[18] As reformers looked to the future during the Second World War, the perception of the 1920s and 30s as a failed reconstruction gathered political momentum. Interviewees incorporated elements of this split vision as they described their childhoods. The children of disabled veterans were sometimes aggrieved that their parents had not been better supported by the state, sentiments sharpened by a myth of betrayal that was overlaid by the progressive vision of the 'people's war' and the greater ambition of post-Second World War reconstruction.[19] Other interviewees, meanwhile, fitted their accounts of growing up between the wars within the narrative of improved housing and new suburban estates.

Veteran status had sometimes helped families to obtain housing, though the move did not always prove beneficial. Allan Pentney's father was quick to take up the offer of a council-built house, but the rent was expensive and the family were forced to move out after getting into arrears. When Norfolk County Council acquired an estate in Lingwood for disabled veterans, John Mingay's father, who had lost an arm, was offered an allotment and a 'little house on

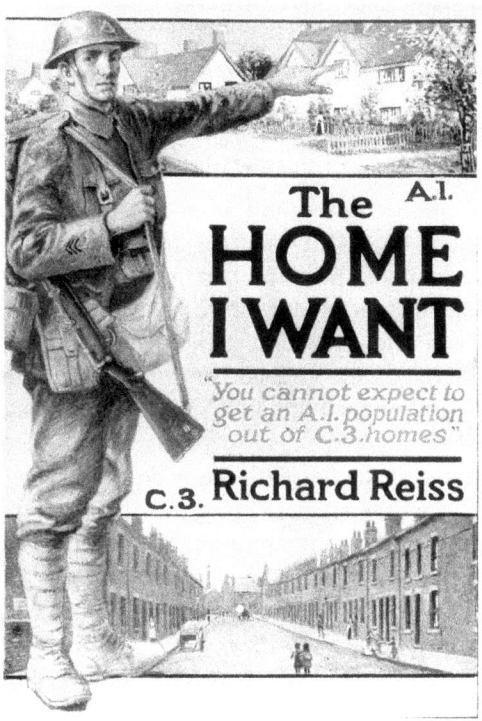

Figure 5.2 Richard Reiss, *The Home I Want*, 1918. Courtesy of the Mary Evans Picture Library. All rights reserved.

the hill'. Veteran networks could be important in obtaining housing. Bill Swann's mother and father moved to the Oswald Stoll mansions after an ex-officer, 'Commander somebody or other', took an interest in the plight of the double-amputee. Kathleen Skin's father bought a plot of land in Cambridgeshire in the late 1920s from a family whose son had died in the war and who were offering land for sale to ex-servicemen. The war was often part of the story of how families got to live where they were, a past inherent in place.

Wealth and income greatly affected the kind of domestic life a family would lead but the crucial factor was whether the father was capable of work. The higher the income and the more stable the employment, the more home could be enjoyed as a place of recovery and renewal. The equation often went the other way for disabled veterans: the more serious the disability, the less likely it was that a father could secure work and the more constrained domestic space and comfort became.[20] The house at Lingwood where John Mingay grew up was 'tiny', cheaply built from asbestos and very cold, the toilet a forty-yard walk from the house. The poultry farm in Thurgoland that the blind charity St Dunstan's found for Ray Burgin's father had no running water – it had to be drawn from a well – and no electricity until after the Second World War. Bill Swann described the flat in the Oswald Stoll Mansions where he lived with his brother, sister and parents as 'basic', yet 'bigger than where we'd come'. One room served as a lounge and eating area, and there was a scullery with a bath covered by a wooden plank which also served as the kitchen bench. There was the 'barest' of furniture; the only item Bill could recall was the chair where his double amputee father spent most of his time. Bill contrasted the cramped interior of the flat with the wide hallways where the disabled men parked their wheelchairs and the impressive façade of the building. A Charity Organisation Society worker who visited the family in the 1920s noted how restricted Bill's father's life had become but made no comment about his children, who were also affected by lack of space and their father's immobility.[21] Bill 'used to play hours and hours of crib with him! And … sometimes it was interesting, but sometimes it was very boring!' The only time the family went out together was on a Sunday when they would walk to Battersea Bridge with his father in his three-wheeled chair: 'So that's about all I can think of … doing things together, yeah.'

Children growing up in fatherless households experienced similarly confined domestic spaces. It was common for war widows to supplement their income by renting out rooms. After Winifred Spray's father died in 1918, her mother gave over an upstairs room and the parlour to tenants, leaving mother and daughter with no private space apart from their bedroom. After Rosemary Game's father died in the 1930s from a war-related rheumatic condition, her mother took in boarders so she could keep the house in Winchmore Hill they had purchased in the 1930s. War loss and disability put pressure on domestic space, and because they were poor, families with the most severely disabled fathers were often the least able to insulate children from suffering. It was 'hard' to hear her father's moans through the thin bedroom walls of their cottage, Marion Armstrong told me.

For interviewees like Marion who had disabled fathers, poor housing was *felt* as a war legacy and expressed the deprivations they had undergone. Brian Mullarkey's father had grown up in 'a fairly large house in the centre of Norwich, in a good housing area', but Brian grew up in a small Victorian terrace, five boys in one bedroom and three to a bed, his mother sleeping with her two daughters, his father occupying a small back room. This was not the fate that the family had expected. His father had purchased an allotment in the early 1920s with the aim of building his own house, but his breakdown put paid to that. The cramped terrace showed how far down in the world his family had fallen: 'Now, that's just to suggest to you that that's how my life should have followed a similar pattern ... but it didn't.' The war, as Brian saw it, was the cause of the family's misfortunes.

At the other end of the scale were families whose housing improved between the wars. Interviewees recalled the excitement of new homes on suburban estates which came within their parents' reach due to cheap credit. They listed the advantages of indoor bathrooms and toilets, hot water services, a bedroom to themselves and a garden. Smith recalled the 'Ideal' coke burner in the indoor kitchen of their new semi-detached in Harrow, while Pat Stamp contrasted their rented house in Forest Gate with their new home in Boreham Wood, which had an indoor toilet and bathroom – 'we'd never had a bathroom before' – electricity, a 'squidgy' kitchen with a boiler in the corner and a large sitting room, 'the first ... we'd seen'. Space and comfort made a home-based childhood more viable, and provided the conditions for 'father time'.[22] Joyce Fey's father, who had been a private in the Machine Gun Corps during the war, went back to his trade as a printer afterwards and by the time Joyce was a girl his income was sufficient to purchase a four-bedroom house in South London: 'the back room wasn't used for very much. And with three brothers, my father bought a snooker table, and a table-tennis table that went on top of it, and we all played games.' The house that Mary Burdett's father built just outside Cambridge had a playroom where she and her brother could bring friends.

The variations in housing described by the interviewees echo the national picture, with some having grown up in poor and overcrowded accommodation and others enjoying the benefits of rising living standards and improved housing. In fact, the situation of the children of war widows and disabled soldiers interviewed for this project was probably little different from that of many working-class families around the country, whose opportunities for domesticity were also constrained by space.[23] Dennis Johnson, whose father was a full-time metal worker in Middlesbrough, shared a bed with his four brothers, while his sister and mother occupied the second bed until their father returned home from night shift. In some respects, the situation of the wounded veteran's family might actually be better than in other poor families, for example if they were able to take advantage of loans or were given preference in housing. Nevertheless, it was often through memories of poor housing that the children of disabled soldiers and war widows sought to convey the personal hardships of the aftermath.

Household routines

Disability and widowhood had profound effects on the roles and responsibilities of family members. Children in fatherless families relied on their mothers for survival, and dependence on a single adult could arouse insecurity. Marion Armstrong's 'biggest fear' after her father died in March 1932

> was if my mother died. That was the biggest emotion. And I used to pass our auntie's house to and from school and I used to look every time we passed because, in those days, if people died, relatives drew the curtains till after the funeral – the house was kept in darkness till after the funeral – and I used to look at this auntie's house and think, 'Oh, my mum hasn't died, because she hasn't drawn the curtains.'

Traditional gender roles were simultaneously reinforced and undermined in households like Marion's. Widows were often forced to find work, the income from their pensions being lower than the wartime separation allowance.[24] Mothers became breadwinners, homemakers and carers in households where fathers could not work. Bill Swann's family could not survive on his father's war pension so his mother 'used to have to go out cleaning and that, and she didn't have the best of health'. Bill hesitated when I asked him to describe his mother. She was not bad-tempered, he said, but her life was 'hard' and there was not much fun at home. 'You never saw her laughing a lot.' Later in life, Brian Mullarkey often thought about what his mother's life must have been like with seven children and an income of thirty-five shillings a week from his father's work pension: 'you know, I often ... I want to know what ... what was going on in her mind, how she coped with it all'. As a child he had not given it any thought; the family was absorbed in getting by. While taking on new responsibilities, a mother might nevertheless maintain traditional routines. Brian's mother used to prepare her husband's breakfast each morning although he had not worked since 1928.

Interviewees from families like these were at pains to convey their mothers' resourcefulness. Eileen Pollock's mother held down three jobs, working as a cleaner in the local school and police station and in a fish and chip shop in the evening. She was 'mother and father to us'. Allan Pentney described his mother's efforts to save her family from 'virtually starving' after his father's business as a boot-repairer failed and they got into debt. She borrowed money from friends to set up a general store in the Norfolk village of North Creake: 'And so she set into work – it was just early days of the War – and she worked like a demon, worked 12, 15 hours a day, running the shop, looking after the family, keeping things going, and helping my father go about his business.' John Mingay described his mother as 'a very energetic person, I mean, it's obvious that with his arm, she did most of the work with the poultry and whatnot, you know'. When she wasn't looking after the poultry she was cooking or making mats and rugs to sell. He had vivid memories of her at work: 'I can see my mother in the scullery with her bucket full of feathers, you know, and all the innards of the chickens and whatnot! Mother used to sit there day after day doing that.'

I thought Harriet Pollock was being rhetorical when she commended her mother for having kept the family out of the workhouse, but as Andrea Hetherington shows, widows sometimes had to resort to the Poor Law and pressure was put on them to have their children placed in an institution to free them up for employment.[25] By necessity, these mothers did tasks that a husband and father would normally do, but disability and widowhood also reinforced traditional expectations about women's place. The children of disabled soldiers conjured a pieta-like figure. It was his mother's 'dedicated life's work to ... to minister unto him, as it were', said

David Smith. A similar image came to John Mingay: 'Oh, I think Mother ... I don't know, she must have been a saint.' Winifred Spray described her war widow mother as a 'wonderful mother', 'sacrificing, really, to me'. These children drew on traditional notions of femininity constructed around duty, care and self-sacrifice to express their gratitude towards their mothers.

The heroism and strength of mothers in the homes of disabled soldiers were admired but could also convey how difficult family life had been. Harriet Pollock broke down in the first few minutes of our interview as she recalled her mother carrying her father downstairs from the bedroom so he could join them for dinner. He could barely stand, and she had to muster the strength of a man. The home lives of disabled men revealed gender scripts at their baldest: the labours of wives were directed to basic survival.

At the same time, a disabled father could have opportunities for 'involved fathering' that a breadwinning father might miss. He might lack money and material comfort, but had time on his hands and was about the house. Ray Burgin's father, for example, used to walk Ray to school and pick him up each afternoon. Marion Armstrong remembered playing with her father when she was home sick from school:

> I never went to bed without he said, 'Good night, me old love!' He'd give me a kiss – I can remember that vividly. And I can remember my mother made everything. But a treat was a bought cake – to us – because we never had ... there was a bakery at the end of the road, and they sold butterfly cakes with fresh cream in, and I remember I was off school, ill, and because I was ... and my dad was in bed ill – one of his ill times – and I got into bed with him during the day, and my mother had brought my dad a butterfly cake ... as a treat, because, as I say, they were treats. And he gave it to me, and I remember her coming in and saying, 'Oh, love, I was giving *you* a treat', and he says, 'Let her have it, she'll enjoy it better than me.' He was a lovely man. He lived for ... his kids.

Her father's wish that Marion should enjoy the treat shows how this disabled father 'lived for ... his kids'. It was not just the opportunity to be with his children that a full-time father at home might enjoy; he might also have time for domestic chores. Eileen Pollock's father would get up early on washing day to posset the clothes and had taught his daughters how to scrub and wash.

Disability and widowhood revealed the war's impact at its starkest, but in other homes, the legacies were benign or even advantageous to domesticity. During the war, their fathers had learned to look after themselves. They could make breakfast with a Tommy cooker, sew buttons on their tunics or darn socks with their 'hussef'. Military service made them capable, but as husbands and fathers, their roles were ancillary to wives. They might help prepare food or wash up, but only cooked in exceptional circumstances, such as when wives were ill or as a treat. Joyce Fey's father would make toffee apples on the weekend. Military experience, however, gave veterans the confidence and ability to cook and clean, and they could take over if necessary. Her mother did all the housework when Rosemary Gitsham was young, but her father quickly adjusted to doing the housework after her mother died.

Grooming, dress and posture bore the imprints of war. Teape's father 'always walked well. And he was always saying ... he was always saying to me, when he used to take me to the bus, you know, "Oh, goodness! Stop bending over! Stand up straight!"' Jefferey Flower's father always had his suits tailor-made, and Jefferey believed that this was a hang-over from his army days as an officer: 'I think it just carried on, because in the Army, you had to pay for your own uniform.' John Mingay remembered his father's advice when he joined up in the Second World War: 'You've got to be smart. Keep yourself dressed.' Fathers impressed the importance of neatness on their children through their own appearance; June Teape recalled a father who was 'beautifully dressed'. Her father, Margaret Reardon told me, was a 'very particular man about cleaning personal items, such as shoes (which he highly polished to the point where you could practically see yourself in them), brushing coats – he would never go out without ensuring things were absolutely clean and fit to wear, and it was very difficult to clean things for him as he got older and was less able to do it himself'.[26] He had worked as a butler before the war, but Margaret believed that his fastidiousness was also due to the war.

Children's shoes bore the signs of military service. When I asked Doris Perley if there was any indication that her father had been in the Army, she replied, 'Oh, shoes had to be polished. Yeah. Always.' Elizabeth Bartholomew's father set up a weekly routine. He would polish the children's shoes before church on Sunday, but during the week they had to do their own: 'oh yes, eight o'clock at night, when the homework was finished, you cleaned and polished your shoes'. He had been a batman in the war and was now instructing his children in the very routines he had performed for his officers. This was a life-long lesson: according to her great-granddaughter, Elizabeth, who was then in her mid-nineties, would pack her shoes with newspaper so they kept their shape. Army habits found their way into homes and were transferred across generations: 'I think those sort of things possibly did rub off', Beryl Manthorp remarked, 'and I think they possibly still do … because … the Army has a standard, hasn't it … and those chaps … who were in the trenches and barracks, I mean, they were … they had to be smart … Part of the training, and I suppose it sticks.'

It was not just their views about health and appearance that marked out military fathers, it was their *manner* of instilling habits. Dennis Johnson's father drummed into his children that they must brush their teeth three times a day: 'That's what the Army teaches you. Teaches you discipline. And you live by numbers.' They could be hard taskmasters. When her father asked them to do something, recalled Elizabeth Burdett, they had to 'jump to it', and he might give them a light slap if they were slow. He had high standards: 'I mean, I remember, for example, cleaning some shoes, and thought I'd made a good job, and … he sort of sent them back because I hadn't done … you know the welt round the bottom there, I hadn't sort of obviously polished round all those bits.' Routines like this could make children feel like army recruits doing bull. Mary Hardie, born in 1912, recalled in an interview with Steve Humphries that as children they used to have to do all the housework and were ordered about by their father, who 'had us all lined up like a regiment of soldiers'.[27] Drilled by veteran fathers, many of the women and men who served in the Second World War were familiar with military discipline long before they joined up.

Neatness, cleanliness and order were aspects of home life that the interviewees immediately recognised as having military connotations, but odd or disquieting aspects of a father's behaviour might also be put down to the war. Dennis Johnson's father was scrupulous about germs: 'with him being in … in the forces, very hygienic, he used to boil water in the dish, he used to put a spoonful of Dettol in. Yeah. Yeah. Yeah, he'd get washed in Dettol. Yeah.' Jean Croft's father would quiz his children about their diet and bowel movements and would lecture them about the need to stay regular. He had become seriously ill with enteritis at Gallipoli, and Jean thought this explained his fixation with bowels. John Morgan's father was particularly strict about the use of water. He had also served in Gallipoli, where water had to be carried on foot and was always in short supply: 'Used to really hurt him if somebody left the tap running.' Looking back, the interviewees tended to regard their fathers' eccentricities sympathetically, as an understandable reaction to wartime experiences.

The accounts given by the children of veterans echo the broader narratives of family life in interwar Britain in many respects. These were fathers who enjoyed being at home and who did some of the domestic work even when they were disabled. Military service had made them competent. Yet their roles at home were supplementary, and as a result, easy for the interviewees to recall. It was expected that mothers and daughters would do the mainstay, which in the homes of disabled veterans might include paid work and 'masculine housework' like gardening and decorating. When it came to domestic habits, the legacies of war lay less in the division of roles than the atmosphere of scrupulous attention to routines, as fathers, having had orders barked at them in the ranks, now took on the mantle of the sergeant-major.

Leisure and play

Discussions of childhood and youth are commonly separated from discussions of parenthood in the social histories of interwar Britain. Play belongs to the child's world, and yet among the interviewees in this study, it was a key point of connection between generations, and as much a part of the adult's as the child's world. While Chapter 6 investigates play from the child's perspective, here I consider its appeal among returned-soldier fathers.

The interviewees described fathers with a wide range of leisure activities and hobbies. John Frost's father introduced him to football, cricket, cribbage, darts and billiards. Joyce Fey's father had interrupted a promising career as a footballer to enlist and resumed his passion after the war, coaching a local South London team and writing a football column for the local newspaper. Sharing her father's passions, Joyce explained, she became a daddy's girl:

> after the War ended, I was his constant companion, I went everywhere with him … he was a footballer, so we went to football a lot. I saw all the greats. I saw … we went to whichever ground in London – we lived in Newell then – and we went to whichever ground in London the best player was playing at, so I saw Stanley Matthews, and… Danny Blanchflower, and all of those, so … yes. And I went to cricket with him, and I'm still a cricket fanatic.

Fathers made toys in the backyard workshops and sheds of suburban houses. Margaret Reardon's father was good with his hands. He made her a doll's house and furniture, and a Jacob's Ladder out of wood and ribbon. Margaret would sometimes see children out in the street with new toys, and if she said to her father '"I'd like, I'd like one of those", he'd, they'd have it ready for me that evening'. Rosemary Gitsham's father made her a toboggan. After building his own home in Newcastle NSW, the Australian veteran and carpenter for the B. H. P. Steelworks Herbert Way began to produce toy furniture and household utilities for his daughter Gwendoline from discarded cigar boxes. He made twenty-three miniature pieces, including a mangle, washing board and wash tank, a bed complete with carved headboard, pillow and blankets, a kitchen dresser with opening doors, lounge settees and a high-backed 'father's chair'.[28] Like the toy industry itself, the doll's house made by Joyce Fey's father was repurposed during the Second World War, becoming a rabbit hutch whose inhabitants she remembered 'appearing through the windows! Yes!'

Like the makers of the Queen Mary Doll's House, whose significance as a war legacy is investigated by Rachel Duffett, these veterans were engrossed in constructing miniature domestic worlds.[29] Absorbed in detail that required dexterity and precision, the maker could become forgetful of self and regain a sense of control in the world. In his essay on the miniature, Steven Millhauser contrasts the fascination it occasions with the 'dread inherent in hugeness'.[30] Trench warfare was characterised by enormity. Men struggled to find the words to encapsulate its thunderous sounds, the skies filled with eerie light and the sensation of the shaking ground. A soldier could hold himself together by focusing on a small object: the tank commander Wilfred Bion recalled an attack at Wytschaete when his gaze locked onto a clump of mud that was swinging from his dug-out roof, suspended by a blade of grass.[31] In the aftermath of a war that had overwhelmed the senses, the attention involved in fashioning small objects like toy furniture or construction models held appeal. As Millhauser concludes of his own fascinations, 'Under the sway of the miniature I contemplate my isolation, and my contemplation is clean, uncorrupted by the impurity of terror.'[32] Instead of pursuing 'fantasies of flight and freedom' from the domestic in the 1920s and 30s, an impulse which Paul Fussell argues in *Abroad* 'can be said to begin in the trenches', the veteran fathers in this study played at home with their children and made domestic miniatures with their own hands.[33]

Sometimes the relationships between fatherhood, recuperation and play can only be seen by looking more closely at individual family histories. Such connections, however, are difficult to establish, for if play was a means of sublimating the war past, a child born afterwards might not discern its relationship to the war. Margaret Seabrook remembered her father as a man with great energy and many passions: 'He wasn't a sitter. He was always doing things.' Margaret described an idyllic childhood living above the family drapers store on Market Square in Lichfield, overlooking Samuel Johnson's house with the Cathedral just behind the rear garden. While their mother stayed back to manage the shop, her father and uncle would take the three children to the seaside in Felixstowe, Scarborough and Sutton-on-Sea.

When her brother was studying prehistoric history at school, they drove to Stonehenge to see the monument. They went on camping trips in the car, taking a fold-up table and picnic hampers. Her father constructed a tennis court in the garden and installed a table-tennis table in the glass-ceilinged atrium of the store. He helped his son grow vegetables in the atrium and cut out a Monopoly board from plywood so the children could make their own set.

His main hobby was photography. He belonged to the photographic society in Lichfield and set up a darkroom where Margaret helped him develop pictures. I arrived at Margaret's home to find albums and picture boards placed around the lounge with shots of Margaret, her older brother and younger sister doing roly-polies and handstands in the garden, camping and at the seaside dressed in one-piece bathing suits.

Figure 5.3 Francis Long playing with his children at the beach. Courtesy of Margaret Seabrook. All rights reserved.

When I asked Margaret if there were many signs of the First World War when she was growing up, she replied that at home, 'It was in the past, but from school, we always used to march to the Memorial Gardens in Lichfield, on November 11th for the service there, and my father's friend … Robert Bridgeman, had been killed in the First World War.' Insofar as there was a memory of the conflict, then, it was associated with public rituals and spaces rather than the family. Yet her father was a casualty. He had been gassed in 1917 and was blind for two months. His sight recovered but he was prone to colds and infections. Throughout her interview, Margaret stressed how academically gifted her father was. He had won a scholarship to King Edward's School in Birmingham and had just completed his first year studying maths at Cambridge when he enlisted. The war ended his university career, however. As Margaret explained, 'he couldn't go back to Cambridge because he wasn't fit and was told that he must do an outdoor job … his parents were advised by a doctor that he was not well enough to return to study and should take up an outdoor occupation.' The family bought him a smallholding, but he did not take to farming and after a couple of years he started in the family business in Lichfield.

Figure 5.4 Margaret Seabrook and her brother playing in the garden. Courtesy of Margaret Seabrook. All rights reserved.

Not being able to return to Cambridge was a great setback, but the emotion that Margaret most associates with her father is joy. Margaret learned to capture the family's joyous moments when she was given her own camera, a Zeiss Ikon on her eleventh birthday. She still has the camera and brought it out to show me. She was also given a photo album that birthday, 'My first shots. September, 1936', and one of the photos in the album shows her father at the beach with her sister and brother. Above it is the caption 'Happy Daddy', double exclamation marks, and in fact the entire album constructs a happy family. Yet when I asked Margaret if her father had a temper, she repeated three times, 'he did have a temper', especially when he was young, and remarked twice on how he 'mellowed' with age.[34] Her father's anger had no place in Margaret's photographic record or memories of childhood, however. The double exclamation marks in the photograph album suggest the part

160   *Historian*

she had played as a child in creating an image of the happy father, an image that she re-enacted in our interview seventy years later.

At one level Margaret's story is about how a returned soldier was able to move on by immersing himself in family life. Her father was fully absorbed in his hobbies and outdoor pursuits. The First World War, as she stated, *was* in the past. And yet perhaps it was not entirely. When I asked Margaret how her father might have felt about not being able to finish his degree at Cambridge, she replied: 'He was very upset about it. He would have liked to have done that … I think he put his mathematics to use in various ways, and he was very good, he made a wireless – before I was born, I think – and he was very good at photography.' Margaret believed that her father's

Figure 5.5 Page from Margaret Seabrook's photo album, 'Happy Daddy!!'. Courtesy of Margaret Seabrook. All rights reserved.

hobbies gave him another outlet for his talents. She had kept her father's hospital tag and the telegram informing his parents that he was severely injured, but these artefacts – held onto by other descendants as positive proof of the war's damaging impact – were incidental to her story. Her father was an energetic, creative, playful and above all a 'happy daddy'.

Leisure, as Margaret's story shows, depended on wealth and physical capacity. Holidays, days out, hobbies and toys required income, and fathers needed to be physically able to join in. Fathers' play often revolved around physical exertion and as a result, men who were disabled could be constrained as fathers too. Dora Kneebone remembered her mother's warning call when games got boisterous: 'It was always, "Dora, mind Daddy's leg"', though he was sometimes up for a game of badminton over the clothesline. Elizabeth Game remembered the time her father was asked to join a tug-of-war match at a holiday camp in Bognor Regis. He had contracted rheumatic fever in the war and had a weak heart. She and her mother had looked on clapping and laughing, but the eleven-year-old Elizabeth was aware that her mother 'was just a touch worried'.

The inability to join in had a particularly great impact on sons. Bill Swann explained that the reason he didn't learn to ride a bike until his late teens, and was hopeless at DIY, was that his amputee father could not show him by example. There was little to be proud of in Brian Mullarkey's father:

> I had a father, but could never be taken as a father in the full sense of the word … engaging. There was nobody to say, you know, 'Come along, I'll show you how to fish', you know, 'Let's go and have a kick about with the football.' You know, 'What do you think of Norwich this week, what they done?' No, none of that … but when I got married, you see, I just didn't really know what a father's duties were, because … I know that there was … you know, affection, and love there even, for me, on his behalf, but that could never be shown. And that's … that's a big miss.

It wasn't just the lack of fathering that was a loss, but the lack of a role model. When I asked Brian who he emulated when bringing up his four daughters, he replied, 'Well, what would Mother have done?' Yet Brian had found a way to compensate for some of these losses. There was a framed photograph on his wall of his father as captain of the local football team, and Brian had kept his boxing gloves, cricket bat, football and dumbbells. He had preserved something of the man his father had been before the war, before Brian knew him, a 'very big man, particularly ... when he was young', and 'a great sportsman too'. As Bill Swann indicates in his regrets about not being able to ride a bike or do DIY, and Brian Mullarkey shows in his comments about becoming a father, these were felt as life-long deficits.

Discipline and violence

Social histories of returned veterans and fatherhood provide contrasting views of the emotional climate in homes between the wars. Historians in Australia and Britain have documented public anxieties about the 'brutalised veteran' and have investigated cases of violence towards wives and children.[35] Courts often showed lenience towards the 'deranged ex-serviceman', his actions excused in a resurrection of the 'unwritten law' which tolerated domestic violence as a normal part of marriage.[36] As Judith Allen comments, 'freedom in the domestic zone had always been one of the spoils of war; and the inter-war home could resemble conceded, even conquered territory'.[37] At the same time, historians of childhood and domesticity note the growing disapproval of corporal punishment in the popular press and advice literature during the 1920s and 30s.[38] Smacking was acceptable, but the emotional impact of beatings was a subject of lively discussion among child experts between the wars.[39] The disapproval of corporal punishment was linked to an image of the modern father as 'benevolent' rather than 'authoritarian'.[40]

The interviewees described fathers who could be 'strict' or 'quite dominant' but spoke about them in largely positive terms. Joyce Fey thought her father was 'a fantastic character'; Rosemary Gitsham had 'a terrific father'; Pat Stamp had a 'good father', and Vic Wiltshire 'a great father'. A good father was defined in negative terms, as one who was *not* violent or aggressive. Brenda Aubrey's father was 'placid' and 'ever so soft', Elizabeth Bartholomew's was 'very nice-natured', Anne-Marie Careless's was 'always kind' and Doris Perley's was 'really gentle' and 'amiable'. They found it difficult to imagine that their fathers had been trained to be violent and had perhaps even killed. Her father so disliked wringing the necks of chickens, Doris Perley told me, that his mother had to ask a neighbour to do it. Dora Kneebone's father was a 'mild-mannered man, he was … so gentle, and … it was so unlike him to want to fight. [*laughs*] He never fought anybody in his life, except in France! [*laughs*]'. Her father was a reluctant recruit, said June Teape, 'he waited, he didn't want to go'. In fact, Walter Hempshall had enlisted in 1915 before conscription was introduced, but June could not square enthusiasm for war with the gentle father she knew. There was an element of idealisation in these descriptions, as Marion Armstrong revealed in this comment about her parents: 'I never can remember a wrong word between them, which is a lovely thought.'

Only two interviewees in the study described fathers who were violent. Neither of them wanted their interviews on the record and were concerned about conveying too negative an impression. In one case the father had sexually abused the interviewee's sister. She described him as 'eccentric' and put his behaviour down to a brain injury. The fact that in her view the war had caused the condition allowed her to tell me what he had done without condemning him. The thirty-five interviewees who agreed that I could use their interviews were largely silent about violence at home. This is striking because aggression and unpredictable tempers are among the most common emotions witnessed today by the wives and children of veterans with PTSD, and British and Australian historians have shown that there were numerous cases of domestic violence among returned veterans in the 1920s and 30s.[41] Given the reservations expressed by the two interviewees above, it seems likely that descendants with a family history of violence may have been reluctant to put themselves forward to be interviewed, especially at a time when the public image of the First World War soldier was as a victim rather than an aggressor.

Self-censorship may also have been at work among those who volunteered their stories. They were just as likely to recall their *mother's* temper as their father's. Her mother wore the trousers, said Dora Kneebone; she was a 'spitfire'. Pat Stamp's mother kept a cane on the dinner table and would smack her children when they misbehaved. She would threaten them by saying 'wait 'til your father gets home', but Pat did not recall ever being hit by her father. In her study of working-class fatherhood in Victorian Britain, Julie Marie Strange observes that corporal punishment was more often a threat than a reality, and that 'A father who chastised with discrimination and logic was, in this reckoning, a caring father.'[42] My interviewees expressed much the same view. John Frost explained that 'if any of us were naughty, we'd see him go to his buckle, his belt, and I never ever saw him undo the belt completely, but that was enough, you know! ... now and again Mum would say, "Now, stop it, or I'll tell your dad", and ... but no.' His father was 'strict in a way, and yet ... you could get ... if you knew how to get round him, you could, you know'. David Smith laughed as he recalled the sound of his one-legged father stumping up the stairs to hit his older brothers for being rowdy at bedtime: 'If he lost his rag, I mean ... I think a child of ... nine or ten would be a bit frightened, yes.' But he only ever hit them through the bedclothes, and David remembered that on one occasion he did the same thing to his daughter when she was being silly and would not go to sleep. Violence was a means of teaching children right and wrong, and looking back, the interviewees felt their fathers had behaved justly. Doris Perley was thrashed by a local policeman when he caught her stealing apples from a local orchard, and was expecting sympathy when she ran home to tell her father:

> That did it. 'Don't you dare touch anything that doesn't belong to you – not even an apple on the ground!' He said, 'Bringing our name into disrepute like that!' And he tanned my backside there and then ... And that's the only time in all my life. He was a very honest man, you know ... very poor ... but always ... he would be ... people didn't touch things that didn't belong to them.

Doris told her story in an approving way, as an example of her father's moral values, values which were also her own.

The ability to control anger was thus seen as an important aspect of what made a 'good father', and like silence, it required willpower. Vic Wiltshire gave a quite different description of the newly returned soldier who had married his mother and the father that he himself remembered. Vic 'never saw him lose his temper', he told me proudly. When Vic lost his little brother while he was out playing with his mates, his father didn't hit me or anything, he just took me up to the Police Station and make me learn the hard way that, 'You shouldn't do this sort of thing.' You know, normally a bloke might hit me, but he didn't. But, I mean, he was … I mean, there's no nicer man than him.

His father had not always been able to control his temper, however. He had been blown up in a trench at Gallipoli and after the war, showed the hyper-startle response typical of the PTSD victim. He was 'hitting my mother … his wife-to-be, when they were courting … because he was shell-shocked, and his reaction to anything was to jump up and hit'. The fact that he had never lifted a finger to his children showed why Vic thought his father 'just perfect'.

The interviewees associated corporal punishment with school rather than home. His father might give them a tap if they were naughty, said George Elders, but home was 'easy' compared with the punishments doled out by his teachers. At school, John Frost was caned for things he hadn't done and became a 'trouble[d] child', desperate to leave as soon as possible. His father by contrast was 'always fair'. Fathers sometimes took their children's side when teachers administered punishments. Pat Stamp's father went to his daughter's school to protest after she was beaten. Jefferey Flower's hand was broken in eight places during a beating:

> 'Right, Flower. What do you write with?' 'Right hand.' 'Left hand out. Don't you dare move!' Oooooooh! He said, 'That was for not obeying me. Put your hand out. This is for telling tales.' Oooooooh! And then kept me out the front. And I … I didn't cry, I couldn't cry in front of the class, I just … all I knew was that my hand was just one searing pain! [*laughs*] I did tell my father, and I did see him at the school a couple of days later. Now, whether that was to tell them I was going to do well in school, or whether it was to say, 'Don't you touch my boy again' … I shouldn't have been caned, and I think he was complaining that I had been caned, because my hand was black and swollen.

Jefferey attributed the violent treatment of pupils at the school to the war: his headmaster had 'had a plate in his head, silver plate, and he'd scream and shout … in front of you'. His own father, it transpired, also had a short fuse when he came back from the war, and in the parlance of PTSD was 'hypervigilant'. As Jefferey explained: 'woe betide anybody who swore in his presence. If his wife were there, or any other ladies, they would find themselves on the deck. Or if anybody took him by surprise. His brother slapped him on the back, in the middle of the street, one day, and the next thing, the brother was on the floor.' I asked Jefferey why he thought his father was like this, and he replied, 'Well, because he reacted. He said … "Well, I've just come out of a war." He said, "When people attack you, you respond."' Unlike his teachers and the headmaster, however, Jefferey's father had learned to contain himself. Respect for their own fathers was sharpened by the experience of brutal veterans outside the home.

Yet their fathers' tempers were not necessarily as equable as the interviewees wished me to believe. The children of disabled men remembered irritated and moody fathers but they put this down to wounds. John Mingay was 'afraid of Father, because he was always … to me, he was always not well, and we had to be careful with him. Mother was the one that sorted us out, she'd … I can hear her saying, "Now, you've got to be careful today, boys, Father ain't too well", because he had trouble with his legs as well as his arm.' On those occasions – which in Mingay's memory seemed like 'always' – they had to tiptoe about the house. Ray Burgin's father never beat him or his mother, but he had a short temper. Ray attributed this to his headaches and frustration at not being able to see: 'the wounds that he had … didn't help, you know'.

Hints of more complicated histories of domestic tension sometimes emerged despite the insistence on peaceable fathers. When I asked Joyce Fey if her father ever lost his temper, she replied instantly, 'he would never have hit anybody. He never hit me, he never hit my brothers that I can remember.' She went on to recall a time when the boys next door had gotten into trouble with the police. Her father had sat her brothers around the table and told them that 'if they were in trouble with the police, it would be *as nothing* to the trouble they would be [in] with him. I shall never forget it! It was … quite incredible – the way he talked to them. You know, he was … they all loved him so much really.' She had been taken aback by the force of her father's tone, and felt it afresh in the interview, leading her to pause and reassert what a good father he was, as if she did not want to end the story on a negative note. When I asked John Mingay about his father's temper, his initial answer accorded with the image of the benevolent father: he was 'strict', and although there were times when he would 'promise' punishment, he never actually hit them. However, John went on to recall that if they talked during meals, his father would pick up a dessert spoon with his good hand and rap them over the knuckles. He paused, then added, 'I'd say he never hit us, but I'm telling you wrong', and he then remembered an occasion when his brother misbehaved and his father 'just picked him up, he put his foot behind him, and shot him down the hall, "Get to bed!" And that scared us, you know.' Talking to me, a First World War historian, the children were drawn to portray their veteran fathers in a positive light and were hesitant about memories that contradicted this image.

The fathers portrayed by the participants in this study bear close relation to J. B. Priestley's 'little man' or George Orwell's Englishman with his 'addiction to hobbies and spare-time occupations, the privateness of English life'.[43] As historians have shown, this image of domesticated masculinity became a national type between the wars, its features more sharply drawn through the contrast with Prussian aggression. The First World War soldier's transition to civvy street in this narrative is one of 'return to the gentle pleasures of hearth and home'.[44] Yet the transition was never as complete as the discourse has it. The interviews reveal how domesticity could function as a place of recovery, but traces of the violent past are harder to discern. The image of peaceable fathers carried weight not just because of the children's personal loyalties to their fathers, but as a national myth. The only topic which regularly aroused hostility in his father, said Jeffery Flower, was the mention of the Germans. Doris Perley's father refused to have sympathy for Germany after the Second World War: 'Bad people had to be punished.' The only time his father ever 'showed his authority' was when Dennis Johnson was called up to do his National Service and it looked like he might be posted in Germany. The authoritarian German was the mirror image of the suburban 'good father', and it was only when it came to his old enemy that the Englishman's own aggression could be freely voiced.

Contemporary attitudes towards parenting also shaped the children's memories. They viewed their fathers in relation to present-day standards which hold that violence of any kind towards children is unacceptable, and they censored memories that contradicted those norms. Moreover, in a climate that is attuned to the traumas suffered by soldiers in the First World War and in which pity is the overriding sentiment of remembrance, they found it difficult to volunteer negative or ambivalent feelings. They wanted me to understand that their fathers were not violent, but were capable of it, and approved the self-control it took them to keep their tempers in check. When they did something wrong, Pat Stamp recalled, 'we'd get a lecture off of him to say, "Now, I don't want to hit you", he said, "but if I do start, I'll not know when to stop, and you'll be sorry", and that was his excuse, so he never hit us.' Remembering times when they had been hit or felt frightened, the interviewees countered with assertions of love or excused violence as a reaction to war wounds. Just as the courts had done in domestic violence cases at the end of the war, they made adjustments for the veteran. They were proud that despite having gone through the 'war to end all wars', *their* father was not brutalised.

In 2014, after hearing a BBC World Service programme in which I talked about the impact of the First World War on the children of veterans, Rosemary Gitsham, whom I had interviewed three years earlier, wrote to me. She was struck by the fact that, despite serving in Gallipoli, Malta and the Somme, her father 'never suffered from shell shock and seemed to be a well adjusted chap, calm and friendly with everyone'. She went on to say that 'As a child of someone who must have suffered greatly I feel grateful that his trauma was not passed on to me. He was a great Dad, the best.'[45] She wanted to pay tribute to her father because of what he had *not* passed on, he was 'the best' because he only shared the positive aspects of his war with her.

The emergence of the 'involved father' in Britain between the wars is usually explained in terms of the decline in separate spheres and the emergence of the companionate marriage, and the demographic and economic shifts that intensified family life and facilitated fathers' time and home-based leisure. Yet as this study shows, the shift was also a product of the First World War. The promise of 'Homes for Heroes' was made in response to the sacrifices of citizens on the home and war fronts during the conflict. Domesticity acquired practical purpose and emotional resonance as a refuge from the past war while the private pastimes of recovery

– gardening, board games, hobbies and holidays – became symbols of national character. As the memories of children who grew up between the wars reveal, however, lived experience was more complex than the national mythology of domestic recuperation allows. Wishing to uphold the image of the benevolent father, they were reluctant to talk about family conflicts and regarded their fathers' occasional eruptions of anger as a legacy of the war that should be respected and not reproved.

Notes

1. S. Pooley and K. Qureshi (eds), 'Introduction', *Parenthood between Generations: Transforming Reproductive Cultures* (New York: Berghahn Books, 2016), 24–6.
2. Pooley and Qureshi, 'Introduction', 26–8; see also Luisa Passerini on transmission that occurs without verbalisation. 'Memories between Silence and Oblivion', in K. Hodgkin and S. Radstone (eds), *Contested Pasts: The Politics of Memory* (London: Routledge, 2003), 248.
3. The role of young women in care is discussed in Chapter 5.
4. IWM Photographs, Walter Hempshall, 2009-03-26/1. Thanks to James Wallis for reproductions of Walter Hempshall's postcards and photographs.
5. Passerini, 'Memories between Silence and Oblivion', 244.
6. J. Sturgeon, '*The Storyteller* by Walter Benjamin Review – a Master Thinker's Fiction', *The Guardian*, 1 August 2016.
7. S. Rose, *Which People's War? National Identity and Citizenship in Wartime Britain 1939–1945* (Oxford: Oxford University Press, 2003); A. Light, *Forever England: Femininity, Literature and Conservatism between the Wars* (London: Routledge, 1991); L. Noakes, *Dying for the Nation: Death, Grief and Bereavement in Second World War Britain* (Manchester: Manchester University Press, 2020), 55.
8. C. Mowat, *Britain between the Wars* (London: Methuen, 1955), 1.
9. S. Kent, *Making Peace: The Reconstruction of Gender in Interwar Britain* (Princeton: Princeton University Press, 1993), 97, 99.
10. Light, *Forever England*, 8. In his study of the interwar popular press, Adrian Bingham describes a shift in perceptions of masculinity that echoes Light. Some of the 'old values' of Imperial masculinity endured but there was increasing scrutiny of its codes and a belief that Great War veterans 'revulsed by brutality' would seek 'a quiet life' of domestic pleasures. *Gender, Modernity and the Popular Press in Inter-War*

Britain (Oxford: Oxford University Press, 2004), 197. Jon Lawrence also argues that ideas of national identity became more temperate and domesticated between the wars. J. Lawrence, 'Forging a Peaceable Kingdom: War, Violence, and Fear of Brutalization in Post–First World War Britain', *Journal of Modern History*, 75: 3 (September 2003), 557–89.

11 D. Cohen, *Household Gods: The British and Their Possessions* (New Haven: Yale, 2009), xii, 188–9.
12 J. Stevenson, *British Society 1914–45* (London: Penguin, 1984), 163.
13 D. Gittins, *Fair Sex: Family Size and Structure in Britain, 1900–39* (New York: St. Martin's Press, 1982), 33.
14 L. King, *Family Men: Fatherhood and Masculinity in Britain c. 1914–1960* (Oxford: Oxford University Press, 2015).
15 Quoted in J. Burnett, *A Social History of Housing 1815–1985* (London: Routledge, 1991), 220.
16 R. Reiss, *The Home I Want* (London: Hodder and Stoughton, 1918).
17 Stevenson, *British Society*, 222.
18 Burnett, *Social History of Housing*, 226.
19 J. Baxendale and C. Pawling, *Narrating the Thirties: A Decade in the Making, 1930 to the Present* (London: Macmillan, 1996), 116–18, 137–9.
20 As Rachel Hasted observes, 'personal wealth greatly affected the outcome and future life chances of First World War disabled veterans'. *Domestic Housing for Disabled Veterans 1900–2014* (London: Historic England, January 2016), 6.
21 D. Cohen, *The War Come Home: Disabled Veterans in Britain and Germany, 1914–1939* (Berkeley: University of California Press, 2001), 108.
22 Gittins, *Fair Sex*, 40; Bingham, *Gender, Modernity and the Popular Press*, 236.
23 Lynn Abrams makes a similar point about the impact of cramped housing on Scottish men's opportunities for a home-centred life. L. Abrams, '"There Was Nobody Like My Daddy": Fathers, the Family and the Marginalisation of Men in Modern Scotland', *Scottish Historical Review*, 78: 206 (October 1999), 224.
24 A. Hetherington, *British Widows of the First World War: The Forgotten Legion* (Barnsley: Pen and Sword, 2018), 34; J. Meyer, '"Not Septimus Now": Wives of Disabled Veterans and Cultural Memory of the First World War in Britain', *Women's History Review*, 13: 1 (2004), 119–20.
25 Hetherington, *British Widows*, 48.
26 Unpublished ms written by Margaret Reardon and given to the author: 'The Families of First World War Soldiers in Twentieth-Century Britain', 2.

27 S. Humphries, *A Labour of Love: The Experience of Parenthood in Britain 1900–1950* (London: Sidgwick & Jackson, 1993), 184.
28 Newcastle Museum, NSW, Herb Way dolls furniture c. 1925, https://newcastle-collections.ncc.nsw.gov.au/museum?page=search#view=list&id=6fd7&terms=%5B%22and%22%2C%5B%5B%22keywords%22%2C%22herb%20way%22%5D%2C%5B%22department%22%2C%22Museum%22%5D%2C%5B%22type%22%2C%22Story%22%2C%22%3C%3E%22%5D%5D%5D. Accessed 1 February 2023. The British veteran Edgar Yarwood produced a striking collection of miniature art deco furniture. H. Beckett, 'Doll's House Furniture Made by a Soldier Blighted by WW1', *Museum Crush*, 12 December 2022, https://museumcrush.org/the-dolls-house-furniture-made-by-a-soldier-blighted-by-wwi/. Accessed 27 January 2023.
29 R. Duffett, 'The War in Miniature: Queen Mary's Dolls' House and the Legacies of the First World War', *Cultural and Social History*, 16: 4 (2019), 431–49; see also R. Duffett, '"Playing Soldiers?": War, Boys, and the British Toy Industry', in L. Paul, R. R. Johnston and E. Short (eds), *Children's Literature and Culture of the First World War* (London: Routledge, 2015), 239–50.
30 S. Millhauser, 'The Fascination of the Miniature', *Grand Street*, 2: 4 (1983), 134.
31 W. R. Bion, *War Memoirs 1917–19* (London: Karnac Books, 1997), 94.
32 Millhauser, 'Fascination of the Miniature', 135.
33 P. Fussell, *Abroad: British Literary Travelling between the Wars* (Oxford: Oxford University Press, 1980), 4.
34 The memories promised by the family photography industry are invariably positive, Annette Kuhn argues: 'They *will* be shared, they *will* be happy – the tone of the seduction is quite imperious.' *Family Secrets: Acts of Memory and Imagination* (London: Verso, 2002), 23; L. Gloyn, V. Crewe, L. King and A. Woodham, 'The Ties That Bind: Materiality, Identity and the Life Course in the "Things" Families Keep', *Journal of Family History*, 43: 2 (2018), 161.
35 C. Emsley, 'Violent Crime in England in 1919: Post-War Anxieties and Press Narratives', *Continuity and Change*, 23: 1 (2008), 173–95; C. Emsley, *Soldier, Sailor, Beggarman, Thief: Crime and the British Armed Services since 1914* (Oxford: Oxford University Press, 2013), esp. chapter 6. On Australia see E. Nelson, 'Victims of War: The First World War, Returned Soldiers, and Understandings of Domestic Violence in Australia', *Journal of Women's History*, 19: 4 (2007), 83–106; S. Garton, *The Cost of War: Australians Return* (Melbourne: Oxford University Press, 1996), 198–200.
36 Nelson, 'Victims of War', 100.

37 J. Allen, *Sex and Secrets: Crime Involving Australian Women since 1880* (Oxford: Oxford University Press, Melbourne, 1990), 155. Raymond Evans concludes that 'Ex-diggers, so often, it appears, carried the war home in combat-ravaged minds and battle-hardened bodies, to inflict it as a private hell upon their wives and children.' 'Masculinism and Gendered Violence', in K. Saunders and R. Evans, *Gender Relations in Australia: Domination and Negotiation* (Sydney: Harcourt Brace Jovanovich, 1992), 203.
38 Bingham, *Gender, Modernity and the Popular Press*, 104, 237.
39 King, *Family Men*, 71–2; D. Thom, 'The Healthy Citizen of Empire or Juvenile Delinquent? Beating and Mental Health in the UK', in M. Gijswit-Hofstra and H. Marland (eds), *Cultures of Child Health in Britain and the Netherlands in the Twentieth Century* (Amsterdam: Rodopi, 2003), 189–212.
40 King, *Family Men*, 145. King argues that the '"bar" of good fatherhood was raised' in inter-war Britain. *Family Men*, 16. On public discourses of domesticity and fatherhood, see M. Collins, *Modern Love: An Intimate History of Men and Women in Twentieth Century Britain* (London: Atlantic Books, 2003), 90–5; Bingham, *Gender, Modernity and the Popular Press*, 237.
41 B. Van der Kolk, *The Body Keeps the Score: Brain, Mind, And Body in The Healing of Trauma* (New York: Penguin Books, 2015), 9–10, 25; Evans, 'Masculinism'; Garton, *Cost of War*; Nelson, 'Victims of War'; Emsley, *Soldier, Sailor*.
42 J. M. Strange, *Fatherhood and the British Working Class, 1865–1914* (Cambridge: Cambridge University Press, 2015), 180–3.
43 G. Orwell, 'England Your England', *The Lion and the Unicorn: Socialism and the English Genius* (London: Searchlight Books, 1941), 39.
44 Lawrence, 'Forging a Peaceable Kingdom', 588.
45 Letter from Rosemary Gitsham to M. Roper, 4 August 2014.

6

Playing at war and being at war

> Postwar shaded into prewar; war remembered or war prefigured was seldom absent.
> – Charles Mowat, *Britain Between the Wars*, 1955[1]

As German bombers rumbled over Lichfield during the Second World War, using the spires on the city's cathedral to guide their path to Birmingham, fifteen-year-old Margaret Seabrook and her sixteen-year-old brother would play Dover Patrol in the family bomb shelter. The naval strategy game, produced by H. P. Gibson between 1920 and the 1960s, was based on the exploits of the Dover Patrol Force, a British Navy unit whose most famous engagement was the Zeebrugge raid on the German U-boat base in 1918. Margaret remembers her brother's passion for Dover Patrol, and his passion too for making a note of every ship that sank during the war, a pastime which she now found 'horrifying'.

As a memory of bombing on the home front, Margaret's account is hardly dramatic.[2] Yet as Margaret herself perceives, the very notion of playing at war as war erupted overhead, the crisscrossing of her brother's interests between a game and the human toll of naval casualties and the telescoping of time as First World War sea battles were re-fought amidst the aerial battles of the Second, now seems extraordinary. Margaret's reminiscence is an example of Charles Mowat's observation, made in the second 'post-war' of the twentieth century, that people's reactions to the later conflict were shaped by the earlier one.[3] Children imagined the First World War while the Second took place around them. It was a source of play but also of military knowledge and attitudes to citizenship, service and nation.

This chapter is about the ways in which children imagined war in their play and the transitions they underwent as the memory of the past war bled into visions of another war, which after 1940 was often fought in the skies above their homes. The Second World War was experienced in different ways by the interviewees according to where they lived. The most graphic accounts of bombing were from those who grew up in cities like Bristol, London and Middlesbrough. John Frost's family were bombed out of their homes in Lewisham three times. For those living in rural areas and small towns like Margaret and her brother in Lichfield, it was more distant. Allan Pentney remembered the 'Woom woom woom' of planes to the north-west of their home in the Norfolk village of North Creake and finding out next morning that Coventry had been bombed, 'a hundred and twelve miles from us'. Age as well as proximity to the fighting shaped their experience.

Almost a quarter of a century separates the youngest from the oldest participants in this study. Around two-thirds were born between 1921 and 1930, fourteen in the first half of the 1920s, within the age range of those who could be called up for military service during the Second World War. Nine were born in the second half of the 1920s, and like Margaret – who joined the Harvest Camps organised by the Ministry of Agriculture – were too young to join up but volunteered in other ways. Seven were born in the first half of the 1930s and reached adolescence during the war, while the youngest had no living memory of the time before the Second World War and were barely of school age by its end. The Second World War had entered the lives of the thirty-five participants at different points, but it was the backdrop of adolescence and early adulthood for the mainstay born in the 1920s.

The first section of this chapter is about war imagined and the fragments of the First World War past that children borrowed from the wider culture and their parents in play. The First World War became more visible during the Second World War, and the second section investigates the earlier war histories that the later conflict exposed. The third section focuses on aerial bombing, the anxieties of children and young people, the survival skills they acquired and how they became military citizens. It is impossible to understand the subjectivities of children born in the 1920s and 30s without a sense of the past war that figured in their imaginings and how this shaped their reactions to the subsequent war.

Playing at war

In 'Playing at War', published in 1990, Graham Dawson develops a framework for thinking about the ways in which children internalise war culture.[4] The essay is an exercise in autobiographical memory, in which Dawson reflects on his childhood fascination with war and the representations of war from which masculine identities are constructed. As a young boy in the late 1950s, he loved to play the cowboy, wearing hats and toting a gun and holster, a persona approved by his family and captured in numerous snapshots. This personal 'masculine pleasure-culture of war' evolved during the 1960s as he became a collector of model soldiers and aircraft, and as he approached adolescence, became fascinated by military figures with socially marginal pasts that echoed Graham's own, such as the outsider-hero Captain Hornblower.

Dawson develops a form of what he calls 'double consciousness' as he reflects on his past, on the one hand reconstructing his childhood play and the fantasies that he invested in it, on the other, critically assessing his formation as a man and the gendered possibilities that the genres of the war hero suggest.[5] War play, he concludes, is an important means through which boys fashion identities *as* boys, a fashioning which shifts as they mature and engage with the materials of war culture – toys, TV shows, films, clothing and comics and popular fiction – in new ways. Through the imagination of war, personas and personal convictions are formed, and writing as he was in the wake of the Falklands/Malvinas war, Dawson was keen to expose the deep roots of popular patriotism.

For Dawson, growing up during the consumer boom of the late 1950s and 60s, the mass market was the primary source of war culture. In the 1920s and 30s, however, toys were mainly accessible to the middle classes, and children acquired their war culture from their elders and objects in the home as well as from commercial sources.[6] A memoir writer who grew up in London during the war recalled how, as he helped his father build an Anderson shelter in the back garden in 1939, 'I got my pistol, and dreamed I was in the trenches, in the Last Lot, and just about to lead my men Over the Top'.[7] Preparing for the war to come, children imagined the past war.

Although largely beyond the means of poor children growing up in Britain between the wars, toys, comics, children's annuals, fiction and the cinema were significant sources of war culture alongside more personal connections.[8] The first half of the twentieth century saw a significant expansion of commercial war culture for children. There was a boom in war games on the eve of the First World War, described by H. G. Wells in his best-selling book of 1913 *Little Wars*, the objective being to knock down wooden soldiers with a tiny cannon, paying strict attention to protocols like the distance that troops could advance and the timing of their manoeuvres. By 1914 around ten million toy soldiers were being produced annually in Britain.[9] During the First World War manufacturers expanded production from soldiers to the new technologies of modern warfare, producing miniatures that included tanks and even an 'exploding trench'.[10] Children were mobilised into war through enthusiasms that combined the military and technical. The connections between war and play were not just in children's heads but were economic. The Lord Roberts Workshops, which claimed to be Britain's largest toy maker in 1919, were set up to offer employment to disabled soldiers and sailors and their dependents.[11] They offered an extraordinarily diverse range of products from an almost full-scale model of a tank in 1917, which was produced for fund-raising purposes, to doll's houses and soft toys.[12] A child clutching their favourite doll or teddy from the Lord Roberts Workshops would have known that it was made by a disabled soldier or his family and had been purchased to help support them. Munitions companies were encouraged to go into toy production at the end of the First World War, but during the Second World War the trend went the other way: facing dwindling markets and a ban on metal materials, toy companies like Lines Brothers and Meccano began to produce parts for bombers, gas masks, life-jackets and munitions.[13] There was a close relationship between war and toy production in the early to mid-twentieth century.

Sales of some military toys declined in the post-war period and there was a trend towards soft toys and construction kits, perhaps influenced by anti-war sentiments and concerns about producing militarised citizens.[14] At the same time, overall consumer spending on toys rose by around a third, and they came within the reach of greater numbers of children.[15] Construction kit companies produced military models alongside civil engineering products like diggers, cranes and hoists. Meccano, for example, included First World

War tanks, ships, submarines and aircraft in its product range.¹⁶ The company played to the war's legacies in children's popular culture, offering models of the BE2 biplane that featured in the *Biggles* novels, and the Fokker Triplane flown by the 'Red Baron'. Toys like these could have a long life, passed down to younger siblings and friends, and sometimes from parents to their children: a First World War model infantry soldier or tank purchased during the First World War could still be in service during the 1940s.¹⁷

Children, as Emily Gallagher notes, innovate through play, yet are 'great cultural conservationists', and in her study 'Digging Deep', she shows how Australian children in the 1920s and 30s drew on the memory of the First World War, digging full-scale trenches in their back yards, role-playing as soldiers, wreaking vengeance on Germans and fashioning tanks, dreadnoughts, machine-guns and bayonets out of materials at hand. A single packet of seeds spread out on the floor could furnish an entire army. Drawing on household utensils, snatches of talk between adults and information acquired through newspapers, magazines and books, children domesticated the past war.¹⁸

They incorporated artefacts from the past war in their play. John Frost's father made a toy gun for him out of the butt of a Lee Enfield, replacing the rifle bolt with a gate bolt. No toy could possess more cachet than an actual weapon used by a father. Raymond Burgin had a 'sort of cowboy pistol' made for him by his blind veteran father, but it was no match for his friend's service revolver, 'a … a real pistol … [*laughs*] not one that he had any ammunition for, of course! It was his father's.' Children played in the sites of the past war. Vic Wiltshire and his friends used to go to a derelict army stable at Pampole Point in Bristol, where they would play cowboys and Indians in the remnants of trenches where horses were washed. Ex-servicemen sponsored the war play of the next generation: Bill Swann's toy soldiers were given to him by an ex-Navy officer who was a volunteer for the disabled veterans charity Lest We Forget.

Playing at war, boys learned about military culture and acquired skills from their fathers. Clive Jones already knew how to tie knots when he joined the Navy, as he used to practise on bits of string with his father, who had been an ordinary seaman during the First World War. Jefferey Flower's father bought him an electrical set with a buzzer and a light and taught him Morse code. Jefferey became animated as he remembered the fun he had with an air rifle bought by his father: 'in the swimming baths they had long corridors, and ... I could shoot candles out ... with this airgun. I had a Hector, it wasn't a very powerful one, but ... I used to stick soldiers up in the garden and psh ... psh ... psh ... psh.' His shooting practice put him at an advantage when he did National Service. Other recruits had trouble with the Bren gun during Basic Training, as they were instructed to only shoot two rounds on automatic: 'If you let it go dunk, dunk, dunk, they'd kick you in the ribs. "I said *two*."' Jeffery, though, had 'a feather touch ... du-dung ... du-dung'. Boys like Jeffery had been immersed in war culture since boyhood and, through their fathers and their games, had already acquired skills in soldiering. As he explained, 'I was shooting from a young age. And in the Army, I got quite good at shooting.'

They also learned from their fathers about the dangers of weapons. Writing for the BBC People's War project, Rob Brown recalled his First World War veteran father's belief that 'the intelligent training of his offspring would make them safer when dangerous munitions were found, and so we quickly learned the difference between live, fired and dummy ammunition and were well drilled in range discipline and "never pointing a gun at anyone", even if it was only a toy cap pistol'.[19] The panic felt by the eleven-year-old John Frost was palpable as remembered the time he picked up his brother's rifle and propped it on the windowsill:

> and I pulled the bolt back, a bullet came up, and I didn't expect that, you know ... because my dad had shown me about rifles, so I knew about pulling the bolt back, but I thought, 'It shouldn't be loaded.' And in panic, I pushed the bolt back, didn't I! [*laughs*] So I pushed the bullet, and there was a woman out in the gardens – because I was facing the gardens, and she was putting her washing out, and I was pointing the rifle, and I thought, 'My God!' ... so I put the rifle back.

John had not expected the rifle to be loaded and had made things worse by pushing the bolt. His confession to his parents set off a chain of admonitions. His father 'was just cross that I'd been so stupid as to do it'. Because the rifle was jammed, his brother had to take it back to the Home Guard, and they told his brother off for leaving the rifle unattended. The domestic authority of the father and the social authority of the military reinforced each other in a way that still unsettles John at the age of eighty-five.

Through play, children learned who was a legitimate target of violence, when violence was justified and how to exercise it. The leaders of the Axis powers were fair game. Jeffery Flower remembers drawing crowds around him at a local fair:

> there was 'Tojo' and 'Goering', and 'Hitler' and 'Mussolini' on a swing, with all their faces, with a stick behind, and you had a ball, and you had to knock these off the swinging platform! And I was good at it, so people were paying me to throw the ball! [*laughs*] I mean, they were only, say, from here to the piano away from you, but you still had to hit the stick dead on the top, for it to go off, and get your prize!

Children learned about the ethics of violence from their fathers. David Smith described a scene that might have come from Savile Lumley's recruitment poster, except it was not a warlike temperament that his father wished to communicate, but the need to treat the enemy humanely:

> Oh, toy soldiers, yes, yes! I had … quite a lot of toy soldiers. And certainly Father never discouraged me from playing soldiers! [*laughs*] There was one occasion, actually, when my elder brother was playing … with the soldiers, and shooting little guns at them with matchsticks in for shells, you know, and … we were playing, and this must have been in the sitting room, because Father was reading the paper by the fire, and this game was going on, you see, and Father looked up, and he said, 'Good Heavens!' he said, 'What are you doing?' And my brother had made a Meccano gibbet, and with springs on, and was hanging somebody, you see! [*laughs*] 'My God!' he said, 'What are you doing?' And my brother said, 'Oh, we're hanging the prisoners!' [*laughs*] And Father was horrified!

His father 'made a joke of it' but was conveying a serious lesson: 'he would sort of say, "God! You don't do that!", you know, "Prisoners of War, you don't hang them!"' The psychological experts who observed children's play during the Second World War found that they often enacted violent fantasies such as this, but through their fathers, they might also learn restraint.

The war's effect was apparent in the ways that parents engaged with their children's play. Other legacies were indirect, consisting of passions that fathers developed during the war and continued in other forms afterwards. Fascination with mobility was a feature of interwar modernity, but there was often a military backstory behind the record-breaking attempts that thrilled public audiences. Malcolm Campbell, whose Blue Bird vehicle tipped 300 mph on the Bonneville salt flats in 1935, was a dispatch rider in the war before becoming a pilot in the RFC. John Alcock and Arthur Brown, the first to make a transatlantic flight in 1919, were military pilots, and they attempted the record in the Vickers Vimy, a modified First World War bomber. The first two British winners of the Schneider Trophy, Henry Charles Biard and Sidney Webster, were also RAF veterans. Planes and aeronautical technology featured regularly in interwar publications like the *Boys Own Paper* and *The Modern Boy*. The ex-RFC pilot and author of the *Biggles* series, W. E. Johns, for example, wrote a spotter's column in the early 1930s called 'What Plane Is That?'[20] The war histories of these men formed part of their celebrity. Airspeed records, and the technology developed for them, foreshadowed the war to come: Britain's iconic fighter plane, the Supermarine Spitfire, evolved from the company's race-winning entries for the Schneider Trophy in the early 1930s.

Veteran fathers followed the exploits of these modern pioneers and passed their enthusiasm on to their children. John Frost and his father were captivated by the mechanical technology of trains, planes, ships and cars. As a boy his father took him to see the 'big train' from Edinburgh, and he once saw *The Mallard* pass through Pickering; 'the telegraph poles were cracking as they went past this open window, and Dad says, "Oh, they must doing [*sic*] over the 100 now!" You know, it was … it was great! And I was always interested in trains with him.' They would look at cars together and go to air shows.

John's father served in the Royal Navy as a stoker from 1912 until 1921 and acquired his mechanical knowledge through working in the engine room. He knew a lot about the design and armoury of naval craft as well. John would occasionally show him photos of Navy vessels, and 'we would talk about it, he'd say, "Oh well, this is that", and "this is that", and he'd tell me what it was about, you know, some of them … had torpedo tubes around the funnel.' He showed John how to draw warships: 'He'd say, "Oh, well, the gun would be farther back than that" he said, "because, don't forget, it's got to turn round. You've got to get that gun round. If you have it too close, they won't be able to fire back that way."'

His father's enthusiasms had given John an entrée to war culture and he maintained his father's love of machines and military technology. Before moving to Middlesbrough, he lived in a bungalow near Biggin Hill where he used to watch the air shows. For his seventieth birthday he did a freefall jump from 10,000 feet, and to celebrate his seventy-fifth he went track racing in a Porsche. As he remarked, 'Well, I like speed, I like driving, you know!' Ties between fathers and sons were often based on enthusiasms that harked back to the past war and retained military associations.

Like John's father, Rosemary Gitsham's father Vernon had a wide range of hobbies and pastimes. He was fascinated by new technology. While serving in France he became interested in aeroplanes, and after a short period as a watchmaker, joined the RAF in the early 1920s and became a flight engineer. Aeronautics was not just a job; speed and flight were his passions, and along with his flight logbooks he kept newspaper cuttings of the transatlantic flight attempts in the 1930s.

Rosemary – his only child – spent her entire career working in aviation. She was able to obtain free flights through her job and had gone on trips to Egypt and the Middle East, the places that had fascinated her father during his war service. On the way into the house, I noticed two Honda Civics from the mid-1990s parked in the garage. I remarked on the fact that they were identical, and she explained that she and her husband kept one for day-to-day use, and the other in pristine condition, a modern classic. Rosemary had maintained her father's fascination with machines, a family legacy that had stretched across almost a century.

The First World War that featured in the games children played in the 1920s and 30s was not just imagined. Its traces were palpable as children held First World War weapons, donned uniforms and army kit and were given advice by their fathers. War play was not detached from the adult world, but a means through which children acquired knowledge in a militarised society and became fighting citizens. The next section considers their memories of the outbreak of the Second World War, a war that was their own, but in which fragments of the First World War reappeared.

The Great War reappears

The Second World War had contradictory effects on the memories of the participants in this study. Looking back in later life, they had vivid memories of the conflict. In part, there was a social explanation for this, as they were among the few remaining eyewitnesses, and their stories were encouraged by communities of remembrance from schools to Armistice Day commemorations. In addition, the intensity of the bombing and the damage and disruption it caused were seared into their minds and impelled their remembering. Aerial warfare, as Helen Jones remarks in her study of civilians on the Home Front, shook mental as well as geographical landscapes and 'it was as if their lives before and after were lived in parentheses'.[21] It was hard enough for my interviewees to recall the time before the war, let alone the aftermath of a war before their time. Even the older respondents – teenagers when the war broke out – had trouble remembering the pre-war years. Rosemary Gitsham mentioned in passing a neighbour who had shell shock, and when I asked her to tell me more, she replied:

> *RG:* I can't remember really. I don't think he often went out. He lived with his sister, you know, and … it's a very long time ago, isn't it!
> *MR:* It is a long time ago. Yes.
> *RG:* I mean, I remember the Second World War like anything … but you're not doing that!

Watching the behaviour and reactions of their parents during the Second World War, they became more conscious of the First World War. Memories of the outbreak in 1939 were sharpened by the recognition that this was the second global conflict that their parents had lived through.[22] As John Mingay recalled:

> I can see it now, we sat and listened to Mr. Chamberlain, 3rd September, saying that 'We are at war', and Father just got up out of his chair and went out. He'd gone about a quarter of an hour, and Mother said, 'John, go and see if you can find him', and so I went out, and he was at the top of our field – we had a smallholding … I went up to Father at the top of the field, he was crying his eyes out. I mean, he'd got this arm in a sling, in a leather sling, which he had to wear all the time, and his … his … his words were to me – I'd never

heard him swear before that, and he said, 'bloody hell', he said, 'All I went through, and now you've got to go and do the same.' And I said to him, 'Well, Father, that's the way it is.'

His father was upset at the prospect of what his sons – John, James, who would be made a POW, and Frederick, who would die in 1944 when his Wellington bomber crashed – were about to be put through. His generation had sacrificed themselves, he had lost an arm, but to what end? There was a sense of foreboding among some. Margaret Reardon's family was on holiday in Lowestoft at the time, and she recalled how her father became 'agitated' watching the Regatta when a German destroyer was seen to turn back from the harbour. 'That's a bad sign', he had said, 'The War is coming.'[23] Her mother came from West Hartlepool and had witnessed the naval raids in 1914: 'she knew about the bombardment. I think they thought the worst was going to happen.'

Rosemary Gitsham's father, who was serving in the RAF at Andover, was posted to a new base the day after war was declared. She, their dog and a 'few bits and pieces' were bundled into the family car and driven to Oxford by her 'terrified' mother, who had only just started taking driving lessons and never drove again. In their different ways, accounts like these record the disquiet that parents felt at the prospect of another war.

In some ways, the Second World War enhanced the authority of veteran fathers. They knew about weapons and defences and were called on for advice in Home Front defence.[24] Their ability to recognise threats, stay cool under fire and make sound judgements in a crisis was valued, and they expected to hold sway in decisions about precautions. Veteran fathers took charge in a battle that encircled the home. His father 'guided us', John Frost explained, and Elizabeth Bartholomew recalled that her father instructed them about 'what we should do and what we shouldn't'.

Doris Perley's father was 'very cool and calm and collected. Tough family I came from!' Bill Swann remembered the disabled veterans living at Oswald Stoll mansions casually tossing incendiary bombs off the roof: 'I mean, they weren't scared.' After hearing an explosion during the first bombing raid in Bristol, Brenda Aubrey ran outside to see an eerie glow. 'Very lights falling!', said her father, the term used by First World War soldiers for incendiary bombs.

While they expected to take charge, the responsibility of protecting the family could be stressful. Joyce Fey remembered her father 'listening, very intently' to the radio news broadcasts, trying to get a sense of the war's progress so that he could take the right precautions, and being annoyed when the children weren't quiet.

Alertness to threats was a hallmark of the old soldier, as Jessica Hammett notes, and some interviewees described being saved by the quick reactions of their fathers.[25] When a German fighter plane suddenly appeared while Joyce Fey and her father were walking on Ranmore Common, 'my father shoved me in the ditch, and there was a horrible rattling noise, I don't know if it was machine-gun fire or what, but he was very quick, and we neither of us were hurt'. John Morgan recalled the squadron of planes that appeared low over a hedge near Bradwell airfield, which John and his brothers assumed were Spitfires: 'You could see the pilots in them, you know, and we're sort of waving to them, until suddenly … Dad suddenly saw, and said, "Get in … get inside!"' John's father was a volunteer in the Observer Corps but his reactions were also sharpened by familiarity with danger.

War service could lead fathers to hold strong views about the best way to keep their families safe, and they were not afraid to ignore government advice.[26] Many preferred to keep the family close. Jefferey Flower's father was an ARP warden, but he decided that his family would be safer under the staircase than in the communal shelter. Rosemary Game, Eileen Pollock and David Smith also used shelters in their homes. George Elders's father in Middlesbrough built a 'bloody big' shelter, as did Margaret Reardon's father in London, while Elizabeth Burdett and her siblings slept throughout the Blitz in the shelter her father constructed in the back garden of their house in Peterborough.

Fathers could be stubborn when it came to safety. Joyce Fey recalled the 'huge row' that broke out between her parents when constructing their Anderson shelter. The instructions had said that the door should open inward, but her father had seen blown-in dugouts in the First World War and thought this was 'daft'. He reasoned that 'If we get buried in it, if we open it inwards, everything will come in on us.' When their shelter was bombed, the family were unable to open the door and had to be dug out, but Fey was convinced that her father had been right: 'So he built it opening outwards, and it ... and we were buried, and they ... nothing came in, and we were safe.'

It was important for the children to feel that their fathers were decisive and in control, and mothers were positioned as the anxious ones. Margaret Reardon's mother developed alopecia and lost her hair.[27] Brenda Aubrey described her mum as 'more nervous, and my dad weren't ... you know, nervous or nothing, you know'. 'Everything always worried her', said Joyce Fey of her mother, who stammered and was a heavy smoker. Joyce conveyed the differences between her mother and father in a memory of the moment after their shelter was bombed. Her mother tried to light a cigarette, and like an NCO instructing his platoon, her father shouted at her to 'Put that out, we don't know how much oxygen we've got.' Behaviour that accorded with gender norms could help contain children's fears, yet the contrast between anxious mothers and capable fathers was not always as clear as the interviewees declared. The return of war could stir up apprehension as well as courage. During the first raid in Bristol, Jefferey Flower told me, his father, who was on his own in the house at the time, finished off half a bottle of whiskey.

The outbreak of the Second World War uncovered new legacies of the First World War. Despite the 'dad's army' mythology of men past their prime, the war on the home front enhanced the authority of fathers in some ways. Their skills and experience became valuable, and the children could see them doing their bit as fire watchers, ARP wardens and observers. Children also witnessed more troubling legacies as a new threat exposed old defences among their fathers. The war as their parents experienced it, however, became less central to the children as they matured and became military citizens themselves.

Being at war

For children growing up in cities like Bristol and London after 1939, playing at war and being at war morphed into one other. Bombing created new opportunities for play and the excitement of venturing into the ruins was remembered by many. After the first raid on Bristol Jeffery Flower walked into the city centre to check out the damage. He remembers being fascinated by a shrapnel-pocked car parked outside the university. Bill Swann went sight-seeing with a friend the day after the 7 August raid on London's docks, and was in the middle of London Bridge when the evening raid began: 'I can remember walking back, and shrapnel would start coming down, and we'd nip into doorways!' Looking back, he found his insouciance rather hard to explain: 'But as I say, we just treated it as something ... natural! [*laughs*]'. Like many children, David Smith and John Frost would collect shrapnel from the anti-aircraft batteries and compete with their friends to see who had the biggest chunks. Sometimes, John recalled with wonderment that was still apparent, 'they were still warm!' John and his friends would hold competitions to see who could construct the longest clip from the bullet cases strewn around London's streets. For a while, John lived in Kent, where he and his friends would rush to the sites of crashed aircraft and cannibalise parts as souvenirs. As he explained, 'I found it exciting.' Girls also rummaged in the ruins. June Teape used to search out for shards of Perspex, the high-tech material used in aircraft screens, hoping to fashion jewellery from it.[28]

The element of danger added to the excitement. As Gabriel Moshenska has argued, for children in the Second World War, play could be a means of managing the traumas of aerial warfare. Sharp shards of hot shrapnel, even unexploded shells, became playthings, and children were attracted by their violent potential. Picking over the ruins was risky, but the dangers were more controllable than the randomness of bombing.[29] Freud provides a possible explanation for children's compulsion to flirt with danger and turn lethal objects into playthings in his 1920 essay 'Beyond the Pleasure Principle'. He describes a game played by a small boy (Freud's grandson Ernst) while his father was away at the war and his mother had momentarily left him on his own. The boy would throw a cotton reel away and then pull it back with evident satisfaction, exclaiming 'Ooh', 'ah', an expression which Freud interpreted as 'fort', 'da', or 'gone', 'there'. As Freud saw it, the game gave his grandson a means of control over his parents' absences, since he was now the one to initiate the separations.[30] This, Freud concluded, might be what drew some patients to remember unpleasant experiences that one might assume they were keen to avoid. Turning the remnants of lethal weapons into collectables, plundering from the wreckage of crashed planes and ducking in and out of shelters during raids, children exercised control over arbitrary violence.

They lived on a knife-edge between excitement and terror, and seventy years on, some of them still showed signs of trauma as they recounted what they saw.[31] A vivid picture came to my mind as George Elders described the scene shortly after a bomb fell outside the school in Staithes: 'there was one lad there, he was laid … just laid on his back, and he'd lost a leg, and he died'. Allan Pentney's speech was halting as he tried to tell me about the time an aircraft crashed outside their home in North Creake: '20 yards away, and it was the middle of the night … *bang*! "What the hell is that?" Jumped up … went outside, went round … the Mosquito landed right in this man's … went down … bang, wallop.'

They were haunted by memories of freak events. Mary Burdett remembers the tale told by the maid who was supposed to look after them in their bomb shelter, about a woman hit in her shelter when the glint of her gold filling caught the eye of a German pilot. Bombing created grotesque landscapes, and the disorder stuck in children's minds. When the Germans bombed Victoria Park in Bristol, said Jeffery Flower, the golden eagle atop the park fountain was set into flight and 'Nobody ever found it. It must have shattered.' There was an element of the uncanny about some of their memories and they doubted themselves. Mary Burdett described the shock of seeing empty space at the end of the terrace where her brother's friend's house had once been. The house had sheared off at the connecting wall, leaving only the bath which jutted out from the edge of the first floor. The vision seemed so bizarre as to be scarcely believable, yet Mary had recently come across a photo of the house in the local newspaper and was astonished to find that it confirmed her personal memory.

Joyce Fey was ten years old when her house in South London was destroyed. Her pauses, unfinished sentences and tremors show the effort it still takes to explain what happened:

MR: What do you remember?
JF: My mother, my father, my little sister – who was just a baby. Erm … it's hard to … I think the bomb actually hit the shelter … because we heard a bang, you know, a sort of … as if it had hit the shelter, and then we seemed to be lifting and dropping. We ended

up in the bottom of a crater. The people next door – there was an old lady and her ... her son and daughter ... well, her daughter and her husband – their shelter was ... was concreted inside, ours wasn't, and they were thrown against the back of the house, and the old lady was decapitated ...
MR: Oh, dear.
JF: ... which was awful. Erm ... and ... we were there for some time. I still have a ... a ... shake. We were there for some time, and ... then we heard noises outside, and somebody came and dug us out. And people at the end of the garden – because there was another row behind us, it was all very terracey, along the Anstey Road was all Victorian terraces, and another Victorian terrace behind us, and they had got out, you know, when the raid ended, and they had ... counted the shelters and realised one was missing, so the only place it could be was in the bottom of the crater, and so they came and looked for us and got us out. There was a baby found on the roof of the house opposite! Yes! Crying ... they heard it crying, and it was up there by itself. Yes.

The scene remains hard to comprehend, the miracle of the family's survival, the entire shelter lifted by the blast and dumped in the bottom of a crater, her neighbour decapitated. Joyce ends with the bizarre story of the baby perched on the terrace roof, a tiny being shot into space from the protective orbit of family and home. City dwellers like Joyce Fey, Jefferey Flower and John Frost talked about the bombing, not just because it was a moment when their personal past had coincided with momentous historical events, but because it was disturbing. Like Freud's grandson with his cotton reel game, they felt compelled to return to the trauma.

Children were not just passive eyewitnesses to destruction, but participants whose hobbies and leisure contributed to the war effort. They helped turf over the ground in their backyards and local parks and tended vegetables. They raised money for war causes.[32] Organisations such as the Boy Scouts and Girl Guides helped with Civil Defence duties like fire-watching and the construction of bomb shelters, while the Girls Training Corps and the Air Training Corps Cadets taught children how to prepare for raids and readied them for military service. Encouraged by the government, Spotters Clubs were set up in 1941 and by 1943 over three hundred were in existence. The clubs drew on children's fascination with aviation, using model aircraft to teach the differences between aircraft and issuing badges and certificates of proficiency to their members.[33] In an extraordinary merging of fictional and actual transmission of war culture, W. E. Johns was commissioned by the Air Ministry to write articles on plane spotting in girls' and boys' papers.[34] School children gathered wreckage from the air war for recycling, but it also formed the basis of personal collections and might be put on display in local shop windows as war trophies. Among Margaret Seabrook's wartime ephemera was her Harvest Camp badge. The camp had special significance for Margaret, not just because she was away from home doing her bit, but because it was where she met her future husband.

The interviewees were proud of their warcraft. They knew how to distinguish British from German planes. 'You can always tell a German plane because the engine's in the front of the planes, always in a straight row', said George Elders. Allan Pentney joined the Observer Corps at eighteen and was proud of his expertise: 'We were very good at aircraft spotting. We knew the aircraft well. At night, of course, we knew the sound of them. But as the day come, we plotted them ... we could see the numbers of aircraft, and reported the numbers. And ... you know, we'd see hundreds at a time going over us! Incredible!' They could identify different types of bombs. 'Breadbaskets', explained John Frost, were 'full of incendiary bombs, and they used to come down in parachutes, and as they hit the ground, the baskets would break open', leaving a strong smell of magnesium. They knew when to take cover. David Smith recalled a moment of family comedy when, hearing the whistle of an approaching bomb during the Blitz, he and his brother dived to the floor, while his father, who was working up north and had come home for the weekend, remained standing. He had not recognised the sound and was puzzled by the antics of his sons, for whom ducking had become second nature. Children's sharp eyesight and ears made them particularly good at sensing danger, and families and the government relied on their alertness.[35]

The legacies of the First World War emerged again when children reached eighteen and were called up. Family history sometimes influenced their decisions. Margaret Reardon joined the ATS because it was Army, and 'that was a family thing ... we were ... an Army family'. Beryl Manthorp's father had been a corporal in the

RASC and was pleased when she joined the ATS and became a PTI instructor in an anti-aircraft regiment, finishing the war as a warrant officer. Bill Swann's father was 'pleased' when Bill decided to volunteer for the RAF rather than wait to be called up. Until then he had considered Bill a 'bit of a softie' and thought that the services would toughen him up.[36] Dennis Johnson felt closer to his father when he was on National Service in the early 1950s than when father and son were living under the same roof: 'I always say to my wife, "You know, I got to know my dad more through when I was in North Africa", yeah. And he wrote to me about once every three or four weeks. I said, "I got to know him more through his letters", yeah.' Veteran fathers knew what their sons were going through during basic training and gave advice. His father never talked about the First World War, John Mingay said, 'until the next war started, and then, I mean, he was full of it then, you know, giving us boys tips of what to do and what not to do'. Dispensing advice gave fathers too old to fight a vicarious role, being a domestic parallel of the 'useful masculinity' they performed in organisations like the Home Guard.

As Penny Summerfield observes in her study of young women in the Second World War, families had varying reactions to the prospect of military service.[37] Despite the myth of old soldiers anxious to have another go at the Germans, some parents were reluctant to join the war effort. Hedley Green's mother was working night shifts during the war, and when his father was asked to do fire-watching duty, he appealed to the local tribunal on the grounds that somebody needed to be at home with their two children. He felt that he and his wife, both ex-service, had done their bit in the First World War. Doris Perley's father volunteered for the police at the outbreak of war so that he could avoid the call-up, as he did not want to leave his family.

Some refused to support their children's wishes to join up. As Summerfield notes, this could reflect a patriarchal culture in the family, with authoritarian fathers being resistant to the state's encroachment on their control over their children's futures, particularly when it came to daughters.[38] Yet resistance could also stem from a wish that their children would not have to go through what they went through. Eileen Pollock recalls her father pleading with his brother not to join up at the start of the Second World War.

June Teape's father, who had seen some bloody sights as an RAMC stretcher bearer in France, did not want her to become a nurse. Others experienced the ambiguities of the First World War's legacies. Beryl Manthorp's mother had been a Red Cross nurse in the First World War and continued to take an active part in voluntary work for the Red Cross after the war ended. During the Second World War, she threw herself into nursing work for the Red Cross. Beryl felt that her mother had given her a mixed message, however, as she had steered Beryl towards the St John Ambulance rather than the Red Cross. Beryl's mother closely guarded the professional skills she had learned in the First World War, and Beryl thought she was uneasy at the prospect of having her daughter on her own patch and 'didn't want to own me'. Her mother seemed to find it difficult to acknowledge Beryl's success in the army and things at home were tense after she returned to Norwich at the end of the war: 'she seemed to have an awful distrust in my ability to look after myself'.[39]

Parents' reactions to their children's service might not only be animated by pride and cooperation with the state, but by rivalry and perhaps even envy, as sons and daughters now had opportunities to contribute to a national cause in a way they could not, and enjoy the kind of esteem and glamour that service on the home front lacked. The wartime divide between the young fit male and the comic 'dad's army' figure had a female counterpart in the contrast between servicewomen turned mothers and housewives, and daughters in uniform determined to show what they could do.[40]

Attitudes to the Germans also revealed the tensions between generations. Many remarked on the enmity expressed by otherwise peaceful fathers and regarded it as a characteristic of that generation. Their fathers' hatred might be a source of awkwardness and embarrassment. Dennis Johnson recalled his father's reaction when Dennis was called up to do his National Service:

> He said, 'If they'd given a posting to Germany, you wouldn't have gone.' 'I wouldn't have gone, Dad?' 'No, you'd have stayed in this house, even if the police come for you, I could chase them. But no way are you going to Germany.' He couldn't stand anybody saying it. And he lost a son there. That was him, you know. I said, 'Well, Dad', I said, 'you know, the War was over ... like ten year ago', you know, but it was still in his mind, you see.

Her father, said Joyce Fey bluntly, 'hated the Germans, full stop, because of ... because of what they were doing'. Jefferey Flower recalled that his 'family weren't exactly liking Germans! So I was ... I was sort of brought up on that sort of tenor, so it made it very awkward for me later on when I went to Germany on business! [*laughs*]'. Her father's view of the Germans was a source of frustration for Rosemary Game too, but looking back she understood that he was reacting to the First World War and how it affected his family:

> His biggest fault ... he was a good man, devout Christian, but his one big flaw was, he hated everything German. Erm ... that, of course, was the result of his generation, and the fact that his little brother had been killed, and he never forgave the entire German nation. I can hear him now, 'The only good German is a dead one!' And as a teenager, of course, I remember wailing to my mother, 'It's not Christian!' you know ... [*laughs*] and she trying to explain ... you know. But you have to be ... you have to be grown up to understand that kind of shift of personality. You don't understand it as a teenager. Everything is black and white.
>
> MR: Can you remember how he was in the lead up to the Second World War?
>
> EG: The same kind of attitude – that you couldn't trust any of them. You know, you simply couldn't trust anything German ... except that he tended to use the word 'Bosch', or 'Hun'. Yeah. In a sense, I think he gave the impression that he wasn't surprised.

When her mother bought a German sewing machine, Rosemary's father ordered her to take it back to the store. He would not forgive. Doris Perley's parents had brought her up to believe that 'the Germans were "bad"' and 'Bad people had to be punished.' Yet when Doris met German lodgers in Dunstan after the war, she found to her surprise that 'they were the most polite people you ever did meet! ... As soon as they got to the corner of the street, off would come their caps and "good morning", that sort of thing.'

Hatred of the Germans was not universal among the First World War generation, however. Despite being made a prisoner of war, George Elders's father was grateful for the care given him by a German doctor, who he said had saved his life after he was hit in the back by shrapnel. Brian Morgan's father did not hold any animosity towards the Germans. He had converted to the Plymouth Brethren between the wars and held to their principles; members of the Brethren could serve but did not carry arms. Vic Wiltshire's father 'often said the best people he ever met were the Germans ... which ... a lot of people say that. But that was him.' Though influenced by a second encounter with the same enemy, individual histories and beliefs also shaped their parents' attitudes towards the Germans.

The interviewees in this study are marked by their location in time, growing up between the two global wars of the twentieth century. The oldest were born when the First World War was only just 'post', became adolescents at a time when war was 'prefigured' and served in their own war. The youngest were born when the Second World War was prefigured and became adolescents during the conflict. For these children, the imagination, experience and memory of war were tightly meshed. They formed their identifications as boys and girls through family histories of service and the hardware and detritus of war as well as through commercial war culture. They bore the legacies of war in different ways. Sons learned warcraft from their fathers, but the ethos of duty and service was transmitted to daughters as well as sons. The wars that children imagined, and which formed them as men and women, British subjects, and military citizens, were in the recent past, and after 1939, waged in the skies above. Their homes became targets and sites of defence, and the things they played with could radiate the very heat of battle. What Rosie Kennedy remarks about children during the First World War is perhaps even more true of children in the Second: they were not simply socialised into military culture from above, they 'also mobilised themselves'.[41] The shared experience of total war and military service could strengthen ties between generations, but also marked moments of disruption and strain as children became combatants, and returned soldiers became 'old soldiers'.

Notes

1 C. Mowat, *Britain between the Wars* (Chicago: Chicago University Press, 1955), 1.
2 For other memories of sheltering in air raids, see the BBC archive *WW2 People's War: An Archive of World War Two Memories*, www.bbc.co

.uk/history/ww2peopleswar/categories/c1161/. Accessed 10 November 2021. See also Gabriel Moshenska on how sheltering became part of children's games. *Material Cultures of Childhood in Second World War Britain* (London: Routledge, 2021), 88, 104.

3 Sue Grayzel demonstrates this in her study *At Home and Under Fire: Air Raids and Culture in Britain from the Great War to the Blitz* (Cambridge: Cambridge University Press, 2012). Aerial attacks during the First World War, she argues, laid the basis for a civilian identity in the Second World War based on home defence.

4 G. Dawson, 'Playing at War: An Autobiographical Approach to Boyhood Fantasy and Masculinity', *Oral History*, 18: 1 (Spring, 1990), 44–53.

5 Dawson, 'Playing at War', 45, 52.

6 J. Morley, 'Dad "Never Said Much" But … Young Men and Great War Veterans in Day-to-Day-Life in Interwar Britain', *Twentieth Century British History*, 29: 2 (June 2018), 209.

7 R. Westall, *Children of the Blitz: Memories of Wartime Childhood* (New York: Viking, 1985), 70.

8 A basic Meccano kit cost more than a third of a labourer's weekly wage. R. Wainman, '"Engineering for Boys": Meccano and the Shaping of a Technical Vision of Boyhood in Twentieth-Century Britain', *Cultural and Social History*, 14: 3 (2017), 384.

9 R. Duffett, '"Playing Soldiers?": War, Boys, and the British Toy Industry', in L. Paul, R. R. Johnston and E. Short (eds), *Children's Literature and Culture of the First World War* (London: Routledge, 2015), 239–48; R. Kennedy, *The Children's War: Britain, 1914–1918* (Basingstoke: Palgrave Macmillan, 2014), 57–61.

10 Duffett, 'Playing Soldiers?', 239.

11 *Games and Toys* (October 1915), 232; *Games and Toys* (January 1919), 248.

12 *Games and Toys* (January 1919), 248; R. Green, 'Dolls Houses from the Lord Roberts Memorial Workshops', *Dolls' Houses Past & Present*, 17 June 2013, www.dollshousespastandpresent.com/issue17june2013p4.htm. Accessed 10 November 2021; British Pathé, 'London's "Tank"', www.britishpathe.com/video/VLVA6MQJP23R2YV7B378CULYTJTYM-DISABLED-SOLDIERS-CONSTRUCT-TANK/query/+LORD+ROBERTS+WORKSHOP. Accessed 10 November 2021.

13 Duffett, 'Playing Soldiers', 241–2.

14 Kennedy, *Children's War*, 62.

15 C. More, *Britain in the Twentieth Century* (London: Routledge, 2006), 109.

16 A selection of interwar Meccano manual covers can be found at www.meccanoindex.co.uk/Mmanuals/1928/Covers.php?id=1614346836. Accessed 10 November 2021.

17 A First World War model tank sits alongside *Biggles* books on the mantle of the boys' bedroom in the Imperial War Museum's 1940s House. 'The 1940s House: The Boys' Bedroom', www.youtube.com/watch?v=-xjXzY-L6s. Accessed 10 November 2021.
18 E. Gallagher, 'Digging Deep: Playing at War in Australia, 1914–1939', *History Australia*, 16: 1 (2019), 169–89.
19 R. Brown, 'Son of a Home Guard Company Commander', BBC archive *WW2 People's War*, article ID: A2356841, contributed on 27 February 2004, www.bbc.co.uk/history/ww2peopleswar/stories/41/a2356841.shtml. Accessed 11 November 2021.
20 H. Jones, *British Civilians in the Front Line* (Manchester: Manchester University Press, 2006), 124.
21 Jones, *British Civilians*, 3.
22 See J. Hammett on First World War veterans' appreciation of 'the seriousness of war'. '"It's in the Blood, Isn't It?" The Contested Status of First World War Veterans in Second World War Civil Defence', *Cultural and Social History*, 14: 3 (2017), 349.
23 For other examples, see L. Smith (ed.), *Young Voices: British Children Remember the Second World War* (London: Viking, 2007), 21, 88.
24 G. Sheffield, 'The Shadow of the Somme: The Influence of the First World War on British Soldiers' Perceptions and Behaviour in the Second World War', in P. Addison and A. Calder (eds), *Time to Kill, The Soldier's Experience of War in the West 1939–45* (London: Pimlico, 1997), 31; Hammett, 'It's in the Blood', 345.
25 Hammett, 'It's in the Blood', 348.
26 Hammett, 'It's in the Blood', 343; P. Summerfield and C. Peniston-Bird on the 'hard-bitten' veteran, *Contesting Home Defence: Men, Women and the Home Guard in the Second World War* (Manchester: Manchester University Press, 2007), 221.
27 Unpublished ms written by Margaret Reardon and given to the author: 'The Families of First World War Soldiers in Twentieth-Century Britain', 8.
28 On Perspex collectors, see Moshenska, *Material Cultures*, 157.
29 Moshenska, *Material Cultures*, 42, 61–2, 141. See also Gallagher on play as a means of managing wartime anxieties. 'Digging Deep', 8.
30 S. Freud, 'Beyond the Pleasure Principle', *The Standard Edition of the Complete Psychological Works of Sigmund Freud*, 18 (1920), 1–64.
31 G. Ben-Ezer, 'Trauma Signals in Life Stories', in K. M. Rogers, S. Leydesdorff and G. Dawson (eds), *Trauma and Life Stories: International Perspectives* (London: Routledge, 1999), 29–45; L. Dodd, '"It Did Not Traumatise Me at All": Childhood "Trauma" in French Oral Narratives of Wartime Bombing', *Oral History*, 41: 2 (Autumn 2013), 37–48.

32 J. Schwitzer and K. Thompson, 'Children in Wartime', *Oral History*, 15: 2 (Autumn 1987), 34.
33 Jones, *British Civilians*, 122. For a personal memory of the Spotting Clubs, see F. W. C. Smith, 'My Memories of WWII', BBC archive *WW2 People's War*, article ID: A4654451, contributed on 1 August 2005, www.bbc.co.uk/history/ww2peopleswar/stories/51/a4654451.shtml. Accessed 11 November 2021.
34 Jones, *British Civilians*, 125.
35 Schwitzer and Thompson, 'Children in Wartime', 33.
36 The belief that the younger generation was 'soft' was common among veterans of the First World War. Morley, 'Dad "Never Said Much"', 16.
37 P. Summerfield, *Reconstructing Women's Wartime Lives: Discourse and Subjectivity in Oral Histories of the Second World War* (Manchester: Manchester University Press, 1998), 43–75.
38 Summerfield, *Reconstructing Women's Wartime Lives*, 53–8.
39 Summerfield also notes cases where mothers had 'used the war to make their own bids for freedom' but blocked their daughters. *Reconstructing Women's Wartime Lives*, 55.
40 See Summerfield on military masculinities and the contrast between civilian and soldier. *Reconstructing Women's Wartime Lives*, 116–21.
41 Kennedy, *Children's War*, 8; S. Audoin-Rouzeau and A. Becker, *1914–18: Understanding the Great War* (New York: Hill & Wang, 2003), 111.

7

Daughters, care and citizenship

The statue sculpted in 1918 by Clare Sheridan (a cousin of Winston Churchill), shows an Australian soldier and a young girl at St Dunstan's, the hostel for blind servicemen set up in 1915 by the publisher Arthur Pearson. The blinded soldier stands at full height, wearing the uniform and slouch hat of the Anzac, his face tilted upwards in a proud pose. The girl, her youth accentuated by the difference in height between them, rests her hand gently around his forearm and looks down at the way ahead.

Sheridan's statue is suggestive of the role of young women in the aftermath of the First World War. Though only in her early thirties, Sheridan had experienced a succession of personal tragedies during the war. She had taken to sculpting after the death of her child in 1914, and shortly after giving birth to a second child the following year, her husband was killed at the battle of Loos. Yet this sculpture, created in the final year of the conflict, depicts not death but the fates of the survivors and the responsibilities that would come to lie on the shoulders of the young. The image of the 'generous self-sacrificing woman', which David Gerber notes is common in representations of the disabled veteran, here encompasses girlhood.[1]

Sheridan's image was one of many during the war to portray a young girl guiding a blind veteran. Her sculpture bears a close relation to a sketch by the renowned Dutch cartoonist Louis Raemakers of a young girl called Ruby Smith, the daughter of the head gardener at St Dunstan's who was known to the men of St Dunstan's as 'Little Ruby'. Ruby's image appeared frequently in St Dunstan's publications and postcards bearing the caption 'Blinded for You'.[2]

Figure 7.1 A girl leading a blind Australian soldier from St Dunstan's Hostel. Model by Clare Sheridan, 1918. IWM Museum Exhibits Collection, Q 66143. All rights reserved.

In 1990, then aged seventy-seven, Ruby recalled her childhood at St Dunstan's:

> I used to go up to them and chat to them and we'd walk around just holding hands and walking along together. If they wanted to go to a certain workshop I knew them all off by heart and where to find everything ... Some of the Australian chaps were quite tall, well-built men and I always remember how my little hand seemed so small in their big hands.[3]

Figure 7.2 Louis Raemaker's sketch of a blind soldier and his guide. Courtesy of Blind Veterans UK. All rights reserved.

Ruby's story was not just known by the staff and men at St Dunstan's, but was widely circulated in publicity and newspapers. Her image became part of the charity's brand and she became a minor celebrity, receiving gifts and letters congratulating her on her service to the men.[4]

This chapter is about the social and emotional expectations that surrounded young women's caregiving after the war, and how these expectations shaped the lives of the daughters of disabled men. Seth Koven has written about the 'affinity' between the 'crippled child' and the disabled soldier, and how children in institutions during the war were drawn into the care of recovering soldiers, being seen to play a key role in the restoration of their morale and the transition from wounded soldier to civilian. The 'affinity', however, was not

Figure 7.3 St Dunstan's postcard 'Blinded for You', 1916. Courtesy of Blind Veterans UK. All rights reserved.

confined to the disabled child, or to the war, but is part of the history of girlhood and adolescence after the war. Girls often feature in representations of the recovery and care of disabled men. In the reminiscence above, Ruby describes the relationship from the blind soldier's perspective of touch, and the feel of her 'little' hand in his. It is a personal representation of the social expectations that surrounded care, which extolled the capacity of girls to put themselves in the place of the unsighted man, to navigate the world he could not see and relate to him in a manner seemingly uncomplicated by condescension or disgust. Ruby describes guiding the men around the grounds of St Dunstan's 'by heart', her ambiguous phrase suggesting the conscientiousness and affection that care should entail.

Thirteen of the interviewees in this study had a father with a war disability, over a third of the sample, a higher proportion than among the general population of ex-servicemen between the wars. Their prominence in the project is partly due to the way it was conceived and advertised. People who had grown up with a disabled veteran father immediately saw the personal relevance of a study about the war's impact on the family and were quick to respond. Disability was a telling legacy in the early twenty-first century public memory of the First World War, and in their family histories victimhood was literally embodied.

Yet the contemporary context of remembrance does not provide a sufficient explanation of their motivations. War disability had far-reaching effects on children, particularly daughters. It created economic and emotional stresses, and gendered obligations that were felt from a young age. The impact was particularly noticeable among the seven daughters of disabled soldiers, most of whom had been drawn into family networks of care that lasted well beyond adulthood. While much has been written about the immediate impact of war disability and how it was treated in the transition from soldier to civilian, here I want to trace the history of care across the twentieth century through the perspective of daughters. What was their experience of disability, and what expectations, tensions and conflicts surrounded the giving of care? What kind of life was possible for women who had helped look after veterans from a young age? The accounts here suggest that daughters' contributions were little recognised beyond the immediate family and neighbourhood, and that, in contrast to Little Ruby, or the young women in organisations like the Girl Guides between the wars, they experienced care as a personal obligation rather than a form of patriotic service.[5] When they compared themselves to other young women in the Second World War, the pressures to help look after disabled fathers and support their mothers were recalled as obstacles to citizenship rather than a means of access to it.

The first section of the chapter discusses the role of children in institutions like St Dunstan's, and the gendered and emotional economies of care within such institutions. As Deborah Cohen shows in her comparative study of disabled soldiers, the voluntary sector played a particularly active role in Britain, stepping in where the state would not.[6] However, charitable support often came with moral strings which included assumptions about gender, age and the appropriate roles of family members in care. The second section investigates the interviewees' memories of childhood, fathers and caregiving, while the third section discusses their experience as adults. The daughters of disabled First World War servicemen look back on their childhoods from a present in which girls have greater freedom from domesticity, and in which children's obligations to help support their parents are no longer assumed. Spanning girlhood on the one hand and late life on the other, the interviews allow us to look beyond the usual chronologies of demobilisation, return and aftermath to reveal how the conflict shaped the lives of descendants across a century.

Gender and the emotional economies of voluntary care

Expectations about age, masculinity and femininity were inherent in the assistance given to blinded ex-servicemen by St Dunstan's, a central tenet being to rehabilitate the man and eschew dependence, a credo summed up in the title of the memoir written by the blinded soldier known as 'Territorial': 'V.O.B.', or victory over blindness.[7] Pearson himself set a standard that veterans were encouraged to follow. Recovering servicemen recount the impression made by his 'jaunty self-confidence' and conviction that the blind should 'not only be as self-reliant as possible but that we should be seen to be self-reliant'.[8]

It was not just the figure of Pearson, but the networks of relationships at St Dunstan's that provided a model of the gender arrangements that should support the disabled soldier. Most of the nurses, guides and family visitors who did outreach work were women. Pearson was the unquestioned father figure, his position as founder and benefactor honoured in the posy of flowers put together by Ruby's father from the gardens of the Regent's Park property, which she would bring him each week. Pearson had lost his sight before the war and relied on the help of the Voluntary Aid Detachment (VAD) Irene Mace, 'the girl who was his nurse, reader and guide'. She exemplified the cross-generational, cross-gender relationships of care that would later characterise those between disabled fathers and their daughters.[9] Irene went on to marry Pearson's right-hand man Ian Fraser, who took over the running of St Dunstan's after Pearson's unexpected death. Fraser and Irene were married on the second anniversary of his wounding in a symbolic act of triumph over misfortune.[10] Like Pearson, Fraser attributed the beginnings of his recovery to Irene's care.[11] From its earliest days, the organisation extended its reach to the home. Editions of *St Dunstan's Review* recorded the marriages of St Dunstan's men and the births of their children, and they wrote back about their experiences as breadwinning fathers and husbands. Many of the occupations that men were trained in, such as basket and mat-making or poultry farming, could be done from home.[12] Pearson insisted that rehabilitation depended on a man's capacity to be productive, and wives and children were drawn into roles that would support his labour. At its farm in the Midlands, for example, St Dunstan's offered training to the wives and relatives of men who had taken up poultry farming.[13]

The value of marriage for the blind serviceman was discussed in a special debate among the inmates of St Dunstan's in July 1917, Pearson emphasising the aspect of care when he stated that if a wife truly loved a St Dunstan's man, she 'loved him both as a mother and as a wife'.[14] When Walter Burgin's poultry farm became too much to manage on his own, the matron at St Dunstan's arranged a date with a sister at the hostel whom he eventually married.[15] Relationships like these were founded on care which was sometimes professional before it became intimate, combined aspects of marriage and maternity, and could establish expectations that transferred across generations.

Domesticity, then – the help of wives and the solidity and emotional security offered by family life – underpinned the treatment offered to the disabled veteran. Yet it was not only women as nurses and wives who figured in his rehabilitation as a citizen and man, but children. In part this was for commercial reasons: the charity's fund-raising postcards of fathers deprived of the sight of their children were intended to solicit the very pity that Pearson and Fraser were otherwise anxious to avoid.

Pearson was quick to recognise that the children of disabled soldiers would need additional support for medical, educational and other costs not covered by the Ministry of Pensions, and employed visitors to ascertain the needs of families through an After Care Fund, established in August 1918. The charity also established a

Figure 7.4 'You've Not Said How I've Growed, Daddy!', Thomas Henry, circa 1916. Courtesy of the Mary Evans Picture Library. All rights reserved.

children's fund to support the educational and medical needs of the dependents of blind servicemen and put on entertainment for them.[16] Bill Swann, who grew up in the Oswald Stoll Mansions in South London which was occupied by disabled veterans and their families, envied the children of St Dunstan's men because they went out on day trips, got gifts at Christmas and gained free admission to football matches.[17] In 1922 and 1923 St Dunstan's ran a beauty pageant for the children's fund. Studio portraits of the winning babies were published in *St Dunstan's Review*, highlighting the pleasures that blind fathers were missing out on, and the need to help support their families.

The value of the child was more than monetary, however. Little Ruby's story is an example of the mobilisation of children into the war effort. As Tammy Proctor and Rosie Kennedy have shown, organisations like the Girl Guides expanded rapidly during the war, teaching girls to sew, cook and clean so they could be useful companions to the soldier.[18] Ruby's help was understood as a form of patriotic duty, an expression of the young girl's gratitude towards men who had, as the St Dunstan's postcards put it, been 'blinded for you'. There is 'no act more sacred, none more patriotic' than the care of the disabled soldier, wrote T. P. O'Connor in his essay for *The Queen's Gift Book*.[19] The care given by children was thought to have qualities that were not typically found in adults. Promoting its baby competition, St Dunstan's commended the cheering effect of being among children: 'we all know what a pleasure and comfort children can be, especially for a blind man'.[20] 'Territorial', who had lost his sight in 1915, recalled in his memoir the help given by the Boy Scouts, who used to run messages, escort the men to buses and trains and row boats for them in the park. It was not their *labour* that he appreciated most, but how the boys contributed to 'the general cheerful atmosphere prevailing everywhere'.[21]

Helpful as the scouts were, in his life outside St Dunstan's it was the unsolicited aid of an eight-year-old girl that made the deepest impression on 'Territorial'. She would appear each morning from a run-down tenement as he was on his way to the tramcar; initially, her brothers would accompany her, but eventually it was just her. He recalled her 'clean and soft' hand in his, and her bravery on one occasion when a herd of bullocks on the loose swept past and she steered him into the safety of a shop. She had kept her cool and 'never let go my hand', he wrote, prompting a man in the shop to commend the girl's 'magnificent' sense of responsibility.[22]

The incident had impressed on 'Territorial' the girl's bravery, but simultaneously too, his own dependence. The help of a young girl could be accepted without the pity that a disabled soldier – schooled by institutions like St Dunstan's to prize his independence and eschew victimhood – might feel when offered help by an adult. The major initial obstacle to his recovery, wrote Lord Fraser, was 'fear of being the object of pity and emotional sympathy', and a feeling that this might 'sap this desire to be self-reliant'.[23] He found it 'irritating to have to be helped' and 'suffered from the fear that people were looking at me in a pitying way'.[24] Representations of the disabled soldier stressed the enervating effects of pity. 'Don't pity the disabled man – find him a job', proclaimed a YMCA poster at the end of the war.[25] The magazine for disabled soldiers, *Reveille*, edited by the novelist John Galsworthy, described the damaging impact of pity. Hospital routines sapped the disabled soldier's independence and threatened to turn him into a child, 'suffering' from patronage.[26] The French pioneer of help for blinded soldiers, Brieux, thought that adults needed to serve an 'apprenticeship' if they were to care properly for the men, and he recounted the comments of a man whose guide invariably left bruises on his arm, the helper clutching him too tight in his anxiety that he might fall over. Do-gooding women were singled out for criticism for their narcissistic sensitivity to horror.[27] Adults' concerns about how to help merely 'stamp in his mental misery', Brieux concluded.[28]

Children, however, were thought to be natural companions for the disabled man. The facially disfigured veteran Stanley Cohen was wary of going out in public but felt able to teach at his local Sunday School, the children being curious rather than revulsed by his condition. 'With children he was safe', remarks his historian Juliet Nicholson.[29] Dependent themselves, children could recognise the disabled soldier's dependence, and their care was assumed to be free from condescension. 'Territorial' admired these qualities in the girl who offered to be his guide, and in his own daughter. She had modelled her behaviour on his from a very young age, tracing her fingers over her books as if reading braille. She was an expert guide by the age of three, and he had often enjoyed her 'sweet company' when out walking, 'her little hand in mine'. The help of young girls was assumed to be given not out of pity, embarrassment or the wish to appear charitable, but as Ruby put it, 'by heart'. The affinity between the child and the disabled soldier was not just 'representational', as Koven concluded, but central to the emotional and institutional economies of care

Idealised depictions like these tell us little about children's feelings at the time, but much about how adults wished them to be. Retrospective accounts suggest that sympathy was not the only reaction that a child felt on encountering a disabled veteran; wounds could be deeply discomfiting. Pam Parish, whose story is told by Juliet Nicholson in *The Great Silence*, dreaded the visits of a local veteran with a facial wound, who their mother encouraged to call by. She would instruct Pam to give the man hello kisses but, repelled by his disfigurement, Pam and her sister would do everything they could to avoid contact with him.[30] The vivid descriptions of wounds given by the participants in this study suggest that, as children, they found war-damaged bodies disturbing. The notion of girlhood in particular as an 'apprenticeship' for care was oblivious to how girls themselves felt, being in essence a form of emotional conscription in a campaign to shore up the wounded veteran.

Daughters, citizens and workers

The changes in the position of young women are much discussed in the social histories of interwar Britain, which document the growth of new employment based on their labour, the significance of their contributions to family incomes in a time of insecure male employment and the emergence of new forms of leisure.[31] Young women were key figures in the rise of the consumer industries, voting with their feet as they left domestic work for factories which offered them higher wages and greater freedom. Their incomes and mobility were further increased by the Second World War and the demands of mobilisation. At the same time, the fall in completed family size, improved housing and the diffusion of labour-saving devices permitted more leisure.[32] The women interviewed by Clare Langhamer recall their youth as a time of relative freedom, with 'no major responsibilities' and 'nobody to bother about'.[33] Sally Alexander has written about the psychological shifts that accompanied economic and social changes in interwar Britain, a new sense of independence and glamour, inspired in part by Hollywood idols, and a clear sense of generational difference between daughters and the domestic concerns of their mothers.[34]

The situation of the daughters of disabled soldiers was often at odds with this picture. Selina Todd notes that the greater freedom afforded to some young women was not just the result of economic shifts, but could arise from emotional considerations between mothers and daughters.[35] The 'maternal aspiration' to provide greater personal freedom was less apparent among the daughters of disabled soldiers, however, who often experienced a rapid transition into domestic roles.[36] A key element was the family's economic situation, as daughters' incomes were critical in homes where a war pension was inadequate or non-existent, and their help at home was needed. Even when money was not short, disability faced young women with expectations of care more familiar to their mothers' generation than to their own. Bill Swann, whose double amputee father needed help with dressing, washing and walking, explained the divisions of labour in his family:

> I think my sister did most of the helping out ... like the girls always got lumbered, didn't they ... yeah, I'm afraid I have a guilty feeling about ... I don't think I ever did really help as much as I should have done, or could have done – not that I was ever asked to, you know, because that's the point ... I think the way they treated kids, the girl was expected to help out, where the boys weren't.

As they looked back three-quarters of a century later, the daughters of disabled soldiers evoked the quality of attentiveness associated with the image of Little Ruby. Brenda Aubrey knew exactly what caused her father problems and why:

> I suppose his stump was about that long [measures with her hands]. And he had a white ... they used to send him a white stump sock – he called them that ... I don't know if that's what they were called, you know – and ... they were fine, but, of course, in the very hot weather, he used to get trouble with perspiration and soreness, you know, but nothing bothered him. He was ... he could ... you know ... hurry and everything, you know, and that's an integral part of my dad, he was ... you know, friendly, and quite a nice ... he wasn't very tall, like me, and quite a nice little man he was really, you know.

Brenda's description of her father repeats the tensions between compassion and admiration at the overcoming of adversity that had characterised discussions at the end of the war. Her mention of the 'trouble' that her father's stump sock caused him brings an immediate counterclaim that 'nothing bothered him'. Brenda goes on to stress how active her father was despite having just one leg, how he could 'hurry and everything', and she finishes with an admiring vision of him as a 'nice little man' in which his disability is discounted. There are two voices here, one attuned to her father's difficulties from a young age, the other wanting to counter a negative image of him as a victim and assert his personal triumph over disability.[37]

Dora Kneebone's account shows how the care given by the daughters of disabled veterans was normalised. They did not necessarily think of themselves as different from other girls growing up in the 1930s. Dora's father had a leg wound and although it caused him pain, he could garden and had a successful career as a printer in the City of London. From a young age, Dora had helped him:

> if he sat down when he came in [from work] ... I thought, 'Oh, I'll go in and take his shoes off for him' ... Thinking back, when I told a girl, a woman, a proper woman, posh woman, in Wembley, that I used to take Daddy's shoes off, she said, 'You took his shoes off for him, Dora?' So I said, 'Yes. Well, he needed to have them taken off, and it was easier for me to do it for him', and she didn't say a word, because she's a ... great church-goer, whereas I skip in and out of church! [*laughs*] Well, yes, I mean, I ... oh gosh ... no, let's not say any more!

Dora's description resonates with Little Ruby's account and the memoirs of 'Territorial'. What is interesting in Dora's account, however, is that the rituals surrounding her father's return seem to have been entirely private, and she was unaware until late in life that personal care like this was not typical among girls of her generation. She felt embarrassed when it was questioned, and in a private settling of scores, took pleasure in thinking herself more Christian than her church-going companion. Dora mentioned her friend's comment three times in our meetings, on one occasion remarking rather angrily, 'didn't she know the story of Christ and the washing of the feet?'[38]

The narratives of these daughters evoke aspects of what Ilany Kogan calls 'primary identification' among the children of Holocaust survivors, who are highly attuned to how their parents are feeling, and who – in a kind of generational reversal – come to feel responsible for alleviating the parent's pain.[39] To an extent, these obligations were felt by sons as well, but as my interviewees note, the housework and personal care in the homes of disabled soldiers usually fell to daughters.[40]

The adolescence and early adulthood of these women were shaped by their negotiations with their mothers about care, and they experienced tensions between obligation and independence. After Marion Armstrong's father died on her ninth birthday, her mother supplemented the family income with sewing and cleaning jobs close to home. As the eldest daughter with two younger siblings, the responsibility to help fell on Marion. She contrasted her situation with that of her older brother, who had won a place at grammar school and went on to become a Squadron Leader in the RAF during the Second World War. Marion passed the first half of the entry examinations for the grammar school, she explained, but the financial burden on her mother was in her mind throughout, and she decided not to complete them: 'there again, you see, this is how it affects a child. I was worried sick for fear I passed, because I knew my mother couldn't afford the uniform.'

Marion left school at fourteen and began work in a local grocers' shop. During the Second World War, she said, 'all I wanted to do was go in the Forces, and learn how to drive', but her brother, who was on overseas service, wrote saying 'Please don't volunteer. My mother's got two of us in.' Her mother was also keen for her to stay at the grocer's because as manageress at a time of rationing, she could get hold of 'more or less what I wanted!'. Her wage, moreover, increased the family income by almost a third: 'I remember how proud I was to give her ten shillings, and I kept 2/6d., and clothed myself. And … oh, she was thrilled.' The fact that Marion could remember the exact amount of her contribution shows the pleasure she felt in being able to support her mother, yet she also framed her story as one of missed opportunities.

When I asked Marion if she had ever felt frustrated or disappointed about not joining up, her reply seemed to cancel out the feelings she expressed earlier in the interview:

> I just accepted it. I really did think I'd get called up, but, of course, the War ended … and, you know, that was it. And the firm wouldn't let me go anyway. But … no, I didn't … no. We grew up … I think … I think because all the relatives were so sorry for my mother, because she nursed my dad for years, as I say, and it was hard … She had it very hard, and I think all the relatives drummed it into us, 'Look after your mother, Marion, because she's had it so hard.' I think we just knew we had to look after her. I just accepted the fact. I never resented her. But … we got on well.

During our interview, Marion played out the different emotional demands that she experienced as the daughter of a disabled soldier. Having expressed the wish to follow her brother into the war, she then rehearsed all the reasons why this was not possible, and explained that she not only 'accepted' her situation, but was proud of the help she gave. Marion's story is a counterpoint to the interwar history of 'maternal aspiration' for daughters. Her mother's needs had been 'drummed in' to her by family and neighbours, and even in late life, in an era where women's career ambitions are encouraged, she found it difficult to acknowledge her desire for greater independence.

Lives of caregiving

To this point, I have focused on the impact of war disability on young women, and how its demands shaped families' reactions to the changing social expectations of young women between the wars. Yet the entire lives of these women had sometimes been dominated by care. The gendered emotional scripts associated with care, moreover, had not only affected them as daughters, but as women, wives and workers.

Brenda Aubrey

There were war-disabled men on both sides of Brenda Aubrey's family, her father having lost a leg in the war and her husband's father being blinded. Brenda was recently widowed when I interviewed her in late 2013 and wanted to tell the stories of two families and two daughters, herself and her sister-in-law Joan. Joan had taken over the care of her father after her mother's death, and eventually father and daughter moved from Bristol to a purpose-built home constructed by St Dunstan's in Brighton. While there, Joan met and married another First World War veteran, George Killingbeck. He was blind and had lost an arm in the war, and had won a British Empire Medal for his work as a braille teacher and fund-raiser for St Dunstan's. Joan then became the caregiver for Killingbeck and her father. The gendered arrangements that were established in the early days of St Dunstan's, with marriages based on care and daughters as carers, were operating within Brenda's family half a century later.

Brenda's interview reveals the emotional expectations that these arrangements placed on her. She recalled an awkward conversation with Killingbeck (her then-brother-in-law):

> *BA:* Well, I remember, we went to Brighton, and George could do everything – vacuum, everything – but he couldn't tie his shoelaces, and I said, 'I'll tie them, George', and I bent down, and he said, 'You don't come … Harold don't come here often enough to see his dad, you know, Brenda', and I said, 'We can't afford it, George.' 'You know we'd always pay him his fare, and there's no need for the three of you to come', he said. And I thought, 'Oh!' But he never told Harold anything, only ever me. He always told me off, you know! [*laughs*] But he was well thought of in St Dunstan's, and he was a Freemason, and … you know, very … he was the Grand Master once …
>
> *MR:* What was his name?
> *BA:* George Killingbeck.
> *MR:* Right … Did you feel a bit guilty when he said that?
> *BA:* Yeah, of course you did. But, I mean, it was so far. We never had a car then, you know, and we were bringing up Elaine [her daughter], and I wasn't working and … you know … Wills' [the tobacco company] money didn't go up too much then. After it did, you know. And you couldn't keep asking them for money, could you – or I wouldn't – not say, 'Could you pay my fare and I'll come and see my dad', you know!

Tensions around gender and care permeate Brenda's story about her encounter with George. An attentive guide, she bends down to tie up his shoelaces, a memory, however, whose utterance seems to imply that the disabled man was dependant, and she immediately counters by assuring me of his competence ('George could do everything'). Brenda was annoyed that Killingbeck had chosen to tick her off rather than her husband, and that he was not sympathetic to their wish to visit Brighton as a family. But she didn't dare criticise him outright, as he was a bigwig in St Dunstan's and a Mason. She is also protective of her *husband's* dignity, as we see in the last sentence when she switches to the first person and imagines the humiliation that Harold would feel having to go cap in hand to St Dunstan's for his train fare.

Brenda's situation shows the kinds of emotional relationships that could develop around the care of disabled soldiers across the lives of women. She experiences them as a daughter, a wife, a daughter-in-law and a sister-in-law. Her role in care moves between the domestic and the institutional through the relationship with St Dunstan's and her in-laws. Her story shows the personal pressures placed on women by the social expectations around care, vulnerable to criticism that they were not doing enough, and feeling accountable to other disabled men because of marriage. It reveals the effects of changing gender norms too, for although in 2013 Brenda was hesitant to give full vent to her feelings about Killingbeck, she was probably more able to express her annoyance then than she would have been as a young wife in the 1950s.

Jean Brown

Jean Brown's story also shows how care for the disabled veteran could extend across life, its networks providing opportunities but also constraining women. After her father was blinded at Arras in 1917, St Dunstan's supported his training as a physiotherapist, and helped him to set up a practice in the family home in Reading which he ran from the drawing room. Jean had watched him working from a young age and decided to train as a physiotherapist herself, taking a job in the Reading hospital. Like Marion Armstrong, her decision to stay close to home was based on conscience and awareness of her mother's situation. Her three brothers were ordained ministers working in parishes across the UK, and Jean felt that 'my mother needed support really … so, erm, yes, I felt that was the right thing'.

After her mother died in 1963, home help took over the care of her father. Jean was unmarried and continued to live at home, and when in 1977 the help became poorly, Jean decided to resign from her job at the Reading hospital to look after her father, who was then in his early nineties. The more infirm he became, the less able she felt to leave the house:

> towards the end, I found it very stressful, and my brother in Cornwall, they said I could go down for a holiday if I could get someone to look after him, and I got one of these nurses … well, a Gardener's Nurse I think it was. Anyway, so I went on this holiday, and then I wished

> I hadn't, because it was not long after that that he died, when I … I came home and, yes, because actually, he said to me, 'I wish you could have another holiday', which was … you know, it was nice of him to think like that, wasn't it.

Listening to Jean, I was struck by the guilt that she still felt about her holiday. She had needed a break yet felt bad when she was away. The memory of her father's 'nice' reaction on her return – not resentful, but sympathetic – makes her even more regretful, a feeling that his death shortly after intensified. A professional carer herself, she recognised that these feelings were inherent to care, and after telling me this, she recalled that as a child, trips to London were surrounded by anxiety as her mother 'always felt she'd got to get back home. Yes. Didn't want to be away too long.' The anxieties of care – felt whether present or absent – were carried by two generations of women.

Jean's life until her father died – where she lived, her choice of career and even retirement – had revolved around the family's efforts to support the disabled veteran. Although she did not say so directly, these responsibilities affected her ability to form romantic attachments as well. At the end of our interview, Jean pointed to a photo on her mantelpiece. It was of a man living a few doors away with whom she had begun a relationship in 2002. For the next ten years, they went out 'and had very nice times together'. When I asked if she sometimes regretted that looking after her father had taken up so much of her life, she responded 'Well, not, not now. I think I did at the time. I sort of felt, "When am I going to be able to do something else?" you know. I think I did a bit.' Having found a way to 'do something else' later in her seventies, she was now less regretful.

As I saw it, the war seemed to cast a shadow across Jean's life. Yet this was not how she saw it; she had cared for her father because she loved him, and her later romance had left her with few regrets. Jean's account reveals the tensions between my focus, as a social historian, on the personal costs of caregiving and Jean's sense of a life lived well enough.

This chapter has considered the impact of the First World War through the perspective of the daughters of disabled soldiers and their experiences of caregiving. Their accounts differ from those of the sons considered in the previous chapter, whose relationships with their First World War veteran fathers had often helped them find their feet in the armed services during the Second World War and in national service.[41] The daughters in this study regarded their help as a private moral obligation. It did not carry the ideological freight of pride in service that the Little Ruby image suggests. They sometimes recalled frustration at the responsibilities it was assumed they would bear, but they were also proud of their care, and regretful when in their eyes it fell short. What emerges from the interviews is a rather different picture of young women's lives in the early to mid-twentieth century than the social histories of the period portray. Where the historical narratives emphasise greater opportunities for girls to define a role as useful citizens, these women record the economic and emotional stresses of disability, the failures of the state, the moral expectations that surrounded voluntary organisations and the pressures to conform to traditional ideals of women's place.

The ways in which demands like these might shape the subjectivities of young women are conveyed by the novelist and feminist Doris Lessing, born in 1919, her father an amputee and her mother a nurse. Lessing's autobiographical writings, from the 1994 memoir *Under My Skin* to the 2007 novel *Alfred and Emily*, convey the place of the war in the psychic landscape of a daughter. She describes how the relationship between her parents began in the aftermath as her mother was nursing her father in hospital. She records her father's manful attempts to flout his disability, riding horses and running one-legged in school races, but also his nightmares and depression. She writes of the discomforts her father's stump caused him with the intimate knowledge of someone who has stood by and imagined what this must feel like. She describes her mother's stoicism, energy, sociability and competence in domestic organisation, an outward display whose cracks were exposed when she had a breakdown. Lessing recalls feeling 'desperately sorry for her', even whilst she planned to run away.[42]

On the face of it, Lessing's life of political activism and rebellion against gender norms contrasts with the lives of the daughters of disabled soldiers in this study, who in their different ways had bowed to social pressures. Yet they all attest to the power of an emotional script that prized the young girl's capacity to identify with the suffering of the soldier. 'Do children feel their parents' emotions?', Lessing asks in the blurb on the dust jacket of *Alfred and Emily*, and continues, 'Yes, we do, and it is a legacy I could have done without. What is the use of it? It is as if that old war is in my own memory, my own consciousness.'[43]

Notes

1 D. Gerber, 'Introduction: Finding Disabled Veterans in History', in D. Gerber (ed.), *Disabled Veterans in History* (Michigan: Michigan University Press, 2012), 9.
2 Blinded Soldiers and Sailor's Care Committee, *Report of St Dunstan's Hostel for Blinded Soldiers and Sailors for the Year Ended March 26th 1916*; 'Little Ruby Drawing: The Story Behind the Iconic Drawing of Little Ruby', http://100objects.blindveterans.org.uk/little-ruby-drawing/. Accessed 5 February 2020. A further variation of the Ruby theme appears on the frontispiece of *The Queen's Gift Book*, a volume produced to encourage donations to Queen Mary's convalescent homes. Two elegant women frame Hugh Thomson's picture, while a blind soldier guided by a young girl are just visible in the background. Thanks to Gary Haines for drawing my attention to this image. Queen Mary, *The Queen's Gift Book: In Aid of Queen Mary's Convalescent Auxiliary Hospitals. For Soldiers and Sailors Who Have Lost Their Limbs in the War* (London: Hodder and Stoughton, 1916).
3 R. Crane, 'Cover Girl 1916: Ruby Crane Talking to David Castleton', *St Dunstan's Review* (January–Feburary 1990), 4–6.
4 Crane, 'Cover Girl 1916', 5.
5 On young women and citizenship between the wars, see T. Proctor, 'Daughters of War: Girl Guides and Service after the First World War', *Twentieth Century British History* (2021), hwab032, doi: 10.1093/tcbh/hwab032, 1–26.
6 Deborah Cohen estimates that war pensions took up around 20 per cent of the annual German budget between 1925 and 1930, compared with 7 per cent in Britain. *The War Come Home: Disabled Veterans in Britain and Germany, 1914–1939* (Berkeley: University of California Press, 2001), 4.
7 F. Reid, *Broken Men: Shell Shock, Treatment and Recovery in Britain 1014–1930* (London: Continuum, 2010); J. Anderson, *War, Disability and Rehabilitation in Britain: 'Soul of a Nation'* (Manchester: Manchester University Press, 2011), 7; J. Meyer, '"Not Septimus Now": Wives of Disabled Veterans and Cultural Memory of the First World War in Britain', *Women's History Review*, 13: 1 (2004), 117–38.

8 Lord Fraser of Lonsdale, *My Story of St Dunstan's* (London: George G. Harrap, 1961), 55.
9 Fraser, *My Story*, 56.
10 Fraser, *My Story*, 64.
11 Fraser, *My Story*, 17.
12 Two interviewees had blind fathers who were trained by St Dunstan's. Brenda Aubrey's father-in-law used to make coconut matting, and Burgin's father had a poultry farm.
13 *St Dunstan's Annual Report*, year ended 31 March 1917.
14 *St Dunstan's Review* (July 1917), 17.
15 See Chapter 5. Burgin's views had clearly shifted by the late 1920s, as in 1917 he had argued that if a St Dunstan's man were to marry, he should have known his wife before being blinded. *St Dunstan's Review* (July 1917), 18.
16 Rob Baker notes, 'St Dunstan's – Name, Function and "Brand" Changes', Blind Veterans UK.
17 Anderson, *War, Disability and Rehabilitation*, 61.
18 R. Kennedy, *The Children's War* (London: Palgrave Macmillan, 2014), 109–16; T. Proctor, 'On My Honour: Guides and Scouts in Interwar Britain', *Transactions of the American Philosophical Society*, New Series, 92: 2 (2002), 71–2.
19 T. P. O'Connor, 'The Blind', in G. Goodchild (ed.), *The Blinded Soldiers and Sailors Gift Book* (London: Jarrow and Sons, 1918), 203.
20 *St Dunstan's Review* (April 1921), 1.
21 Territorial, 'From Ypres to V. O. B.', 58. MS, Blind Veterans UK.
22 Territorial, 'From Ypres', 127–8.
23 Fraser, *My Story*, 20.
24 Fraser, *My Story*, 48.
25 Young Men's Christian Association, 'The Red Triangle Employment Bureau for Ex-Service Men', Imperial War Museum poster, Art IWM PST 13211, www.iwm.org.uk/collections/item/object/10. Accessed 5 February 2020.
26 J. Galsworthy (ed.), *Reveille: Devoted to the Disabled Soldier and Sailor* (August 1918), 8.
27 G. Buckley, 'From the Man's Point of View', in Galsworthy (ed.), *Reveille*, 193.
28 Buckley, 'From the Man's Point of View', 191.
29 J. Nicholson, *The Great Silence 1918–1920: Living in the Shadow of the Great War* (London: John Murray, 2009), 63.
30 Nicolson, *Great Silence*, 49–50. On children's reactions to wounds, see also M. Larsson, *Shattered Anzacs: Living with the Scars of War* (Sydney: UNSW Press, 2009), 132–4.

31 S. Alexander, 'Becoming a Woman in the 1920s and 1930s', in S. Alexander, *Becoming a Woman and Other Essays in Nineteenth and Twentieth Century Feminist History* (London: Virago, 1994); C. Langhamer, *Women's Leisure in England, 1920–1960* (Manchester: Manchester University Press, 2000); K. Milcoy, *When the Girls Come Out to Play* (London: Bloomsbury Academic, 2017); S. Todd, 'Young Women, Work and Leisure in Interwar England', *The Historical Journal*, 48: 3 (2005), 55.
32 Todd, 'Young Women'; Milcoy, *Girls Come Out to Play*, 42. See also K. Holden, 'Family, Caring and Unpaid Work', in I. Zweiniger-Bargielowska (ed.), *Women in Twentieth Century Britain* (London: Routledge, 2001), 134–48.
33 Langhamer, *Women's Leisure*, 50.
34 Alexander, 'Becoming a Woman'.
35 Todd, 'Young Women', 790; Milcoy, *Girls Come Out to Play*, 41.
36 Their situation was akin to the daughters of lone mothers interviewed by Penny Summerfield in her research on servicewomen in the Second World War, who also 'struggled to reconcile their understandings of a daughter's duty towards her mother with their sense of having been exploited, economically and emotionally'. *Reconstructing Women's Wartime Lives: Discourse and Subjectivity in Oral Histories of the Second World War* (Manchester: Manchester University Press, 1998), 62. The eldest daughters of disabled soldiers in Australia, comments Larsson, were liable to become 'mother's right hand'. *Shattered Anzacs*, 130.
37 See Chapter 1 and C. Gilligan, R. Spencer, M. K. Weinberg and T. Bertsch, 'On the Listening Guide: A Voice-Centred Relational Method', in P. M. Camic, J. E. Rhodes and L. Yardley (eds), *Qualitative Research in Psychology: Expanding Perspectives in Methodology and Design* (Washington, DC: American Psychological Association, 2003), 157.
38 Notes on interview with Dora Kneebone, 27 February 2015.
39 I. Kogan, 'The Second Generation in the Shadow of Terror', in M. Gerard Fromm (ed.), *Lost in Transmission: Studies of Trauma across the Generations* (London: Karnac, 2012), 5–8.
40 Langhamer, *Women's Leisure*, 95; Milcoy, *Girls Come Out to Play*, 40–1; Summerfield, *Reconstructing Women's Wartime Lives*, 47.
41 J. Morley, 'Dad "Never Said Much" But ... Young Men and Great War Veterans in Day-to-Day-Life in Interwar Britain', *Twentieth Century British History*, 29: 2 (June 2018), 199–224.
42 D. Lessing, *Alfred and Emily* (London: Fourth Estate, 2008), 156.
43 Lessing, *Alfred and Emily*, dust jacket.

Part IV

Descendant

8

Father and son on Bob's war

The following three chapters draw at points on my personal memories of researching Robert Henry Roper's war and are framed by two bereavements. I was twenty when I did my first interview with Granddad in March 1980, and in early September that year, we drove up to his home town of Beechworth to visit the places he frequented as a child and the cemetery in Yackandandah where his ancestors were buried. Returning to the pub that night, Granddad said he felt cold and couldn't warm up, and a fortnight later he was admitted to the Heidelberg Repatriation Hospital with heart problems. He died on the morning of my twenty-first birthday party, having written me a cheque and this note: 'you get one 21st birthday only Make it a happy one Granny + I are barracking hard for you + your future Love from us both'. The second bereavement was in June 2016 when my father died from pancreatic cancer days short of his ninetieth birthday. In many ways it was a good death: he was diagnosed in February, and in March my sister Lyndal and I – both of us resident in the UK – were able to join our sister Cath and our stepmother Robyn and be with dad in Melbourne when he was still relatively well.

Dad had begun to work on his father's war records in the late 2000s after more than a decade of genealogical research that included trips to Norfolk and Campbelltown in Scotland from where the Ropers had emigrated in the 1860s. Whereas my focus was singular – Granddad's war and its family legacies – for my father, the First World War was initially a source of additional evidence for the genealogist. Preparing the Epilogue of my 2009 book *The Secret Battle*, I made copious notes during phone calls as Dad related stories that his father, aunts and cousins had told him about the Roper family in Beechworth. He was quick to obtain the service records of his father and two uncles when they were digitised in the mid-2000s. In 2013 he transcribed his father's handwritten memoirs of Gallipoli and in 2015 he transcribed his memoir of the Camel Corps.[1] He began to track down the service records of Granddad's mates and immersed himself in the published histories and unit diaries of the Camel Corps. He was fascinated by the insubordination of Number Two Company as they roamed the Libyan and Sinai deserts without the weight of military hierarchy to keep them in check.[2] In September 2015 we took a trip to the Australian War Memorial (AWM) in Canberra to look up the records of Granddad's commanding officer George Langley, the man Granddad had accused of routing Number Two Company by sending them into the frontline at the Second Battle of Gaza in 1917 as a punishment for their rebelliousness. We discovered that in the 1930s, Langley, then a schoolmaster, had hoped to borrow files from the AWM to write a history of the Cameliers, but C. E. W. Bean put a stop to it.[3] Dad came to the 'Love and Sorrow' conference at Melbourne Museum in September 2015 where I gave a lecture on Granddad's home life after the war and the role of suburban domesticity (and my grandmother) in his recuperation.[4]

Our efforts were not exactly collaborations, more like histories of the same man pursued in parallel by a son and grandson. As Dad remarked on more than one occasion, I was more interested in explaining the man than his war. Dad was the better military historian, and I remember looking up at him in the 'Love and Sorrow' conference for confirmation that I'd got the facts right about his uncles' war service. It probably wasn't easy for Dad to sit in silence as I described his home life as a boy to the audience. He told me later that he missed some of the lecture as I was talking too quickly. In an email written that night, he offered some amendments, but he also said that the talk had had a powerful impact on him and captured his father 'in all his contradictoriness'.[5]

I was disconcerted when in late 2015, another First World War historian approached my father for an interview about 'Bob'. I emailed Dad to voice my concern that the history I had encouraged, preserved and researched over the past thirty-five years might be given over to a stranger. Dad thought his father's memoirs deserved publication and was disappointed that I had not made much progress on that front. I was disappointed that although Dad also felt a sense of ownership towards his father's war history, he was willing to pass his research and experience as a descendant to an outsider. But his reaction also gave me pause to wonder why, despite our numerous conversations about his father since 1980, and despite interviewing British descendants since 2011, I had not thought to interview him until my visit in 2015. The grandson's experience of the war's afterlife would be at the centre of the history that I imagined writing. My father's memories would supplement it, but he would be an observer of the professional historian's efforts rather than the star witness or co-author.

There was a backstory to my feeling of proprietorship. I had just turned thirteen when, at the beginning of December 1972, my father sat us all down and announced that he was leaving. A bewildering chain of events followed. By January 1973 my mother, two sisters and I had moved out of the house in Bundoora where we had lived for the past four years and were installed in a weatherboard house that needed work, on a scrubby half-acre plot in the outer suburb of Montmorency.

None of us knew anyone local. It was a difficult and depressing time. Granddad and Granny deeply disapproved of Dad's behaviour and stepped into the breach left by his departure. Granny would phone us every week; they helped sort out repairs on the house and property and took us on holidays to resorts around Victoria. When the weather turned unseasonably cold during a summer holiday in Mt Beauty – our first without Dad – they drove up from Melbourne to deliver blankets. In my mid-teens, bike rides from Montmorency to Surrey Hills, a cooked midday meal and time spent sitting on the garden bench overlooking the vegetable patch or watching Granddad write his memoirs of Gallipoli were a welcome relief from the sometimes-desolate atmosphere at home. Well before the breakup, however, I had sought Granddad's attention: a photograph from 1964, when I was around five years old, shows the three Roper children sitting with Granddad on the garden bench at Kent Road. I am nestling up to him while Cath is immobilised in splints from a recent operation, and Lyndal is writing.

History gave me another means of being part of my grandfather's world as I reached my late teens. I would accompany him to the Anzac Day reunions at the Shrine of Remembrance after

Figure 8.1 Granddad with the Roper grandchildren at Surrey Hills, circa 1964. We are sitting on the garden bench outside the sleepout where Granddad wrote his war memoirs. From left to right: Lyndal, Mike and Cath. Author's own. All rights reserved.

the march, and I encouraged him to write a memoir of his service in the Camel Corps. It was Cath and me who drove out to Dad's house in Wattle Glen in September 1980 to pass on the news that Granddad was in the Repat and dying. I would be the one to hold the manuscript copies of his Gallipoli and Camel Corps memoirs after his death.

Dad tolerated my bid to become his father's historian, and his comments and research often took me in creative directions. He liked my first published paper, written as an undergraduate student in 1980, where I sought to relate Granddad's hatred and the bitterness of his politics to the injustices he experienced at the hands of his commanding officers in Gallipoli and the Middle East. At that time, he was a social worker looking after children in care and felt his father's temper could be explained in other ways too. He wondered what it might have to do with his mother. What about his early years? Those comments set me thinking about the limits of legacy history, a theme that the next two chapters explore. The patrilineal order was to some extent restored when I left Australia for

Figure 8.2 Reconstituted family in the backyard at Montmorency, circa 1977. From left to right: Granddad, Lyndal, Ailsa, Granny, Cath and Mike. Author's own. All rights reserved.

the UK and passed Granddad's memoirs and my notes on his early history to Dad for safekeeping. Yet there remained moments where our interests clashed, and as Bean's terse exchange with Langley shows, wrangles over the historical record and who possesses the authority to settle it were not just a family affair, but are endemic to the pursuit.

Dad and I were absorbed in a process of imaginative reconstruction in our research, a reconstruction of the man, a reconstruction of his war and a reconstruction of what the war did to him. What was it that drove us? We were compelled in part by the wish to explain the imprint he left on us. Poring over the military records, my father was trying to fathom the origins of his father's left-wing politics and contempt for authority, issues that had brought the two of them into conflict during the 1950s and 60s when my father

Figure 8.3 Granddad on horseback in the Anzac march, circa 1977. Granddad is second to the left of the walking photographer. He became a member of the Light Horse after the Camel Corps was disbanded in mid-1918. He had not always been happy to join the march. In the 1930s, he told me, 'We used to go into the City, into where they were holding them, and we wouldn't go any further' (R. H. Roper interview, 'Great Depression', 1980). Author's own. All rights reserved.

was working for the Australian Security Intelligence Organisation. Family history came to serve different functions as I grew older and my circumstances changed. My experiment in oral history as a twenty-year-old helped explain the volcanic temper that made me wary of the grandfather I loved. Hearing him talk about Lone Pine and the Middle East campaign, I thought I had discovered the roots of his disenchantment. When I asked him in 1980 what he was expecting as they prepared to go into battle at Lone Pine, he replied: 'I was expecting more humanity … But our officers … they were just brutes.'[6] Hearing him talk about that first night on the Peninsula, and being the very age he was then, I could project myself into the scene on the evening of the attack and wonder how I would have coped.

In 2001, twenty years after granddad's death, now aged forty-three and with a one-year-old daughter, scenes of Kent Road came to mind when I was recuperating after a stay in hospital with pneumonia. I was immersed in a feverish reminiscence and began writing what would become a thirty-thousand-word memoir which opened with our journey to Beechworth and Granddad's death. I was not only mourning his death but my youth. When Dad and I began to collaborate in the lead-up to the Centenary, I was in my mid-fifties and destined to stay in the UK. Our research on Bob provided new material for reveries of my Melbourne childhood. Re-reading the war memoirs that dad had transcribed, I could summon Granddad in the sleepout at his rolltop desk. With my 1980 analogue tape recordings now digitised, I could hear again the clank of crockery and cutlery on tape, and Granny asking Cath if she wants more cake. I could conjure Granny bent over the stove, her wooden spoon almost worn away on its right side, and Granddad sitting at the head of the grey-flecked Laminex table with its aluminium bevel, tut-tutting as he listens to the ABC radio news. My nostalgic rumination, however, would be tethered by evidence and historical discipline.

Our research on Bob became a way for Dad and me to stay in touch and the Centenary gave our efforts added purpose. Government sponsorship of digitisation had liberated military records on a hitherto unimaginable scale – attestation papers that listed occupation, religion and vital data, records of where men served and what medical problems they had and records of their health after the war.[7] For my father's generation, being the child of a survivor acquired the kind of social cachet that was once attached to the veteran, and this made it more difficult for Dad to resist the approaches of interested historians. He took to attending the annual Anzac Day ceremony at the local war memorial, his own and his father's medals pinned to his chest, and would remember a man who – an itinerant labourer, Gallipoli veteran, Camelier and railwayman – seemed to embody the legend. On a damp morning on 25 April 2015, the Centenary of the Landing, he presented a wreath at the war memorial in Diamond Creek on behalf of his local branch of the retirement organisation PROBUS. A month later I was sending Dad dispatches from Gallipoli as I toured the battlefields with military historians from around the world.

The months on either side of the anniversary of the Landing saw us exchange emails every couple of days as we tracked the movements of Number Two Company and the fates of its officers and men. New information kept coming to light. In February 2015, Janet Butler, who was working on a history of the Camel Corps, got in touch to say that she had found a thirty-three-page memoir of Bob's service in Gallipoli and a memoir of his service in the Camel Corps in the Liddle Collection at Leeds University.[8] This was an archive I had visited during my research on British families in the First World War, but I'd never thought to look up my own grandfather's name in the catalogue. He had apparently submitted the manuscripts to Eric Liddle through a comrade in the Camel Corps Association after Liddle toured Australia inviting veterans to submit material. I had not reckoned on the colonial networks of which my grandfather, despite his hatred of the British officer class, was clearly part. In a letter to Liddle in January 1979, Granddad mentioned that my sister Lyndal was in Tübingen doing research for her PhD on the Reformation and that I was in my first year of history at Melbourne University: 'it is he who persuaded me to write about my mates + doings in the Infantry, Camel Corps, + Light Horse'.[9] This seemed to give me more credit than was warranted, as Lyndal and I both remembered Granddad writing his memoirs of Gallipoli in the mid-1970s, and at that point, I was in my early teens and had no particular interest in history. Bizarrely, however, in 1979 when Grandad wrote to Liddle, I was certainly interested in his war, yet had no knowledge of the memoirs I had supposedly encouraged him to write. The family always assumed that we possessed the only copy of his Gallipoli memoirs, and in my recollection, it was the Camel Corps memoir that I urged him to write in 1978, not the Gallipoli memoir. Even more puzzling, Granddad explained to Liddle that his Gallipoli memoir was based on a diary that he destroyed in 1954 because it 'contained many contentious articles' and that before doing so he had extracted from it 'dates of different and important events'.[10] We knew that Bob had kept what my father called a 'black book' in his bedside cabinet, a 'record of officers' misdeeds' and mutinies by the men in Number Two Company.[11] Yet Lyndal and I thought we could remember him burning it in the incinerator at the bottom of the yard at Kent Road in the mid-1970s, a good twenty years after he claimed to have destroyed it. A family with two professional historians and an ex-civil servant with a scrupulous eye for the record seemed incapable of piecing together the history of Granddad's war writing, let alone his war.

During 2015 our family was engrossed in deep questions of memory and source: was it more accurate to treat Granddad's war writings as a contemporary or a retrospective record? Did he have the black book at hand when he wrote the first versions of his memoirs? My father felt sure that they were a faithful rendition of the black book with the most contentious incidents left out and for him, their value rested on this. After all, they gave precise details of dates and events, and it did not seem credible that he had reconstructed the detail from memory. 'I cannot accept', he wrote, that his father would have destroyed the black book 'without writing up a sanitized version'.[12] Yet it was clear that Granddad was altering the story with each new rendition. The Liddle memoir looked to be a polished-up version of the memoir that the family possessed. Granddad consults external sources, adjusts some dates, and introduces 'slanguage', writing for example that he cursed the water-carrying Salvation Army minister McKenzie 'in real Australian bullock driver's language'.[13] He expands his descriptions of themes that were by then part of Anzac folklore about Gallipoli, such as the poor food and flies. Introducing himself and his memoir to a professional historian in Britain, he mentions his grandchildren's historical interests. I am astonished at the intensity of his efforts. Completing the Camel Corps memoir, he told his fellow Old Camelier Rex Hall in 1978, had been 'a strain, my 82 Year old [sic] fingers stiffen up & my eyes get weak'.[14] On the back of that, however, he went on to re-write his memoir of Gallipoli for Liddle, posting instalments in January and May 1979. He was engaged in a ceaseless re-writing of his war in the last two years of his life. What animated him was the passing of his generation. He was now the last surviving member of Number Two Company, he told Liddle in January 1979, and had attended a dinner of the Gallipoli Legion last week at which there were just fifty-seven men. 'In a few years [sic] time the 1914–18 soldier will be extinct', he reflected.[15]

The expanding networks of genealogy and digitisation continued to yield new information after 2015, and bit by bit, I was led to reconsider my grandfather, my wish to claim him as a father figure and to be his historian. Dad and I had always assumed that Bob and Alice met in 1920 when they were working at the St Kilda Road

Barracks, and I had written confidently in 2009 that their marriage in 1923 was 'conceived amid recuperation'.[16] Yet early in 2018, the Roper children were put in touch with a family that had discovered a blood match through DNA sampling. Looking on Ancestry.com, I was astonished to find that they had posted the very same studio photograph of Granddad in uniform that stood on my bookshelf as a teenager.

It transpired that Bob was not only grandfather to me, Lyndal and Cath, but had three other grandchildren too. He had had a relationship with a woman called Catherine Toohey and had fathered a child, Kathleen, born in 1921. On a visit to Melbourne in 2018, my sister Cath and I met with the three Toohey descendants – all of us Bob's grandchildren – in a café in Seddon in the western suburbs. I wondered what Dad, who had lost his brother Lin in 1951, would have made of the news that he also had a half-sister. The charge of hypocrisy was one that Granddad often liked to level. He never forgave his mother for walking out on the family and had

Figure 8.4 Robert Henry Roper studio portrait held by the Roper and Toohey families. Author's own. All rights reserved

cold-shouldered his only living son for (as he saw it) deserting his wife and three children. Yet it now appeared that, probably unbeknown to him, Granddad had done a similar thing.

The digitisation of official records and the proliferation of amateur and professional genealogy networks over the past two decades have allowed family historians to launch out in new directions. Their research, coupled with the personal experience of the survivors, can sometimes reveal hidden effects of the First World War that have escaped historians. It can direct new light onto the collective past and national mythologies and challenge accepted historical understandings.[17] At the same time, family history is also an intensely personal activity with a past of its own. It is important to understand who chronicles the war in the family and why, how they bear that history, and how historical research affects family relationships. Such pursuits are often animated by loss, as we seek to resuscitate the dead and find a place for them in the historical record.

Preparing to write this chapter, I went back to my emails and the transcripts of my interviews with Dad for the first time since his death. I am not yet ready to hear the recording of his voice. Now it is my father, rather than my grandfather, that I wish to bring to life, and it is hard to reckon with him being gone. Historical research requires rigour, all that seeking out traces, piecing them together and putting them into context. It is a discipline to which my father and I were committed, but our reconstructions were also reveries. As such, they tell us as much about the desires of the dreamers as the past they dream of. Every family historian has a backstory about how their interests developed, and their efforts to place an ancestor in history are often about finding a place for themselves in the family when that family is no more.

Notes

1 R. H. Roper, 'Gallipoli Memoir'; R. H. Roper, 'Camel Corps Memoir', 1978. MS in author's possession.
2 According to my grandfather, two months into the desert campaign the men in Number Two Company drew their rifles on their commanding

officer after he threatened to shoot a lance-corporal who refused to mount his camel and do ceremonial drill. R. H. Roper, 'Camel Corps Memoir', 1978, 4; A. Eldans to Major Smith, 28 March 1916: AWM4, AIF Unit War Diary, Number Two Company Imperial Camel Corps (hereafter ICC), January to August 1916, 11/11/1, Part 1. His successor Robert Dyett wrote to his superior officers in June 1916 them that 'I have had several bad cases of either disobedience, obscene language or even violence to NCOs this week. I have one court martial pending, and have applied for another. At the general's request I have forwarded to him a list of men who cannot be trusted to carry out patrol work.' R. Dyett to CO Imperial Camel Corps, Sollum, 3 June 1916: AIF Unit War Diary, as previous note.

3 Langley's account was eventually published by his widow in 1976. G. and E. Langley, *Sand, Sweat and Camels: The Story of the Australian Camel Corps* (Adelaide: Lowden, Kilmore, 1976).

4 M. Roper, 'The Bush, the Suburbs and the Long Great War: A Family Memoir', *History Workshop Journal*, 86 (Autumn 2018), 90–113.

5 W. S. Roper email, 17 September 2015.

6 R. H. Roper interview, 'First World War', 1980.

7 On the scope and use of digitised pension files, see J. McCalman, R. Kippen, J. McMeeken, J. Hopper and M. Reade, 'Early Results from the "Diggers to Veterans" Longitudinal Study of Australian Men who Served in the First World War: Short- and Long-Term Mortality of Early Enlisters', *Historical Life Course Studies*, 8 (2019), 52–72; B. Scates, 'How War Came Home: Reflections on the Digitisation of Australia's Repatriation Files', *History Australia*, 16: 1 (2019), 190–209. On the ethical issues surrounding the use of British pension files, see J. Meyer and A. Moncrieff, 'Family Not to Be Informed? The Ethical Use of Historical Medical Documentation', in A. Hanley and J. Meyer (eds), *Patient Voices in Britain, 1840–1948* (Manchester: Manchester University Press, 2021).

8 R. H. Roper, 'Recollections of First World War Service with the Imperial Camel Corps' (1979), Liddle Collection 1914–18, University of Leeds: LIDDLE/WW1/ANZAC/AUST/REC/46; 'R. H. Roper Gallipoli Memoir', Liddle Collection: LIDDLE/WW1/EP/062/21.

9 R. H. Roper to E. Liddle, 30 January 1979, Liddle Collection: LIDDLE/WW1/ANZAC/AUST/REC/46.

10 R. H. Roper to Liddle, 30 January 1979.

11 W. S. Roper interview, 'Early Life', September 2015.

12 W. S. Roper email, 8 November 2015.

13 R. H. Roper, 'Gallipoli Memoir', Liddle Collection: LIDDLE/WW1/ANZAC/AUST/REC/46, 28.

14 R. H. Roper, 'Camel Corps Memoir', 1978.
15 R. H. Roper to Liddle, 30 January 1979.
16 M. Roper, *The Secret Battle: Emotional Survival in the Great War* (Manchester: Manchester University Press, 2009), 317.
17 For considered reflections, see B. Ziino, '"A Lasting Gift to His Descendants": Family Memory and the Great War in Australia', *History & Memory*, 22: 2 (2010), 125–46; C. Holbrook and B. Ziino, 'Family History and the Great War in Australia', in B. Ziino (ed.), *Remembering the First World War* (Abingdon: Routledge, 2015), 39–55. Scates discusses the democratising potential of digitised repatriation records in 'How the War Came Home', 190–209.

9

Dysentery and the Anzac legend

> The condition of the men of the battalion was awful. Thin, haggard, as weak as kittens, and covered with suppurating sores. Practically every man had dysentery. The total strength of the battalion was two officers and 170 men. If we had been in France every man would have been sent to hospital.
> — *Medical Officer Captain Luther, 1915*[1]

> So we got to bed, about two hours later we were hauled out and we went up into the trenches, and we saw the poor buggers, you should have seen the fellows that were there, our blokes, you'd have thought they were ghosts.
> — *Robert Henry Roper 1980, remembering his first night at Gallipoli*[2]

When we were children, Granddad would often talk – and write – about the horrors of battle at Lone Pine in Gallipoli, where he embarked as part of the Sixth Reinforcement to the Second Infantry Battalion on 5 August 1915. After rushing the Turkish trenches at 5.30 pm the following day, he became separated from his unit and spent the night on his own in a shallow sap, piling up dead bodies from the battle to create a defence. Granddad eventually found his unit and was told that he was one of twenty-three survivors of the 150 men who had gone into battle. This was a statistic that, like the toll of casualties after the Second Battle of Gaza, he could reel off the tip of his tongue, even though he often found it difficult to bring words to mind. As he looked back in my interview with him in 1980, sixty-five years later, the effect of being plunged into murderous fighting was apparent to me and my sister Cath. Granddad's voice broke as he told us how he felt after being directed to a dugout to get some sleep: 'I just remember howling [*long silence*]'. He described feeling numb, symptoms that today we associate with PTSD. His shorthand reference for Lone Pine was 'wanton murder'.[3]

The toll taken by the fighting at Lone Pine was clear, yet there were other memories about which he barely spoke. In the 1980 interview he recalls the shock of seeing how emaciated the men who landed on 25 April had become. This is the only time in the interview that he refers to dysentery, and the reference is oblique. Yet the service records show that he was one of the victims, admitted to the Field Ambulance after just three weeks on the peninsula.[4] Granddad's written memoirs of Gallipoli are also allusive: he only mentions the word dysentery twice in a text of over twenty thousand words. In the humorous style of the Anzac, the entry for the end of August has him parading sick not with diarrhoea and vomiting as the service records have it, but with a gum boil, and deciding not to have his tooth removed when he sees the dentist's forceps, rusty with the gore of Lone Pine.[5] The first mention of dysentery is in November when the division was at rest in Lemnos for three weeks and is a comment on the *absence* of the condition: 'our nerves are still shattered, most of us are putting on weight, nobody is suffering from dysentery, but I think most of us are suffering from lethargy'.[6] The second reference is in December as they prepare to withdraw from the peninsula, and this time he counts himself among the victims.[7]

Despite Granddad's felicity, the impact of the epidemic is apparent on closer examination of his memoirs. Gallipoli's cost is counted not only in the number of corpses but in the men's declining health. Welcoming the reinforcements on 4 August, the OC of the battalion comments on their 'clean + healthy appearance', and granddad goes on to reflect that 'they were physically ill and I was physically fit, but my morale was in a hell of a mess'.[8] When he sees his younger brother Charlie at Lone Pine at the end of October, he notes that 'He is much subdued, painfully thin and of course is lousy, but cheerful.'[9] Given the stoic image of the Anzacs, the beginning of the sentence cannot be left to stand without a follow-up assertion of his brother's morale. Granddad's writings are dotted around with references to unappetising rations, the spoiling of food by flies and weakened comrades. Yet only once does he say that he had dysentery himself, and he never tells his reader what it was like.

Granddad is hardly unusual, for the ghost of the dysenteric hangs over the entire campaign. His doubled-up figure can be glimpsed but his testimony is elliptical; the term 'laconic', often used for the Anzacs, is befitting. Perhaps because of his silence, cultural historians have focused on the heroic mythology of the Anzacs that was constructed by journalists like Ellis Ashmead-Bartlett and Charles Bean, rather than the epidemic in which the myth was mired. Yet as military and medical historians have shown, dysentery played a fateful role in the campaign.[10] The tragic human consequences were vividly – and angrily – described by A. G. Butler, the ex-medical officer and official historian of the Australian Army medical services, who believed that the rapid deterioration of the health of the Anzac forces played 'an important – possibly a determining part in the campaign'.[11] Unlike veterans, the women who had nursed them gave graphic accounts of the state to which victims could be reduced. Sister Mary Fitzgibbon was on the *Essequibo* ferrying soldiers from Helles to the base at Mudros:

> The wounded were easy enough to deal with, but the sick! They were in a terrible state, all suffering from dysentery and enteric. Their insides had simply turned to water, and all they had been able to do for them on shore was tie their trousers tight round their legs with pieces of string. We had to rip their trousers off with scissors, and then we washed the boys as best we could.

She went on,

> I'll never forget them. Just pouring with dysentery – sick, miserable, and in terrible pain. It was pitiful to see them, so weak, and blood and water pouring out of them. We had medicine that we gave them, but we could really do very little for them.[12]

The effects were not just physical but mental: the stomach and emotional states are closely linked, and the gut problems experienced by soldiers at Anzac sapped their morale.[13] Diaries document the malaise that accompanied stomach troubles. The victims, as Butler observed in 1930, were struck by both 'physical and mental nausea'.[14] When Patsy Adam-Smith interviewed Alan Gourlay in 1976, he told her that he had become so weak that he could not walk without help. His service records however reveal that the toll was mental as much as physical, for he was admitted to hospital on 8 October 1915 with 'Nervous Breakdown'.[15]

Wasting away in fact, the dysenteric subsequently became largely invisible in the Anzac legend of soldiers who were among the finest specimens of manhood and military prowess in the world. The history of dysentery prompts questions about the memory work that Charles Bean set in train to 'sanitise' the epidemic that brought Australian soldiers to their knees.[16]

The experience of dysentery

Men typically gave brief indications of their poor health in letters and diaries written from the Peninsula, but little more. On 2 September 1915, Bean reported in his diary that he had diarrhoea and that the condition was 'running through the whole camp'. On 9 September he writes, 'Tummy still sore. Bazley [his batman and later assistant at the Australian War Memorial] in same way.'[17] Oral testimonies tend to reveal more than diaries, letters or memoirs, and the discussion here draws on the interviews with Australian veterans conducted by Patsy Adam-Smith at the State Library of Victoria in the 1970s, and interviews with British veterans conducted by the Imperial War Museum between the 1970s and late 1980s.[18] Social history brought the ordinary soldier's experience of the campaign to the fore, and interviewers asked the survivors direct questions about how they coped during the epidemic. The survivors looked back from an age where attitudes towards bodily functions were arguably more relaxed, but even so, half a century on the subject remained difficult to broach. Just as Granddad did, these veterans talked more freely about others than themselves.

In the following excerpt from an interview with the British veteran Cecil Meager, his middle-class interviewer asks a question about the state of the men's health, and Meager confides a personal detail. The interviewer senses his discomfort and moves to reassure him:

> *Interviewer:* It must have been very difficult when you had dysentery.
> *Meager:* Oh yes, it was.
> *Interviewer:* Did you find that men used to foul themselves up?
> *Meager:* Yeah. *I* did.
> *Interviewer:* Did you?

Meager: Oh yes ... Yes.
Interviewer: Well, I imagine you couldn't help it. Could you?
Meager: Oh no, you couldn't, no. No, it was, well, it just came on, and that was that [*chuckles*].
Interviewer: That must have been very difficult, bearing in mind you didn't have other clothes to change into.
Meager: No, there weren't any clothes.
Interviewer: So you just had to put up with it.
Meager: Had to put up with it. Yeah. It was awful [*voice trails off, almost inaudible*]. I, I, I ...
Interviewer: I imagine it must have been rather degrading for you.
Meager: Oh it was. I know I wasn't the only one, but still. It was, considering from, that ... the family life you'd had, before, you know, when you'd been brought up as we were, you know.[19]

Meager went on to say that the condition had made him very low and assented when the interviewer suggested the word 'depressed' to him. In that state, he explained, 'you wanted to ... get out of it, you know'.[20]

Veterans were spare in their language, but their adjectives convey the abject state to which they had been reduced: 'terrible' and 'really awful'; 'very bad', 'horrible'.[21] It was 'one of the worst things' about being on the peninsula, Alan Gourlay told Patsy Adam-Smith, worse than the fighting. The British recruit Frederick Caokes was shot through the stomach and although relieved to get away from the fighting, it was 'more this, the lack of water, the thirst, and the conditions we were living in, the flies and the dysentery. It was awful really.'[22] Just as the toll taken by the epidemic exceeded that inflicted by weapons, so too in the men's minds, the horrors of their living conditions could eclipse the horrors of battle.

Diarrhoea undid the work of civilisation. When the Australian Imperial Forces (AIF) arrived in Egypt *en route* to Gallipoli, the odours and filth impressed on them the superiority of the European.[23] On the peninsula, however, their facilities were just as primitive, and the filth was their own. The stench of dead bodies and excreta – Granddad called it the 'Gallipoli death odour' – marked their removal from civilised society.[24] The exposed coast and lack of back areas meant that it was not feasible to construct the kind of pits that the army provided on the Western Front. Orders issued on 4 June 1915 specified a number of hygiene and sanitation measures, including the construction of deep pits, the covering of excreta with soil and the use of cresol, but the geography, the demand on latrines due to the men's chronic diarrhoea and the exposure of the latrines to fire made this impossible.[25] Gourlay recalled that 'The latrines just consisted of a big hole dug in the ground with an A frame over it and a rail you're supposed to sit on, and all they'd do to keep the smell down was to put lime in it. The place was a mass of flies.'[26] Words like 'just', and 'all they'd do' convey the contrast between the facilities they were used to and what they had on the peninsula.

The failure to cover the latrines early in the campaign, moreover, was one of the principal reasons for the spread of gastrointestinal disease.[27] As summer approached and men fell ill, the amount of uncovered excreta proliferated. The sicker they became, the more the flies fed on their excreta and spread the disease.[28] Problems quickly dogged the new lines after the August campaign, with the result that the condition of reinforcements like my grandfather deteriorated more quickly than the original forces.[29]

The capacity to separate food from dirt is a mark of a civilised society, yet on the peninsula, it was impossible to sustain. Every Gallipoli veteran remembers the flies. 'Unbearable', 'detestable things', said James Page, while Stanley Parker Bird heard about the 'colossal swarms' of flies even before he reached the peninsula.[30] Flies pestered them as they sought rest, and they ingested them through open mouths as they slept.[31] British soldiers were perhaps less inured to the fly than the Anzac, but feelings of disgust permeate Australian accounts too. What unnerved the men was that the fly travelled from excrement and the bodies of the dead to their food. It was 'the horrible thought', James McPhee told Adam-Smith, that 'the latrines, even for a fly, were only a short flight away'.[32] Because cooked food could not be got up to the men and they had to prepare it individually amidst the swarms of flies, in effect they made themselves ill. 'It may be conjectured that in the soldiers' mess-tin was to be found the most important passive agent in the cycle of infection', wrote Butler in 1930.[33] His assessment expressed a visceral sensation in medical terms: both the mouth and anus, William Miller reminds us, 'are vulnerable to contamination and are highly dangerous contaminators'; the men's knowledge that they might be ingesting food tainted with the shit and bodily remains of others threatened bodily and psychic boundaries.[34]

The breaching of these boundaries is signalled in representations of the watery brown apricot and plum jam which was a staple of their rations. Granddad conveys its similarity to their runny excreta in a reference to 'Dicken's diarrhoea', a corruption of 'Deakin's diarrhoea', named after the English jam and marmalade manufacturer.[35] Yet these colloquialisms also perhaps connoted the explosive effects of ingesting the fly-blown mixture, and the role of

Figure 9.1 David Barker, 'APRICOT AGAIN!'. The staring eyes and gritted teeth of the Anzac convey the men's discontent about their monotonous rations. However, Barker's drawing gives little hint of the visceral disgust occasioned by apricot jam because of its resemblance to diarrhoea and the part played by the fly-blown runny mixture in the spread of the epidemic. Courtesy of Bridgeman Images. All rights reserved.

the jam in a malign transmission from human waste and remains to the living:

> You had to fight the flies, big green flies, bigger than blowflies. They used to come off the dead bodies out in front in swarms, and if you opened a tin of jam, or anything else, it was a case of fight them off while you got a bit of jam onto a biscuit to try and eat it.[36]

The men may have had only a rudimentary sense of germ theory at the time, but some victims later became students of the disease. Gourlay gave a detailed account to Adam-Smith of the treatments available at the time – castor oil with lemon, bismuth and chlorodyne – and how much they had improved with the advent of sulphur drugs and antibiotics.[37]

It was not just the toileting and eating conventions of a civilised society which were breached at Gallipoli; the sickness also struck their social identities as men. The bodily toll is recounted in exact memories of the difference between their enlistment weight and weight after becoming ill: 'Oh, when I went on the peninsula, I was eleven stone. When I went off [laugh] I was six stone six', said Cecil Meager.[38] Caokes was twelve stone when he joined up, and reckoned he weighed seven stone five in hospital.[39] For the Anzacs, who were forging a reputation in the campaign as soldiers and men, the decline was not just personal but collective. 'It's absolutely piteous to see great sturdy bushmen and miners almost unable to walk through sheer weakness, caused by chronic diarrhoea, or else one mass of Barcoo rot', wrote the sapper Cyril Lawrence. 'We are all the same, all suffering from sheer physical weakness.'[40]

Dysentery was an intensely humiliating condition. As the British recruit Horace Manton recalled, 'you was loose all the time. Course I had to drop out, we was marching once, I had to drop out. Couldn't walk any further.'[41] The victim might make as many as fifteen or twenty trips a day to the latrine, and if he was not able to reach the latrine or take emergency relief in time, he might soil himself. His backside would become raw. 'Blood comes away with you at the finish', James Tolley explained.[42]

Like the collective memory of 'Deakin's diarrhoea', the horror and disgust associated with the condition are conveyed in a story which may have been a 'latrine furphy', but whose repetition at the time and later conveys the state to which it brought the men at Gallipoli. In an interview in 1987, Manton explained:

> What they did, they put two posts up there, and a plank across, and they dug a trench, and you used to have to go, and of course when you've got dysentery you're running all the time, some of the poor blighters fell in the trench, they did, it was that bad, sitting on this plank they just fell into the trench. It was terrible, really, this dysentery, you could see them go into this ... and the smell, terrible.[43]

The man is rescued by his comrades in some versions of the story; in others, the victim drowns in excrement.[44]

'Whatever their source', comments Rachel Duffett, 'digestive problems brought a particular type of misery to the men in the trenches.' For the victims, the inability to contain their bodily fluids, and disgust at the sight and smell of their excreta contributed to their distress.[45] Their humiliation is evident in the timorous way that Gallipoli veterans approached the subject in interviews half a century after the conflict. Tomlinson would not be drawn when his interviewer asked how he managed: 'I don't remember really, finding places ... I don't know.' All he would say was that the facilities were 'very primitive'.[46] When the British stretcher bearer Tolley was pressed about the state of the men being evacuated from the peninsula with dysentery he hesitated, searching for felicitous phrases: you 'had to just do the best you could, you'd wrap them up, you know what I mean to say, and use something best you could, but they was in a mess, I can assure you. Very primitive.'[47] Joseph Murray recalled the shame of the onlooker and the victim: 'its [sic] degrading to see a pal with his trousers down, and he can't walk, and you're dragging him to the latrine ... shockingly degrading for anybody'.[48] Dysentery weakened them physically and emotionally. The effects could continue for months, and as the next chapter explains, sometimes contributed to long-term conditions like jaundice and nervous complaints. Nobody was immune. After succumbing to dysentery in early September, Bean was diagnosed with 'a sort of epidemic jaundice' in November when he was compiling the entries for what would become *The Anzac Book*. The episode kept him in bed and left him exhausted at the slightest exertion, while General Hamilton was reputed to have suffered the effects of dysentery for years afterwards.[49]

Failures of care

The military, operational and medical failures that contributed to the dysentery outbreak have been well documented by historians, many of them following Butler's trenchant analysis in the *Official History of the Australian Medical Services*. Yet dysentery was, in one sense, simply the most telling sign of the army's overall inability to provide for basic needs in diet, hygiene and sanitation. Water was always in short supply, as the many memories of feeling parched attest, and this may have increased their vulnerability to infection.[50] Water could not be spared for keeping clean, and the men grew filthy.[51] They had to adjust to a level of personal hygiene that, even for the bush recruit, was probably more basic than they had known as civilians. Among the victims of dysentery, the shortage of water was doubly felt, as recovery depends on rehydration and they had to clean their soiled backsides with their hands.[52]

Resentment about water tended to centre on the labours of carting it, two petrol tins at a time, up the steep and exposed escarpments. For men who were sick and working in the heat of summer, these labours were arduous.[53] Granddad relates a story about the Salvation Army chaplain William McKenzie, who was known for offering to help the men carry water, and whose story was told on Anzac Day school broadcasts during the 1960s. According to Granddad, McKenzie only carried his water for a couple of yards. He 'eases the burdens of sick, tired water carrying diggers […] Big Mac the *saint* of Gallipoli. I was mean enough to think I was perhaps carrying up part of his bathwater & we got barely enough to drink.'[54] The McKenzie myth, along with Bean's light-hearted sketches of water carriers in *The Anzac Book*, defuses the hostility that the task aroused.[55]

Food was another aspect of army provision that caused resentment. The remoteness of the peninsula and the lack of a back area meant that supplies of fresh food were rare and soon spoiled. Most of the time they relied on their iron rations of bully beef and tack, a high-fat diet which provided them with an adequate calorific intake but quickly became monotonous and distasteful.[56] Granddad's description of the aftermath of Lone Pine contains a comment on food which, for many years, seemed to me a puzzling non-sequitur:

> I bedded down alongside Snow Reynolds, tried to think of what happened since we arrived on Gallipoli about seventy hours previously. I remember sobbing like hell and being wakened from a heavy sleep at 8 or 9 am – 'For God, King and Country?' Why? Breakfast – Bacon, hard biscuits, liquid apricot jam. Tea. All sorts of devices were used to try & beat the flies from the food, as for the tea, as soon as the lid was lifted from the dixy the flies would make one rush in to it, it was then poured into our dixy-lids, we would skim the flies off try to drink it unadulterated.[57]

The horror of battle was mixed up in Granddad's memory with disgust at his poor food. It was not just the bloodshed that had led him to question patriotism. The violence of Gallipoli had furnished a lesson in what he used to call 'man's inhumanity to man', but so did the food that the army saw fit to give them and the conditions in which they had to eat it.

The army's failures of care were further exposed once the epidemic caught hold. The most serious cases were supposed to be evacuated to Australia, but many were sent to England instead or got no further than Cairo.[58] Sick men were kept in transit for long periods because there was no base hospital on the peninsula and there were insufficient hospital ships, while the base camp hospitals in Lemnos, Malta and Egypt soon became overrun.[59] Bean was quick to recognise the implications of this, noting at the end of June that around a hundred men a day were going off sick and that it could take a month before they returned to their units. On 27 July 250 men left the peninsula sick, and Bean, clearly exasperated, comments that 'men who ought to be back in 6 days are not back in 6 weeks'.[60] Hygiene in the overcrowded hospitals was poor, with the dysentery cases packed tight together in bell tents and others contracting the disease from the victims.[61] 'There is a tremendous lot of amoebic dysentery up here + very large numbers catch it on this unhealthy spot', wrote the consulting physician for Mudros Hospital, Lieutenant W. H. Willcox, to the consulting physician to the War Office, Sir Robert Ross, on 21 October 1915.[62] Those who got back from the base camp hospitals spread the word about getting lost in the system, and the men reached the conclusion that the slow return of their comrades was due to the army's inefficiency, rather than because they were not fit to return.[63]

Dysentery and the Anzac legend 245

EACH ONE DOING HIS BIT
Drawn by W. OTHO HEWETT

Figure 9.2 Otho Hewett, 'Each One Doing His Bit'. Hewett's drawing depicts in patriotic terms the part played by their iron rations. My grandfather, however, thought Fray Bentos 'the lousiest bully made' and intimates his disgust in a racist furphy ('furphy' is Australian slang for a rumour, usually untrue): 'just before we left the Peninsula we read in an English newspaper that a Black Boy had fallen into a Vat of boiling corned beef at the Fray Bentos plant in America. I wondered if we got any of that Vat.' The fantasy here is of civilised men reduced to cannibalism, a bitter comment on the army's uncaring contempt for the Anzacs.
R. H. Roper, 'Gallipoli Memoir', 24. All rights reserved.

In response to the logistical problems of evacuating sick men, and to relieve pressure on the hospitals, official policies encouraged the treatment of men *in situ*. Among the Anzacs, who saw that the army was not managing the evacuation and who did not want to be absent from their mates, an informal culture developed of not reporting sick. It became a point of honour to try and 'stick it out'.⁶⁴ This subsequently became the cornerstone of the Gallipoli legend, stated by Granddad in 1980 as the life-creed 'never leave your mates'.⁶⁵

From an epidemiological standpoint, letting sick men stay on the peninsula was counterproductive as it increased the spread of the infection and contributed to the weakening of the remaining forces. On 24 August the Assistant Director of Medical Services noted that 'I have never seen men out of hospital looking so ill as a large proportion of the men do here'. When Alan Gourlay arrived on the peninsula in September, he was also struck by the men's reluctance to go off sick: 'some of the fellas there, their eyes were staring and their hair had all gone thin, they looked like living skeletons. They didn't report sick. They should have.'⁶⁶ Thomas Yarr, Deputy-Director of the Medical Services Eighth Corps, wrote a note to Sir Ronald Ross describing the state he was in after suffering from dysentery for seven weeks, 'acute for a week with blood in his stools, then subacute'. By the end, he said, 'I became a mere bag of bones and had to walk with a stick + am not strong yet'.⁶⁷ His note was written 'sympathetically', as he wanted to convey to Ross the state to which the men who had stayed on active service had been reduced. A man's decision to report sick was not simply individual. Much as he might desire a way out of his suffering, he did not want to let his comrades down. Men were caught up in the conflict between self-preservation and loyalty. Granddad reports on 2 December that 'It is getting very noticeable that anybody who reports sick seem to be evacuated. I am thinking seriously of having my name put on the list. Must have a talk to Bro Charlie & my mates & see what they think.'⁶⁸ In the event, he was given orders to help prepare for the evacuation. From the men's point of view, the final evacuation in December was simply the formal sanction of individual and collective deliberations about whether to report sick that had been taking place since early summer.

The concept of 'moral harm' – coined by the psychiatrist Jonathon Shay in his study *Achilles in Vietnam* – speaks to the shortcomings of care noted by soldiers and medical officers during the Gallipoli campaign. Shay observes that the anger of veterans is often expressed as betrayal, a feeling that the army has not acted as a responsible 'trustee'.⁶⁹ An army's responsibilities, he says, include not just the safeguarding of life and limb, but the maintenance of day-to-day comfort and subsistence, and moral harm occurs when military leaders fail to preserve these standards. Anger, then, may not only be a response to the moral compromises involved in killing or witnessing atrocities, but can stem from deprivations of various kinds – food, water and the standards familiar to civilian life – when it is perceived that these deprivations are due to the indifference, disrespect or incompetence of commanding officers.[70]

Bean, although anxious to rein in criticisms among the men, was clear about who was responsible for the epidemic. 'The fault happens in this case', he wrote on 18 November 1915, 'to be purely and simply the hopeless weakness, want of imagination, and above all want of moral courage among the British staff.'[71] Butler's appraisal of the medical services in 1930 was excoriating, and although a cautious and reserved man, he did not spare the experts.[72] He criticised the army for its ignorance about the true causes of the epidemic. The fly, he states, was known to be the culprit from the time of the South African wars. Yet the Mediterranean Expeditionary Force (MEF) officers at Gallipoli insisted on their own theories: intestinal chill, an excess of onions and wholemeal biscuits and – most vexatious for Butler – the Director of Medical Service's view that dysentery was caused by the men's habit of sea bathing. The theories they put forward, Butler comments acidly, covered every cause 'except the true one'.[73]

The MEF, Butler believed, had been slow to recognise the seriousness of the outbreak and reluctant to take measures that would help deter the flies.[74] Care of sick and wounded men was affected by a 'lack of firm capable direction'.[75] Butler was scornful of the medical experts who arrived from London 'in dozens' during August, and whose 'fine system of central laboratories' to diagnose the disease and increase sanitary precautions were too late to stem the tide of disease. The experts, Butler concluded, did little but 'clothe in scientific language the fact of a *debacle*'.[76] It was the death of the fly with the change of seasons, not the 'formidable weight of talent, scientific and administrative', that turned the tide.[77]

What animated Butler's criticisms was not the tactical errors that have preoccupied military historians of the campaign, but its human cost. Pity pulls against the stances of medical objectivity and historical distance. In the following passage, for example, Butler describes the principal causes of the outbreak. He begins with the role of food in transmission of the disease, then moves to the condition of the latrines. At this point Butler invites the reader to sympathise with the plight of the victims:

> It may be conjectured that in the soldiers' mess-tin was to be found the most important passive agent in the cycle of infection. Meanwhile the efforts to restrict the access of flies to excreta in the latrines were even less effective. Few latrines at Anzac were not exposed to direct or indirect fire, and many men were killed or wounded there. The plight of the unfortunate dysenteric, forced to relieve himself every half-hour or so, may be imagined.[78]

The chapters on disease at Gallipoli open with a description of the Anzacs in May, taken from the mouth of the man Butler regarded as partially responsible for their decline:

> 'Superb specimens', General Hamilton considered them. 'Fit as fiddles, hard as nails' a regimental medical officer records. The outbreak of sickness due to camp and other conditions in Egypt had quite subsided, and had on the whole left little mark. 'Unfits' had been eliminated; the force was healthy.[79]

Butler emphasises the health of the Anzacs at the beginning of the account in order to highlight their subsequent undoing. The narrative elicits the reader's sympathy through the contrast with the Anzacs of August, who, he tells us, were 'just skin and bone; hands, arms, and legs covered with septic sores; ill with dysentery; had to work in the trenches on bully-beef, bacon, and biscuits'.[80] Through the quotation from Captain Luther with which this article begins, Butler introduces the contentious notion that the lack of care shown to the Australians was a mark of their social inferiority as Colonial subjects.[81]

Butler's feelings about the way the men were treated lead him towards a critique of the Anzac myth's premise that the final evacuation was a success. In a particularly sharp remark, he undermines the only redeeming feature of the whole campaign: 'The retreat from Gallipoli (it may almost be said), is embodied as distinctly, if less dramatically, in the sick wastage of September, October, and November as in the actual strategic "evacuation" of the peninsula.'[82] Questioning the mythology of the withdrawal as a military accomplishment, Butler reminded his readers of the toll taken by sickness. Butler's account of the campaign is a catalogue of failures of care.

It was these that animated his analysis of the medical and logistical issues, and his tone was condemnatory. The army's treatment of the men at Gallipoli was blameworthy, and the injuries they suffered were not just physical and mental, but moral.

Sanitising the Anzacs

As Graham Seal has shown, the Anzac legend has two elements which exist in close relation, a formal version which elevates the moral and military virtues of the Australian soldier, and a more critical, anti-authoritarian underside borne of the 'exigencies of suffering', which circulates in the informal spaces of the veteran reunion and the home.[83] The final part of this chapter reflects on how the dysentery epidemic appears within these twin cultural legacies. The allusive references of memoir writers like my grandfather, and the solicitous replies of veterans when oral historians asked them about the condition, suggest that both the ceremonial and oppositional versions of the legend functioned to foreclose the memory of dysentery. It went underground, to be recovered by descendants like me and my father as we trawled the service records. This hidden quality, and the sanitising impulse in both the ceremonial and vernacular narratives of Anzac, points to the significance of the legend as a kind of 'reaction formation'. This concept was first expounded by Freud in 1894, who described it as a defence mechanism that blocked an unacceptable emotion by asserting its opposite in a 'counter symptom'. Reaction formations are a normal feature of children's development during the pre-adolescent phase: through the actions of the super-ego, or internalised authority figures, the infant's delight in and curiosity about the body's functions is converted into feelings of shame and disgust. Shame might be buried in extreme conscientiousness, disgust in tidiness or greed in excessive generosity.[84] The original impulse, now repressed, nonetheless animates these counter-behaviours and persists in the insistent assertion of its opposite. The clue to the presence of a reaction formation is the compulsive and exaggerated character of counterclaims.

Such a description might apply to the Anzac mythology, in which a trauma – the actual miring of Australia's manhood in shit – was covered over by assertions about physical capability and character.

Bean's efforts to construct the Australian soldier as an exemplar of manhood while the plans for evacuation were being drawn up have been well documented, and generations of historians have critically appraised his romantic depictions of the Anzac. They have identified behaviour and social tensions that the legend excluded and have considered its impact on the wider society.[85] The legend received its strongest promotion when the Anzac forces were most diminished: it was a legend of masculinity that emerged from its apotheosis. At the very moment when Bean was suffering from diarrhoea in late August, and noting the worsening health of Australian soldiers, his diary upheld the Anzacs as 'possibly the very best in the world' and condemned the Tommy as 'a very poor feeble specimen of a man'.[86] Bean's prose elevated the Anzacs as they were brought low; suffering and sickness were sublimated into fantasies of endurance and determination. Thinking with Freud, we might see Bean's work not merely as a response to the strategic and national humiliation of military evacuation, but to the sight and stench of bodily evacuation and the palpable unmanning of the Anzacs.

Produced on Gallipoli and published the following year, the *Anzac Book* contains numerous depictions of unshaven and shabbily dressed men. Bean's sketches show bare-chested men of all shapes and sizes dressed in improvised shorts, their leggings trailing behind them, but none looks like Captain Luther's 'kittens' of August.[87] Rather, the men's haphazard get-up illustrates national virtues of informality and lack of attention to military niceties.

Recollections of men crowded around the latrines or soiling themselves were unrepresentable in a volume destined for circulation to loved ones at home. There is a single passing reference to 'Gallipoli trot' in Edgar Wallace's poem *Anzacs*, which, however, also enshrines the Anzac as a national hero that 'The children unborn shall acclaim'.[88] The memory trace of dysentery persists in the *Anzac Book*'s portrayals of dishevelled insouciance, a trope that gives the merest hint of the 'intestinal holocaust' described by Butler in the *Official History*.[89]

The repressed memory of sickness is also apparent in the narratives of Australian historians, even those who have engaged critically with the vision Bean helped create. Les Carlyon's introduction to the 2010 edition of the *Anzac Book* discusses the 'harsher realities' that Bean sought to exclude from the volume

Figure 9.3 C. E. W. Bean, 'Turkish Divisional Orders'. British and Turkish forces were stretched to the limits by summer, but Bean here produces a riposte to Turkish rumours. Chests thrust out and muscles toned, the athleticism of the Anzacs is highlighted by their state of undress. Shorts were preferred in the heat but were easier to remove when men were taken ill. All rights reserved.

(including the sickness epidemic). Carylon uses the word 'sanitised' twice in the space of two paragraphs to describe these efforts, seemingly unconscious of the scatological facts that underly his metaphor. Lloyd Robson was one of the first historians to probe the powerful cultural resonance of the Anzac soldier, but at times his discussion comes close to repeating the mythology, such as when he claims that the first recruits to the AIF were 'selected from the best physical specimens of the many who rushed to volunteer and rally to the empire'.[90] In his 1974 book *The Broken Years*, Bill Gammage celebrates the fortitude of the Anzacs in a manner that downplays the impact of dysentery. His narrative of the state of the Anzacs in July entails a strange conjoining of Australian nationalism, Edwardian manliness and the stigma surrounding the shirker:

The sick rate was far greater than the wound rate, and threatened to incapacitate the entire Corps. Yet many soldiers stayed in the trenches rather than suffer the long delays in returning fit men to the front, so that by early August probably half the force was sick, and none of it was equal to the strain of a prolonged battle.

A few men surrendered to these afflictions, by malingering or by self-inflicting wounds, and although most doggedly carried on a general malaise settled upon the army.[91]

The behaviour of the Anzacs during the summer of 1915 establishes some of their central moral qualities as men and soldiers. To surrender to sickness is to show weakness and let down your mates. Charles Bean sometimes had more insight into the dysfunctional effects of the myth than the historians who followed him. In his chapter on the 'Sickness of the Army', for example, he discusses the reasons why attempts to keep the men healthy failed. Overwhelmed by the scale of evacuation that was needed once the outbreak began to spread, the medical authorities sought to foster an 'ideal' among the men of 'holding out and performing their duties as long as they had strength to "carry on"; a policy never difficult of application to these troops, since, even in later years, when war service had lost its glamour and its conditions were often detested, their mettle and inborn aversion to "giving in" almost invariably inclined them to struggle to the end against sickness'.[92] Bean admires the men's fortitude, yet is in no doubt that it was a response to official prompting and the failure of the medical evacuation in the summer. The men's persistence was in fact part of the problem, for 'it made impossible one method of coping with the epidemics, and undoubtedly increased both dysentery and enteric by retaining among the troops innumerable sources of infection'.[93]

The flipside of Seal's ceremonial mythology is the demotic version of Anzac, a testier and more oppositional stance that clashes at times with official narratives. Just as the demotic legend suggests, granddad's anger took the form of contempt for hypocritical officers who put their own safety above their men's. Anger reversed the tables, making moral exemplars of the weak and channelling the emotional aftermath of death and sickness into righteous contempt. Passing Brigade Headquarters on the way back to his unit after tunnelling, Granddad witnesses the following scene:

Out came Major King smoking a cigar, said he was ready, the two men unstrapped the stretcher, spread it out on the ground & lowered Major King onto it, then one to each end they lifted their cigar smoking burden & started off to the Beach. Those two men looked as if they should be carried & King looked big enough & healthy enough to carry both of them. How morally low can some men who have power get?[94]

Here was an object lesson in hypocrisy, a symbol of the toll exacted by their officers as sick men carried out duties which should never have been asked of them. Like the official narrative of Anzac, however, the demotic version positioned the soldier as stoic. It covered over the personal memory of being unwell and had no place for those who could not endure.

In my early twenties, I understood Granddad's creed 'never leave your mates' as an abstract political principle rather than an injunction borne of bodily experience. Anger was the emotional legacy of the First World War most familiar to my father and his brother growing up in the 1930s, and to the grandchildren growing up in the 1960s. As my grandfather's historian, I still struggle against the mythological weight of the hardy bush hand and crack shot to imagine the frightened and sick nineteen-year-old on the peninsula. Yet perhaps vestiges of Granddad's experience of dysentery were transmitted in our family and my historical pursuits. As a child, I was often anxious when visiting the toilet at our grandparents' house, as we were under strict instructions to use at most a couple of squares of toilet paper. I would worry that I might not have enough to clean myself or might take too much. Until writing this chapter I considered this parsimony to be borne of shortage in the Great Depression, but it might equally be viewed as a reaction formation, harking from a time in my grandfather's life when the flow of excreta felt unstoppable. When I returned to the study of the First World War in the late 1990s, two decades after Granddad's death and my interviews with him and now a British historian, I wrote an essay about the shame of dysentery and how this led the officer Lyndall Urwick to re-remember and re-write his war from the mid-1950s to the early 1980s.[95] Our family may not consciously have known of Granddad's bouts of sickness and their aftereffects, but it is interesting that my attention was drawn to another veteran whose writing functioned to contain his memory of dysentery. In Freud's formulation, did logorrhoea supplant diarrhoea?

Notes

1 Quoted in A. G. Butler, *Official History of the Australian Army Medical Services in the War of 1914–1918* (Melbourne: Australian War Memorial, 1930–1943), Vol. I, 321.
2 R. H. Roper interview, 'First World War'.
3 R. H. Roper, 'Gallipoli Memoir', in personal possession, 10.
4 Service record of Robert Henry Roper, National Archives of Australia (hereafter NAA): B2455, 13.
5 R. H. Roper, 'Gallipoli Memoir', 13.
6 R. H. Roper, 'Gallipoli Memoir', 16.
7 R. H. Roper, 'Gallipoli Memoir', 23.
8 R. H. Roper, 'Gallipoli Memoir Manuscript Diary Account', Liddle Collection LIDDLE/WW1/EP/062/21. https://explore.library.leeds.ac.uk/special-collections-explore/407442. Accessed 2 February 2020.
9 R. H. Roper 'Gallipoli Memoir', 18.
10 A. Wishart, '"As Fit as Fiddles" and "as Weak as Kittens": The Importance of Food, Water and Diet to the Anzac Campaign at Gallipoli', *First World War Studies*, 7: 2 (2016); M. Tyquin, *Gallipoli: An Australian Medical Perspective* (Newport, New South Wales: Big Sky Publishing, 2012); M. L. Lewis and S. R. Leeder, 'Public Health at Anzac Cove', *Medical Journal of Australia*, 202: 7 (20 April 2015), 384–5; G. Sheffield, 'Shaping British and Anzac Soldiers' Experience of Gallipoli: Environmental and Medical Factors and the Development of Trench Warfare', *British Journal for Military History*, 4: 1 (2017), 23–43; M. Harrison, *British Military Medicine in the First World War* (Oxford: Oxford University Press, 2010); R. Prior, *Gallipoli: The End of the Myth* (New Haven: Yale, 2010).
11 Butler, *Official History*, 206.
12 Quoted in L. Macdonald, *The Roses of No Man's Land* (London: Penguin, 1993), 117–18.
13 Wishart, 'As Fit as Fiddles', 154. Dysentery, Peter Stanley observes, 'weakened more than bowels and bodies. It sapped men's minds.' Quoted in Wishart, 'As Fit as Fiddles', 157. On the relationship between the stomach and emotional disturbances, see M. Roper, 'Re-Remembering the Soldier Hero: The Psychic and Social Construction of Memory in Personal Narratives of the Great War', *History Workshop Journal*, 50: 1 (Autumn 2000), 181–204; A. Carden-Coyne and C. Forth, 'Introduction: The Belly and Beyond', in A. Carden-Coyne and C. Forth (eds), *Cultures of the Abdomen: Diet, Digestion and Fat in the Modern World* (London: Palgrave Macmillan, 2005), 1–11; R. Duffett, *The Stomach for Fighting: Food and the Soldiers of the Great War*

Dysentery and the Anzac legend 255

(Manchester: Manchester University Press, 2012); R. Duffett, 'Ingestion and Digestion on the Western Front', in N. J. Saunders and P. Cornish (eds), *Modern Conflict and the Senses* (London: Routledge, 2017), 171–82.

14 Butler, *Official History*, 243.
15 A. J. E. Gourlay interview with Patsy Adam-Smith, 1976. SLV, MS 10530/TMS 134; 'Casualty Form – Active Service', service record of A. J. E. Gourlay, NAA: B2455.
16 Michael Tyquin speculates on the function of the legend in absorbing the traumas of Gallipoli. M. Tyquin, 'In Search of the Unseen Wound', in T. Frame (ed.), *Moral Injury: Unseen Wounds in an Age of Barbarism* (Sydney: University of New South Wales Press, 2015), 25–6.
17 K. Fewster (ed.), *Bean's Gallipoli: The Diaries of Australia's Official War Correspondent* (Crows Nest, New South Wales: Allen & Unwin, 2009), 197–9.
18 I used Adam-Smith's *The Anzacs* (Melbourne: Penguin, 1991) to direct me to her interviews at the State Library of Victoria. British interviewees were identified through a keyword search of interview summaries using the terms 'dysentery' and 'Gallipoli'.
19 C. C. Meager interview with Lyn Smith, 1984, IWM Oral History 8326, 3/5. www.iwm.org.uk/collections/item/object/80008123. Accessed 29 November 2021.
20 Meager interview, 3/5.
21 Meager interview, 2/5; C. Tomkinson interview with Peter Hart. IWM Oral History 7497, 3/3. www.iwm.org.uk/collections/item/object/80007299. Accessed 29 November 2021; H. Kahan interview with Patsy Adam-Smith, 16 December 1975. SLV, MS 11033/TMS 147; J. McPhee interview with Patsy Adam-Smith, 1976. SLV, MS 10495/TMS 123–4.
22 F. Caokes interview with Jan Stovold, 1984, IWM Oral History 8287, 1/1. www.iwm.org.uk/collections/item/object/80008087. Accessed 29 November 2021.
23 R. White, 'Europe and the Six-Bob-a Day Tourist: The Great War as Grand Tour, or Getting Civilised', *Australian Studies*, 5 (1991), 122–39; R. White, 'Sun, Sand and Syphilis: Australian Soldiers and the Orient, Egypt, 1914', *Australian Cultural History*, 9 (1990), 58.
24 See D. Dendooven, 'Trench Crap: Excremental Aspects of the First World War', in Saunders and Cornish (eds), *Modern Conflict and the Senses*.
25 Butler, *Official History*, 236.
26 Gourlay interview, 1976.
27 There was no sanitary section at Anzac cove until August 1915. Butler, *Official History*, 233.

28 Tyquin, *Gallipoli: An Australian Medical Perspective*, 63; Sheffield, 'Shaping British and Anzac Soldiers' Experience', 31.
29 Butler, *Official History*, 341.
30 J. Page, interview with Peter Hart, 1993. IWM Oral History 13083, 3/3. www.iwm.org.uk/collections/item/object/80012806. Accessed 29 November 2021; Bird, 1984, 2/7, 21.
31 H. Bruckshaw, *The Diaries of Private Horace Bruckshaw, 1915–1916* (London: Scolar Press, 1979).
32 McPhee interview, 1976.
33 Butler, *Official History*, 240.
34 W. I. Miller, *The Anatomy of Disgust* (Cambridge, MA: Harvard University Press, 1997), 96.
35 R. H. Roper, 'Gallipoli Memoir' (Liddle Collection), 19; Wishart, 'As Fit as Fiddles', 153; P. Adam-Smith, *The Anzacs* (Melbourne: Penguin, 1991), 138.
36 C. Newman interview with Roger McDonald, 1978. SLV, MS 11405/TMS 528; R. Mills interview with Patsy Adam-Smith, 1976. SLV, MS 10500/TMS 129–130; Caokes interview, 1984.
37 Gourlay interview, 1976.
38 Meager interview, 1984, 2/5.
39 Caokes interview, 1984.
40 Quoted in L. Carlyon, *Gallipoli* (Sydney: Pan Macmillan, 2001), 313–14.
41 H. Manton, interview with Lyn Smith, 1987. IWM Oral History 9756, 2/4. www.iwm.org.uk/collections/item/object/80009540. Accessed 29 November 2021.
42 J. Tolley, interview with Peter Hart, 1989. IWM Oral History 10404, 4/4. www.iwm.org.uk/collections/item/object/80010183. Accessed 29 November 2021.
43 Manton interview, 1987, 2/4. Meager described a nearly identical scene:

> *Interviewer*: How did it affect you when you had dysentery? How did you feel?
> *Meager*: Oh, you lost all … you had no go in you at all. And if I may say, and I know it isn't a very pleasant thing to say, but there was a trench, and there was a pole, you see, and we used to have to sit on the pole, and some of them, if you don't mind me saying so, fell in it. Oh it was dreadful. That was, I think that was worse than the fighting really. (Meager interview, 1984, 2/5)

44 P. Liddle, *Men of Gallipoli: The Dardanelles and Gallipoli Experience, August 1914 to January 1916* (London: Allen Lane, 1976), 162; P. Hart, *Gallipoli* (New York: Oxford University Press, 2011), 230; P.

Fitzsimons, *Gallipoli* (Melbourne: William Heinemann, 2014), 446; J. Murray interview with Peter Hart, 1984. IWM Oral History 8201, 12/45. www.iwm.org.uk/collections/item/object/80008002. Accessed 29 November 2021.
45 Duffett, 'Digestion and Indigestion', 176; Duffett, *Stomach for Fighting*, 166; Miller, *Anatomy of Disgust*, 9, 69.
46 Tomkinson interview, 1984, 3/3.
47 Tolley interview, 1989, 3/4.
48 Murray interview, 1984, 12/45.
49 Fewster (ed.), *Bean's Gallipoli*, 233–6, Carlyon, *Gallipoli*, 318.
50 Butler, *Official History*, 239; Wishart, 'As Fit as Fiddles', 142.
51 Sheffield, 'Shaping British and Anzac Soldiers' Experience', 27, 31.
52 Murray interview, 1994, 12/45; S. Flint, G. Harper and N. Wilson, 'The Gallipoli Gallop: Dealing with Dysentery on the "Fringes of Hell"', *Microbiology Australia*, 35: 3 (January 2014), 141.
53 B. Gammage, *The Broken Years: Australian Soldiers in the Great War* (Melbourne: Penguin, 1975), 64; Wishart, 'As Fit as Fiddles', 143.
54 R. H. Roper, 'Gallipoli Memoir', 15. For a contrasting view, see M. McKernan, 'McKenzie, William (1869–1947)', *Australian Dictionary of Biography* (Canberra: National Centre of Biography, Australian National University, 1986), https://adb.anu.edu.au/biography/mckenzie-william-7391/text12851. Accessed 29 November 2021.
55 Wishart, 'As Fit as Fiddles', 148.
56 Duffett, *Stomach for Fighting*, 161.
57 R. H. Roper, 'Gallipoli Memoir', 10.
58 Butler, *Official History*, especially 254–80.
59 Tyquin, *Gallipoli: An Australian Medical Perspective*, 92.
60 Fewster (ed.), *Bean's Gallipoli*, 171–2, 178.
61 Captain William Brown, based at Suvla, wrote of '12 cases of dysentery in a bell tent, the inside of it one black mass of flies for about 2 feet down from the top, and the men packed so that one had to edge one's feet in between them when stooping to examine them. They had barely enough water to drink.' Quoted in Harrison, *British Military Medicine*, 196.
62 W. H. Willcox to Sir Ronald Ross, 21 October 1915, Ross Collection, London School of Hygiene and Tropical Medicine (LSHTM), 137/162/112.
63 Tyquin, *Gallipoli: An Australian Medical Perspective*, 95; Butler, *Official History*, 371.
64 Butler, *Official History*, 364.
65 R. H. Roper interview, 'Great Depression', 13.
66 Gourlay interview, 1976.

67 T. Yarr to Sir R. Ross, 23 August 1915, Ross Collection, LSHTM, 137/57/113.
68 R. H. Roper, 'Gallipoli Memoir', 21.
69 J. Shay, *Achilles in Vietnam: Combat Trauma and the Undoing of Character* (New York: Scribner, 2003), 10.
70 Shay, *Achilles in Vietnam*, 19.
71 Fewster (ed.), *Bean's Gallipoli*, 232.
72 S. Garton, 'Anzac Health: A. G. Butler and the Writing of the Official Medical History of Australia During the 1914–18 War', *Working Papers in Australian Studies*, 93 (1994), 97–8. Garton raises the intriguing possibility that Bean's editorial hand may have contributed to the energetic moralism of Butler's account.
73 Butler, *Official History*, 245, 236, 253.
74 Butler, *Official History*, 253, 240.
75 Butler, *Official History*, 260.
76 Butler, *Official History*, 362.
77 Butler, *Official History*, 350, 360.
78 Butler, *Official History*, 240.
79 Butler, *Official History*, 228.
80 Butler, *Official History*, 352.
81 Butler, *Official History*, 321.
82 Butler, *Official History*, 341.
83 G. Seal, *Inventing Anzac: The Digger and National Mythology* (St Lucia: University of Queensland Press, 2004), 3–4.
84 S. Freud, 'Inhibitions, Symptoms and Anxiety', *The Standard Edition of the Complete Psychological Works of Sigmund Freud: Volume XX* (London, Vintage, 2001), 102, 115, 157; C. Galatariotou, 'The Defences', in S. Budd and R. Rushbridger (eds), *Introducing Psychoanalysis: Essential Themes and Topics* (London: Routledge, 2005), 21; Miller, *Anatomy of Disgust*, 2.
85 L. Robson, 'The Origin and Character of the First A.I.F. 1914–18: Some Statistical Evidence', *Australian Historical Studies*, 61 (1973), 737–49; L. Robson, 'The Australian Soldier: Formation of a Stereotype', in M. McKernan and M. Browne (eds), *Australia: Two Centuries of War and Peace* (Canberra: Australian War Memorial in association with Allen and Unwin Australia, 1988), 313–37; D. A. Kent, 'The Anzac Book and the Anzac Legend: C.E.W. Bean as Editor and Image-Maker', *Historical Studies*, 21: 84, 376–90; R. Gerster, *Big Noting: The Heroic Theme in Australian War Writing* (Melbourne: Melbourne University Press, 1987); Seal, *Inventing Anzac*; A. Thomson, *Anzac Memories: Living with the Legend* (Melbourne: Monash University Press, 2013).
86 Fewster (ed.), *Bean's Gallipoli*, 196, 200.

87 C. E. W. Bean (ed.), *The Anzac Book* (Sydney: University of New South Wales, 2010), 21, 29.
88 Bean (ed.), *Anzac Book*, 113.
89 Butler, *Official History*, 359; Bean (ed.), *Anzac Book*, 113.
90 Robson, 'The Australian Soldier', 322.
91 Gammage, *Broken Years*, 65.
92 C. E. W. Bean, *Official History of Australia in the War of 1914–1918, Vol. II: The Story of Anzac* (Sydney: Angus and Robertson, 1924), 373–4.
93 Bean, *Official History*, 374–5.
94 R. H. Roper, 'Gallipoli Memoir', 13.
95 M. Roper, 'Re-Remembering the Soldier Hero'.

10

Legacies of dysentery

In February 1939 the Gallipoli veteran Horace Anelay Brown wrote to the Repatriation Department for help.[1] He had experienced bouts of colitis and dysentery in Gallipoli and a succession of illnesses afterwards, including heart problems. He needed help to move about and wondered if the Repatriation Department could give him a travel allowance so he could run his car. His sole means of support was the war pension and he had been out very little in recent years as 'when I have been out, I have had a bad conscience about it because I felt I could not afford to run the car and was robbing my wife and my family to do so'. His wife, 'whose hands are already full', had been forced to attend to family business that 'with the help of the car, I could have seen to myself'. The condition that Horace suffered from was not just physical; it affected his sense of himself as a man. His wife was now the breadwinner and, feeling that the family could not bear the cost of his mobility, he had become, he said, 'a prisoner in my home'. There was yet further humiliation in having to expose his domestic situation to officials, who after deliberating, decided that they could not support his request.[2] Horace died a year later, aged fifty.

This chapter investigates the long history of the dysentery outbreak at Gallipoli among men like Horace Brown, whose national standing as Anzacs was at odds with the health problems they suffered from after the war, invisible wounds that could bring them low physically, mentally and socially, as Horace's letter intimates. By 1937, over 40 per cent of returned soldiers in Australia had applied for a pension, and the 'stomach cases' were a significant proportion among them.[3] Yet as the official historian of the medical services, R. A. Butler, admitted in 1943 as he looked back on over twenty years of repatriation practices, gastric cases were a 'serious problem' because they were difficult to diagnose.[4] Drawing on the pension files, the chapter describes the kinds of medical conditions that repatriation doctors attributed to the epidemic, and how they and veterans perceived the relationship between war service, emotions and the stomach. The Gallipoli legend shaped the negotiations between veterans and repatriation officials. On the one hand, the returned soldiers were national heroes who deserved public sympathy and support, but on the other, claimants had to contend with a masculinised image of the Anzacs that was at odds with how they felt, and explain themselves to officials who had high regard for self-reliance and were wary of sapping the spirit through benefits.[5] A study of the stomach problems suffered by veterans reveals the emotional cost of national silence about the state of the Anzacs by December 1915 and the reasons for their withdrawal. The long-term effects of dysentery were medically established, but the victims had no collective identity. Their pain was individual and internal, felt in the stomach and enacted in long drawn out and sometimes fractious negotiations with repatriation officials who were apt to dismiss their condition as 'neurotic embroidery'.[6]

The discussion here is based on the analysis of 127 case files of First World War veterans. The sample, undertaken in mid-2019, included the digitised files of all men with the surnames Brown, Green and White. Many were among the so-called 'Albany convoy', the first contingent of five thousand Australian soldiers who departed from Western Australia in November 1914, and applied for a pension or benefits after the war.[7] From this sample, I identified cases where stomach problems were among the symptoms reported by claimants. This allowed a broader understanding of how medical officials understood these conditions and how applicants, their families and advocates constructed their cases for support as each side responded to the memory of Gallipoli and the long-term effects of the war.

Medical Legacies

The stomach was a contested site between the wars: while the repatriation doctors in Australia looked for organic explanations of gastric problems, many medical practitioners in Britain and the United States, influenced by psychology, psychoanalysis and sociology, were convinced that the cause was often emotional. Among the practitioners of what became known as psychosocial medicine, the stomach was an eloquent organ. In 1941, Stewart Wolf and Harold Wolff began a seventeen-year collaboration with a man called 'Tom', who had accidentally swallowed boiling hot chowder as a child, burning through his stomach wall, and whose gastric fistula allowed Wolf and Wolff to observe the activity in his stomach. Tom was employed in the researchers' laboratory, and this enabled them to monitor him hour by hour and week by week. Tom's fistula gave Wolf and Wolff a window onto the workings of his stomach, and onto his emotions too, and how they were related to the 'situational factors' of his home and work life.[8]

In a study of Tom published in 1943 as *Human Gastric Function*, Wolf and Wolff concluded that the stomach was a sensitive register of emotions. Feelings of fright or depression were associated with reduced gastric motor activity; anger and resentment with 'hyperactivity in the stomach'.[9] The acidic activity that accompanied anger, they concluded, could be a contributory cause of ulcers.[10] In an appraisal of the study in 1981, almost forty years after its publication, Stewart Wolf concluded that it confirmed the 'conventional wisdom' – depicted by painters, poets and philosophers extending back as far as the beginning of the Christian era – that stomach troubles 'are brought on by the stresses of life'.[11]

Wolf and Wolff's research took place at the high point of public concern about stomach ailments. In the decade between 1929 and 1939, peptic ulcers were identified as the cause of death in more than forty-three thousand cases registered in England and Wales.[12] During the Second World War, soldiers in the USA and Britain presented to military doctors with stomach troubles in numbers that would have astonished their First World War counterparts: 709 soldiers were discharged from the British Army by the end of 1915 with peptic ulcer compared with 23,574 by the end of 1941.[13] A further study during the Second World War found that of the 14 per cent of patients in a British military hospital who had been diagnosed with stomach disorders, over half had peptic ulcers.[14] Ulcers, and their supposed connection to the stresses of modern life, were matters of concern to doctors across the Western world.

At a witness seminar in 2000, the consultant Dr John Paulley located the problem in the social conditions of the early to mid-twentieth century. The First World War generation, he maintained, had experienced the traumas of war, a difficult demobilisation and economic uncertainty. The 1920s and 30s were 'an intensive period of distress for people who had high expectations of "a country fit for heroes to live in"'. Their dashed hopes had laid the psychosomatic ground for the mid-century rise in stomach complaints.[15] Much the same observation had been made by British doctors during the Second World War, who suggested that the re-igniting of anxieties among Great War veterans could be a significant factor in the eruption of stomach ulcers.[16] Yet even in the 'age of stress', when stomach problems were often among the symptoms reported by Australian veterans diagnosed with 'neurasthenia' or 'debility' and R. A. Butler reckoned that up to 80 per cent of the veterans coming forward had mental conditions, the repatriation doctors were reluctant to entertain the notion that the stomach might register the emotional aftermath of war.[17]

The case histories of the veterans studied here suggest that gastrointestinal diseases during the war could contribute to health problems afterwards. When Horace Brown approached the repatriation in 1927, he had 'sharp attacks of pain' in his gut, vomiting and diarrhoea. He was breathless, exhausted and had heart pains.[18] Investigating further, the doctors found that food would quickly pass through his duodenum and small intestine, rather than remaining there for six hours as was normal.[19] This would account for his feelings of weakness, but the doctors discovered that in addition to liver damage, he had an enlarged heart.

What could have precipitated his condition? Horace joined the Mediterranean Expeditionary Force on 9 May 1915. He was twenty-four years old and a stockman, five foot nine and a half and with a chest measuring thirty-five inches – the kind of man that C. E. W. Bean praised as a model of Australian manhood. Yet after just three weeks on Gallipoli, he went sick with colitis, was evacuated to a hospital in Malta for five weeks and then transferred to a London hospital for a further thirteen weeks. He resumed active service in France in April 1916 but was ill with dysentery and diarrhoea on numerous occasions in the second half of 1916 and was reported to be 'very nervous'. He returned to Australia in August 1917 marked fit for home service only on grounds of 'Dysentery and Debility'.[20] Examining him in 1927, specialists concluded that dysentery had contributed to Horace's condition. Dr Mason cited findings from the Ministry of Pensions in Britain, where Gallipoli veterans had also presented with chronic infections of the alimentary canal and damage to organs including the heart, lungs and liver. He thought it possible that Horace's cardiac weakness, diarrhoea and debility were due to 'an amoebic condition resulting from infection during wartime service'.[21] A second specialist, Dr Edmeades, opined that the enlarged liver was 'probably due to an intra-hepatic ... abscess: the fact that he had dysentery on Gallipoli makes it likely'.[22] Dysentery seemed to have left Horace with a legacy of chronic health problems that shortened his life.[23]

John Irwin White's stomach pain was also accompanied by other symptoms, in his case related to age as well as the effects of dysentery. He had enlisted in 1914 at the age of nearly fifty, but his health broke down during the war and he was discharged in 1917 on grounds of 'senility'. He had suffered from bouts of diarrhoea and gastritis in France and later contracted influenza and malaria. Attacks of weakness and vomiting at night left him 'quite unable' to return to his old job. The repatriation doctors noted that he had diarrhoea 'more frequently than he should. Sequent probably to dysentery of Gallipoli.'[24] As he grew older, White's stomach problems were of less concern to the doctors than his chest and heart, and they adjusted his pension accordingly.

'Nervy men ... were a haunting presence in post-war Australia', remark Bruce Scates and Melanie Oppenheimer, and the men who haunted the repatriation hospitals in the 1920s and 30s were often suffering from their nerves.[25] Like Horace Brown, they slept poorly and were prone to nightmares, mood swings and anxiety. Gastric problems commonly featured in cases of fatigue and weakness, symptoms of a general breakdown in health. One such case was Fred Green, who applied for help from the repatriation with 'nervous debility'. He had been laid up with dysentery for three weeks at Lemnos and contracted enteric fever at the end of the war which left him 'weak and miserable'. He had no energy or appetite, felt shaky and became 'easily upset'.[26] Another was Frederick Green, who sought help from the repatriation with 'stomach trouble'. On investigating his claim, the repatriation officials determined that he was suffering from neurasthenia. However, they did not accept that this was a war condition, as there was 'nothing pointing to any physical disease'.[27] Known colloquially as 'burnt-out veterans', the symptoms experienced by men like Frederick Green and Fred Green were not just physical, but in Butler's words were 'mental and moral' as well.[28] Challenging though they were to the doctors, Gallipoli veterans were familiar with the mental malaise that accompanied gastric conditions. In 1973, Donald William Lechte, who arrived on the peninsula in August 1915, recalled how low dysentery had made him feel: 'I didn't care if it killed me or not. When one has dysentery for a couple of weeks one wouldn't mind being dead anyway.'[29]

The Repatriation Department took a narrow empirical approach when evaluating stomach claims.[30] The fact that a man had contracted a gastric condition on active service was not enough: his post-war illnesses had to be directly attributable to it. The reasoning behind the reduction of John Irwin White's entitlement for gastritis in 1933 was that his condition was 'not stated definitively anywhere to have been due to dysentery particularly'.[31] Faced with ambiguous evidence, the repatriation officials sometimes opted to limit the department's liability. The pension case submitted by William John Brown's wife after his death in 1938 depended on a link between his bowel cancer and dysentery at Gallipoli. Reviewing the evidence, Senior Medical Officer Dr Minty decided that William John's death was not service-related. He accepted the claim of dysentery but argued that the files did not show clear evidence that William John had suffered from recurrent colitis since the war, although he had a report from a specialist in Brisbane who stated that William John had 'recurrent attacks of diarrhoea usually in the early morning for years since the war'. Dr Minty also disputed the claim that there was a link between William John's colitis and bowel cancer, arguing that the very ubiquity of dysentery at Gallipoli weighed against his case: 'Granted that ex member had Dysentery on the Peninsula (and very few escaped it), the evidence on the file does not indicate that this became Chronic.' Attacks of morning diarrhoea, he stated, 'occur quite commonly in the Community' and usually had their origins in 'dietary indiscretions'.[32] Brown's gastric troubles, he seemed to imply, were largely of his own making. Officials debated how long the effects of dysentery might last. After Fred Green's death at the age of eighty-four, a repatriation doctor commented wryly that, far from shortening his life, Green's neurotic concern about his health, and abstemious lifestyle, were probably 'responsible for his longevity'.[33]

The level of proof required by the doctors created a bureaucratic trail that, for some individuals, consists of three hundred pages or more. The paucity of medical records increased the burdens on staff and applicants, the hospital files of Australian soldiers having been destroyed in a fire in London in 1919, a situation that led R. A. Butler to describe the challenge of determining war-relatedness as akin to making 'bricks without straw'.[34] Applicants often had to obtain their own evidence. After William Montagu Brown died in September 1932, his widow applied for a pension on the grounds that doctors in the Perth Hospital thought his chest pain 'was possibly due to illness on service – Dysentery'.[35] She supplied testimonies from Brown's friends and colleagues. Mr Dickson from the Skipper Bailey motor company, who had known William early in the war, recalled his shock on seeing him in 1920 as 'a very big difference was noticeable'. Alice Ryman, his typist for seven years, stated that for 'the whole of this time he was never really well' and on occasion would have to lay up for days at a time. Another employee of Skipper Bailey, Mr Briggs, also testified to William's ill health and, perhaps seeking to pre-empt the moral prejudices of the repatriation officials, wrote that he was 'a good living man' who spent most of his leisure in the garden, and 'seldom drank liquor except for medicinal purposes'.[36]

Despite this battery of testimony, the repatriation officials decided that William's death from cardiac failure could not be put down to his war service. William's stepson, a high school teacher in Geraldton, initiated a further appeal in 1939. Perceiving that the problem lay in the lack of evidence about Gallipoli, Mr Prance managed to track down a comrade from the Twelfth Battalion who had served with William. Mr Richardson stated that he had known William for around four months and that 'his health commenced to fail rather rapidly, and he was forced to receive medical attention often'. He remembered him being evacuated through illness.[37] Prance also obtained testimony from Captain Patterson who was in 'direct command' of William at the Department of Repatriation and Demobilisation in London during 1920 and recalled that on one occasion William had collapsed in his office. William's disability,

Patterson asserted, was 'directly due to wounds and sickness caused by war service'.[38] Prance did his best to strengthen his mother's case, but the repatriation officials decided that this new evidence did not justify altering the original decision. Even a comprehensive array of testimony about an ex-serviceman's health in the war and afterwards, submitted by an adept petitioner and a military man himself (Prance had joined the RAAF Engineering School in 1939), failed to satisfy the repatriation officials.

Although centred on the individual veteran, the application process sometimes became a collective effort as friends, families, colleagues and ex-comrades were drawn into supporting the petitioner. The tone of testimonials was sometimes angry, particularly when the case went to appeal. Arthur Harold Green had served in the First as well as the Second World Wars and was on final leave in 1943 when he underwent an emergency operation for a perforated duodenal ulcer.[39] After his death from peritonitis later in 1951, his wife applied for a widow's pension on the grounds that his ulcer had been caused by his war service.[40] Dr Macleod Murphy submitted a note to the department stating that Arthur Harold had been gassed in the 1914–18 war and had suffered from stomach problems afterwards. His recent trouble had arisen twelve days after he was discharged from the army, and 'it is quite obvious that he had his trouble whilst in the army and it is equally ridiculous to suggest that it developed after his discharge'. It was also therefore 'quite obvious' that Arthur Harold was entitled to treatment by the Repatriation Department.[41] Macleod Murphy wrote another scathing letter to the deputy-commissioner after the appeal was refused. The only reason he could see for the application being rejected was 'the usual stupidity of officialdom'.[42]

In part, the repatriation culture was adversarial because of the standards of proof required for a claim to succeed. Historians have noted that the department's judgements, while they purported to be objective, were based on moral judgements about character, lifestyle and dislike of dependence.[43] At the same time, the focus on disease and aetiology could mitigate moralising tendencies. The tone of the reports was typically factual and terse. Officials might attribute a man's digestive problems to his lifestyle, as Dr Minty did when he put William John Brown's morning diarrhoea down to 'dietary indiscretions', or they might note lifestyle issues but not see them as material, the intention being in the main to ascertain causality.⁴⁴

At a time when mental illness was stigmatised, the narrow focus on physical symptoms and evidence could have positive effects. Taking observations and case histories from outpatient clinics into account, and drawing on the evidence from GPs and specialists, the process aspired to bureaucratic criteria. The Repatriation Department was hardly in the vanguard of medical practice between the wars and while its officials tended in Scates and Oppenheimer's words to be 'Distrustful of quack theories from Vienna', in adhering to organic explanations, they may also have been less apt to pathologise.⁴⁵

Two evidence reports on the same veteran, thirteen years apart, illustrate the difference between the empirical approach typically adopted by the repatriation officials between the wars and a psychosomatic approach. The 1935 report on Fred Green explained that he was suffering from 'palpitation of the heart with tightness of throat at night, nervy, easily upset, not emotional, cannot sleep in the dark (has a light all night), frontal headaches last 2 yrs'. It diagnosed nerve and gastric trouble.⁴⁶ The tone was descriptive and did not abstract Fred's symptoms into a mental illness. His 1949 Hospital File notes, by contrast, are littered with psychological jargon. They describe Fred as a 'well adjusted obsessive compulsive Personality, who was maladjusted at the age of 9yrs by the death of his Mother and experienced aggravation by War Service', and was now suffering from an 'anxiety state concerning fear of heart disease'.⁴⁷ Assessments based on a methodology of reporting mental symptoms alongside physical ones, with a bias towards organic explanations, at least avoided the additional stigma of psychological labels.⁴⁸

The reluctance to embrace psychological explanations did not always work in the veteran's favour, however. As Scates and Oppenheimer point out, lack of training in psychiatry and suspicion of psychoanalysis could lead the repatriation doctors to treat neuroses as 'at best a moral failing, at worst calculated malingering'.⁴⁹ During William Reginald Brown's fortnightly medical assessments, his doctors observed that he was beginning to adduce additional nervous symptoms. He had initially approached the hospital in 1938 feeling 'shaky and depressed' and 'sick in the stomach', but it seemed to the doctors that under observation he was acquiring new symptoms, telling them for example that he 'jumps at sudden noise'.

They doubted the veracity of his complaints: 'Is inclined to answer in the affirmative to all leading questions and exaggerate the severity and duration of his symptoms.'[50] The repatriation doctors probably assumed that William Reginald was exaggerating his troubles in order to increase his chance of a pension, but for a contemporary psychological expert, suggestibility would be an aspect of a mental condition rather than a reason to doubt the truthfulness of a claim. The officials' reluctance to entertain psychological explanations was particularly problematic when a man's state of mind affected his capacity to give a credible account of his symptoms and their connection to the war.

Reporting on nervous conditions but not pursuing psychological explanations, the approach of the repatriation doctors reflects in Kate Blackmore's words an 'obsession with medical taxonomy'.[51] Rather than seeking the origins of stomach problems in early history or a traumatic event and treating them as physical enactments of mental pain, they focused on disease, exposure and symptoms. In this respect, the repatriation culture was consonant with that of the returned soldiers, who valued their privacy and often wanted their problems to be recognised as medical and not emotional. For the repatriation doctors, the dysentery cases were in some ways more straightforward than the general run of men suffering from nerves or debility, as this was a disease whose after-effects were medically established. They were less confident – and more suspicious – of men whose emotional disturbances seemed to have no clear physiological foundation.[52]

Social legacies

The interactions between claimants and repatriation officials were thus shaped by a medical and bureaucratic culture that looked for organic explanations of stomach problems and demanded evidence of them that was often hard to obtain. But they were also shaped by the Anzac ideal of 'courage and self-help', the counter-image of the burnt-out digger and the personal humiliation of dysentery and its aftermath.[53] Scates and Oppenheimer, in their studies of soldier settlement and pension records, describe the deep anger among veterans and their families towards the government officials charged with repatriation.⁵⁴ State parsimony and suspicion that ex-servicemen were trying it on encouraged a 'moral economy' among petitioners, who justified their claims for assistance in terms of a 'fair go' for the service they had given their country.⁵⁵ This economy, Scates and Oppenheimer conclude, was a legacy of the unionised culture of early twentieth-century Australia. Others have argued that the antipathy between officials and claimants was conjunctural, brought about by the difficult task that faced repatriation officials, particularly during the Depression years, in reaching a compromise between entitlement and keeping a tight string on the public purse.⁵⁶ While the burden of proof was supposed to lie with the Repatriation Department, in practice it lay with the most vulnerable.⁵⁷ War pensions, concludes Blackmore, 'became the terrain over which a protracted civil war was fought'.⁵⁸

The discontents of repatriation, however, did not just stem from the popular influence of unionism or injustices in the adjudication of claims. They also emanated from guts and minds that were in turmoil. Anger went right back to the army's failures to look after them on the peninsula. 'We were all fed up to the teeth with everything', the Gallipoli veteran Rollie Mills told Patsy Adam-Smith in the 1970s, the flies, the poor food, the lack of water, the lice and the dysentery.⁵⁹ Appealing the Repatriation Department's decision not to award him a pension, Fred Green insisted that he was 'free from any nervous condition' before he joined the Medical Corps and that the stress of four years in operating theatres and postmortem was the cause of his nerve trouble and gastric trouble. He was 'on the decline because of the war'.⁶⁰ William Montagu Brown's widow stated that 'From the time I married Brown in 1918 he was more or less a sick man.'⁶¹ Reports like these were meant to convince the repatriation officials that the veteran had suffered long-term effects and was entitled to a pension, but the emotion was not simply strategic. Claimants were angry because of what the men were put through in the war, their health problems afterwards and what families had to do to support them.⁶²

The angry tone of petitioners echoed the resentments of the Gallipoli campaign. The very title of Butler's chapter on the outbreak in the *Official History* conveyed a moral judgement. He called it 'The Disease Debacle at Gallipoli'. In the chapter Butler quotes an Australian Medical Officer, who in September 1915 was reputed to have said of the army's belated attempts to get a grip on the epidemic, 'you may as well have spat on a bushfire'.[63]

In the Gallipoli memoirs that my grandfather wrote in the early 1970s, he remarked under the poignant date 17 December 1915, the eve of the withdrawal: 'Many of my mates lie in this accursed land & I wonder if they can judge & if so what is their judgment? I am tired, lousy, & suffer from dysentery. I would love to get an opinion from the late Reverend Digges La Touche.'[64] The clergyman Everard La Touche had travelled with my grandfather from Australia to Gallipoli as part of the Sixteenth Reinforcement that arrived on the peninsula on 5 August. According to Granddad, despite La Touche's protected status as a man of religion, he had insisted on going with his men into the Lone Pine attack on 6 August but was almost immediately hit in the stomach by machine gun fire. La Touche was one of only two men of religion who Granddad respected. The rest, along with most of his officers, are charged with hypocrisy and indifference to the fate of the ordinary soldier. The tone is angry and moralising, suggesting that Granddad – who as a fourteen-year-old itinerant worker had gotten himself confirmed at St Patrick's Cathedral in Melbourne – experienced the war as a shattering of belief systems. It is no accident that he should elect La Touche, killed before he was able to see the full horrors of Gallipoli, to judge the conduct of those who ran the campaign. It is no accident either that the memory of dysentery should feature in his final reckoning, a failure of care so disastrous that it precipitated the withdrawal. The link that a single veteran in his seventies made between dysentery, neglect and moral injury may seem slight in terms of historical evidence, but it points to the shadow that the 'accursed land' of Gallipoli had cast over ethical beliefs and the duties of care owed to citizen soldiers.

Although often adversarial, relationships between applicants and departmental officers (like those between regimental officers and men) were complex because of their shared histories. The policy when establishing the repatriation system was that where possible the officials should also be veterans. Others argued that the military-style culture within repatriation departments exacerbated conflict, as claimants were often assumed to be malingering. The Senior Medical Officer Dr Hastings Willis remarked in 1942 that 'the majority of the departmental clients were not "heroes", but plain men and many of them not as much "wounded" as they wished to be'.[65] But the fact that many of the repatriation staff were veterans meant that some had suffered from the very diseases they were now treating. *The Dark Pocket of Time*, Kate Blackmore's carefully researched study of repatriation, reveals the extent of this. Among the Departmental Medical Officers in Sydney, Leslie Cowlishaw had contracted dysentery in Gallipoli and Sydney Vere Appleyard had contracted trench fever in 1917 that developed into chronic nephritis.[66] Charles Arthur Courtenay, the Principal Departmental Medical Officer in Victoria, had reported sick at Gallipoli on 24 September with shell-shock and had subsequent bouts of 'debility' and 'neurasthenia', conditions that would later exorcise the repatriation officers because of their emotional basis and the difficulty of ascertaining causality. Courtenay was known to be hard on 'pension wranglers' and was disliked by applicants, and one can speculate that his personal history of nervous troubles may not have been unconnected to his uncompromising attitude towards other suffering veterans.[67]

Shared experience of overseas service, however, and the physical and mental stresses it imposed, could also facilitate common understanding as the identity of veteran cut across the identities of applicant and bureaucrat. The pension files give occasional glimpses of the respect shown towards Gallipoli veterans, in phrases like '1914–18 man' or simply 'Anzac'.[68] When John Irwin White appeared before a medical board in February 1917 with vomiting, diarrhoea and debility, the doctors noted that he had been 'on Gallipoli from the landing to the evacuation', then in France during 1916, and that he 'was always been able to carry on, until towards the end, when he broke down'. The medical board concluded that cumulative exhaustion was often to be found among such men.[69] In 1922, respect for those with war service was formally incorporated in the Repatriation Department's medical taxonomy, which distinguished between the neuroses of men with mental and physical constitutions that were fragile prior to enlistment and those of men who had given 'long continued battlefield service'.[70] At one end of the hierarchy stood the Gallipoli men who fought through the war without going off sick; at the other, those who did not see action overseas. When Frederick Green applied for a pension in 1936 on grounds of stomach trouble and neurasthenia, the medical officers on his panel concurred with the unsympathetic judgement of Dr

Crowe. Green's service, he explained, 'was in England only' and he had not experienced any illness sufficient to 'cause or predispose him to any gastric condition'. His complaints were most likely due to 'his post war habits'.[71] The implication seemed to be that Green was drawing on the public awareness of stomach problems after Gallipoli to try it on.

While a Gallipoli man might expect a better hearing from the repatriation officials than a non-combatant, the legacies of dysentery pulled in different directions. Evaluating the post-war policies towards 'war damaged' men, R. A. Butler was concerned about the impact of state support. As the previous chapter shows, his assessment of the campaign highlighted the poor organisation of hygiene and medical facilities. He described strong men brought to their knees by dysentery and emphasised the disservice done to them by the absence of proper medical care. Although sympathetic to the plight of Australia's citizen soldiers, however, Butler's attitude towards pensions was conservative and Victorian: he worried that they would sap the very qualities that had made the Anzacs heroes at home and abroad.[72] 'It cannot be too strongly emphasised', he writes, 'that, in prevention of nervous disorder as in its cure – the positive aids to self-help will be of greater value to the soldier than any artificial support. And his help must take the form of *helping him to work, and making it worth his while, morally and economically to do so*.'[73] At the same time, Butler acknowledged that many of the cases coming forward could not be put down to constitutional weakness or opportunism and that the Repatriation had to respond to the 'popular emotion' surrounding the Anzacs' 'fight' for justice.[74] Butler derided claims circulating in the popular press about the 'burnt out digger', a condition which he felt was a social construction, charitable bodies such as the Returned Sailors and Soldiers Imperial League of Australia being 'in part, the creators of the hypothesis'.[75] Yet as he noted, the Repatriation Department had its own diagnostic equivalent in the term 'debility'.[76] Butler worried that the Anzac would be made dependent by aid, but he also saw that medical men like himself must adjust to a new post-war spirit of public generosity towards the veteran, a sentiment which he called 'the human touch'.[77]

The social legacies of Gallipoli were double-edged. On the peninsula, sick men had been reluctant to be taken out of the line, and

Bean and other journalists had praised their efforts to keep going.[78] This, along with the Anzac's regard for his mates and casual disregard for authority, had become core tenets of the Anzac identity and were policed by the Anzacs themselves. As the Gallipoli veteran Charlie Byrne explained to a repatriation doctor, 'one was not game to go on sick parade unless he had his guts hanging out. His mates saw to that, for no man liked the appellation of a malingerer.'[79] Stoicism created a problem when it came to assessing claims after the war, however, since there was often no medical evidence on men who had stayed in the line.

What often ensued was a search, sometimes decades later, for veterans who could attest to a man's illness. A witness might draw on the Anzac ideal of forbearance to assist an ex-comrade's claim. Because there was no evidence on the files to suggest that William John Brown had been sick at Gallipoli, the officials assessing his widow's pension claim in 1938 sought a testimonial from his commanding officer. Writing more than twenty years after the event, Lieutenant Colonel Bourne emphasised the respect owed to men who had stayed at their posts: William John, he stated, 'had a long tour of duty on Gallipoli – almost seven months continuous and suffered from dysentery'. His war service 'appeared to tax him greatly though he never spared himself and had a distinguished record … He got very thin and weak and so far as I remember appeared to have contracted some stomach trouble.'[80]

The Anzac legend shaped claims about the impact of dysentery. It was not easy for men esteemed for their manly independence to confess to anonymous bureaucrats that they had upset stomachs, were anxious and felt weak. They were often coming forward with stories that revealed their inability to live a life that accorded with the legend.[81] John Irwin White had been a boundary rider and fencer before the war, but since coming home had 'bad' periods where he was 'unable to do any work, sometimes so ill that he thinks he is going to die'.[82] It could feel demeaning to expose domestic troubles to officials and the very thought deterred some from approaching the repatriation.

As with claims during the war, often there was no medical evidence of stomach complaints afterwards to support a claim. As they had done at Gallipoli, the men claimed to have simply put up with the pain or resorted to their own medications. Applying for a widow's pension after William Montagu Brown's death in 1932, his wife explained that they assumed his chest pain was 'due to indigestion and for which we used home remedies'.[83] The couple only discovered that William's condition might be war-related when it became so serious that he was forced to seek medical help. Francis John White provided the repatriation officials with a log of his self-medication from the war until 1933. His dysentery returned periodically after 1915 but 'the condition did not appear severe enough for further hospital treatment'. During 1919–20 he had 'treated myself when stomach troubled me with Sa. Magnesia, Mother Siegals [sic] Syrup, etc., and I also took different nerve tonics. I conducted my own grocery business and used medicines from my own stock'. When the condition flared up in the late 1920s, he 'had no medical attention but relied on home treatment and patent remedies'. He had purchased stomach remedies from a chemist in Corryong, who might be able to 'furnish evidence in my support'.[84] The Gallipoli legend of men who had bravely managed their own troubles persisted in the ways that veterans and their families responded to health problems afterwards. Many could probably not afford to see a doctor, and, stoic Anzacs that they were, took care into their own hands.

Accounting for William Henry White's death in 1943 at the age of forty-nine, his wife explained that although his 'nerves were in a very bad state due to shell-shock', he was 'of such a nature that he would not consult a doctor'.[85] William Montagu Brown objected to doctors, his wife explained, and had avoided the Repatriation Department because he was concerned that they would assume he was 'after more pension' and he did not want to be labelled a scrounger.[86] Veterans internalised the stigmas surrounding malingering and benefit dependence, and this could lead them to steer clear of the Repatriation Department altogether.[87] A returned soldier might act in the Anzac spirit of self-reliance and treat his own ailments, but he might also add weight to his claim and play to the perceived values of the Repatriation Department by putting the lack of medical evidence down to self-reliance. The negotiations were political and strategic and revolved as much around considerations of masculinity, morality, anger and shame as medical taxonomies of cause and symptom.

In 1976, at the age of eighty-one, Roley Mills was interviewed about his early memories of Gallipoli. He remembered 'fellows going down to the latrine, suffering from dysentery, and coming back, could hardly walk, and evidently, one of the boys, it was too much for him. I saw him, I didn't see him do it, but I saw him a minute after it was done, he put a bullet through the calf of his leg. And he was in terrible pain, he was only a lad, and he started to cry.'[88] It is unclear whether Mills himself caught dysentery, but it is surely significant that his account moves from the wretched state of the victims to the memory of a man who could bear no more. Here was the antithesis of the Anzac hero, a soldier reduced to a weeping boy who would shortly be tried for cowardice. These were the kinds of memories that ex-servicemen had to live with, memories of their own enfeeblement and of seeing their comrades come undone. This was the underbelly of the Anzac legend, a memory which would surface in plaintive calls on the Repatriation Department.

In her study of shell shock, Tracey Loughran remarks on the backwards-looking perspective of military doctors in Britain, and much the same can be said of the repatriation culture in Australia. Many of its doctors had trained before the war, and 'employed the same conceptual strategies for handling psychological theories already in use before 1914'.[89] Their frameworks of understanding did not encompass the living circumstances and emotions of the claimant, but at the same time, the number of ex-servicemen coming forward with gastric and nervous troubles forced them to acknowledge that such conditions were physical and emotional and could not be put down to pension-wrangling. In addition to the medical legacies, the social legacies of Gallipoli shaped interactions between claimants and officials. Between the wars, the repatriation system became a 'parallel welfare state' with comparatively generous levels of benefit given in recognition of the sacrifices made by the Anzacs. A veteran could approach the department confident of a certain amount of respect for the '1914–18 man'.[90] Yet the experience was often humiliating. The men gave up any claim to manly self-reliance as they described embarrassing symptoms to anonymous officials and tried to convince them that they were unable to be breadwinners and required help from the state. The Repatriation Department was the one public institution in post-war Australia where the havoc that Gallipoli had played on guts and minds was known, but despite the intention to help veterans recover, it often aggravated the wounds of a disastrous campaign.

Notes

1. The term 'repatriation' is used uniquely in Australia to describe the return and reintegration of soldiers after military conflict, as well as the government policies and offices charged with their care. For a history of the term, see C. Lloyd and J. Rees, *The Last Shilling: A History of Repatriation in Australia* (Melbourne: Melbourne University Press, 1994), Introduction, 1.
2. 'Letter from Horace Anelay (H. A.) Brown to Deputy Commissioner', Repatriation Department, Brisbane, 6 February 1939, National Archives of Australia (hereafter NAA), BP709/1, M2430 PART 2, 121–2.
3. M. Larsson, *Shattered Anzacs: Living with the Scars of War* (Sydney: University of New South Wales Press, 2009), 215; S. Garton, *The Cost of War: Australians Return* (Melbourne: Oxford University Press, 1996), 83.
4. A. G. Butler, *Official History of the Australian Army Medical Services in the War of 1914–1918*, Vol. III (Melbourne: Australian War Memorial, 1930–43), 813.
5. M. Crotty and M. Larsson (eds), *Anzac Legacies: Australians and the Aftermath of War* (North Melbourne, Victoria: Australian Scholarly Publishing, 2010), 7; on the fear of benefit dependence, see J. Murphy, *A Decent Provision Australian Welfare Policy, 1870 to 1949* (London: Routledge, 2016), 117–18.
6. Butler, *Official History*, Vol. III, 833.
7. B. Scates, State Library of Victoria blog, 'Bringing the War Home: Repatriation Records and the Family Historian – Don Grant Memorial Lecture', 18 August 2015, https://blogs.slv.vic.gov.au/family-matters/bringing-the-war-home-repatriation-records-and-the-family-historian-don-grant-memorial-lecture/. Accessed 30 November 2021; B. Scates, 'How War Came Home: Reflections on the Digitisation of Australia's Repatriation Files', *History Australia*, 16: 1 (2019), 198.
8. S. Wolf and H. Wolff, *Human Gastric Function* (Oxford: Oxford University Press, 1943), 89, 112.
9. Wolf and Wolff, *Human Gastric Function*, 116, 127.
10. S. Wolf, 'The Psyche and the Stomach: A Historical Vignette', *Gastroenterology*, 80: 3 (1981), 609.
11. Wolf, 'Psyche and Stomach', 605.
12. J. N. Morris and R. M. Titmuss, 'Epidemiology of Peptic Ulcer Vital Statistics', *The Lancet*, 244 (30 December 1944), 841.
13. E. Jones, 'Stomach for the Peace: Psychosomatic Disorders in UK Veterans and Civilians 1945–55', in M. Jackson (ed.), *Stress in Post-War Britain* (London: Routledge, 2017), 133.

14 I. Miller, 'The Mind and Stomach at War: Stress and Abdominal Illness in Britain c. 1939–1945', *Medical History*, 54: 1 (2010), 97, 99.
15 D. A. Christie and E. M. Tansey (eds), *Peptic Ulcer: Rise and Fall. Wellcome Witnesses to Twentieth Century Medicine* (London: The Wellcome Trust Centre for the History of Medicine at UCL, 2002), 11.
16 G. Draper, 'The Emotional Component of the Ulcer Susceptible Constitution', *Annals of Internal Medicine*, 16: 4 (April 1942), 638, 643, 647.
17 B. Scates and M. Oppenheimer, *The Last Battle: Soldier Settlement in Australia 1916–1939* (Cambridge: Cambridge University Press, 2016), 6, 176.
18 H. A. Brown, 'Report by S. F. McDonald', Repatriation General Hospital Windsor, 18 February 1927, NAA: BP709/1, M2430, 260.
19 H. A. Brown, 'Radiographic Report', Dr Mason, 3 February 1927, NAA: BP709/1, M2430, 14.
20 H. A. Brown, 'Army Form B. 179', 17 October 1917, 2, NAA: BP709/1, M2430, 232.
21 H. A. Brown, 'Report by Dr Mason', 3 February 1927, NAA: BP709/1, M2430, 10.
22 H. A. Brown, 'Report by Dr Edmeades', 6 February 1927, NAA: BP709/1, M2430, 11.
23 H. A. Brown, 'Summary of Particulars of Application for Assistance', 1 May 1940, NAA: BP709/1, M2430, 101.
24 J. I. White, 'Report', Dr W. H. Steel Medical Officer, 2 February 1922, NAA: BP709/1, M10733, 13. Despite the medical notes stating that he was 'on Gallipoli from the landing', there was some doubt about whether White had served in Gallipoli, and his medical records only record gastritis in France. 'Pte E. O'Hanlon Unofficial Memo', 24 July 1915, NAA: BP709/1, M10733, 78.
25 Scates and Oppenheimer, *Last Battle*, 176.
26 Fred Green, 'Extract from Client Form 20E', 21 May 1935; 'Report from Dr A. A. McKay', 21 May 1935, NAA: D363, M9123, 120–1; 'Memorandum for the Secretary, Repatriation Commission from Acting Deputy Commissioner', 23 August 1935, NAA: D363, M9123, 124; Dr O'Brien, 'Report on Discharge, Repatriation Commission, SA Branch, Keswick', 15 December 1936, NAA: D363, M9123, 112.
27 Frederick Green, 'Letter from Deputy-Commissioner J. C. McPhee to Frederick Green', 31 July 1935, NAA: D363, M9123, 96.
28 Butler, *Official History*, Vol. III, 83; on the 'burnt-out digger', see Lloyd and Rees, *The Last Shilling*, chapter 12, 'Organisation and Money', 21.
29 D. W. Lechte, 'Recollections', ca. 1973 (MS), SLV, MS10701.
30 K. Blackmore, *The Dark Pocket of Time: War, Medicine and the Australian State, 1914–1935* (Adelaide: Lythrum Press, 2008), 149, 179.

31 J. I. White, 'Recommendation of Dr W. E. E. Langford', 12 January 1933, NAA: BP709/1, M10733, 16.
32 W. J. Brown, 'Report by Dr. E.D. Ahern', 14 April 1938, NAA: BP709/1, M36103, 11; W. J. Brown, 'Summary of Particulars, Recommendation by C.C. Minty', 6 August 1938, NAA: BP709/1, M36103, 8.
33 Fred Green, 'No. 8 Repatriation Board. Reason for Determination', 28 June 1979, NAA: D363, M9123, 15.
34 Scates and Oppenheimer, *Last Battle*, 147; Butler quoted in Blackmore, *Dark Pocket*, 168.
35 W. M. Brown, 'Communication from Widow', 3 December 1932, NAA: PP2/8, M24115, 190–1.
36 W. M. Brown, 'Communication from Mr H. Briggs', 12 December 1932, NAA: PP2/8, M24115, 173.
37 W. M. Brown, 'Mr Richardson to Deputy Commissioner', 17 May 1939, NAA: PP2/8, M24115, 196.
38 W. M. Brown, 'Captain C. A. Patterson to Deputy Commissioner', 30 November 1940, NAA: PP2/8, M24115, 197.
39 A. H. Green, 'Letter from Arthur Harold Green to Deputy-Commissioner, Repatriation Commission', 15 March 1951, NAA: B73, M3595, 73.
40 A. H. Green, 'Olive Green Record of Evidence', 29 October 1951, NAA: B73, M3595, 49.
41 A. H. Green, 'Dr. I. S. Macleod Murphy Clinical Notes', 5 October 1951, NAA: B73, M3595, 53–4.
42 A. H. Green, 'Dr. I. S. Macleod Murphy to Deputy-Commissioner of Repatriation', 19 November 1951, NAA: B73, M3595, 40. As early as 1919, publications such as the Returned Soldiers and Sailor's League of Australia's *Digger's Gazette* had criticised the repatriation department for being 'saturated with officialdom'. P. Paynton, *'Repat': A Concise History of Repatriation in Australia* (Canberra: Department of Veterans' Affairs, 2018), 34.
43 Scates and Oppenheimer, *Last Battle*, 149, 167; Blackmore, *Dark Pocket*, 143.
44 W. J. Brown, 'Summary of Particulars, Recommendation by C.C. Minty', 6 August 1938, NAA: BP709/1, M36103, 8.
45 Scates and Oppenheimer, *Last Battle*, 178.
46 Fred Green, 'Report of Dr. A. A. McKay, SMO', NAA: D363, M9123, 121.
47 Fred Green, 'Memorandum for Deputy Commissioner', 9 November 1949, NAA: D363, M9123, 110.
48 Alistair Thomson describes how his grandfather Hector's family doctor leaned towards a diagnosis of encephalitis rather than 'exhaustion psychosis' on similar grounds, as it helped avoid the stigma of mental

illness and did not imply a character defect. Thomson, *Anzac Memories: Living with the Legend*, 2nd edn (Melbourne: Monash University Press, 2013), 262.
49 Scates and Oppenheimer, *Last Battle*, 178.
50 W. R. Brown, 'Copy of Form 14A, Drs T.D. Freedman and J. W. Freedman', 19 May 1950, NAA: B73, H6309, 77.
51 Blackmore, *Dark Pocket*, 179.
52 On the difficulties of establishing the entitlements of the 'nerve cases', see Scates and Oppenheimer, *Last Battle*, 177.
53 Butler, *Official History*, Vol. III, 838.
54 B. Scates and M. Oppenheimer, '"I Intend to Get Justice": The Moral Economy of Soldier Settlement', *Labour History*, 106 (May 2014), 231, 240; Blackmore, *Dark Pocket*, 156; Thomson, *Anzac Memories*, 286–7.
55 Scates and Oppenheimer, 'Moral Economy', 231, 240.
56 Lloyd and Rees, *The Last Shilling*, chapter 12, 'Organisation and Money', 7; Thomson, *Anzac Memories*, 287.
57 Blackmore, *Dark Pocket*, 169.
58 Blackmore, *Dark Pocket*, 156.
59 R. Mills interview with Patsy Adam-Smith, 1976, SLV, MS 10500/TMS 129–30.
60 Fred Green, 'Letter from Claimant', 1 June 1935, NAA: D363, M9123, 121.
61 W. M. Brown, 'Communication from Widow', 3 December 1932, NAA: PP2/8, M24115, 171.
62 Larsson, *Shattered Anzacs*, 97–9.
63 Butler, *Official History*, Vol. I, 351.
64 R. H. Roper, 'Gallipoli Memoir', 23.
65 Blackmore, *Dark Pocket*, 156.
66 Blackmore, *Dark Pocket*, 159–60.
67 Blackmore, *Dark Pocket*, 163–4.
68 E.g. John Herbert Brown, 'Army Form D2', 13 December 1918, NAA: B73, M40293, 16.
69 J. I. White, 'Medical Report on an Invalid. Army Form B.179', 20 February 1917, NAA: BP709/1, M10733, 83.
70 Scates and Oppenheimer, *Last Battle*, 179.
71 Frederick Green, 'Report from Dr Crowe', 24 October 1935, NAA: D363, M9123, 58–9.
72 M. Tyquin, 'In Search of the Unseen Wound', in T. Frame (ed.), *Moral Injury. Unseen Wounds in an Age of Barbarism* (Sydney: University of New South Wales Press, 2015), 25.
73 Butler, *Official History*, Vol. III, 833. Original emphasis.
74 Butler, *Official History*, Vol. III, 802.

75 Butler, *Official History*, Vol. III, 816.
76 Butler, *Official History*, Vol. III, 838.
77 Butler, *Official History*, Vol. III, 822.
78 See previous chapter.
79 Quoted in Scates and Oppenheimer, *Last Battle*, 148.
80 W. J. Brown, 'Communication from Lt. Col. G. H. Bourne', 27 June 1938, NAA: BP709/1, M36103, 14.
81 The damaged veteran, Crotty and Larsson note, was a 'discomforting counterpoint to the independent and masculinized hero of Anzac lore'. *Anzac Legacies*, 7; Tyquin, 'In Search of the Unseen Wound', 28.
82 J. I. White, 'Form K', 7 August 1918, NAA: BP709/1, M10733, 11.
83 W. M. Brown, 'Widow's Statement', 26 September 1932, NAA: PP2/8, M24115, 189.
84 Frances John White, 'Extract, Form U (Claimant)', 13 October 1933, NAA: B73, M24941, 77–8.
85 W. H. White, 'Widow's Further Letter', 14 October 1943, NAA: B73, R40203, 10.
86 W. M. Brown, 'Widow's Statement', 26 September 1932, NAA: PP2/8, M24115, 189.
87 Scates and Oppenheimer, *Last Battle*, 147.
88 R. Mills interview with Patsy Adam-Smith, 1976. State Library of Victoria, MS 10500/TMS 129–30.
89 T. Loughran, *Shell-Shock and Medical Culture in First World War Britain* (Cambridge: Cambridge University Press, 2017), 77, 113.
90 Murphy, *Decent Provision*, 110.

11

Stomaching peace

Granddad's twisted little finger was a common enough sight among the Roper grandchildren. He used to tell us that he was lucky to have the finger, as the doctor was about to amputate it when he was distracted by more serious casualties coming into the clearing station after the Second Battle of Gaza.[1] Granddad was forgotten – just as he was the evening of the attack at Lone Pine when he became separated from his unit – but the finger was spared. This, and a pitted scar on his shoulder from an embedded bullet, a wound also received at Gaza, weren't the only legacies of the First World War on Granddad's body, however. He also had a six-inch scar across his belly, a wound incurred in 1950 in an operation to relieve chronic indigestion.[2]

On his visit to the Caulfield Repatriation Department outpatients' clinic in 1949, Granddad told the doctors that he had suffered from stomach troubles since the 1920s. In 1926 he had a five-day fit of hiccoughing and vomiting, and since then experienced bouts of 'scalding epigastric discomfort and flatulence', especially after eating fatty or seasoned foods. The pain became worse after 1939 and he was less able to manage it through his diet. He often felt bloated after meals and the pain would continue into the night. Six days earlier an attack had 'doubled him up, rolled around, perspired freely and seemed feverish'. The medical report stated that Granddad had suffered from repeated bouts of dysentery and jaundice at Gallipoli and 'ever since' had periods when his eyes were yellow.[3] He was admitted to the Heidelberg Repatriation Hospital on 5 February 1950 and after an investigative laparotomy, underwent surgery on 17 February 1950 to remove his gall bladder. Granddad was discharged on 6 March 1950 with a diagnosis of 'fine cirrhosis of liver and cholecystitis (mild)'.[4]

Though minor in medical terms, Granddad's stomach troubles reveal a singular history, the repatriation doctors concluding that they were 'due to war service' at Gallipoli.[5] The case opens questions that officials then, and historians now, are professionally charged to investigate: what counts as a war legacy? The scar on Granddad's belly bore a complex relation to his war. He never blamed the war for his indigestion, dysentery never figured in the war stories he told us as children and only Granny knew of the scar. The legacy accepted by the Repatriation Department was unknown to his family. Despite living with his indigestion and his outpourings of bile towards politicians and businessmen, I never imagined that the two might be connected. The war legacies that I traced were social and political but not somatic. Yet again, however, it is possible that the war counts for too much even in a case like Granddad's where the condition was officially recognised. As the previous chapter attests, the opening of rich archives like the pension files during the past decade can tempt the historian to follow the path taken by the repatriation officials, delimiting the field of causality to the war and ignoring lives before and after which are in any case harder to document.[6] Stephen Garton comments that for veterans and their descendants, attributing problems to the war 'helped people to understand the unfathomable events of ordinary lives made extraordinary by their participation in war', and the same could be said of historians.[7] The legacies of war could, and can still, count for too much.

Born in 1896, Granddad was the fourth child in a family of eleven children. His father was a farm bailiff at the Beechworth mental asylum and money was always short. His mother, who had given birth each year between 1893 and my grandfather's birth, struggled. She had had her own issues as a child: her father, an asylum doctor, committed suicide, and some of her early years were probably spent in care. His sisters and Granddad himself believed that for one reason or another, his mother had him 'snouted' (to 'snout' is an antiquated Australianism for holding a grudge). Granddad was sometimes fed bread and dripping when his brothers and sisters got better food. During an exceptionally cold winter, his mother sent him off to school in the snow without shoes.[8] Granddad would often tell us this story, and it was one he told his son too, who as Dad put it, 'grew up with my father's hatred of his mother'.⁹ Granddad left home when he was twelve and a half and took a job shooting crows on local farms. His mother, who had racked up debts with the local storekeepers, left the family shortly afterwards and moved to Melbourne. Between 1910 and when he signed up, Granddad travelled the eastern coast of Australia working as a casual farm labourer and sometimes as a clerk at the Kew mental asylum. He sent money back to his father, and he returned to Beechworth for a while, perhaps to help care for his seven younger, now motherless, siblings. He erased the memory of his mother. The Gallipoli memoir records how grateful he was to receive letters from his *father's* 'Australian eleven'[10] and after the war he never attempted to make contact with his mother although they were both living in Melbourne. His early life was characterised by what might now be called 'maternal deprivation', a family stretched to the limits financially and emotionally, where the siblings had to look after one another and his mother had it in for him. Apart from Granddad's stories about his mother's grudges, he had a memory of the bushfire on Christmas Day 1899 that struck the farm in Wooragee.[11] As they took flight in a buggy, a burning branch fell on his mother. Her hair caught fire and Granddad, who was then three and a half years old, burst out laughing. Could this be a screen memory, a fantasy that turned his mother's hatred of him into contempt towards her? Was it a recollection of the moment she took against him, or simply the hysterical outburst of a terrified child? Granddad had already witnessed traumas when he signed up in Liverpool in April 1915 and had a history of resentment towards those who should have looked after him.

When I interviewed him in 1980, however, it was the war rather than his childhood which took my attention. I thought it explained his habitual suspicion and fury towards the powers that be. After all, his entire working life was spent in the ranks. Employed by the Victorian Railways, he suffered the humiliation of demotion during the Great Depression when he was reduced from assistant station master to operating porter and car cleaner and his wages were cut by 10 per cent. It took him five years and a post in the remote Malley town of Birchip, to regain a post as assistant station master (hereafter ASM), and during thirty-seven years of service, he never rose above that rank.

In our first interview in 1980, Granddad talked about the impact of the Great Depression on the returned servicemen in Frankston, the outer suburban town where my uncle Lin was born in 1924 and my father Stan in 1926. Granddad and Granny were able to recall the names of each of the '1914 men' who lost their houses due to the pay cut: 'the Guards and the Operating Porters, I think they were two bob above the basic wage, a week, so that ... [*long silence, sighs*] ... one, two, three ... There was five of them. Just had to let their houses go. Out of Frankston.'[12] Granddad said nothing about the War Service Home Loan that had allowed him and other veterans to purchase properties in the first place or the preference they were given in secure government jobs.[13]

Granddad and a schoolteacher, also an ex-serviceman, had helped set up a branch of the Labour Party. The schoolteacher was 'bitter', and so was Granddad: 'You know I was bitter at the, I used to hate the bloody heads.' The importance of hatred as a legacy of the war was apparent from the opening moments of the interview, in a story that symbolises the oppression of the worker and hypocrisy of the bosses:

> it was rotten, the whole thing was rotten. I also told you that this fellow up above, I don't think I'll mention his name. Take Murdoch – you leave that there. This man, they came home from a picture [theatre]. Now the railways carted all those rich blokes those times ... And they came off the last train ... and this individual's father said, they'd had a few pots [beers] too – I had me barrier gate locked – they went into a bit of a confab, and this peanut, he said, 'well gentlemen, we've got the bloody worker now where we want him. See that we keep him there!' And that was the type of man that used to go to church on Sunday.[14]

Granddad's hostility towards the capitalist rivalled that towards his officers, and in retirement, he devoted considerable time to his hatred of the latter. His two most reviled figures were Colonel Langley, Commander of the First Australian Company of the Camel Corps, and General Murray, the Commander-in-Chief of the Egypt Expeditionary Forces. Granddad's tone was contemptuous as, in our second interview, he explained how Murray tried to direct the Second Battle of Gaza from Shephard's Hotel in Cairo, 180 miles away. When Murray finally decided to go up the line, the hospital train coming back from Gaza was shunted into a siding:

> *Granddad:* There was a train load of troops in the desert for eight hours, and you know, blokes had died, and the flies got to them and they just threw them over, out over the trucks – we were in open trucks, not, no carriages. *Blood and guts.* Our train was shunted into a siding, I don't know how many men were on that train, but it'd be 500 at least.
> *Mike:* ... Just waiting for him to come through. So he just made things worse, didn't he.
> *Granddad*: Yes, well when they knew he was coming up they cleared the whole of the line. They were told to clear it. All the stupid bastards ... What they did, the whole of the railway chaps that were in charge of the railways, the chaps that were in charge of communication [their priority], was to get General Murray to the front line ...
> *Mike*: Regardless ...
> *Granddad*: Yes, and he was to travel the absolute maximum. He wanted to get there, because he must have had some feelings that he might ... he might have been shot when he got to the front line anyway.[15]

At the age of eighty-four, a frail old man with months to live, his hatred remained fierce. What animated it was a moral injury, the memory of dying men piled onto open trucks ('no carriage') on a train stalled so that Murray could salvage his reputation. He describes a perverse ethical order in which those formally charged with the care of others are malign.

Granddad's view of the Great Depression and Australian politics mirrored his view of the war. His tone of bitterness and betrayal resonates with what Paul Fussell described in *The Great War and Modern Memory* as 'paranoid melodrama', a mode of political and psychological polarisation that Fussell believed trench warfare had brought about.[16] In Granddad's recollections of his life after the war, the antithetical relations between bosses and workers replaced those between officers and men.

Granddad seems to have seen his decision to join the Labour Party, become a union representative and stay among the rank and file as a response to the moral injuries of the war. When I asked why he thought he never got a promotion beyond ASM, he replied:

> See I know this much, that in the army, I never got promotion, the whole of the [war]. And officers told me that I wouldn't get. Because I was not the right type ... As a chap told me ... after the war finished,

'you know', he said, 'that you would never take to discipline', and he said, 'I've got your pedigree', and he said, 'you'd never leave your mates'. And I said 'no, and I wouldn't leave them now'.

Mike: [*approvingly*] Yeah![17]

Working for the Victorian Railways, Granddad's job was similar in many ways to the army. He was an anonymous cog in a rule-bound bureaucracy, the only humanity to be found in the comradeship among workers. His was a binary social order, split between the rank-and-file and the powers that be. The war had shaken his moral foundations and the emotional tone of his post-war politics repeated his wartime hatred. There was no worse crime than being a 'turncoat', and he singled out the politician Joe Lyons, who had left the Labour Party during the crisis of 1929 to form the United Australia Party in a coalition with opposition parties, as a special object of hate. Lyon's fate, in Granddad's imagination, would be the one faced by deserters in the war, and that the coward General Murray should have faced: 'Yes, turned, twisted, the bloody bastard. They should of [*sic*] shot him.'[18]

In some respects Granddad's life followed the trajectory that the gastric consultant Dr John Paulley identified as the psycho-social ground of the mid-century epidemic in stomach trouble: a difficult return and readjustment followed by an economic crisis in the 1930s that brought hardships that social policies failed to address.[19] Even in old age, he was in a semi-constant state of irritation about the world, clucking and shaking his head over news broadcasts at mealtimes, pushing Granny's offers of food away, prone every now and then to volcanic rage. His anger was constitutional. Had he had a fistula and been a patient of Wolf and Wolff's, they might have seen a stomach that was in a semi-constant ferment of acid production.[20] It may not just have been dysentery at Gallipoli that caused his gastric pain, but the effort it took afterwards to contain his hatred of generals, bosses and politicians. However his stomach pain also coincided with troubles in his personal life and, viewed from a psycho-social perspective, might have contributed to it. The genealogy of his illness led not only back to the war, but to events that followed it.

When Granddad went to the Repatriation Department in 1949, he told them that his pain had worsened during the past eighteen months.[21] This was a time of considerable stress for the family, as Lin had suffered from what my father, in the parlance of the 1970s, called a 'schizophrenic episode'. The relationship between Granddad and Lin had never been easy. Dad describes Lin as a 'dreamy' boy who Granddad felt needed to toughen up. Dad had a searing early memory of when Lin, then around eight or nine years old, went missing, and his mother called his father back from the station to help search for him. They eventually found Lin asleep in the privet hedge, and Dad hid under the dinner table as his father gave Lin a thrashing and his mother tried to get between them. 'It was ... it was, it was terrible to ... terrible to behold.'[22] His father was out of control: 'it was a real rage ... and he just got the razor strop and just laid into Lin'.[23] Granddad bullied Lin throughout his adolescence. Dad remembered him 'flying into a temper' when Lin turned up to the dinner table unshaven, and when he came home on leave during the war, 'something or other suddenly just blew up out of nothing, and ... and Dad hopped into him, and I mean, Lin couldn't, like, he tried to defend himself but he couldn't'.[24] Lin returned to Surrey Hills in October 1945 after serving in the Royal Australian Air Force in Canada and resumed his degree in commerce at Melbourne University the following February, but in mid-1946 he had a breakdown. He thought he was a prophet and began writing on the walls. Dad shared a bedroom with Lin and remembers how frightened he felt when Lin tried to switch off the light by unscrewing the light bulb. Lin was admitted to the mental asylum in Mont Park and received shock treatment at Royal Park. My father remembers the 'panic' surrounding Lin's admission, as his parents sought to keep his illness a secret from all but the family: 'what we had to do, above all, was protect him to the fullest degree we could against ... stigma. So that we didn't want anybody to know that he was in mental hospital.'[25] This was the family drama that was unfolding when Granddad's stomach pains worsened.

Lin appeared to make a recovery, finishing his degree, beginning work as a public servant and planning his engagement. On 17 April 1950, however, the day before Granddad was due to return to work after the cholecystectomy operation, Lin was involved in a car accident in a quiet suburban street a couple of miles from Surrey Hills. The impact spun Lin's car into the driveway of a nearby house and sent Lin through the windscreen. He was taken to Prince Henry's

Hospital in a coma but died on 21 April. The coroner reported a verdict of accidental death.

There is no direct evidence on the repatriation files of the tragedy that had enveloped Granddad. He saw the repatriation officials for post-operative check-ups, and a report of a meeting with his doctors on 4 April concluded that he was fit for work with 'incapacity negligible'.[26] Yet it is clear that something then affected Granddad's recovery, as there is a note on 27 April stating that the railway's medical officer had given him 'recreation leave' until 13 May 1950 as he 'felt unequal physically to the task' of resuming work.[27] The medical officer in charge endorsed this, determining that 'State of General debility post-operative warrants certificate of incapacity to 15/5/50'. Reading the phrase 'unequal physically', the historian of repatriation would surely assume that Granddad's difficulties were due to the surgery. We cannot know whether he told the railway and repatriation officials that he had lost his son and they discreetly used the operation as a means of getting him additional leave, or if he did not want to tell them and so couched his problems in physical terms, or if he really felt he was struggling with the physical after-effects of the surgery. The files simply report – as they had done for scores of First World War veterans – that he was suffering from 'general debility'.[28] Granddad's operation, minor though it was, shows how the emotional troubles of veterans could be concealed by a medical paradigm of organic illness that was adhered to by both claimants and doctors.

We have little record of Granddad's feelings about Lin's death, apart from a phone call with my father who was in Germany at the time, which would bring my father to tears as he remembered his father's voice. Yet Dad was also angry about the way his father treated Lin, and thought he must have reproached himself: 'I don't know how he lived with that, how did he live with the way he treated Lin, when Lin died?'[29] Granddad had plenty of private troubles when he approached the repatriation hospital complaining of stomach ache, and they were ones which made him a bully, not a victim.

The war's legacies might seem remote in this interpretation, which points to family problems, and the shame, guilt and loss surrounding them, as emotional stresses during the period of Granddad's treatment at the repatriation hospital. Nonetheless, the moral aftermath of Gallipoli echoed in the family, and no more so than in the memory of Lin's death. Granddad rarely talked about it, but he told me on one occasion that Lin was killed by the son of a wealthy businessman who did not have a licence, had taken his father's sports car without permission and was speeding. XXXX's father had hired a top lawyer, and the police accepted his version of events. Lin was stitched up. My father's version when I interviewed him in 2015 (also a received memory as he was in Germany at the time) differed in minor points but conveyed a similar moral message. In Dad's account, injustice is represented in the size of the vehicles that collided: 'XXXX was driving a big American car which, I understood, he'd ... he'd nicked, you know, from his father ... like it was his father's car, and Lin was in the little Austin Seven and he got wiped out.'[30]

The records of the inquest expose some elements of the family story as fiction. XXXX was sixteen, but not unlicensed; he had begun driving before the mandatory minimum age for a driving licence was introduced. The vehicle, as my father correctly remembered, was American, a Buick sedan and not a sports car as I had recalled it. Yet the inquest records also hint that my grandfather was not the only one to feel moral outrage at Lin's death. At the scene of the accident, XXXX did not give a statement to police, but was instead allowed to give an interview later at the local police station, accompanied by his legal counsel. XXXX claimed that he smelled alcohol on Lin. This was disputed by the woman who took Lin into her house after the crash, a nurse. In the following days, two residents from the site of the crash measured the length of the skid marks left by the Buick and reported this information to the police, who did not appear to have made their own record. The inference I draw from this is that the neighbours seemed to think XXXX was speeding and was responsible for the accident. To them, XXXX's accusation that Lin had been drinking was a moral slur that must be challenged. In part, the inquest records bear out the family story of the accident as an unequal struggle. But they also suggest that, in the aftermath of the two world wars, my grandparents were not the only Australian citizens to perceive a traumatic event in terms of the harm done to the little man by an establishment that sought to exculpate itself from guilt.

Granddad went back to the gastroenterology consultant on four occasions in the two years after his operation, each time complaining of 'upper abdominal discomfort'. Throughout this period, he was dealing with the loss of Lin and the stress of the inquest, experiences that confirmed his embittered worldview. Like the comrades he had left on the Peninsula, Lin's life was sacrificed; like many of Granddad's officers in the war, XXXX was a coward from a posh background who had pulled strings to get himself off the hook; like the military system, the legal system was unjust. Lin's accident repeated the moral injuries committed by his officers and the bosses and revealed the truth of a world divided between decent ordinary folk and the malevolent rich.

It is impossible to identify the true causes of Granddad's stomach pain and what role, if any, the war played in them. The cholecystectomy did not cure him. Granddad went to the repatriation hospital in May 1952 complaining of heartburn and indigestion that often kept him awake, and twenty-two years later, at the age of seventy-eight, he was still suffering from these symptoms.[31] There is a possible explanation for his troubles that owes nothing at all to the war: the condition was congenital. Like my grandfather, my father could not manage spicy foods or alcohol and often had an upset stomach. When he was in his early fifties – the age when my grandfather's stomach troubles were first diagnosed – Dad was told he had an ulcer. I began to suffer from chronic indigestion in my early fifties and was eventually diagnosed with oesophageal reflux, the same condition noted on Granddad's repatriation files in 1970.[32] The stomach conditions reported by three generations of Roper males are products of different times and places. In 1948 Granddad's problems were explained as a physiological after-effect of Gallipoli. In the 1970s my father's complaints were attributed to stress and he used to take a gloopy pink liquid called Pepto-Bismol to relieve the symptoms. Rates of stomach ulcers have plummeted since the discovery of the *H. pylori* bacteria, and among my generation, gastric reflux is commonly diagnosed, with sufferers being given proton pump inhibitor drugs (PPIs) to help reduce the production of stomach acid. Reflux has replaced the ulcer as the stomach ailment of the contemporary age, with PPIs among the most widely sold drugs in the world. Turning the Freudian legacy of emotional origins on its head, there is a strain of thought that holds that our moods are greatly influenced by what we eat, and that well-being depends on harbouring the 'good' probiotic bacteria in our guts. Anxiety and depression in this approach can be treated through diet. As the authors of a recent study assert, 'it is not inconceivable that gut problems are even the roots of Freudian repression. The secret hiding at the core of a patient's problems might not be an abusive parent but rather an abusive microbiota.'[33]

What does this case tell us about the legacies of war and how historians assess them? The repatriation files form an exceptionally rich source of personal and medical data and have shed new light on the longer histories of return and the transition from soldier to civilian. Extensive though they are, however, they form a limited snapshot and at most a succession of snapshots of medical diagnoses and the interactions between officials and claimants. The records give little insight into the personal lives of the applicants, the kind of lived history that any descendant grows up with. The sorry stories they document may also lead to distorted perceptions of veteran health, the historian treating the most severe cases as if they are, in Janet McCalman, Rebecca Kippen, Joan McMeeken, John Hopper and Michael Reade's words, 'speaking for the full veteran population'.[34]

The war was a relatively brief period in the lives of men like my grandfather who survived to old age. By bringing together family memory with the repatriation files, I have tried to broaden the lens from four years of war, forestall direct conclusions about what counts as a war legacy and open questions about the war's relationship to events before and after. Psychodynamic work on trauma points in this direction: the meaning and personal consequences of a trauma, it asserts, need to be understood in relation to early defences against anxiety that are overwhelmed in a way that 'provides confirmation of those deepest universal anxieties'.[35] The shock does not determine the legacy. The dysentery epidemic at Gallipoli was an individual and social trauma, but the impact on survivors cannot be deduced from the event. In Granddad's case, we also need to consider cross-generational histories of desertion and hatred, bullying, the stigma of mental illness and the impact of losses that had nothing to do with war.

Yet this interpretation, which leans on psycho-social understandings, is just one way of assessing a legacy. Indeed, my motivation to want to pick up the trail of Granddad's early life that my father had pointed out in 1980, and pursue somatic explanations, is itself a family legacy. The psycho-social lens was transmitted to the three Roper children by my dad, the spy turned minister and then social worker, whose study bookshelves were lined with the works of Freud, Rollo May and Carl Rogers, whose humanistic therapy encouraged people to trust their 'gut reactions'. Others might favour different epistemologies of the stomach, genetic inheritance perhaps, or a gut nurtured on a subsistence diet that suffered after the war from the spoils of prosperity, too much starch and red meat and not enough roughage. Perhaps after all, Granddad was obeying a gut instinct when he would shake his head in irritation as Granny offered him more food.

Hatred and a deep sense of moral betrayal are emotions that ran through my grandfather's life and helped him navigate it, from the mother who bullied him to the hypocrisy and cowardice of his officers and the economic hardships suffered by his comrades in the 1930s to the coroner's verdict on the death of his son. These emotions sometimes appear in the pension records as veterans sought recompense from the state for illnesses they believed were war-related and battled with officials over the justice of their claims. The war may not have been the only cause of their grievances, but it made sense of them, while the collective ethos of unionism and a 'fair go' helped them vocalise discontent. Among the Gallipoli men, the emotional force of repatriation claims harked back to the intimate personal experience of nerves and guts in turmoil, conditions that were driven from public consciousness by shame and the heroic mythology of the Anzacs. But despite its horrors, the roots of Granddad's hatred were not sown at Gallipoli alone: each veteran coped with the memory in different ways, drawing on their own pre-war family scripts and experiences to make sense of a national tragedy, a medical debacle and a moment of abject personal suffering.

Notes

1 R. H. Roper, 'Camel Corps Memoir', 14.
2 R. H. Roper, 'Medical Notes', 8 November 1974, NAA B73: H81128.
3 R. H. Roper, 'Report from Dr B. W. Costello', 9 December 1949, NAA B73: H81128. A summary of Granddad's war service from 1920 states

that he contracted dysentery three times at Gallipoli. 'Medical Report on an Invalid', 8 January 1920. Service Documents, NAA B73: M81128.
4   R. H. Roper, 'Report from S. McLennan, Medical Superintendent, Repatriation Hospital Heidelberg Out-Patient', 20 April 1950, NAA B73: H81128.
5   R. H. Roper, 'Letter from Deputy Commissioner H. C. Laussen to R. H. Roper', 5 June 1950, NAA B73: H81128.
6   The 'Diggers to Veterans' study supplements the military and pension records with vital data from across the lives of veterans and will allow rounded assessments of veteran health. J. McCalman, R. Kippen, J. McMeeken, J. Hopper and M. Reade, 'Early Results from the "Diggers to Veterans" Longitudinal Study of Australian Men Who Served in the First World War: Short- and Long-Term Mortality of Early Enlisters', *Historical Life Course Studies*, 8 (2019), 52–72.
7   S. Garton, *The Cost of War: Australians Return* (Melbourne: Oxford University Press, 1996), 30.
8   W. S. Roper email to M. Roper, 18 February 2007.
9   M. Roper notes on phone call with W. S. Roper, 30 March 2015.
10 The reference to the 'Australian Eleven' is cricketing slang. R. H. Roper, 'Gallipoli Memoir', 32.
11 'Tremendous Bush Fires', *Adelaide Advertiser*, 27 December 1899.
12 R. H. Roper interview, 'Great Depression', 1980, 4.
13 On the privileges given to veterans, see McCalman, Kippen, McMeeken, Hopper and Reade, 'Early Results', 70.
14 R. H. Roper interview, 'Great Depression', 4.
15 R. H. Roper interview, 'First World War', 4.
16 P. Fussell, *The Great War and Modern Memory* (Oxford: Oxford University Press, 1975), 76.
17 R. H. Roper interview, 'Great Depression', 12–13.
18 R. H. Roper interview, 'Great Depression', 10.
19 D. A. Christie and E. M. Tansey (eds), *Peptic Ulcer: Rise and Fall. Wellcome Witnesses to Twentieth Century Medicine* (London: The Wellcome Trust Centre for the History of Medicine at UCL, 2002), 11.
20 S. Wolf and H. Wolff, *Human Gastric Function* (Oxford: Oxford University Press, 1943).
21 'Report from Dr B. W. Costello', 9 December 1949, NAA B73: H81128.
22 W. S. Roper interview, 'Early Life', 134.
23 W. S. Roper interview, 'Early Life', 8.
24 W. S. Roper interview, 'Early Life', 52.
25 W. S. Roper interview, 'Early Life', 76.
26 R. H. Roper, 'Outpatient Report', S. McClennan Medical Superintendent, 20 April 1950, NAA B73: H81128.

27 R. H. Roper, 'Case Sheet', 27 April 1950, NAA B73: H81128.
28 R. H. Roper, 'Outpatient Clinic', 1 June 1950, NAA B73: H81128.
29 W. S. Roper interview, 'Early Life', 135.
30 W. S. Roper interview, 'Early Life', 103.
31 R. H. Roper, 'Medical Report', 9 May 1952; 'Medical Report', 13 February 1968; 'Medical Report', 15 April 1970; 'Report', 8 November 1974, NAA B73: H81128.
32 R. H. Roper, 'Request and Report Form', 11 March 1970, NAA B73: H81128.
33 S. Anderson, J. Cryan and T. Dinan, *The Psychobiotic Revolution: Mood, Food and the New Science of the Gut-Brain Connection* (Washington, DC: National Geographic Partners, 2017), 27, 147.
34 Initial findings from the 'Digger to Veterans' project indicate that while men who were discharged as medically unfit or partially disabled had higher than average mortality rates, the mortality of First World War veterans who were discharged fit was not significantly worse than the national male average. McCalman, Kippen, McMeeken, Hopper and Reade, 'Early Results', 59.
35 C. Garland (ed.), *Understanding Trauma: A Psychoanalytical Approach* (London: Karnac, 2002), 11.

Epilogue

One of the few First World War stories that John Frost's father told was about how his ship the *Leander* was hit by a torpedo in the Indian Ocean:

> *JF:* He was off duty, and … well, he was upset, because he was on deck when the torpedo had hit, so he was safe, and the torpedo went straight in the engine room, where he would have been … if he'd have been on duty. And it was funny. During the War, I was evacuated, and Mum and Dad came down one weekend, and during that weekend their communial [*sic*] air raid shelter was hit, so he said, 'I should have been there.' And he said, 'That's not gonna happen again! *You* are coming home.' So I came home and finished the Blitz! [*laughs*]
> *MR:* What did he mean, 'You're coming home', 'It's not going to happen again'?
> *JF:* Because … I think he felt he should have been there.
> *MR:* But … he'd escaped.
> *JF:* Yeah, I know!
> *MR:* But he felt he shouldn't escape?
> *JF:* Well …
> *MR:* Or you shouldn't escape?
> *JF:* Well, he just brought me home. He … felt that he'd left his mates. I think that's the only way I can think of it, you know, he'd deserted them.

As my questions to John indicate, at this point in the interview I was finding it hard to follow the thread: why would his father have taken him back to London from the safety of Kent in the middle of the Blitz? John's interpretation was that his father was trying to avoid repeating what happened on the *Leander*. During the Second World War, he went on to explain, his father would become agitated when John's older brothers were on night duty in the Home Guard: 'Well, he wasn't relaxed – if you can be relaxed in bombing, perhaps that's the wrong word – but when we were all together, he was more relaxed, more … yeah, "It doesn't matter." He kept saying he wanted us together, he didn't like us being split up.' Here, apparently, was a traumatic enactment that explained why his father felt compelled to keep the family under one roof despite the risks.

At the end of our interview, John gave me a CD with files of his father's service records and ship logs put together by a researcher at the National Archives. John couldn't open the disc and hoped that I might be able to convert the files into a different format. On accessing them I found that – just as John had told me – his father was a crew member on a boat called *Leander*. However, this *Leander*, built in 1882, was a depot ship for torpedo boat destroyers and during 1915–16 when his father was serving on the ship, it was stationed in the Scapa Flow area. It was not in the Indian Ocean and was not torpedoed. Searching the internet, I discovered that a New Zealand Navy light cruiser called the *Leander*, built in 1930, was hit by a five-hundred-kilogram torpedo during the Battle of Kolombangara in the Indian Ocean in July 1943, killing twenty-six men in the boiler room.[1] These details fitted John's story exactly but were from the wrong war.

It is impossible to reconstruct the circumstances through which an incident in the Second World War was relocated in family memory to the First World War. Had John's father substituted the HMNZS *Leander* for the HMS *Leander*? Or had John, who was fifteen in 1943, followed the contemporary press reports of body parts blown around the boiler room and buried at sea and projected them back onto his father's war?[2] Alternatively, had he come across the story while searching on the internet for ships called *Leander*, as I had done? The origins of the story, however, are less important than John's conviction that it was true. *Something* in his father's war history, he felt, had affected his reactions during the Blitz. The family had been bombed out of their home three times, and John's own bed frame, he told me, was damaged when the chimney collapsed onto it. The family stayed together but from John's account, it seemed that they were lucky to survive. Attempting to make sense of the family's fate, John had drawn on an event from the wrong war and after the Blitz. His account of his father's motives was also a post hoc construction, based on a trauma discourse that took root within popular culture from the 1970s. Looking back, John concluded that his father must have been suffering from survivor's guilt.

Silence was the First World War legacy mentioned most often by members of the second generation. The traces were oblique. John remembered his father's ominous aphorisms: 'Water's cold wherever you are!'; '"Water's a funny thing", he said. "If you're above it and looking down", he said, "don't look down too long, because it'll draw you down."' Far from being exceptional, John's 'mistake' reveals a situation typical of generations that live amidst mysterious signs. Like many other descendants, he had consulted historians and drew on proximate stories and later explanatory frames to make sense of an absent presence. Diagnostic categories such as 'PTSD' would prove particularly salient: children born in the wake of the First World War knew well enough that the emotional impact of violence could be delayed. Trauma discourse made intuitive sense to the members of a 'post' generation.

They looked back on the child's experience of puzzlement and not knowing, and as adults, turned to history to fill in the gaps. They had played their part in upholding silence. They had not asked questions when their mothers and fathers were alive and often defended family silences. Best leave well alone. That their mothers and fathers had tried to shield them from knowledge about the war, that they did *not* go on about it, was the mark of good parents. Equally, it was the mark of a good father that while he might have killed or watched men die a violent death, he was not violent at home. Complicit in silence, however, the children were left searching belatedly for answers. To be approached by the oral historian as a witness *in lieu* was doubly perplexing. Not only were they not witnesses of the war I was enquiring about, but their 'communicative memory' was thin, and stories from their own war sometimes had to suffice.[3]

Children born in the 1920s and 30s lived their entire lives after the First World War but are nonetheless part of its history. They embodied their parents' hopes and fears. June Teape was an only child, she told me, because her parents were increasingly fearful of a second global cataclysm. They 'did their bit' in the aftermath. Dora

Kneebone saw nothing unusual about her evening ritual of taking off her father's shoes and looking away from the scars on his legs; Margaret Reardon soon learned not to flinch at her father's stories of men sinking to their deaths in mud. Daughters learned that it was their role to support their fathers. Unlike the wartime drama of shells, mud and trenches, the children's part in the aftermath was mundane, habitual and sometimes not even recognised by them as a war legacy.

Born in July 1919, Doris Lessing wrote that she had lived with 'my father's emotion, a very potent draught, no homeopathic dose, but the full dose of adult pain. I wonder how many of the children brought up in families crippled by war had the same poison running in their veins from before they could even speak.'[4] Lessing's memoirs reveal the intimate truth of Marx's famous epithet in *The Eighteenth Brumaire of Louis Bonaparte* that the 'tradition of all dead generations weighs like a nightmare on the minds of the living'.[5]

Marx's statement is perhaps even more true of the third and fourth generations, who inherit deep structures of collective memory about the two world wars but whose 'communicative memory' is more distant, conveyed perhaps through a grandparent, or increasingly, a descendant with no direct connection to the survivors. Without a lived history of the war, these descendants lean heavily on the histories they learn at school or through commemoration and the media. This became apparent during *Meeting in No Man's Land* in 2016 when the participants and organisers were brought face-to-face with different national memory traditions. German descendants were genuinely puzzled by the paraphernalia of British commemoration, the poppies, medals, monuments, two-minute silence on Armistice Day and services across the country on Remembrance Sunday. The British descendants saw how much the Second World War – which in their national tradition was a necessary fight against fascism – continued to preoccupy the German descendants. Insofar as there was a 'national' memory of the First World War in Germany, it was not a war to end all wars, but a precursor to the rise of Hitler, and could not be explained away as senseless slaughter. We learned how deeply these different national histories of war and commemoration (or lack thereof) had impinged on us all. There were shared emotions of mourning and respect for the dead, but the German descendants felt that their country's guilt had to be acknowledged and explained to their British counterparts. Their wars were in the family, and a source of generational conflict, in ways the British found hard to fathom.

Successor generations must therefore contend with legacies of war that weigh more heavily as traditions of memory solidify. Yet as Marx also insisted, descendants make their own histories through their very immersion in 'circumstances existing already, given and transmitted from the past'.[6] This study has captured descendants as they consulted military archives and digital platforms, displayed and rearranged the war memory in their homes and took part in Centenary events. As they did so, they worked on the damage of the past. Marie-Anne Careless, whose French mother and British father met during the First World War, had a traumatic time during the Second World War. The family tried to flee to Britain from the Nazis in 1940, and her father was imprisoned. Today Marie-Anne surrounds herself with objects that symbolise and have survived the disruption and losses of the two world wars.[7] At the end of our interview, Marie-Anne put on the ring that her father smuggled out from prisoner of war camp.[8] For German descendants like Hanne and Dieter, it felt therapeutic to reconstruct the history of their grandfathers' roles in the First World War. It helped them understand the events that had turned soldiers barely out of their youth into domestic tyrants. Descendants create First World War histories of many kinds, histories of growing up in the shadows, histories of family patriarchy and histories that may challenge received assumptions, as Marion Armstrong and Harriet Pollock did when they criticised the treatment of their disabled fathers by the pension authorities.

Precisely because the First World War has been a 'nightmare on the minds of the living' in the Western world during the past century, it has also been a fertile source of creativity and cultural regeneration. This book has shown how descendant historians, novelists, poets and filmmakers have worked the war in the family into new public representations of the conflict. Cultural institutions facilitate the translation of personal stories into heritage and history. During the Centenary, organisations like Age Exchange and the Imperial War Museum's Lives of the First World War set out to convert the family archives of descendants into digital form. Recorded audio and filmed interviews and digitised images of photos, letters and war ephemera could be shared and introduced to new generations. Transmission, I learned during the research for *Afterlives*, is not just a matter of family relationships and early socialisation but can become a collective social experience. It is not just about what fathers and mothers told or did not tell their children, but about the descendants' attempts to piece together the First World War past and create communities of commemoration. A study of descendants must therefore pursue not only the biography of the speaker and the times of which they speak, but the time in which they tell, the traces of the past to which they attend, the groups they create and the communities that coax their stories from them and listen.[9]

Afterlives questions the notion that the memory of past events can be meaningfully separated into fleeting stories told within the family and history that endures in museums, schools or university curricula. Descendants seek out their historian, as I discovered when I was deluged with phone calls, emails and texts from elderly descendants in 2011. The journey of transmission from the private to the public begins with an invitation to ventriloquise, or the search for a ventriloquist. Narrating the voices and silences of past generations, the descendant calls on the historian to articulate the experience of afterlife on their behalf. The historian of descendants must account for the haunting of the past, but in so doing, takes part in a cultural movement that transforms the personal afterlives of war in the family, home, and domesticity into a collective history.

At the same time, family histories of war cannot be fully explained in terms of the contemporary historical culture and the wish to find a place in the record for an ancestor. In undertaking them, descendants try to settle with their personal past and reflect on who they are and what made them. Genealogy is sometimes a therapeutic pursuit. The final section of *Afterlives* offers an account of one such pursuit, as my father and I set about researching the First World War history of his father and my grandfather. My forty-year 'family romance' with Bob's war, I came to realise, was not just a means of claiming a place for him in social history, but of replacing the father who had left my mother and the family in 1973. During the Centenary, Dad and I established an uneasy alliance as we ferreted out service records, pension files and war diaries, each of us trying to understand the judgemental and disapproving, funny and warm, explosively angry and sometimes cruel man that Bob was, and how far the war was responsible for all his contradictions. Military records gave us a handle on the man and the long-term impact of service on his health. That Bob was an Anzac provided an immediate connection to the national past and gave purpose to our research. What though of those who have a war in the family, but no war story in the culture with which they can identify, and who lack the bureaucratic (and archival) paraphernalia that surrounds the soldier's war? In March 2016 I did an interview with my mother Ailsa, who at that time was living in her own home in the Melbourne suburb of Northcote, but suffering from dementia which resulted in her moving to a care home in December 2016. Mum began with her memories of the Second World War, telling me in almost an embarrassed way that 'as far as we were concerned, you know, the family wasn't affected by the War'. Her father had not served in either war, and there was no history of war trauma in the family: 'I was never exposed to anybody who had terrible War experiences – as far as I can recollect.'

She described how strange it felt when she and my father were courting and she began to visit his family home in Surrey Hills. On weekends the parlour at Kent Road would be set aside for Bob and his Camel Corps comrade Stan McCallum to reminisce:

> the two War men would have a little room of their own, and the rest of us would be either out in the garden, or helping in the kitchen or whatever … and that was … I mean, they used to sit there and go … through their War experiences … and, you know, I guess I realised, in later years, how important that must have been because you … you would have to get that out and it'll be open … you know, a person that you could talk to about the War must have been enormously important.

The differences between my father's family and her own were summed up by Mum's memory of the two 'War men' whose talk went on in a sacrosanct space. Her narrative faltered as she tried to compare Bob with her own father:

> MR: What were your first impressions of Dad's father?
> AR: He was somebody I was very unused to [*laughs*], because there wasn't anybody like that in my family. You know, there was the whole War experience, which I'd been kept out, because my dad

... so there was all of that ... then there was the ... you know, the down-to-earthness of him. Erm ...

The reason why Mum felt 'kept out' of the Anzac story was that her father Eric came from a family of conscientious objectors. His father William, a farmer from Youarang in Northern Victoria, was chair of the local anti-conscription campaigns in 1916 and 1917. He was at the centre of a case at Cobram Court in November 1916 when the buggy he and the anti-conscription campaigner Adela Pankhurst were travelling in was pelted with rotten eggs and other missiles as they returned late in the evening from an anti-conscription meeting in Katamatite. Brought to the witness stand by Mr Morrison, who led the men's defence, the local constable was unsympathetic to William Sefton's cause. He reported that many of the residents regarded Sefton 'as a pro-German'. Sefton had four sons of military age, he told the court, and 'had said that sooner than let them fight against the Germans he would see them shot'.[10] Sefton's attitude, the constable seemed to imply, was a monstrous travesty of paternal and national sentiment. The court discharged the twelve defendants (who included three servicemen) with a caution, and they were asked to pay compensation into a fund for the Red Cross, but pro-conscription residents set up a subscription fund and the assailants ended up in pocket.[11] It transpired that the young men had only pleaded guilty in the first place so that their case could be heard. They were 'respectable men', said Mr Morrison, who had been 'incensed' at the disloyalty shown by Sefton and Miss Pankhurst and were determined to 'teach them a lesson'. Conscription had split the local community and made pariahs of those who opposed it, the incident at Katamatite – like those in towns and cities across Australia – exposing what Joan Beaumont calls 'raw emotional violence of a kind rarely seen in public life'.[12]

At the time of the 1916 conscription referendum William's son Eric was twenty and teaching at Echuca High School on the New South Wales border. Because of his stance on conscription, he was given white feathers and yelled at by people in the street. The local recruitment officer called him out of his class on more than one occasion and gave him a lecture on why he should enlist. 'I was estranged in the town the only friends I had were a few Catholics even my own church had sermons aimed at chaps like me', he wrote to his granddaughter Chris (my cousin) in 1970.[13]

The reason why Eric wrote to Chris in 1970 was that she had recently taken part in Vietnam moratorium marches in Brisbane. At last, there was a common cause in the family:

> I tell you all this to show that you, with your protests are merely carrying on what was started 55 years ago. I haven't talked about this much, firstly because when things were tough you could be arrested for the slightest protest by anyone. It has influenced my whole life because 12 Mary St left no doubt in my mind that they thought me 'yellow' + although I married their daughter, I was something to be ashamed of – I simply ignored their displeasure + went straight ahead, + tried to live a normal life. How far I succeeded can be judged by your mother + Ailsa.[14]

'12 Mary St' was the Californian bungalow in the middle-class suburb of Hawthorn where my mother's grandparents the Jenkinses lived. When I interviewed my mother in 2016, it was clear that the split between her father and the Jenkins family had been a source of deep distress for Mum and her sister. Mum put the antagonism down to social class: the home in Cecil St Kew where she and Jean grew up was small and made of timber, her father adding do-it-yourself extensions as the family expanded. The house at 12 Mary St was made of brick and her aunty Teddy owned a car and had sponsored the education of the two daughters at the Methodist Ladies' College, an elite private school. The Jenkins family clearly outclassed Eric as breadwinners and respectable citizens.

In his letter to Chris in 1970, however, Eric attributed the divisions in the family not to social class but to the after-effects of the First World War. His 'whole life' had been coloured by the refusal to serve his country, but this was a history that, unlike the stories shared by Australian veterans in parlours, pubs and Anzac Day reunions, could not be told. He believed that the First World War had been fought to keep Germany from contesting the British domination of trade. Military conflict, he told Chris, 'brings the worst to the top + gives licence to men whose animal instincts they haven't learned to control – hence the concentration camp horrors etc.'. But he had kept his views to himself because of the stigma surrounding conscious objectors in Australia's world wars, and just 'tried to live a normal life'.[15] He hoped his success as a man could be judged by his behaviour as a father. The war in the family was decoupled from its afterlife; in my interview with Mum in 2016 she insisted that by contrast with her father-in-law Bob, who was a war veteran and union man and had strong convictions 'on right and wrong', her father 'was only about family really'. What Eric told Chris in 1970, however, was that his moral stance on the war had been too explosive to share with his family. My mother internalised the notion that there was no war story in the family, yet her early life and that of her older sister had been shaped by the Jenkins family's disapproval of Eric because he had refused to serve his country and Eric's humiliation and anger at being treated as a coward by his in-laws. In a statement that echoes the 1916 and 1917 battles over conscription, my mother described how her father was engaged in a 'battle' with the aunt who took them on expensive holidays and attended the parent–teacher sessions at their school, a 'battle not only for her [his wife Vera], but for the children as well [Mum and Jean]'.

Mum's story shows the personal suffering and inter-generational legacies of silence that could follow from experiences in the First World War that did not fit the frames of public memory. It was a war story that could not be told as a war story. The legacies in Mum's family were not about what military service did to fathers, but what it meant to refuse to serve, a moral stance that could not be articulated and was the antithesis of the Anzac who had volunteered for his country and manfully endured the brutality of modern warfare.

My mother's family serves as a counterpoint to the histories in this book which take the soldier's war as the point of origin.[16] If my mother had been asked to contribute to the oral history project that I began with British descendants in 2011, she might have replied that she had no war story to tell. The Centenary began to open the space for stories like hers that had been kept silent by descendants and ignored within commemoration. The point of historical research, however, is not just to broaden the range of public representations of the First World War. The discovery of a hitherto 'hidden history' does not in itself advance historical understanding much beyond the surface reassurance of democratic inclusivity. The work of descendant history also entails trying to fathom how the First World War – remembered, mythologised, unrecognised or forgotten – has travelled in the family in the century since the Armistice and how it shaped the descendants as political subjects, consumers and producers of First World War heritage and as sentient beings.

Notes

1. Ministry for Culture and Heritage site NZHistory, 'HMS Leander', https://nzhistory.govt.nz/war/hmnzs-leander/recovery-and-repair. Accessed 12 December 2021.
2. This theory is not borne out by a search of *The Times* around the time of the incident. The only mention of the *Leander* in 1943 is a list of awards given to crew members during the battle, which suggests that the incident was not widely known at the time.
3. J. Assmann, 'Communicative and Cultural Memory', in A. Erll and A. Nünning (eds), *Cultural Memory Studies: An International and Interdisciplinary Handbook* (New York: de Gruyter, 2008), 109–19.
4. D. Lessing, *Under My Skin: Volume One of My Autobiography to 1949* (London: Harper Collins, 1995), 10.
5. K. Marx, 'The Eighteenth Brumaire of Louis Bonaparte', in T. Carver (ed.), *Marx: Later Political Writings* (Cambridge: Cambridge University Press, 1996), 32.
6. Marx, 'Eighteenth Brumaire', 32.
7. David Parkin argues that the mementoes of displaced people can help effect the 're-personalisation' of relationships and memory after displacement. D. Parkin, 'Mementoes as Transitional Objects in Human Displacement', *Journal of Material Culture*, 4: 3 (1999), 303.
8. See Chapter 2.
9. Santanu Das makes a similar observation about the 'powerful but subterranean' presence of First World War memories in India today. 'In order to salvage such memories and materials', he says, it is 'essential to reach out to families and the community, the first step to coax private memories into the more public domain of what Jay Winter and Emmanuel Sivan have called "remembrance."' S. Das, *India, Empire, and First World War Culture: Writings, Images, and Songs* (Cambridge: Cambridge University Press, 2018), 21.
10. *Benalla Standard*, 17 October 1916, 3; *Herald*, 18 November 1916, 3; *Numurkah Standard*, 22 November 1916, 2.
11. *Numurkah Leader*, 24 November 1916, 1.
12. J. Beaumont, *Broken Nation: Australians in the Great War* (Sydney: Allen and Unwin, 2014), 242. See also the discussion of regional violence in R. Bollard, *In the Shadow of Gallipoli: The Hidden History of*

Australia in World War I (Sydney: University of New South Wales Press, 2013), 71–98, 142–56.
13 Letter from Eric Sefton to Christine Brewer, 21 June 1970.
14 Eric Sefton to Christine Brewer, 21 June 1970.
15 Eric Sefton to Christine Brewer, 21 June 1970.
16 For critiques of soldier-centred histories, see S. Grayzel, 'AHR Roundtable: Who Gets to Be in the War Story? Absences and Silences in *They Shall Not Grow Old*', *American Historical Review*, 124: 5 (December 2019), 1782–88; L. Noakes and J. Wallis, 'The People's Centenary? Public History, Remembering and Forgetting in Britain's First World War Centenary', *The Public Historian*, 44: 2 (2022), 56–81.

Appendix I
Afterlives interview profiles

The information below was compiled from ancestry.com, military records and my interviews. Special thanks to James Wallis for his help with this research. The place and date of the interview are given in brackets after the interviewee's name.

Abbreviations

ARP: Air Raid Precautions
ATS: Auxiliary Territorial Service
CWGC: Commonwealth War Graves Commission
RAMC: Royal Army Medical Corps
RASC: Royal Army Service Corps
RASCM: Royal Army Services Mechanical Transport
WRNS: Women's Royal Naval Service

Armstrong, Marion (Middlesbrough, 2013)

> B. 1923. Father Arthur Lindsey (b. 1887 Loftus, miner) was discharged from the army in December 1917 and died in 1932 from complications due to a wound on his eye. Married in 1918, three children. Arthur's pension was discontinued after his death, as he married after he was wounded. Mother worked as a cleaner and did sewing. Brother Eric joined the RAF in WW2 and was killed at the end of the war. Marion worked in a grocery shop during WW2 but wanted to join up. She married at twenty-nine, her husband's father was blinded in WW1 and got a 50 per cent pension. Husband ran a coal merchant's business.

Aubrey, Brenda (Bristol, 2013)

B. 1927. Father Frederick Bennett (b. 1894 Bristol, miller), married in spring 1915 and enlisted in Royal West Kent Regiment in November 1915. He was discharged after his leg was amputated at the top of the thigh. He received a pension and worked at Wills Tobacco in the sorting room with other disabled servicemen. Married in 1926, two children. The family's income was sufficient to buy a new house in 1935. Brenda left school at fourteen and worked for Wills stripping tobacco. Her husband Harold's father was blinded in WW1. Brenda's sister-in-law cared for Harold's father and married a blind WW1 ex-serviceman, George Killingbeck, who worked for the blind charity St Dunstan's.

Bartholomew, Elizabeth (Felixstowe, 2011)

B. 1916. Father John Andrew Campbell (b. 1883 Glasgow, pre-war regular in Highland Light Infantry, later engineman). John joined the Seaforth Highlanders in November 1914 and was an officer's batman. Married 1910, five children born between 1912 and 1923, Elizabeth was conceived during father's home leave. John worked as a stevedore after the war. The family were bombed out of their home in Glasgow during WW2. Elizabeth was a clerk in the army during WW2 and two of her brothers were navigators in the RAF.

Brown, Jean (Reading, 2014)

B. 1924. Father Arthur Henry Brown (b. 1886 London, clerk) served with the Queen's Westminster Rifles. He was blinded in May 1917 and trained as a physiotherapist at St Dunstan's, later opening a practice in the family home at Reading. Married 1912, four children. Jean served in the WRNS during WW2 and was stationed at Cowes and Whale Island correcting signalling manuals. She trained as a physiotherapist at King's College between 1947 and 1950 and worked at the Royal Berkshire Hospital. Jean resigned after her mother's death in 1977 and became a full-time carer for her father.

Burdett, Mary (Cambridge, 2011)

B. 1934. Father George William Stanley Burdett (b. 1899 Peterborough) served as a motor mechanic in the RASCM. Married 1925, two children. George established a machine tool company in Peterborough after the war and became a member of the Institution of Mechanical Engineers in 1937. Senior Warden in ARP during WW2. Estate valued at £28,000 at his death in 1962. Mary was a social worker prior to retirement.

Burgin, Ray (Bristol, 2013)

B. 1931. Father Walter Burgin (b. 1884 Sheffield, decorator, married 1909, wife died 1911) served as a sapper in the Royal Engineers and was discharged in 1917 after being blinded. Walter received a 100 per cent pension. He was trained by St Dunstan's as a poultry farmer. In 1928 he married Grace Marsden, a nurse from St Dunstan's, who helped run the farm. The family moved to Brighton when Ray was seven and his father retired. Ray was living in Brighton during WW2 and trained as a lighting engineer. After his wife's death in the 1960s, Walter Burgin lived with Ray, his wife and two children.

Careless, Marie-Anne (Droitwich, 2015)

B. 1938. Father Charles Ernest Couch (b. 1895 Cambridge, railwayman) served as a private in the Suffolk Yeomanry. He met his wife in Hazebrouck during the war and in 1925 got a job as a gardener at CWGC cemetery in Bertincourt. Marie-Anne and her parents tried to escape to Britain in WW2 but were captured by the Germans at the coast and her father was imprisoned at Frontstalag 220 in St Denis from July 1940 until 1944. Marie-Anne and her mother were interned in Paris. Marie-Anne and her parents returned to Bertincourt after the war to find that their furniture and possessions had been taken. Her older brother was in hiding for much of the war and died from the effects aged twenty-nine. Marie-Anne worked for the CWGC before she married.

Elders, George (Middlesbrough, 2013)

B. 1926. George Pierson Elders (b. 1894 Sleights, sailor's apprentice) enlisted in the Yorkshire Regiment in November 1914. He was shot in the back and was a prisoner of war. Returned from the war underweight. Married in 1925, two children, listed in 1839 as a labourer and Air Raid Warden in Sleights. George recalls bombing in Whitby during WW2 and he later served in the Navy as a stoker.

Fey, Joyce (Bristol, 2013)

B. 1931. Father Albert Edwin Hunt (b. 1898 London) was a private in the Machine Gun Corps. Married 1920 in Camberwell, five children born between 1921 and 1937, worked as a printer at the *Camberwell and Peckham Times*. War interrupted his sporting career and he remained keen on sport, especially football. During WW2 the family were bombed out of their house in Peckham and survived the blast in a shelter built by her father. Father was a domineering character, mother shy and under-confident. Against her father's wishes, Joyce went to university to study science and became an industrial chemist.

Flower, Jeffery G. (Bristol, 2013)

B. 1930. Father George Edward (b. 1894 Bristol, laboratory assistant) joined the Gloucester Regiment and served in the Middle East and the Western Front where he was wounded when a bomb fell on his section. He was jittery and prone to hit out after his return from the war. Jefferey recalls the shrapnel wounds on his body. George Edward married Constance Payne in 1923, two children, worked as a wage clerk at Caxton's Printworks. He was an ARP warden during WW2 and had to put out a fire on the roof of their house after it was set alight by an incendiary bomb. Jeffery had kept his father's cane, shell cases, hospital label and a service revolver which his father kept loaded. Jeffery did National Service in East Africa and studied chemistry at Bristol University.

Frost, John (Middlesbrough, 2013)

B. 1928. Father George James (b. 1894 Deptford) was a stoker in the Navy from 1912 to 1921. After the war, George worked as a stoker for the manufacturing company Stones. The family of five lived in Lewisham and were bombed out of their house three times during WW2. John was evacuated to Kent during the Blitz but his father brought him back to London. He was a hydraulic valve engineer before retiring.

Game, Elizabeth (Middlesbrough, 2013)

B. 1925. Father Ralph Oswald Burn (b. 1891, postal clerk in 1911) had heart problems due to rheumatic fever contracted in WW1 and was invalided out of the Royal Engineers in 1917. His brother, John Culbertson Burn (b. 1897) was killed in action in Flanders in August 1918. Ralph married Winifred Lucas in 1922, lived in Winchmore Hill and had three children between 1925 and 1932. He died aged fifty-three in November 1944. After his death, Winifred rented rooms to lodgers and became a dinner lady and clerical assistant. Elizabeth trained as a language teacher and worked in state and private schools during her career. She married in 1950 and her husband worked for ICI.

Gitsham, Rosemary (Felixstowe, 2011)

B. 1935. Father Vernon Ewart (b. 1893 Hornsey) served with the Royal Fusiliers in Egypt, Gallipoli and France. After the war, he trained with Mappin and Webb as a watch repairer and jeweller and in 1924 he joined the RAF as a flight engineer. Married Dorothy Minnie Bowes, tax office clerk in 1925 in Romford. Rosemary was an only child. Vernon was stationed at RAF bases in the Mediterranean and around the UK and specialised in seaplanes. He retired to the house in Felixstowe where Rosemary grew up and now lives. Rosemary joined British European Airways in 1955 after she left college and worked in aviation throughout her career. She had a motorcycle license and for her fiftieth birthday, she organised a balloon trip. She is a member of the Martlesham Heath Aviation Society.

Green, Hedley (Colchester, 2015)

B. 1930. Father Ernest Arthur Green (b. 1893 Colchester) served in the Suffolk Yeomanry and became a bus driver after the war. Mother Evelyn Maud Tuffin served in the Queen Mary's Army Auxiliary Corps and ran an Officer's Mess in France in 1918. Hedley joined the Navy when he was fifteen and served for fourteen years before becoming a civil servant.

Johnson, Dennis (Middlesbrough, 2013)

B. 1933. Father William John Johnson (b. 1884 Ebbw Vale, shoemaker) married in 1907 and was living in Darlington when the war broke out. He served as a driver in the RASC for the duration of the war and had gunshot wounds on his buttock and back. His wife died in childbirth in 1916 and his three children were placed in an orphanage. William John remarried in 1920 and had two further sons. He worked as a night watchman. One of the sons from his first marriage, also in the RASC, died in 1940 at Dunkirk. Dennis was a centre lathe operator with British Steel before he retired.

Jones, Clive (Felixstowe, 2011)

B. 1923. Father Arnold Edward Jones (b. 1889 Ludlow, ironmonger) was an ordinary seaman in the Royal Naval Volunteer Reserve, married in 1921 and ran a butcher and grocer's shop in Onibury after the war. Clive began a geography degree at Cambridge, joined the Navy in 1942 and was commissioned as a sub-lieutenant in 1943. He was at Omaha Beach shortly after the landing in 1944. He taught liberal studies at a further education college prior to retirement.

Kerslake, Mary (Little Melton, Norfolk, 2014)

B. 1939. Father Frederick Allen Tunnah (b. 1893 Rhos, Denbighshire) was a private in the RAMC. Mother Ivy Deane served in the Queen

Mary's Army Auxiliary Corps. They were married in 1925 and lived in Hove. Frederick was a traveller but during WW2 he was employed by the Ministry of Works and the family moved around for father's work, based for part of the war at an ammunition dump in Rhos. Mary was ordained as a Church of England Minister in 2006 and was active in her local church in Hethersett.

Kneebone, Dora (Ipswich, 2015)

B. 1925. Father Alfred Uttin (b. 1876 Camberwell, compositor) joined the Bedfordshire Regiment in March 1915 and was discharged with a leg wound in 1918 aged forty-three. Mother witnessed zeppelin raids and her brother lost an eye and was a POW during WW1. Father's brother lost an arm in WW1 and lost his wife and daughter in WW2. Dora grew up in Wembley.

Manthorp, Beryl (Norwich, 2014)

B. 1921. Father Harry Albert Manthorp (b. 1893 Colchester, commercial clerk) was a corporal in the RASC and served in Egypt, Salonika and Greece. His brother Richard Walter was killed in 1915. Harry was a building merchant in Norwich after the war. Beryl was a physical training instructor with the ATS during WW2 and in 1954 she set up the Guildhall School of Dancing in Norwich with help from her father. Beryl published *Towards Ballet: Dance Training for the Very Young* in 1980 (the book is still in publication).

Marriage, June (Norfolk, 2014)

B. 1933. Grandfather George James Elston (b. 1890 Northampton, carman) served as a private in the Suffolk Regiment and was killed in action in April 1917. June's mother (b. 1911) lived with her maternal grandparents until age fifteen when her mother remarried.

Mingay, John (Sheringham, 2013)

B. 1917. Father Henry Mingay (b. 1890 Catfield, general labourer), enlisted in the Norfolk Regiment in 1914 and was discharged in 1916 due to a gunshot wound. His arm was amputated above the elbow. Family had a smallholding on settlement scheme in Lingwood for disabled veterans. John Jr served as a lance corporal in a tank regiment from 1939 to 1945. His brother Frederick Eric died in a plane crash in 1944 and another brother James was a prisoner of war in Germany. John was a teacher prior to retirement.

Morgan, Brian (Holt, 2013)

B. 1932. Father Gerald Bede Morgan (b. 1895 Southminster) was a private in the Essex Regiment, served at Gallipoli and in Egypt. Two half-brothers were killed in WW1, Gerald was shot through the shoulder and another brother was wounded. Married Gladys in 1921 and joined the Plymouth Brethren. The family of eight lived on a smallholding settlement at Mayland, Essex. The eldest daughter stayed with the Brethren but the rest rebelled and had little contact with their parents once they left home. Brian left school at fourteen and was apprenticed as a carpenter. He later became a builder.

Mullarkey, Brian (Sheringham, 2013)

B. 1927, one of seven children born between 1918 and 1928. Father Albert (b. 1889 Norwich, insurance clerk) came from a well-off local family. He joined the Essex Regiment and fought at the Somme. Returned to the Norwich Union after the war but had a breakdown and retired with ill health in 1930. He never applied for a war pension and the family lived on his work pension. He spent most of his time inside the house and neglected his appearance. Family believed he was suffering from shell shock; he would tremble during thunderstorms and during bombing in WW2. One of Brian's brothers was killed in a motorbike accident in 1937, another in 1944 when serving in the Navy. Brian was a firefighter prior to retirement.

Pentney, Allan (Aylsham, Norfolk, 2011)

B. 1925. Father Thomas (b. 1891 Burham Thorpe, Norfolk, farm horseman) was injured on Somme in 1916 and his leg was amputated above knee. Married Beatrice Parnell in December 1919, whose three brothers had served in the same company as Thomas. He trained as a boot repairer, but his business failed in the early 1930s. Mother's friends lent her money so she could open a general store in North Creake. Allan was a carpenter and worked in the construction industry before retiring.

Perley, Doris (Middlesbrough, 2013)

B. 1930. Father Henry Gedling (b. 1899 Lanchester) enlisted underage and was discharged in April 1915. Re-joined as a private in the Royal Scots Regiment, his pension card in 1918 states that he had nephritis aggravated by war service. Married Edith Mardon in 1921. Employed as a labourer after the war and moved from Middlesbrough to Sunbury-on-Thames during the Great Depression in search of work, the family followed him a year later. She was an amateur dancer and trained as a teacher, and was working as a supply teacher when she retired.

Pollock, Harriet (Middlesbrough, 2013)

B. 1922. Father William Smithson (b. 1894 Sadberge, foundry worker) enlisted in the Durham Light Infantry in 1912 and was discharged in 1915 with 'tubercular lung'. He married in 1919, lived in Stockton-on-Tees. William was unable to work after the war and was eventually bedridden. Harriet's mother nursed him. William's disability pension was stopped after his death in 1938 aged forty-three. Harriet's mother worked as a cleaner, the family had to sell off some furniture after William's death and Harriet left school at fourteen. During WW2 she worked in a grocer's store. Her father's youngest brother Joe was killed in Italy during WW2 and Harriet's own husband, a WW2 veteran, died from war-related injuries in 1979 when he was fifty-seven. Harriet was a full-time mother.

Reardon, Margaret (Cambridge, 2015)

B. 1920. Father Arthur George Chapman (b. 1885 Trumpington, attendant at Fulbourn Asylum) served as a private in the Grenadier Guards. His brother was killed in France in 1917. Margaret's mother came from Hartlepool and remembered the air raids. Father became Chapel Clerk at Trinity College after the war. Mother and father were Air Raid wardens during WW2. Margaret joined the Land Army at twenty-one, trained with the Royal Signals Service and was based at a wireless station in Douglas on the Isle of Man.

Seabrook, Margaret (Wendover, 2017)

B. 1925. Father Francis Long (b. 1895 Lichfield) won a County Scholarship awarded by King Edwards High School in May 1914 and was expecting to go up to Cambridge when the war broke out. He enlisted as a sapper in the Royal Engineers and was discharged after being gassed in September 1917. Married Daisy Dunning in 1922, who was a teacher. Francis and Daisy worked in the family drapers store in Lichfield and the family lived above the shop. Francis was an ARP warden in WW2. Margaret was a Farm Camp volunteer and subsequently trained as a domestic science teacher.

Skin, Kathleen (Cambridge, 2011)

B. 1920. Father William Cecil Skin (b. 1887 Guernsey) enlisted as a Regular in the Second East Lancashire Regiment in October 1906 and entered the war on 6 November 1914. His medal card states that he was discharged in July 1915 'due to sickness'; Kathleen states that he was blinded in one eye, deaf in one ear and walked with a leg iron. William's brother was serving in the Navy and was killed in 1915. William went to South Africa after the war and in 1922 moved to a property in Wickford, Essex owned by his father. His occupation is listed as clerk. The family later moved to Wimpole in Cambridgeshire. William was often hospitalised with malaria and money would be deducted from his pension to cover the cost, leaving the family short of money. William began to lose his memory when Kathleen was around ten and spent long periods of time in Fulbourn Mental Hospital.

Smith, David (Bristol, 2013)

B. 1929. Father Alexander George Smith (b. 1890 East Ham, accounts clerk) enlisted in the London Regiment as a private. He was wounded in September 1916 and his leg was amputated above the knee. He was not expected to survive. Married Doris Percival in 1920. She was a Red Cross nurse and nursed Alexander. Caring for him became her 'life's work'. Father often had shooting pains in his stump. He worked in the Ministry of Pensions and the family lived in a semi-detached in Harrow. David studied at Cambridge and was an insurance broker specialising in education prior to his retirement.

Spray, Winifred (Kennington, Oxford, 2011)

B. 1915. Father John Hickson (b. 1884 Nottingham, carpenter) married Florence in 1913 and joined the Royal Engineers as a sapper. He died of wounds in December 1917 when Winifred was two and a half. Florence received a widow's pension and worked as a cleaner and took in lodgers. Winifred was not told that her father had died. She is not sure if she has a memory of him, but she often dreamed about him and wrote an essay about her dreams before our interview. As a child, Winifred sometimes felt ashamed of her mother because her clothes were shabby. Winifred trained as a children's nurse and married in 1945.

Stamp, Pat (Norwich, 2014)

B. 1923. Father Harry John Wood (b. 1895 Upton Park) enlisted in the Middlesex Regiment. He had 'holes in his legs' due to shrapnel, found walking painful and used a walking stick. He could not do jobs around the house like gardening and decorating. John was a clerk in the War Office, retired at fifty-five because of ill-health. Mother worked for Selfridges during WW1, and in an armament factory. Parents married 1920, three girls and two boys. In early 1939 the family moved from Forest Gate to a new 'modern' house in Boreham Wood, Hertfordshire. Pat left school at fourteen and worked in the Co-Op during WW2. She tried to join the WRNS but was rejected as her occupation was protected. She was an ARP warden but felt that by comparison with her brother, who had joined the navy, her wartime experience was a bit 'boring'.

Swann, Bill (Peterborough, 2011)

B. 1922, sister born 1916. Father Herbert Swann (b. 1883 Bradford, barman/grocer) joined the Northumberland Fusiliers. Herbert married Rosa Meaker in 1915. His first son was born in 1916 and in October 1917 he was wounded at Ypres, losing both legs above the knee and his right arm. Two further children were born after the war and Bill was the youngest. The family of five lived in a two-bedroom flat in the War Seal Mansions in Fulham. Herbert died at sixty-four, partly from his wounds. Bill volunteered for the RAF in 1941 and served in the RAF Regiment on airfield defence. He worked for Thomas Cook as a clerk after leaving the RAF.

Teape, June (Felixstowe, 2011)

B. 1928. Father Walter Hempshall (b. 1894 Calverton Notts, hosiery factory worker) served in the RAMC during WW1 in France and East Africa, where he contracted blackwater fever and malaria. He returned to Calverton after the war, married in 1924 and worked as a machinist. He used to nurse sick people in the village, including his sister-in-law who had terminal cancer. Walter helped set up a Fire Service unit in Calverton during WW2 but tried to dissuade June from volunteering. June trained as a teacher and taught liberal studies at a further education college prior to her retirement.

Wiltshire, Victor (Bristol, 2013)

B. 1924. Father Albert Victor Wiltshire (b. 1895 Bristol, tailor's trimmer) joined the Gloucestershire Regiment. He was gassed during the war and had a bayonet wound in his side. He was demobilised in 1919 with malaria, but according to Vic he also suffered from shellshock and would lash out at people. He married in 1921 and set up a boot repair business. Two of his brothers were killed in WW1. Vic served in the RAF during WW2 and was an advertising accounts manager prior to retirement.

Appendix II
Meeting in No Man's Land interview schedule

(These are a guide and can be added to or changed slightly depending on the interviewee's background etc.)

Please could you tell us your name and where you were born and grew up?

You've come to share a family history that relates to the First World War. Who is the principal relative /or ancestor you have come to tell us about?

Did you know them personally – or someone who was close to them?

If you knew them personally, can you tell us what kind of person they were? Where were they born? What were they doing before the First World War? (Follow-up questions if possible)

What do you know of their experience of the First World War? (Follow-up)

In what way were they or their family members affected by the war, either at the time or afterwards? (Follow-up questions if appropriate)

How did you come to learn of their experience of the First World War? How was the story passed down to you?

Do you have any photos or letters or other artefacts that relate to your father/mother or grandfather/grandmother etc. and their experience of the First World War?

Please show us … and describe what you have brought. (Follow-up questions where appropriate)

Do you have anything that your ancestor wrote during the war or after, about any aspect of their experience? If so, could you read an extract for us from a letter/ postcard …?

Did they pass on a song or a saying from their wartime experience?

Did they share with you or a relative any specific experience from the First World War that has remained in your memory through the years?

Can you tell us why you wanted to share your family history of the First World War? Why is it important to you?

Do you feel that your ancestor's experience of the First World War has in some way affected subsequent generations within your family? In what way?

If you could only choose one artefact among those you have brought to show us, which would you choose and why?

What is your personal view of the First World War and how in your country people choose to remember or commemorate it?

How do you imagine that your views of the First World War might compare with those of the British/German descendants you will be meeting?

You have chosen to take your family history from the First World War and share it with the descendants of former enemies. Why did you feel you wanted to do this?

Select bibliography

Documentary records

Archives

Australia

Australian War Memorial, Imperial Force Unit War Diaries, 1914–18
National Archives of Australia (NAA), World War I Personal Service Records
NAA, World War I Repatriation Records
State Library of Victoria, World War I Collection

United Kingdom

Blind Veterans UK
Liddle Collection (First World War), University of Leeds
Mass Observation Archive, University of Sussex, 2014 Directive. Part 1. The First World War, www.massobs.org.uk/images/Directives/Autumn_2014.pdf
Sir Ronald Ross Collections, London School of Hygiene and Tropical Medicine
Manuscripts in personal possession
R. H. Roper, 'Gallipoli Memoir'
R. H. Roper, 'Camel Corps Memoir'

Newspapers

2014–18

The Age
The Boston Globe
The Guardian

The Observer
Der Spiegel International
The Telegraph

1914–18

The Benalla Standard
The Herald
The Numurkah Leader
The Numurkah Standard

Interviews

Interviews by the author

A. E. Roper, 'Early Life', March 2016
R. H. Roper, 'Great Depression', 1980
R. H. Roper, 'First World War', 1980
W. S. Roper, 'Early Life', September 2015
W. S. Roper, 'Career', February 2016

Archived interviews

State Library of Victoria (SLV)

Gourlay, A. J. E., interview with Patsy Adam-Smith, 1976. SLV, MS 10530/TMS 134

Kahan, H., interview with Patsy Adam-Smith, 16 December 1975. SLV, MS 11033/TMS 147

McPhee, J., interview with Patsy Adam-Smith, 1976. SLV, MS 10495/TMS 123–124

Mills, R., interview with Patsy Adam-Smith, 1976. SLV, MS 10500/TMS 129–130

Newman, C., interview with Roger McDonald, 1978. SLV, MS 11405/TMS 528

Imperial War Museum (IWM)

Bird, S. P., interview with Peter Hart, 1984, IWM Oral History 7375. Available www.iwm.org.uk/collections/item/object/80007177. Accessed 29 November 2021

Caokes, F., interview with Jan Stovold, 1984, IWM Oral History 8287. Available www.iwm.org.uk/collections/item/object/80008087. Accessed 29 November 2021

Manton, H., interview with Lyn Smith, 1987. IWM Oral History 9756. Available www.iwm.org.uk/collections/item/object/80009540. Accessed 29 November 2021

Meager, C. C., interview with Lyn Smith, 1984, IWM Oral History 8326. Available www.iwm.org.uk/collections/item/object/80008123. Accessed 29 November 2021

Murray, J., interview with Peter Hart, 1984. IWM Oral History 8201, 12/45. Available www.iwm.org.uk/collections/item/object/80008002. Accessed 29 November 2021

Page, J., interview with Peter Hart, 1993. IWM Oral History 13083. Available www.iwm.org.uk/collections/item/object/80012806. Accessed 29 November 2021

Tolley, J., interview with Peter Hart, 1989. IWM Oral History 10404. Available www.iwm.org.uk/collections/item/object/80010183. Accessed 29 November 2021

Tomkinson, C., interview with Peter Hart, 1984. IWM Oral History 7497. Available www.iwm.org.uk/collections/item/object/80007299. Accessed 29 November 2021

Internet sources

M. Barrett, 'Sent Missing in Africa: Briefing Paper for *The Unremembered*', www.michelebarrett.com/wp-content/uploads/2019/11/Sent-Missing-in-Africa.pdf

BBC online, *WW2 People's War: An Archive of World War Two Memories*, www.bbc.co.uk/history/ww2peopleswar/categories/c1161/

British Council, *Remember the World as Well as the War: Why the Global Reach and Enduring Legacy of the First World War Still Matter Today*, 2014, www.britishcouncil.org/sites/default/files/remember-the-world-report-v4.pdf

Byng-Hall, J., 'Family Scripts: A Concept Which Can Bridge Child Psychotherapy and Family Therapy Thinking', https://icpla.edu/wp-content/uploads/2015/04/Byng-Hall-J.-Family-Scripts.pdf

Dowd, V., 'The Birth of *Oh! What a Lovely War*', *BBC News Magazine*, 12 November 2011, www.bbc.co.uk/news/magazine-15691707

Holbrook, C., 'How Anzac Day Came to Occupy a Place in Australians' Hearts', *The Conversation*, 24 April 2017, https://theconversation.com/how-anzac-day-came-to-occupy-a-sacred-place-in-australians-hearts-76323

Honest History, 'Kaching! Australia's Anzac Centenary Spend Hits $A562 Million', 11 January 2016, http://honesthistory.net.au/wp/kaching-australias-anzac-centenary-spend-hits-a562-million/

Melody, H., 'Ted Hughes and War', www.bl.uk/20th-century-literature/articles/ted-hughes-and-war

Middlebrook, M., 'The Writing of the First Day on the Somme', December 2004, https://web.archive.org/web/20060215034015/http://www.fylde.demon.co.uk/middlebrook2.htm

Noakes, L., 'Centenary (United Kingdom)', in U. Daniel, P. Gatrell, O. Janz, H. Jones, J. Keene, A. Kramer and B. Nasson (eds), *1914–18 Online: International Encyclopaedia of the First World War*, Berlin 2019, https://encyclopedia.1914-1918-online.net/article/centenary_united_kingdom?version=1.0

Books and articles

Abrams, L., *Oral History Theory* (Abingdon: Routledge, 2010).

Abrams, L., '"There Was Nobody Like My Daddy": Fathers, the Family and the Marginalisation of Men in Modern Scotland', *Scottish Historical Review*, 78: 206 (October 1999), 219–42.

Adam-Smith, P., *The Anzacs* (Melbourne: Penguin, 1991).

Alexander, S., 'Becoming a Woman in the 1920s and 1930s', in S. Alexander, *Becoming a Woman and Other Essays in Nineteenth and Twentieth Century Feminist History* (London: Virago, 1994).

Alexievich, S., *The Unwomanly Face of War* (London: Penguin, 2017).

Allen, J., *Sex and Secrets: Crime Involving Australian Women since 1880* (Oxford: Oxford University Press, Melbourne, 1990).

Allport, A., *Demobbed: Coming Home after the Second World War* (New Haven: Yale University Press, 2009).

Anderson, J., *War, Disability and Rehabilitation in Britain*: '*Soul of a Nation*' (Manchester: Manchester University Press, 2011).

Ashplant, T. G., 'Fantasy, Narrative, Event: Psychoanalysis and History', *History Workshop Journal*, 23: 1 (1987), 165–7.

Assmann, J., 'Communicative and Cultural Memory', in A. Erll and A. Nünning (eds), *Cultural Memory Studies: An International and Interdisciplinary Handbook* (New York: de Gruyter, 2008), 109–19.

Audoin-Rouzeau, S. and Becker, A., *1914–18: Understanding the Great War* (New York: Hill & Wang, 2003).

Bar-On, D., *Fear and Hope: Three Generations of the Holocaust* (Cambridge, MA: Harvard University Press, 1995).

Barrett, M. and Stallybrass, P., 'Printing, Writing and a Family Archive: Recording the First World War', *History Workshop Journal*, 75: 1 (2013), 1–32.

Bashforth, M., 'Absent Fathers, Present Histories', in P. Ashton and H. Keen (eds), *People and Their Pasts. Public History Today* (Basingstoke: Palgrave Macmillan, 2009), 203–23.

Baxendale, J. and Pawling, C., *Narrating the Thirties: A Decade in the Making, 1930 to the Present* (London: Macmillan, 1996)

Bayer, M., 'Commemoration in Germany: Rediscovering History', *Australian Journal of Political Science*, 50: 3 (2015), 553–61.

Bayer, M., 'Remembrance Revisited? The First World War Centenary in Germany', *Cultural Trends*, 27: 2 (2018), 136–41.

Bean, C. E. W. (ed.), *The Anzac Book* (Sydney: University of New South Wales, 2010).

Bean, C. E. W. (ed.), *Official History of Australia in the War of 1914–1918* (Sydney: Angus & Robertson, 1921–42).

Beaumont, J., *Broken Nation: Australians in the Great War* (Sydney: Allen & Unwin, 2014).

Beaumont, J., 'Commemoration in Australia: A Memory Orgy?', *Australian Journal of Political Science*, 50: 3 (2015), 536–4.

Beckett, H., 'Doll's House Furniture Made by a Soldier Blighted by WW1', *Museum Crush*, 12 December 2022, https://museumcrush.org/the-dolls-house-furniture-made-by-a-soldier-blighted-by-wwi/. Accessed 27 January 2023.

Ben-Ezer, G., 'Trauma Signals in Life Stories', in K. M. Rogers, S. Leydesdorff and G. Dawson (eds), *Trauma and Life Stories: International Perspectives* (London: Routledge, 1999), 29–45.

Berezin, M., 'Secure States: Towards a Sociology of Emotion', *Sociological Review*, 50: 2 (2002), 33–52.

Bertaux, D. and Thompson, P., 'Family Myth, Models and Denials in the Shaping of Individual Life Paths', in D. Bertaux and P. Thompson (eds), *Between Generations: Family Models, Myths and Memories* (Oxford: Oxford University Press, 2005), 1–13.

Bingham, A., *Gender, Modernity and the Popular Press in Inter-War Britain* (Oxford: Oxford University Press, 2004).

Bion, W. R., *War Memoirs 1917–19* (London: Karnac Books, 1997).

Bloch, A., 'How Memory Survives: Descendants of Auschwitz Survivors and the Progenic Tattoo', *Thesis Eleven* (September 2021), 1–11.

Bohleber, W., 'Transgenerational Trauma, Identification and Historical Consciousness', in J. Straub and J. Rüsen (eds), *Dark Traces of the Past: Psychoanalysis and Historical Thinking* (New York: Berghahn, 2011).

Bollard, R., *In the Shadow of Gallipoli: The Hidden History of Australia in World War I* (Sydney: University of New South Wales Press, 2013).

Borland, K., '"That's Not What I Said": Interpretive Conflict in Oral Narrative Research', in S. Gluck and D. Patai (eds), *Women's Words: The Feminist Practice of Oral History* (New York: Routledge, 1992), 63–76.

Bottero, W., 'Practicing Family History: Identity as a Category of Social Practice', *British Journal of Sociology*, 66: 3 (September 2015), 534–56.

Bourke, J., *An Intimate History of Killing: Face-To-Face Killing in Twentieth-Century Warfare* (London: Granta Publications, 1999).

Bruckshaw, H., *The Diaries of Private Horace Bruckshaw, 1915–1916* (London: Scolar Press, 1979).

Buckerfield, L. and Ballinger, S., *The People's Centenary: Tracking Public Attitudes to the First World War Centenary 2013–2018* (London: British Future, 2019).

Butler, A. G., *Official History of the Australian Army Medical Services in the War of 1914–1918* (Melbourne: Australian War Memorial, 1930–43).

Byng-Hall, J., *Rewriting Family Scripts: Improvisation and Systems Change* (New York: Guilford Press, 1995).

Carlyon, L., *Gallipoli* (Sydney: Pan Macmillan, 2001).

Cartwright, D., 'The Psychoanalytic Research Interview: Preliminary Suggestions', *Journal of the American Psychoanalytical Association*, 52: 1 (Winter 2004), 209–42.

Clifford, R., 'Families after the Holocaust: Between the Archives and Oral History', *Oral History*, 46: 1 (Spring 2018), 42–54.

Clifford, R., *Survivors: Children's Lives after the Holocaust* (New Haven: Yale University Press, 2020).

Cohen, D., *Family Secrets: The Things We Tried to Hide* (London: Penguin, 2013).

Cohen, D., *Household Gods: The British and Their Possessions* (New Haven: Yale, 2009).

Cohen, D., *The War Come Home: Disabled Veterans in Britain and Germany, 1914–1939* (Berkeley: University of California Press, 2001).

Collins, M., *Modern Love: An Intimate History of Men and Women in Twentieth Century Britain* (London: Atlantic Books, 2003).

Crotty, M. and Larsson, M. (eds), *Anzac Legacies: Australians and the Aftermath of War* (North Melbourne, Victoria: Australian Scholarly Publishing, 2010).

Damousi, J., 'Why Do We Get So Emotional About Anzac?', in M. Lake and H. Reynolds, with M. McKenna and J. Damousi, *What's Wrong with Anzac? The Militarization of Australian History* (Sydney: New South Books, 2010).

Das, S., *India, Empire, and First World War Culture: Writings, Images, and Songs* (Cambridge: Cambridge University Press, 2018).

Dawson, G., 'Playing at War: An Autobiographical Approach to Boyhood Fantasy and Masculinity', *Oral History*, 18: 1 (Spring, 1990), 44–53.

Dawson, G., *Soldier Heroes: British Adventure, Empire and the Imagining of Masculinities* (London: Routledge, 1994).

Dendooven, D., 'Trench Crap: Excremental Aspects of the First World War', in N. J. Saunders and P. Cornish, *Modern Conflict and the Senses* (London: Routledge, 2017), 183–95.

Dodd, L., '"It Did Not Traumatise Me at All": Childhood "Trauma" in French Oral Narratives of Wartime Bombing', *Oral History*, 41: 2 (Autumn 2013), 37–48.
Duffett, R., 'Ingestion and Digestion on the Western Front', in N. J. Saunders and P. Cornish (eds), *Modern Conflict and the Senses* (London: Routledge, 2017), 171–82.
Duffett, R., '"Playing Soldiers?": War, Boys, and the British Toy Industry', in L. Paul, R. R. Johnston and E. Short (eds), *Children's Literature and Culture of the First World War* (London: Routledge, 2015), 239–48.
Duffett, R., *The Stomach for Fighting: Food and the Soldiers of the Great War* (Manchester: Manchester University Press, 2012).
Duffett, R., 'The War in Miniature: Queen Mary's Dolls' House and the Legacies of the First World War', *Cultural and Social History*, 16: 4 (2019), 431–49.
Duffett, R. and Roper, M., 'Making Histories: The Meeting of German and British Descendants of First World War Veterans in "No Man's Land", Bavaria, 2016', *The Public Historian*, 40: 1 (2018), 13–33.
Emsley, C., *Soldier, Sailor, Beggarman, Thief: Crime and the British Armed Services since 1914* (Oxford: Oxford University Press, 2013).
Emsley, C., 'Violent Crime in England in 1919: Post-War Anxieties and Press Narratives', *Continuity and Change*, 23: 1 (2008), 173–95.
Erll, A., 'Locating Family in Cultural Memory Studies', *Journal of Comparative Family Studies*, 42: 3 (2011), 303–18.
Evans, R., 'Masculinism and Gendered Violence', in K. Saunders and R. Evans (eds), *Gender Relations in Australia: Domination and Negotiation* (Sydney: Harcourt Brace Jovanovich, 1992), 200–21.
Faimberg, H., *The Telescoping of Generations: Listening to the Narcissistic Links between Generations* (London: Routledge, 2005).
Fewster, K., *Bean's Gallipoli: The Diaries of Australia's Official War Correspondent* (Crows Nest, New South Wales: Allen & Unwin, 2009).
Figlio, K., 'Oral History and the Unconscious', *History Workshop Journal*, 26: 1 (1988), 120–32.
Fisher, T., 'Fatherhood and the British Fathercraft Movement 1919–39', *Gender & History*, 17: 2 (2005), 441–62.
Foster, A. M., '"We Decided the Museum Would Be the Best Place for Them": Veterans, Families and Mementos of the First World War', *History and Memory*, 31: 1 (Spring/Summer 2019), 87–117.
Francis, M., 'Attending to Ghosts: Some Reflections on the Disavowals of British Great War Historiography', *Twentieth Century British History*, 25: 3 (2014), 347–67.
Freud, S., 'Beyond the Pleasure Principle', *The Standard Edition of the Complete Psychological Works of Sigmund Freud*, Vol. XVIII (London: Vintage, 2001), 1–64.

Freud, S., 'Inhibitions, Symptoms and Anxiety', *The Standard Edition of the Complete Psychological Works of Sigmund Freud*, Vol. XX (London: Vintage, 2001), 77–175.

Freud, S., 'Screen Memories', *The Standard Edition of the Complete Psychological Works of Sigmund Freud*, Vol. III (London: Vintage, 2001), 303–23.

Freund, A., 'A Canadian Family Talks about Oma's Life in Nazi Germany: Three-Generational Interviews and Communicative Memory', *Oral History/Forum d'histoire orale*, 29 (2009), 1–26.

Frie, R., *Not in My Family: German Memory and Responsibility after the Holocaust* (Oxford: Oxford University Press, 2017).

Frosh, S., *Hauntings: Psychoanalysis and Ghostly Transmissions* (Basingstoke: Palgrave Macmillan, 2013).

Fulbrook, M., *Dissonant Lives: Generations and Violence through the German Dictatorships* (Oxford: Oxford University Press, 2011).

Fussell, P., *The Great War and Modern Memory* (Oxford: Oxford University Press, 1975).

Galatariotou, C., 'The Defences', in S. Budd and R. Rushbridger (eds), *Introducing Psychoanalysis: Essential Themes and Topics* (London: Routledge, 2005).

Gallagher, E., 'Digging Deep: Playing at War in Australia, 1914–1939', *History Australia*, 16: 1 (2019), 169–89.

Gammage, B., *The Broken Years: Australian Soldiers in the Great War* (Melbourne: Penguin, 1975).

Garton, S., 'Anzac Health: A. G. Butler and the Writing of the Official Medical History of Australia during the 1914–18 War', *Working Papers in Australian Studies*, 93 (1994), 97–109.

Garton, S., *The Cost of War: Australians Return* (Melbourne: Oxford University Press, 1996).

Gerber, D., 'Introduction: Finding Disabled Veterans in History', in D. Gerber (ed.), *Disabled Veterans in History* (Michigan: Michigan University Press, 2012).

Gerster, R., *Big Noting: The Heroic Theme in Australian War Writing* (Melbourne: Melbourne University Press, 1987).

Gilligan, C., Spencer, R., Weinberg, M. K. and Bertsch, T., 'On the Listening Guide: A Voice-centered Relational Method', in P. M. Camic, J. E. Rhodes and L. Yardley (eds), *Qualitative Research in Psychology: Expanding Perspectives in Methodology and Design* (Washington, DC: American Psychological Association, 2003), 157–72.

Gittins, D., *Fair Sex: Family Size and Structure in Britain, 1900–39* (New York: St. Martin's Press, 1982).

Gloyn, L., Crewe, V., King, L. and Woodham, A., 'The Ties That Bind: Materiality, Identity and The Life Course in the "Things" Families Keep', *Journal of Family History*, 43: 2 (2018), 157–76.

Goltermann, S., 'On Silence, Madness, and Lassitude: Negotiating the Past in Post-War West Germany', in E. Ben-Ze'ev, R. Ginio and J. Winter (eds), *Shadows of War: A Social History of Silence in the Twentieth Century* (Cambridge: Cambridge University Press, 2010), 91–114.

Gordon, A., *Ghostly Matters: Haunting and the Sociological Imagination* (Minneapolis: University of Minnesota, 1997).

Grayzel, S., 'AHR Roundtable: Who Gets to Be in the War Story? Absences and Silences in *They Shall Not Grow Old*', *American Historical Review*, 124: 5 (December 2019), 1782–8.

Grayzel, S., *At Home and under Fire: Air Raids and Culture in Britain from the Great War to the Blitz* (Cambridge: Cambridge University Press, 2012).

Green, A., 'Intergenerational Family Stories: Private, Parochial, Pathological?', *Journal of Family History*, 38: 4 (2013), 387–402.

Hall, R., 'Emotional Histories: Materiality, Temporality and Subjectivities in Oral History Interviews with Fathers and Sons', *Oral History*, 47: 1 (Spring 2019), 61–71.

Hammett, J., '"It's in the Blood, Isn't It?" The Contested Status of First World War Veterans in Second World War Civil Defence', *Cultural and Social History*, 14: 3 (2017), 343–61.

Hanna, E., Hughes, L. M., Noakes, L., Pennell, C. and Wallis, J., *Reflections on the Centenary of the First World War: Learning and Legacies for the Future*. Project Report, AHRC, 2021.

Hareven, T., 'Cycles, Courses and Cohorts: Reflections on Theoretical and Methodological Approaches to the Historical Study of Family Development', *Journal of Social History*, 12: 1 (Autumn 1978), 97–109.

Harrison, M. (ed.), *The Centenary of the First World War: How the Nation Remembered* (London: DCMS Centenary Publications, 2019).

Harrison, M., *The Medical War: British Military Medicine in the First World War* (Oxford: Oxford University Press, 2010).

Hart, P., *Gallipoli* (New York: Oxford University Press, 2011).

Haslam, N. and McGrath, M., 'The Creeping Concept of Trauma', *Social Research: An International Quarterly*, 87: 3 (Fall 2020), 509–31.

Hass, A., *In the Shadow of the Holocaust: The Second Generation* (Ithaca: Cornell University Press, 1990).

Hasted, R., *Domestic Housing for Disabled Veterans 1900–2014* (London: Historic England, 2016).

Hetherington, A., *British Widows of the First World War: The Forgotten Legion* (Barnsley: Pen and Sword, 2018).

Hirsch, M., 'The Generation of Postmemory', *Poetics Today*, 29: 1 (2008), 103–28.

Hirsch, M., *The Generation of Postmemory: Writing and Visual Culture after the Holocaust* (New York: Columbia University Press, 2012).

Hirschfeld, G., Krumeich, G. and Renz, I. (eds), *Encyclopaedia of The First World War* (Paderborn: Ferdinand Schoningh Verlag, 2003).

Hoffman, E., *After Such Knowledge: A Meditation on the Aftermath of the Holocaust* (London: Vintage, 2005).

Holbrook, C., *Anzac: The Unauthorised Biography* (Sydney: University of New South Wales Press, 2014).

Holbrook, C. and Reeves, K., 'Making Sense of the Great War Centenary', in C. Holbrook and K. Reeves (eds), *The Great War: Aftermath and Commemoration* (Sydney: University of New South Wales Press, 2019), 1–21.

Holbrook, C. and Ziino, B., 'Family History and the Great War in Australia', in B. Ziino (ed.), *Remembering the First World War* (Abingdon: Routledge, 2015).

Holden, K., 'Family, Caring and Unpaid Work', in I. Zweiniger-Bargielowska (ed.), *Women in Twentieth Century Britain: Social, Political and Cultural Change* (London: Routledge, 2001), 134–48.

Holloway, W. and Jefferson, T., *Doing Qualitative Research Differently: Free Association, Narrative and the Interview Method* (London: Sage, 2000).

Humphries, S., *A Labour of Love: The Experience of Parenthood in Britain 1900–1950* (London: Sidgwick & Jackson, 1993).

Jacobs, M., *D. W. Winnicott* (London: Sage, 2008).

Jeffery, K., 'Commemoration in the United Kingdom: A Multitude of Memories', *Australian Journal of Political Science*, 50: 3 (2015), 562–67.

Jones, E., 'Stomach for the Peace: Psychosomatic Disorders in UK Veterans and Civilians 1945–55', in M. Jackson (ed.), *Stress in Post-War Britain* (London: Routledge, 2017), 131–45.

Jones, H., *British Civilians in the Front Line* (Manchester: Manchester University Press, 2006).

Joseph, B., 'Transference: The Total Situation', *International Journal of Psychoanalysis*, 66: 4 (1985), 447–54.

Kant, V., 'Remembering Gallipoli in Contemporary Turkey', in B. Ziino (ed.), *Remembering the First World War* (Abingdon: Routledge, 2015).

Kennedy, R., *The Children's War: Britain, 1914–1918* (Basingstoke: Palgrave Macmillan, 2014).

Kent, D. A., 'The Anzac Book and the Anzac Legend: C. E. W. Bean as Editor and Image-Maker', *Historical Studies*, 21: 84 (1985), 376–90.

Kent, S., *Making Peace: The Reconstruction of Gender in Interwar Britain* (Princeton: Princeton University Press, 1993).

Kidd, J. and Sayner, J., 'Unthinking Remembrance? Blood Swept Lands and Seas of Red and the Significance of Centenaries', *Cultural Trends*, 27: 2 (2018), 68–82.

Kidron, C., 'Breaching the Wall of Traumatic Silence: Holocaust Survivor and Descendant Person–Object Relations and the Material Transmission of The Genocidal Past', *Journal of Material Culture*, 17: 1 (2012), 3–21.

King, L., *Family Men: Fatherhood and Masculinity in Britain, 1914–1960* (Oxford: Oxford University Press, 2015).

Kogan, I., 'The Second Generation in the Shadow of Terror', in M. G. Fromm (ed.), *Lost in Transmission: Studies of Trauma across Generations* (London: Karnac, 2012), 5–21.

Kohut, T., *A German Generation: An Experiential History of the Twentieth Century* (New Haven: Yale University Press, 2012).

Kuhn, A., *Family Secrets: Acts of Memory and Imagination* (London: Verso, 2002).

Kuhn, A. (ed.), *Little Madnesses: Winnicott, Transitional Phenomena and Cultural Experience* (London: Bloomsbury Publishing, 2013).

LaCapra, D., *Writing History, Writing Trauma* (Baltimore: Johns Hopkins Press, 2001).

Lake, M., Reynolds, H. with McKenna, M. and Damousi, J., *What's Wrong with Anzac? The Militarization of Australian History* (Sydney, New South Books, 2010).

Langhamer, C., *Women's Leisure in England, 1920–1960* (Manchester: Manchester University Press, 2000).

Larsson, M., *Shattered Anzacs: Living with the Scars of War* (Sydney: University of New South Wales Press, 2009).

Lawrence, J., 'Forging a Peaceable Kingdom: War, Violence, and Fear of Brutalization in Post–First World War Britain', *Journal of Modern History*, 75: 3 (September 2003), 557–89.

Lessing, D., *Alfred and Emily* (London: Fourth Estate, 2008).

Lessing, D., *Under My Skin: Volume One of My Autobiography to 1949* (London: Harper Collins, 1995).

Lichtenstein, J., *The Berlin Shadow* (London: Scribner, 2020).

Liddle, P., *Men of Gallipoli: The Dardanelles and Gallipoli Experience, August 1914 to January 1916* (London: Allen Lane, 1976).

Light, A., *Forever England: Femininity, Literature and Conservatism between the Wars* (London: Routledge, 1991).

Lloyd, C. and Rees, J., *The Last Shilling: A History of Repatriation in Australia* (Melbourne: Melbourne University Press, 1994).

McCalman, J., Kippen, R., McMeeken, J., Hopper, J. and Reade, M., 'Early Results from the "Diggers to Veterans" Longitudinal Study of Australian Men Who Served in the First World War: Short- and Long-Term Mortality of Early Enlisters', *Historical Life Course Studies*, 8 (2019), 52–72.

McCartney, H., 'Commemorating the Centenary of the Battle of the Somme in Britain', *War and Society*, 36: 4 (2017), 289–303.

McCartney, H., 'The First World War Soldier and His Contemporary Image in Britain', *International Affairs*, 90: 2 (2014), 299–315.

McHugh, S., 'The Affective Power of Sound: Oral History on Radio', *Oral History Review*, 39: 2 (Summer/Fall 2012), 187–206.

McKenna, M. and Ward, S., '"It Was Really Moving, Mate": The Gallipoli Pilgrimage and Sentimental Nationalism in Australia', *Australian Historical Studies*, 38: 129 (2007), 141–51.

Meyer, J., '"Not Septimus Now": Wives of Disabled Veterans and Cultural Memory of the First World War in Britain', *Women's History Review*, 13: 1 (2004), 117–38.

Meyer, J. and Moncrieff, A., 'Family Not to Be Informed? The Ethical Use of Historical Medical Documentation', in A. Hanley and J. Meyer, *Patient Voices in Britain, 1840–1948* (Manchester: Manchester University Press, 2021).

Milcoy, K., *When the Girls Come Out to Play* (London: Bloomsbury Academic, 2017).

Miller, I., 'The Mind and Stomach at War: Stress and Abdominal Illness in Britain c. 1939–1945', *Medical History*, 54: 1 (2010), 95–110.

Miller, W., *The Anatomy of Disgust* (Cambridge, MA: Harvard University Press, 1997).

Millhauser, S., 'The Fascination of the Miniature', *Grand Street*, 2: 4 (1983), 128–35.

Moeller, R. G., 'On the History of Man-Made Destruction: Loss, Death, Memory, and Germany in the Bombing War', *History Workshop Journal*, 61: 1 (Spring 2006) 103–34.

Mombauer, A., 'The German Centenary of the First World War', *War and Society*, 36: 4 (2017), 276–88.

Morley, J., 'Dad "Never Said Much" But … Young Men and Great War Veterans in Day-to-Day-Life in Interwar Britain', *Twentieth Century British History*, 29: 2 (June 2018), 199–224.

Moshenska, G., *Material Cultures of Childhood in Second World War Britain* (London: Routledge, 2021).

Mosse, G., *Fallen Soldiers: Re-Shaping the Memory of the World Wars* (Oxford: Oxford University Press, 1990).

Mowat, C., *Britain between the Wars* (Chicago: Chicago University Press, 1955).

Murphy, J., *A Decent Provision Australian Welfare Policy, 1870 to 1949* (London: Routledge, 2016).

Nelson, E., 'Victims of War: The First World War, Returned Soldiers, and Understandings of Domestic Violence in Australia', *Journal of Women's History*, 19: 4 (2007), 83–106.

Nicholson, J., *The Great Silence 1918–1920: Living in the Shadow of the Great War* (London: John Murray, 2009).
Noakes, L., *Dying for the Nation: Death, Grief and Bereavement in Second World War Britain* (Manchester: Manchester University Press, 2020).
Noakes, L., '"My Husband Is Interested in War Generally": Gender, Family History and the Emotional Legacies of Total War', *Women's History Review*, 27: 4 (2018), 610–26.
Noakes, L. and Wallis, J., 'The People's Centenary? Public History, Remembering and Forgetting in Britain's First World War Centenary', *The Public Historian*, 44: 2 (2022), 56–81.
Olechnowicz, A., *Working-Class Housing in England between the Wars: The Becontree Estate* (Oxford: Oxford University Press, 1997).
Oppenheimer, L. and Hakvoort, I., 'Will the Germans Ever Be Forgotten? Memories of the Second World War Four Generations Later', in E. Cairns and M. D. Roe (eds), *The Role of Memory in Ethnic Conflict* (Basingstoke: Palgrave Macmillan, 2003), 94–105.
Parkin, D., 'Mementoes as Transitional Objects in Human Displacement', *Journal of Material Culture*, 4: 3 (1999), 303–20.
Passerini, L., 'Memories between Silence and Oblivion', in K. Hodgkin and S. Radstone (eds), *Contested Pasts: The Politics of Memory* (London: Routledge, 2003), 238–54.
Pennell, C., 'Taught to Remember? British Youth and First World War Centenary Battlefield Tours', *Cultural Trends*, 27: 2 (2018), 83–98.
Phillips, A., *Winnicott* (London: Penguin, 2007).
Pooley, S. and Qureshi, K. (eds), *Parenthood between Generations: Transforming Reproductive Cultures* (New York: Berghahn Books, 2016).
Portelli, A., 'The Death of Luigi Trastulli: Memory and the Event', in A. Portelli (ed.), *The Death of Luigi Trastulli and Other Stories: Form and Meaning in Oral History* (New York: State University of New York Press, 1991).
Portelli, A., 'Uchronic Dreams: Working-Class Memory and Possible Worlds', in P. Thompson and R. Samuel (eds), *The Myths We Live By* (London: Routledge, 1990).
Proctor, T., 'Daughters of War: Girl Guides and Service after the First World War', *Twentieth Century British History* (2021), hwab032, 1–26.
Proctor, T., 'On My Honour: Guides and Scouts in Interwar Britain', *Transactions of the American Philosophical Society*, New Series, 92: 2 (2002).
Reid, F., *Broken Men: Shell Shock, Treatment and Recovery in Britain 1014–1930* (London: Continuum, 2010).
Reynolds, D., *The Long Shadow: The Great War and the Twentieth Century* (London: Simon & Schuster, 2013).

Roberts, E., *A Woman's Place: An Oral History of Working-Class Women 1890–1940* (Oxford: Wiley-Blackwell, 1995).

Roberts, E., *Women and Families: An Oral History 1940–1970* (Oxford: Wiley-Blackwell, 1995).

Robson, L. L., 'The Australian Soldier: Formation of a Stereotype', in M. McKernan and M. Browne (eds), *Australia: Two Centuries of War and Peace* (Canberra: Australian War Memorial in association with Allen & Unwin, 1988), 313–37.

Robson, L. L., 'The Origin and Character of the First A.I.F. 1914–18: Some Statistical Evidence', *Australian Historical Studies*, 61 (1973), 737–49.

Roper, M., 'Analysing the Analysed: Transference and Counter-Transference in the Oral History Encounter', *Oral History*, 31: 2 (Autumn, 2003), 20–32.

Roper, M., 'The Bush, the Suburbs and the Long Great War: A Family Memoir', *History Workshop Journal*, 86 (Autumn 2018), 90–116.

Roper, M., 'Re-Remembering the Soldier Hero: The Psychic and Social Construction of Memory in Personal Narratives of the Great War', *History Workshop Journal*, 50: 1 (Autumn 2000), 181–204.

Roper, M., *The Secret Battle: Emotional Survival in the Great War* (Manchester: Manchester University Press, 2009).

Rose, S., *Which People's War? National Identity and Citizenship in Wartime Britain 1939–1945* (Oxford: Oxford University Press, 2003).

Roseman, M., *Generations in Conflict: Youth Revolt and Generation Formation in Germany 1770–1968* (Cambridge: Cambridge University Press, 1995).

Roseman, M., 'Surviving Memory: Truth and Inaccuracy in Holocaust Testimony', in R. Perks and A. Thomson (eds), *The Oral History Reader*, 3rd edn (Abingdon: Routledge, 2016), 320–34.

Rosenthal, G., 'Biographical Research', in C. Seale, G. Gobo, J. F. Gubrium and D. Silverman (eds), *Qualitative Research Practice* (London: Sage, 2004), 49–65.

Rosenthal, G., 'German War Memories: Narrability and the Biographical and Social Functions of Remembering', *Oral History*, 19: 2 (Autumn 1991), 34–41.

Rosenthal, G. (ed.), *The Holocaust in Three Generations; Families of Victims and Perpetrators of the Nazi Regime* (London: Bloomsbury, 1998).

Rosenthal, G., 'Reconstruction of Life Stories: Principles of Selection in Generating Stories for Narrative Biographical Interviews', *The Narrative Study of Lives*, 1: 1 (1993), 59–91.

Rosenthal, G., 'Veiling and Denying the Past: The Dialogue in Families of Holocaust Survivors and Families of Nazi Perpetrators', *History of the Family*, 7 (2002), 225–38.

Runia, E., '"Forget About It": "Parallel Processing" in the Srebrenica Report', *History and Theory*, 43: 3 (October 2004), 295–320.
Samuel, R. and Thompson, P., 'Introduction', in R. Samuel and P. Thompson (eds), *The Myths We Live By* (London: Routledge, 1992).
Saunders, N., 'Bodies of Metal, Shells of Memory: "Trench Art" and the Great War Re-Cycled', *Journal of Material Culture*, 5: 1 (2000), 43–67.
Saunders, N., 'Material Culture and Conflict: The Great War 1914–2003', in N. Saunders (ed.), *Matters of Conflict: Material Culture, Memory and the First World War* (London: Routledge, 2004).
Scates, B., 'How War Came Home: Reflections on the Digitisation of Australia's Repatriation Files', *History Australia*, 16: 1 (2019), 190–209.
Scates, B., *Return to Gallipoli: Walking the Battlefields of the Great War* (Cambridge: Cambridge University Press, 2006).
Scates, B. and Oppenheimer, M., *The Last Battle: Soldier Settlement in Australia 1916–1939* (Cambridge: Cambridge University Press, 2016)
Scates, B., Wheatley, R. and James, L., *World War One: A History in 100 Stories* (Melbourne: Penguin, 2015).
Schwab, G., *Haunting Legacies: Violent Histories and Transgenerational Trauma* (New York: Columbia University Press, 2010).
Schwitzer, J. and Thompson, K., 'Children and Young People in Wartime', *Oral History*, 15: 2 (Autumn 1987), 32–7.
Seal, G., *Inventing Anzac: The Digger and National Mythology* (St Lucia: University of Queensland Press, 2004).
Sheffield, G., 'The Centenary of the First World War: An Unpopular View', *The Historian* (Summer 2014), 22–6.
Sheffield, G., 'The Shadow of the Somme: The Influence of the First World War on British Soldiers' Perceptions and Behaviour in the Second World War', in P. Addison and A. Calder (eds), *Time to Kill: The Soldier's Experience of War in the West 1939–45* (London: Pimlico, 1997), 29–40.
Sheffield, G., 'Shaping British and Anzac Soldiers' Experience of Gallipoli: Environmental and Medical Factors, and the Development of Trench Warfare', *British Journal for Military History*, 4: 1 (2017), 23–43.
Sheftel, A. and Zembrzycki, S. (eds), *Oral History Off the Record: Toward an Ethnography of Practice* (London: Palgrave, 2013).
Sieder, R., 'A Hitler Youth from a Respectable Family', in D. Bertaux and P. Thompson (eds), *Between Generations: Family Models, Myths and Memories* (Oxford: Oxford University Press, 2005), 99–121.
Smith, L. (ed.), *Young Voices: British Children Remember the Second World War* (London: Viking, 2007).
Spence, D., 'Rain Forest or Mud Field?', *International Journal of Psychoanalysis*, 79 (1998), 643–7.

Stamenova, K. and Hinshelwood, R. D., *Methods of Research into the Unconscious* (Abingdon: Routledge, 2018).
Stanley, P., *Bad Characters: Sex, Crime, Mutiny, Murder and the Australian Imperial Force* (Sydney: Pier 9, 2010).
Stein, A., *Reluctant Witnesses: Survivors, Their Children and the Rise of Holocaust Consciousness* (Oxford: Oxford University Press, 2014).
Stevenson, J., *British Society 1914–45* (London: Penguin, 1984).
Strange, J. M., *Fatherhood and the British Working Class, 1865–1914* (Cambridge: Cambridge University Press, 2015).
Summerfield, P., 'Culture and Composure: Creating Narratives of the Gendered Self in Oral History Interviews', *Cultural and Social History*, 1: 1 (2004), 65–93.
Summerfield, P., *Histories of the Self: Personal Narratives and Historical Practice* (Abingdon: Routledge, 2019).
Summerfield, P., *Reconstructing Women's Wartime Lives: Discourse and Subjectivity in Oral Histories of the Second World War* (Manchester: Manchester University Press, 1998).
Summerfield, P. and Peniston-Bird, C., *Contesting Home Defence: Men, Women and the Home Guard in the Second World War* (Manchester: Manchester University Press, 2007).
Szreter, S. and Fisher, K., *Sex Before the Sexual Revolution: Intimate Life in England 1918–1963* (Cambridge: Cambridge University Press, 2010).
Tate, T. and Kennedy, K., *The Silent Morning: Culture and Memory after the Armistice* (Manchester: Manchester University Press, 2013).
Tebbutt, M., *Being Boys Youth, Leisure and Identity in the Inter-War Years* (Manchester: Manchester University Press, 2012).
Thom, D., 'The Healthy Citizen of Empire or Juvenile Delinquent? Beating and Mental Health in the UK', in M. Gijswit-Hofstra and H. Marland (eds), *Cultures of Child Health in Britain and the Netherlands in the Twentieth Century* (Amsterdam: Rodopi, 2003), 189–212.
Thompson, P. with J. Bornat, *The Voice of the Past*, 4th edn (Oxford: Oxford University Press, 2017).
Thomson, A., *Anzac Memories: Living with the Legend*, 2nd edn (Melbourne: Monash University Press, 2013).
Tint, B., 'History, Memory and Intractable Conflict', *Conflict Resolution Quarterly*, 27: 3 (Spring 2010), 239–56.
Todd, S., 'Young Women, Work and Leisure in Interwar England', *The Historical Journal*, 48: 3 (2005), 789–809.
Todman, D., *The Great War: Myth and Memory* (London: Hambledon and London, 2005).
Tonkin, E., *Narrating Our Pasts: The Social Construction of Oral History* (Cambridge: Cambridge University Press, 1992).

Twomey, C., 'Trauma and the Reinvigoration of Anzac', *History Australia*, 10: 3 (2013), 85–108.
Tyquin, M., *Gallipoli: An Australian Medical Perspective* (Newport, New South Wales: Big Sky Publishing, 2012).
Tyquin, M., *Gallipoli: The Medical War. The Australian Army Medical Services in the Dardanelles Campaign of 1915* (Sydney: University of New South Wales Press, 1993).
Tyquin, M., 'In Search of the Unseen Wound', in T. Frame (ed.), *Moral Injury: Unseen Wounds in an Age of Barbarism* (Sydney: University of New South Wales Press, 2015), 19–31.
Van der Kolk, B. A., *The Body Keeps the Score: Brain, Mind, and Body in the Healing of Trauma* (New York: Penguin Books, 2015).
Van Emden, R., *The Quick and the Dead: Fallen Soldiers and Their Families in the Great War* (Bloomsbury: London, 2011).
Volkan, V., 'The Intertwining of the Internal and External Wars', in M. G. Fromm (ed.), *Lost in Transmission: Studies of Trauma across Generations* (London: Karnac, 2012).
Wainman, R., '"Engineering for Boys": Meccano and the Shaping of a Technical Vision of Boyhood in Twentieth-Century Britain', *Cultural and Social History*, 14: 3 (2017), 381–96.
Wallis, J., 'Great-Grandfather, What Did *You* Do in the Great War?', in B. Ziino (ed.), *Remembering the First World War* (Abingdon: Routledge, 2015), 21–39.
Webster, J., Tolson, L. and Carlton, R., 'The Artifact as Interviewer: Experimenting with Oral History at the Ovenstone Miners' Cottages Site, Northumberland', *Historical Archaeology*, 48: 1 (2014), 11–29.
Welzer, H., 'Collateral Damage of History Education: National Socialism and the Holocaust in German Family Memory', *Social Research*, 75: 1 (Spring 2008), 287–314.
Westall, R., *Children of the Blitz: Memories of Wartime Childhood* (New York: Viking, 1985).
White, R., 'Europe and the Six-Bob-a-Day Tourist: The Great War as Grand Tour, or Getting Civilised', *Australian Studies*, 5 (1991), 122–39.
White, R., 'Sun, Sand and Syphilis: Australian Soldiers and the Orient, Egypt, 1914', *Australian Cultural History*, 9 (1990), 49–80.
Wilson, R., *Cultural Heritage of the Great War in Britain* (Aldershot: Ashgate, 2013).
Wilson, R., 'Still Fighting in the Trenches: "War Discourse" and the Memory of the First World War in Britain', *Memory Studies*, 8: 4 (2015), 454–69.
Winnicott, D. W., *Playing and Reality* (London: Penguin, 1988).
Winter, D., *Death's Men: Soldiers of the Great War* (London: Penguin, 1978).

Winter, J., 'Commemorating Catastrophe', *War and Society*, 36: 4 (2017), 239–55.

Winter, J., 'Forms of Kinship and Remembrance in the Aftermath of the Great War', in J. Winter and E. Sivan (eds), *War and Remembrance in the Twentieth Century* (Cambridge: Cambridge University Press, 1999), 40–61.

Winter, J., 'Sites of Memory and the Shadow of War', in A. Erll and A. Nünning (eds), *Cultural Memory Studies: An International and Interdisciplinary Handbook* (New York: de Gruyter, 2008), 61–74.

Winter, J., 'Thinking about Silence', in E. Ben-Ze'ev, R. Ginio and J. Winter (eds), *Shadows of War: A Social History of Silence in the Twentieth Century* (Cambridge: Cambridge University Press, 2010), 3–31.

Winter, J., *War Beyond Words: Languages of Remembrance from the Great War to the Present* (Cambridge: Cambridge University Press, 2017).

Wishart, A., '"As Fit as Fiddles" and "As Weak as Kittens": The Importance of Food, Water and Diet to the Anzac Campaign at Gallipoli', *First World War Studies*, 7: 2 (2016), 131–64.

Wolnik, K., Busse, B., Tholen, J., Yndigegn, C., Levinsen, K., Saari, K. and Puuronen, V., 'The Long Shadows of the Difficult Past? How Young People in Denmark, Finland and Germany Remember WWII', *Journal of Youth Studies*, 20: 2 (2017), 162–79.

Woodham, A., King, L., Gloyn, L., Crewe, V. and Blair, F., 'We Are What We Keep: The "Family Archive", Identity and Public/Private Heritage', *Heritage and Society*, 10: 3 (2017), 203–20.

Yow, V., '"Do I Like Them Too Much?": Effects of the Oral History Interview on the Interviewer and Vice-Versa', *Oral History Review*, 24: 1 (Summer 1997), 55–79.

Yow, V., 'What Can Oral Historians Learn from Psychotherapists?', *Oral History*, 46: 1 (Spring 2018), 33–42.

Ziino, B., '"A Lasting Gift to His Descendants": Family Memory and the Great War in Australia', *History and Memory*, 22: 2 (2010), 125–46.

Ziino, B., 'Introduction: Remembering the First World War Today', in B. Ziino (ed.), *Remembering the First World War* (Abingdon: Routledge, 2015), 39–55.

Index

Note: 'n' after a page reference indicates the number of a note on that page. Bold page references refer to figures.

1914–1918 project 99

Abrams, Lynn 10–11, 170n.23
Adam-Smith, Patsy 6–7, 236–8, 241, 270
Addison Act, 1919 146
affiliative ties 77–8
Age Exchange 1, 18–19, 65, 132, 301
    see also *Meeting in No Man's Land* project
air raids 48–9
Alexander, Sally 207
Alexievich, Svetlana 42, 55
Allen, Judith 162
Ally (*Meeting in No Man's Land* participant) 109, 111, 113, 116, 117
Amiens, Battle of 100
amnesia, as social defence 70
amnesiac soldier trope 39–40
Ancestry.com 7, 230
Angelika (*Meeting in No Man's Land* participant) 121, 130–1
anti-war feeling 120–2
Anzac Day 89, 93, 223–4, **226**, 227
Anzac legend 6–7, 17, 32–3
    courage and self-help ideals 269
    and dysentery 235–53
    never leave your mates ethos 246, 253
    sanitising function 249–53, **251**
    stoic image 235
    versions 249–53

Appleyard, Sydney Vere 272
Armistice Day 89, 100, 182, 300
Armstrong, Marion 1, 14, 50–1, 64, 76, 148–50, 152, 163, 210–11, 213, 309
Ashmead-Bartlett, Ellis 236
Assmann, Jan and Almeida 63–4
Aubrey, Brenda 63, 81, 162, 183, 208, 211–13, 310
audio recording 35–6
Australia
    Act of Federation 93
    Centenary spending 92
    German community 101
    National Archives 96, 106n.34
    national narrative 92–6, 100–2
Australian Remembrance Trail 95
Australian Security Intelligence Organisation 226
Australian War Memorial 7, 93–4, 106n.34, 222
authoritarianism 126–8

Baillieu, Ted 94–5
Barker, Pat, *Regeneration* trilogy 5
Bartholomew, Elizabeth 162, 183, 310
Bashforth, Martin 134n.8
battlefield pilgrimage 93–5, 106n.38
Bayer, Martin 90
BBC World Service 168
Bean, Charles 237, 242–4, 247, 250, **251**, 252, 263

bearing memory 115–19
Beaumont, Joan 7, 304–6
Benjamin, Walter 143
Bennett, Frederick 310
Berezin, Mabel 136n.29
Beuys, Joseph 123
Bingham, Adrian 169n.10
Bion, Wilfred 157
Blackmore, Kate 269, 270, 272
blind veteran tropes 47–8
Blood-Swept Lands and Seas of Red exhibition 98
Blunden, Edmund 111
Bourke, Joanna 25n.44
British Film Institute 19
Brittain, Vera 111
Brown, Arthur Henry 310
Brown, Horace Anelay 260, 263–5
Brown, Jean 62, 213–14
Brown, William 257n.61
Brown, William John 267–8, 274
Brown, William Montagu 266–7, 270, 274–5
Brown, William Reginald 268–9
Burdett, Elizabeth 154, 184
Burdett, George William Stanley 310
Burdett, Mary 62, 66, **67**, 149, 187, 310
Burgin, Ray 47–8, 81, 142, 145, 148, 152, 166, 177, 311
Burgin, Walter 203, 311
Burn, John Culbertson 312
Burn, Ralph Oswald 312
burnt-out veterans 265, 269
Butler, A. G. 236, 239, 243, 247–8, 250
Butler, Janet 228
Butler, R. A. 260–1, 263, 266, 270–1, 273
Byng-Hall, John 61
Byrne, Charlie 274

Camel Corps 222, 228, 229, 231–2n.2
Camel Corps Association 228
Cameron, David 90, 92, 98

Campbell, John Andrew 310
Campbell Ross, John 1
Caokes, Frederick 238, 241
caregiving
 adolescence and early adulthood 209–11
 emotional economies 202–7
 emotional expectations 212
 emotional relationships 211–13
 and gender 202–7, 211
 girls 197–216, **198–200**, **204**
 lived experience 211–14
 and maternal aspiration 207–8
 moral obligation 201, 215
 and primary identification 209
 tensions 208–12
 voluntary sector 201–2
Careless, Marie-Anne 45, 78–80, **79**, 85n.36, 162, 311
Caritas 109
Carlyon, Les 250–1
Cartwright, Duncan 34
Centenary 2–3, 8, 18–19, 71, 227, 306
 Australia 92–6, 100–2
 counter-movements 97–8
 funding 92
 Germany 89–92, 100–2
 Great Britain 89–102
 national differences 100–2
 national narratives 89–102
Chapman, Arthur George 316
Charity Organisation Society 148
children, mobilisation 205
Children of the Great War project 110, 128
Chilton, Charles 5
Chris (*Meeting in No Man's Land* participant) 111
Christel (*Meeting in No Man's Land* participant) 101, 112, 121, 129, 131, **131**
civil defence workers 48–9
Clark, Alan 96, 133
Clark, Christopher 90–1
Clifford, Rebecca 32
Cohen, Deborah 144, 201, 216n.6
Cohen, Stanley 206

commemoration
  Australia 92–6, 100–2
  Centenary 2–3, 8, 18–19, 71
  communities of 302
  diversity 101–2
  Germany 89–92, 100–2
  Great Britain 90, 96–102
  motivations 132
  national differences 100–2
  national narratives 89–102
communicative memory 53, 63–4, 80, 114–15
communities of exchange 81
conscientious objectors 304–6
contemporary witnesses, relationships with 3–4
corporal punishment 162, 164
Couch, Charles Ernest 311
counter-narratives 48–9, 115, 128–32, **130**, **131**, 303–6
Courtenay, Charles 272
Cowlishaw, Leslie 272
creativity, and oral history 40–3, 53, 55n.2
Croft, Jean 154–5
crying 76
cultural memory 53, 63–5, 114–15
cultural milieux 10–11
cultural producers 64–5
cultural scripts 32–3
cultural store 37–40, 53

Dachau 92
Danzinger, Kurt 33
Das, Santanu 307n.9
daughters, caregiving 197–216, **198–200**, **204**, 218n.36
  adolescence and early adulthood 209–11
  emotional economies 202–7
  emotional expectations 212
  emotional relationships 211–13
  and gender 202–7, 211
  lived experience 211–14
  and maternal aspiration 207–8
  moral obligation 215
  and primary identification 209
  tensions 208–12

Dawson, Graham 25, 37, 175
Dean, Ivy 73
Delia (*Meeting in No Man's Land* participant) 123–4, 128, **130**
demobilisation 167, 263
demographic trends 144–5
deposited representation 76
Der Spiegel 89
Diana (*Meeting in No Man's Land* participant) 115, 123, 124, 128–9
Dieter (*Meeting in No Man's Land* participant) 109, **111**, 126–8
digital technologies 19, 36, 99, 102, 117, 301
disabled fathers 65, 68, 74, 75, 142, 145–9, 152, 161, 166, 201, 207–16
  see also caregiving
discipline 162–6
Dixon, George 63
domestic
  ephemera 19, 78, 81, 92, 123
  house-worlds 78
  leisure 155–62, **158**, **159**, **160**
  miniatures 156–7
  recuperation 169
  routines 15, 143, 150–5
  space 148–50
  tension 166
  violence 163, 165
domesticity 144–5, 167–9, 203
Duffett, Rachel 7–8, 18, 110, 156, 242
dysentery epidemic, Gallipoli campaign 235–53, 282, 292
  bodily toll 241
  diarrhoea 238–9
  experience of 237–42, **240**, 257n.61, 275–6
  failures of care 243–9, **245**
  food contamination 239–41, 247–8
  hospitals 244–5
  humiliation 241–2, 260
  hypocrisy 253
  in situ treatment 245–6
  medical legacies 261–9

memory trace 250
mental effects 236, 241
moral harm 246–7
national silence 261
sanitising legends 249–53, **251**
social legacies 260–76
war pensions 260–1

Elders, George 63, 72, 74, 165, 184, 187, 189, 192, 311
Ellenbogen, Marianne 33
Ellis, Charles 236
Elston, George James 314
emotional codes and cultures 10, 48, 68–70, 211, 215
emotional community 102, 132, 136n.29
emotional demands on interviewee 46–7
emotional distance between historian and interviewee 24n.31
emotional economy 84n.26, 201–7
emotional enactments 14, 61
emotional expectations 69–70, 199, 212
emotional experience 11, 14, 115
emotional investments 10, 15
emotional labour 71, 134n.8
emotional states
 interviewer and interviewee 34–5, 50, 51, 54
 and stomach 236, 261–2
 and stresses 201, 215, 262–3, 268, 289
emotional ties 115, 116
emotions and remembering 31–2
empathetic understanding, limits of 12
employment 147–8
Europeana website 117
Evans, Raymond 171n.37
Ewart, Vernon 312–13
experiential method in oral history 53–5
eyewitness, presumed value of 41

fabulation 41
Faimberg, Haydée 75–6

family historians 3
family histories 231, 302–3
family life 150–5
 discipline 162–6
 leisure 155–62, **158–160**
 violence 162–8
family loyalties 13
family memory 92
family scripts 61
family secrets, disclosure 65
family size 144–5
family stories 10–11
family transmission 61–82
 and cultural memory 63–5
 and gender 70–5
 Germany 11–12, 76–7
 silence 65–70, 82
 and trauma 75–8, 81–2
 and war heritage 78–81, **79**
 and war legacies 62
fantasy 31, 35, 38, 41, 42, 77, 284
father figures 139, **140**, 141–3
fathering, lack of 161–2
fatherless households 148, 150–2
fathers
 authority 183, 185
 fear of 166
 good 143, 162–4
 household routines 152–5
 involved 152, 168–9
 leisure 155–62, **158–60**, 168–9
 and play 179–81
 and Second World War 183–5, 190–3
 tempers 166–7
 violence 162–8
femininity 73, 144, 152, 202
Fey, Joyce 66, 149, 153, 155–6, 162, 166, 184–5, 187–8, 192, 311–12
films and filmmakers 6
First World War Engagement Centres 102
Fischer, Franz 91
Fischer, Gérard 101
Fisher, Kate 32
Fitzgibbon, Mary 236
Flower, George Edward 312

Index

Flower, Jefferey 48–9, 66, 78, 80, 153, 165–7, 177–9, 184–7, 192, 312
forgetting 11, 13, 46, 54, 90, 125, 141–3, 145
Franziska (*Meeting in No Man's Land* participant) 101
Fraser, Ian 203, 205–6
Freud, Sigmund 14, 37, 185–7, 249, 250
Frie, Roger 8, 22n.21
Friedrich, Jorge 22n.21
Fromelles mass graves 95
Frost, George James 312
Frost, John 50, 155, 163–5, 174, 177–81, 183, 186, 293, 297–9, 312
Fulbrook, Mary 11
Fussell, Paul 17, 97, 157, 286

Gallagher, Emily 177
Gallipoli campaign 15–18, 93, 95, 100, 154–5, 165, 227–9, 231–2n.2
  apricot and plum jam 240–1, **240**
  battle of Lone Pine 17, 234–5, 243–4, 271
  casualties 234, 235
  death odour 238–9
  dysentery epidemic 235–53, 282, 292
  dysentery epidemic legacies 260–76
  evacuation 248
  failures of care 243–9, **245**
  flies 239, 257n.61
  food 243–4, **245**
  food contamination 239–41, 247–8
  hypocrisy 253
  Indian troops 18
  latrines 239, 248
  moral harm 246–7
  personal hygiene 243
  sanitising legends 249–53, **251**
  water supplies 243
Galsworthy, John 206
Game, Elizabeth 66, 161, 184, 312
Game, Rosemary 4, 148, 192
Gammage, Bill 251–2
Gaza, Second Battle of 222, 282, 285–6
Gedling, Henry 315–16
gender
  and caregiving 202–7
  and family transmission 70–5
  gender roles 150–2
  generation, definition 20n.2
  see also family transmission
generational affinities 119
generational tension 48–9
Gerber, David 197
Germany 8, 300–1
  ambivalence 92
  Centenary spending 92
  denazification 122
  domination of Second World War 92
  family transmission in 11–12, 76–7
  heroising tendency 131
  history of extremism 101
  learned history 13
  Meeting in No Man's Land project 7–8, 109–34
  national narrative 89–92
  Nazi heritage 8, 10–15, 23–4n.31
  and Second World War 90–1, 101, 112
  Second World War silence 125–31, 133, 135n.18
  shame and complicity 8, 112
  war heritage 92, 117–19
  war pensions 216n.6
ghosts 78
Gilligan, Carol 49
Girl Guides 201, 205
Gitsham, Rosemary 2, 153, 156, 162, 168, 181–3, 312–13
Gitsham, Vernon 181
Goltermann, Svenja 122, 135n.18
good father trope 143, 162–4
Gordon, Avery 78
Gourlay, Alan 236, 238, 241, 246

Great Britain
  Centenary spending 92
  national narrative 90, 96–102, 132–3
Green, Arthur Harold 267
Green, Ernest Arthur 313
Green, Fred 264–6, 268, 270
Green, Frederick 264–5, 272–3
Green, Hedley 67, 72–4, 77, 190, 313
Grey, Mr 46–7
Guardian, The 99–100
guilt 8, 12, 13, 15, 76, 91, 92, 112, 122, 125, 131, 212, 214, 289, 290, 301

hallucinations 40
Hammett, Jessica 49, 184
Hanne (*Meeting in No Man's Land* participant) 8, **10**, 112, 114–15, 125–6
Hardie, Mary 154
Hareven, Tamara 9–10
Heard, Rob 98–9
Helmi, Nardine 101
Hempshall, Walter 4, 142, 163, 318
Henry, Thomas **204**
Heritage Lottery Fund 98, 102
Heritage Lottery Fund heritage projects 18
heroising tendency, German descendants 131–2
Hetherington, Andrea 151
Hewett, Otto **245**
Hickson, John 11, **12**, 317
hidden history, Roper family 306
Hilary (*Meeting in No Man's Land* participant) **111**, 113, 120
hinge generation 75, 115
Hirsch, Marianne 30, 77
Hirschfeld, Gerhard 90
historians
  and family histories of war 6–7
  and research on war legacies 231
history, lessons from 115, 119–23
history from below 9–10, 59n.60

history making of descendants 5, 19, 116–19, 222–31
Hitler Youth 118, 126
Hoffman, Eva 75, 77
Holbrook, Carolyn 95, 96
holidays 161
Holloway, Wendy 57n.19
Holocaust, the 13–14, 91
Holocaust survivors 33, 59n.49
  child survivors 32
  children of 30
  family reunification 32
  and primary identification 209
  and trauma 77–8
home life, forward projection 139, **140**
homes 43–4, **44**, 45
Homes for Heroes scheme 146
Honest History 95–6
Hopper, John 292
household routines 150–5
housing 44, 145–50, **147**, 170n.23
Hughes, Ted 5, 21n.9
humanity, restoring and sustaining 115, 128–32
Humphries, Steve 154
Hunt, Albert Edwin 311–12
Hunt, Tristram 98

identification 76, 209
illusions and transitional objects 37, 38, 42
imagination
  descendants 6, 14, 35, 55, 77, 81
  historians 36
  and play 175, 193
  public 95
imaginative reconstruction 43, 225–6
Imperial War Graves Commission 102
Imperial War Museum 4, 7, 99, 237, 301
incomes 147–8, 151
injustices, exposing 120
inter-generational transmission 77, 85n.39, 98, 112, 116, 141–3, 306

interviews 18, 35, 53–4
  effects on interviewer 14, 17, 33, 35, 40, 45, 46, 58n.42, 237
  identifying voices 49–52
  interpreting 32
  interviewee motivations 52–5, 64–6
  listening to 54
  locations 43–4
  Meeting in No Man's Land project 110, 319–20
  relationships within 30–55
  and remembering 40–3
  smoothing tendency 55
  and unconscious projects 52
  understanding difficulties 46–9
  and war heritage 45
involved fathering 152, 168–9

Jackson, Peter 6
Jarvis, Camilla 1–2, **3**, 8, 18
Jarvis, Eileen 1–2
Jarvis, Léonie 1–2
Jarvis, Philip 1–2
Jean, Brown 310
Jefferson, Tony 57n.19
Johnson, Dennis 68–9, 150, 154, 167, 190, 191, 313
Johnson, Sydney 69
Johnson, William 68–9, 313
Jones, Arnold Edward 313
Jones, Clive 65, 177, 313
Jones, Helen 182
Joseph, Betty 34, 52
Jürgen (*Meeting in No Man's Land* participant) **114**, 125

Kästner, Erich 1, 89
Kennedy, Rosie 193, 205
Kent, Susan 144
Kerslake, Mary 73, 80, 313–14
Keys, Brian 4–5
Kidron, Carol 135n.20
killing, contradictory emotions of 25n.44
Killingbeck, George 211–13
Killingbeck, Joan 211–13
kindness 143

King, Laura 145
Kippen, Rebecca 292
Kneebone, Dora 69, 72, 76, 80, 144, 161, 209, 299–300, 314
Kogan, Ilany 76, 209
Kohut, Thomas 23–4n.31
Koven, Seth 199, 206
Krumeich, Gerd 90

La Touche, Everard 271
LaCapra, Dominick 59n.49
Land Army 73
Langley, George 222
Lawrence, Cyril 241
Lawrence, John 170n.10
Leakey, Josh 69
learned history 4, 13, 77, 110
Lechte, Donald William 265
legacies 1, 2, 8, 33, 61–2, 69–70, 73–6, 78, 101, 125, 127, 128, 139, 141, 144, 149, 155, 180, 185, 189, 193, 216, 253, 292
  of dysentery epidemic, Gallipoli campaign 260–76, 282–3, 287–92
  naming of 62–3
legacy history, limits of 224
leisure 128–9, 155–62, **158–60**, 168–9
Les (*Meeting in No Man's Land* participant) 120–1, 123
Lessing, Doris 215–16, 300
Liddle, Eric 17, 228, 229
Light, Alison 144
Linde (*Meeting in No Man's Land* participant) 64, 115, 128, 129
Lindsey, Arthur 309
Listening Guide 49–52
Littlewood, Joan 5, 111
lived history 4, 13, 64, 77, 89, 292, 300
living memory, final remaining links to 1
Lloyd, Sarah 18
Lloyd George, David 146
Local Government Board 146
Long, Francis 157–61, **157**, **159**, **160**, 316

Long Long Trail, The (BBC radio programme) 5
Lord Roberts Workshops 176
loss, emotion of 5, 6, 8, 14, 69, 96, 132, 231, 288–9, 292
Loughran, Tracey 276
Love and Sorrow conference 222
Lumley, Savile, 'Daddy, what did you do in the Great War?' 139, **140**, 143
Lyons, Joe 287

McCallum, Stan 303–6
McCalman, Janet 292
McCartney, Helen 99
Mace, Irene 202–3
McHugh, Siobhán 35–6
McKenzie, William 243
McMeeken, Joan 292
McPhee, James 239
Mangin, Anthelme 40
Manthorp, Beryl 154, 189–91, 314
Manthorp, Harry Albert 314
Manton, Horace 241, 242
Marga (*Meeting in No Man's Land* participant) 122, 123
Mariana (*Meeting in No Man's Land* participant) 117
marriage 145, 203, 213
Marriage, June 68, 314
Martin (*Meeting in No Man's Land* participant) 111, 113, 117, 119
Marwick, Arthur 73
Marx, Karl 300, 301
masculine housework 145
masculinity 33, 49, 143, 144, 167, 169n.10, 190, 202, 250, 275
Mass Observation 4, 71
May, Rollo 293
May, Theresa 100
Meager, Charles 237–8, 241, 256n.43
Meccano 176–7
medals 8, **10**, 80
medical legacies, dysentery epidemic, Gallipoli campaign 261–9, 282–3, 287–92

Meeting in No Man's Land project 7–8, 19, 78, 91, 100–1, 109–34, 300
  aims 109–10
  anti-war message 120–1
  bearing memory and making history 115–19
  counter-narratives 115, 128–32, **130**, **131**
  declarations of peace 122–3
  funding 109
  identifications with First World War 122–3
  interview schedule 319–20
  interviews 110
  lessons 115, 119–23
  motivations 115–16, 119–20, 131–2
  participants 110–16, **111**, 132, 133
  resident historians 110
  shared perception 114–15
  war heritage 116
memorial books 1–2
memory 14, 229
  bearing 115–19
  preserving 119
  public 10–11
  temporal displacement 297–9
Mendes, Sam 6
mental illness 7, 62–3, 268
methodology 18, 35–6, 53–5
Middlebrook, Martin 6
military culture 193
  and play 177–8
Miller, William 239
Millhauser, Steven 156–7
Mills, Rollie 270, 275–6
Mingay, Frederick 183
Mingay, Henry 314
Mingay, James 183
Mingay, John 74, 146–8, 151–3, 166–7, 182–3, 190, 314
misremembering 33, 297–9
mobility, fascination with 180–1
Mombauer, Annika 91
moral ambiguity 112–13
moral betrayal 293

moral economy 270
moral harm 246–7
Morgan, Brian 192–3
Morgan, Gerald Bede 315
Morgan, John 184, 315
mortality, descendants 63
mortality rates 295n.34
Mosse, George 135n.16
mothers 44, 71–2, 155, 163–4, 185, 191, 196n.39
 and disabled veterans 145, 150–2, 201, 207, 209, 218n.36
 resourcefulness 33
 war experiences 71–4
 and widowhood 150–2
motivations 5
 for care 201
 for commemoration and remembrance 109–33
 interviewee 52–3
 for researching war 4–5, 293
 unconscious 15
 see also Meeting in No Man's Land project
Mowat, Charles 173
mud 66, 141
Mullarkey, Albert 67, 315
 breakdown 61–2
Mullarkey, Brian 67, 139, 141, 149, 151, 161–2, 315
 father's breakdown 61–2
Müller-Hohagen, Jürgen 112
Munich, Soviet Republic 129
Murphy, Macleod 267
Murray, Joseph 242

narrative context in interviews 34–5
narrative methodology 55
National Heritage Lottery 109
national identity 170n.10
national narratives 89–102, 113
 Australia 92–6, 100–2
 differences 100–2
 Germany 89–92, 100–2
 Great Britain 90, 96–102, 132–3
 Nazi Germany 8, 10–15, 23–4n.31, 90, 91, 112, 125–6, 129–31

nervy men 264–5
Nicholson, Juliet 206, 207
No Glory campaign 97–8
Noakes, Lucy 71, 84n.26
non-purposive state (Winnicott) 42
nurses 202

O'Connor, T. P. 205
Oh, What a Lovely War! 5, 96, 111
Omaha beach 46–7
online research tools 7
on-site observations 54
Oppenheimer, Melanie 264, 268–70
oral history 9–11
 directions 41–2
 experiential method 53–5
 and fantasy 35, 38, 41, 42, 56n.10, 57n.18
 identifying inaccuracies 33
 as intermediate space 36–43
 interview relationships 36–43, 54–5, 59n.59
 interviewee motivations 52–3
 interviewer and illusions 43
 narrative context of 34–5
 and repetition 50
 and re-remembering 33
 as testimony 29–35
 triangulation 32
 understanding difficulties 46–9
Owen, Wilfred 5
ownership, sense of 223

pacifism 21, 120–1, 304–7
parental authority 49–50, 183, 185
Parish, Pam 207
Parkin, David 307n.7
participant history 19
Passchendaele 99–100
Passerini, Luisa 142–3
Patch, Harry 1
patriotism 133
Paulley, John 263, 287
Pearson, Arthur 197, 202–3
Pennell, Catriona 97
Pentney, Allan 66, 145, 146, 151, 174, 187, 189, 315
Pentney, Thomas 315

Perley, Doris 73, 153–4, 162–4, 167, 183, 190, 192, 315–16
Peter (*Meeting in No Man's Land* participant) 113, 124
Pheasant Wood Commonwealth War Graves cemetery 95
Phillips, Adam 40
pity of war narratives 3, 97, 132
play 37
    child perspective 173–93
    father's perspective 155–62, **158, 159, 160**
    lessons of 178–9
    masculine 175
    and military culture 177–8
    parental engagement 179–81
    and risk 178–9
    and Second World War 173
    sites 177
    toys 175, 176
    and violence 179
    war play 173, 175–81
Pollock, Eileen 151, 152, 190–1
Pollock, Harriet 44, **44**, 143, 151, 152, 184, 316
Pooley, Siân 141
popular memory 5, 11, 13, 15, 74
Portelli, Alessandro 34, 41, 42, 55, 56n.10
'postmemories' 30
primary identification 209
Proctor, Tammy 205
psychoanalysis 49, 52, 54, 75, 82, 262, 268
psychological defences 35, 77
PTSD 62, 70, 163, 165, 235, 299
public memory 7, 10–14, 89, 96, 201, 306

qualitative software packages 57n.19
Queen Mary Army Auxiliary Corps 73
Qureshi, Kaveri 141

Raemaker, Louis **199**
Rainer (*Meeting in No Man's Land* participant) 118–19

reaction formations 15, 249
Reade, Michael 292
Reardon, Margaret 66, 141, 153, 156, 183–5, 189, 316
recuperation, and play 157–61, **157, 159, 160**
Reiss, Richard, *The Home I Want* 146, **147**
Relatives Database 95
remembering
    and creativity 41–3
    and emotions 31–2
    and experience 29–35
    and interviews 40–3
    and historical imagination 36–43
remembrance 63, 91, 134n.6, 201
Remembrance Sunday 300
Renz, Irina 90
repatriation culture 267
Repatriation Department 260, 265, 268, 270, 273, 275, 276, 282–3, 287–8
Reveille 206
Reynolds, David 3–4, 97
Roberts, Elizabeth **44**
Robson, Lloyd 251
Rogers, Carl 293
role models, lack of 161–2
Roper, Ailsa 303–6
Roper, Charlie 235
Roper, Michael
    death of father 221
    death of grandfather 221, 227
    family separation 223
    interviews father 223
    reconsideration of grandfather 229–31
    researches grandfather 221–31
    war legacies **9**, 15–19, 24n.39
Roper, Robert Henry 15–18, 94, **224–6, 230**, 302
    battle of Lone Pine 17, 234–5
    birth 283
    death 221, 227
    dysentery 235–7
    father and son research 221–31, 302–3

first interview 221
Gallipoli memoir 222–5, 227–9, 231–2n.2, 235–6, 240, 243–4, **245**, 246, 252–3, 271, 284
hatred 285–6, 293
imaginative reconstruction 225–6
life trajectory 283–7
and Lin's death 288–91
PTSD 235
reconsideration of 229–31
scars 282, 283
sense of moral betrayal 293
service records 222
stomach troubles 282–3, 287–92
temper 226
war legacies 15–18, 282–3, 287–92
Roseman, Mark 33, 133
Rosemary (*Meeting in No Man's Land* participant) 116
Rosenthal, Gabriele 11
Royal Army Service Corps 66, **67**
Russian campaign 4–5
Ruth (*Meeting in No Man's Land* participant) 116, 120, 121, 128

St Dunstan's Hostel 197–9, **198**, 200, **200**, 202–6, 211–14
St Dunstan's Review 203–5
Samuel, Raphael 9–10
Saunders, Nicholas 58n.45, 81, 136n.25
Savill, David 7–8, 124
scars 2, 123, 142, 282
Scates, Bruce 264, 268–70
Seabrook, Margaret 157–61, **157**, **159, 160**, 173, 189, 316
Seal, Graham 249, 252
second generation, situation of 12, 19, 30, 53, 54, 61–82, 101, 299
Second World War 90, 121–2, 297–300
attitudes to the Germans 191–2
bombing 173–4
children's involvement 188–9
dominates memory 92
excitement 185–7
experience of 174
and fathers 183–5, 190–3
First World War visibility during 174, 182–93
German denial 101
German shame 112
German silence 125–31, 133, 135n.18
memories 182–93
outbreak 68, 182–3
and play 173
prisoners of war 79
seventy-fifth anniversary 90–1
stomach troubles 262
Secret Battle, The (Roper) 221–2
secretiveness 69
Sefton, Eric 304–6
Sefton, William 305–6
self-censorship 163
sexual abuse 163
shame 112, 293
Shay, Jonathon 246–7
shell-shock 62, 165, 168, 182, 276
Sheridan, Clare 197, **198**
Shrouds of the Somme installation 98–9
silence 11, 21n.13, 76, 129–31, 133, 135n.18
breaking of 115, 124–8
and family transmission 65–70, 82
inter-generational legacies 125–8, 306
paternal 141–3
shared histories of 123
upholding 299
Simpson and his donkey 16
Skin, Kathleen 29–31, 33–5, 41–2, 52, 147, 316–17
Skin, William Cecil 316–17
Smith, Alexander George 317
Smith, David 58n.44, 63, 66, 145, 149, 152, 164, 179, 184, 186, 189, 317
Smith, Ruby 197–202, 205, 209, 215, 216n.2

Smithson, William 316
soldier-centred perspective 71, 74–5
Somme, Battle of the 6, 96–7, 120–1
sources 32–3, 229
Special Operations Executive (SOE) 31
Spence, Donald 54, 59n.59, 59n.60
Spray, Winifred 11–12, **12**, 41, 74, 148, 317
   home 43–4
   memories of father 37–40
   and parental authority 49–51
   voices 49–50
   war heritage 80
Stamp, Pat 68, 71–2, 142, 149, 162–5, 168, 317–18
stomach ulcers 291–2
Strange, Julie Marie 164
subjectivity 11, 33, 36, 47–8, 52, 78
substitution 41
Summerfield, Penny 190, 218n.36
survivor's guilt 299
Swann, Bill 65–6, 68–70, 74, 147, 148, 150–1, 161, 162, 183, 186, 190, 204, 207–8, 318
Swann, Herbert 318
Szreter, Simon 32

Teape, June 4, 74, 142, 153, 163, 191, 299, 318
temporal displacement 297–9
'Territorial' 205, 206, 209
testimony, oral history as 29–55
Theodora (*Meeting in No Man's Land* participant) 91–2, 112, 113, 121, 125, 129–30, 132
They Shall Never Grow Old (film) 6
third generation, situation of 13, 77, 80, 101, 110, 116, 143, 300
Thompson, Paul 9–10
Thomson, Alastair 7, 32–3, 279–80n.48
Todd, Selina 207

Todman, Dan 21–2n.15
Tolley, James 241
Tonkin, Elizabeth 33
toy production 176
toy soldiers 176
transcription 35
transference 30, 52
transitional objects 36
transmission
   inter-generational 9, 141
   public and private 302
   studies and theories of 10–15, 75, 77, 82, 141–3, 305
   unconscious 76–7
   see also family transmission
trauma
   collective 249, 292
   culture 70, 95, 299
   and experience 25n.44, 46–7, 62, 187–8
   and family transmission 75–8, 81–2, 124, 127, 168
   theories 75–8, 292
trench art 78
Tunnah, Frederick Allen 313–14
Tyne Cot 100

uchronic dream 34, 41
unconscious 32, 34, 57n.21
   motives 14, 15, 52
   projects 52
   and transmission 76–7, 81
unsettlement, feelings of 67–8
Urwick, Lyndall 253
Uttin, Alfred 314

Vansina, Jan 64
veterans, last 1
veteran's return tropes 38–9, **38**, **39**
victimhood 205
violence 162–8
   downplaying 17
   and play 179
voices 49–52, 55
Voices of the Great War 18

Walder, Dennis 21n.9
Wallace, Edgar 250

Wallis, James 100, 106n.38
war culture, sources of 175–6
war heritage 1–2, 4–5, 8, **10**, 116–18, 123, 298–307
  and communicative memory 80
  documenting 3–4
  domestic utility 78
  family transmission 78–81, **79**
  Germany 92, 117–19
  in homes 45
  household routines 153–5
  journeys 81
  preservation 119
  therapeutic value of 58n.45
war pension claims, dysentery epidemic 260–76
Way, Herbert 156
Weinrich, Arndt 90
Wells, H. G. 176
Welzer, Harald 13, 15, 131
Western Front Association 98, 100
White, Francis John 275
White, John Irwin 264, 265, 272, 274, 278n.24
White, William Henry 275
widows 150–2
Willcox, W. H. 244

Willis, Hastings 271–2
Wiltshire, Albert Victor 318
Wiltshire, Victor 162, 164–5, 177, 193, 318
Winnicott, Donald 36–7, 40, 42, 48–9, 53
Winter, Denis 6
Winter, Jay 63, 134n.6
Wolf, Harold 262
Wolf, Stewart 262
Wolfgang (*Meeting in No Man's Land* participant) 92, 129
women 163–4
  changes in position 207
  domestic role 144
  responsibilities 150–2
  war experiences 71–4
Wood, Harry John 317–18
wounds 2, 72, 74–5, 81, 123, 135n.20, 282

XXXX 290, 291

Yarr, Thomas 246
Yow, Valerie 46, 58n.38, 58n.42

Ziino, Bart 64, 95, 96

EU authorised representative for GPSR:
Easy Access System Europe, Mustamäe tee 50,
10621 Tallinn, Estonia
gpsr.requests@easproject.com

www.ingramcontent.com/pod-product-compliance
Ingram Content Group UK Ltd.
Pitfield, Milton Keynes, MK11 3LW, UK
UKHW021820291225
466492UK00004B/15